VIRTUES AND PASSIONS IN LITERATURE

Excellence, Courage, Engagements, Wisdom, Fulfilment

Edited by

ANNA-TERESA TYMIENIECKA

The World Phenomenology Institute, Hanover, NH, U.S.A.

Published under the auspices of
The World Institute for Advanced Phenomenological Research and Learning
A-T. Tymieniecka, President

Springer

Library of Congress Cataloging-in-Publication Data is available

ISBN 978-1-4020-6421-0 (HB)
ISBN 978-1-4020-6422-7 (e-book)

Published by Springer,
P.O. Box 17, 3300 AA Dordrecht, The Netherlands.

www.springer.com

Printed on acid-free paper

All Rights Reserved
© 2008 Springer
No part of this work may be reproduced, stored in a retrieval system, or transmitted in any form or by any means, electronic, mechanical, photocopying, microfilming, recording or otherwise, without written permission from the Publisher, with the exception of any material supplied specifically for the purpose of being entered and executed on a computer system, for exclusive use by the purchaser of the work.

TABLE OF CONTENTS

ACKNOWLEDGEMENTS   vii

THEMATIC STUDY

LAWRENCE KIMMEL / Literature and the Passion of Virtue   xi

SECTION I

TSUNG-I DOW / Historical and Contemporary Virtues As Reflected in Chinese Literature   3

BERNARD MICALLEF / Revisiting the Traditional Virtues of the Hero: A Phenomenological Study of Wilfred Owen's Disabled Soldier   15

VICTOR GERALD RIVAS / Beauty, Taste, and Enlightenment in Hume's Aesthetic Thought   49

SECTION II

EVGENIA V. CHERKASOVA / Virtues of the Heart: Feodor Dostoevsky and the Ethic of Love   69

BRUCE ROSS / The Willing Subject and the Non-Willing Subject in the *Tao Te Ching* and Nietzsche's *Hyperborean*: Taoist and Deconstructive Challenges to the Idea of Virtue   83

REBECCA M. PAINTER / Virtue in Marilynne Robinson's *Gilead*   93

SECTION III

ALIRA ASHVO-MUÑOZ / Inherent and Intentional Inquiries on Virtues   115

RAYMOND J. WILSON III / Striving and Accepting Limits As Competing Meta-Virtues: Goethe's *Faust* and Ibsen's *The Wild Duck*   123

PETER WEIGEL / Happiness, Division, and Illusions of the Self
in Plato's *Symposium* — 135

ANNIKA LJUNG-BARUTH / The Virtue of Responsibility:
Femininity, Temporality, and Space in Michael Cunningham's
The Hours — 159

SECTION IV

VICTOR GERALD RIVAS / Enlightenment, Humanization,
and Beauty in the Light of Schiller's "Letters on the Aesthetic
Education of Man" — 171

LAWRENCE F. RHU / Beyond Adaptation: Stoicism,
Transcendence, and Moviegoing in Walker Percy
and Stanley Cavell — 199

JOHN BALDACCINO / Between the Ironic and the Irenic:
Happiness, Contingency, and the Poetics of Recurrence — 211

RAJIV KAUSHIK / Phenomenological Temporality
and Proustian Nostalgia — 225

SECTION V

JAIMIE JANDOVITZ / Art and Awareness — 245

ENRICO ESCHER / The Image in the History of Thought — 253

MARTIN HOLT / The Narrative Model — 265

WILLIAM ROBERTS / Political Symbolism
in the Saint Antoine Gate — 291

MÜNIR BEKEN / Music Theory and Phenomenology of Musical
Performance. A Case Study: Five Notes in Joël-François
Durand's *un feu distinct* — 305

NAME INDEX — 311

ACKNOWLEDGEMENTS

The studies published in this volume stem mainly from the 30th International Conference of the International Society of Phenomenology and Literature. It was held May 24 and 25, 2006, at Harvard University Divinity School, Cambridge, Massachusetts. The topic was "Historical and Contemporary Virtues As Reflected in Literature," but a more innovative title has been judged to be more appropriate for this volume. My sincere thanks to all of the authors and speakers for their ingenious contributions going reflectively through the contemporary transformations in approaches to life and excavating the ancient sedimentations of cultural molding while they maintain a focus on selfhood and personhood. Thanks go to Jeff Hurlburt for his editorial help and to Springer for the copyediting and proofreading of the volume.

A-T. T

THEMATIC STUDY

LAWRENCE KIMMEL

LITERATURE AND THE PASSION OF VIRTUE

Let others complain the age is wicked; my complaint is that it is wretched, for it lacks passion.

Kierkegaard

INTRODUCTION

There has always been a reasonable concern that passion constitutes a challenge to the ordeal of civility—that passion and pathology are close cousins if not twin siblings. But in a time and place where political correctness seems to be replacing moral sensibility and political biases are hawked as the morality of family values, it is reasonable to redirect attention to a world of literature in which morality has never been reduced to norms of social currency and where virtue still embodies a passion of commitment that aspires to excellence.

As a codicil to Nietzsche's argument for the moral imperative of revaluing all values, our own time begs recourse to a world of literature in which actions are not simply recast in the idols and ideologies of the age—a diverse and contradictory world that holds some promise of rediscovering a moral touchstone for critical understanding. Moral insight, not social respectability, has always been the appeal of literature, and we would do well to rediscover its sustaining spring. The world's great literature is a resource for stretching imagination to test the limits of moral intelligibility. Setting aside the commanding and comfortable authority of prescriptive righteousness in favor of a broader and deeper understanding of the complex virtues of moral life is a risk of literature well worth taking. It demands only that we search for a moral compass informed by literature and life no less than politics and polls. In this light I will proceed to analyze the idea of virtue in its original meaning of "human excellence," which requires passion in its expression.

Although my primary point of departure is the archaic literature and not the classical philosophy of Greek culture, a good deal of the earlier literature is in concert with Aristotle's "virtue ethics," which contends among other things that virtue is not a function of action but an activity of the person. It is the excellence of character that defines the moral life and virtue of human beings, not the correctness of a particular action. If we are to speak meaningfully of virtue, of the excellence of a human being, we require an understanding of the full range of passions of which human beings are capable. There is an apparent contradiction in the usual way of understanding moral virtue, the resolution of which will help to make this point.

The character of Achilles portrayed in Greek literature is of whole cloth: The excellence or virtue of his character includes his faults as well as his "virtues." This is no less true of Odysseus or of Oedipus: Their faults are also their strengths. The virtue of these exceptional characters transcends and is not defined by observance of normative prescription. A simpler way of putting this is that the excellence of a human being is not limited to or discovered by an analysis of his or her several virtues. Moral excellence is manifest only in the fullness of its expression, in the "vices" no less than the "virtues" of the person. Part of the task of this essay is to resolve the apparency of this contradiction.

I

Philosophical literature from the time of Plato regards passion (*pathos*) as a *happening*—as passive, as an experience that interferes with the active rationality of virtue. Passion here is most often associated with pain and pleasure; to the degree it is associated with desire (again as something that is passively *suffered*), its occurrence is a challenge to be overcome by rational deliberation and control.

The question to which this essay is a response is whether there is rooted in the literature of Greek Epic and Tragedy a different account to be given of virtue/excellence, one in which the passion of the hero is not passive suffering but an active engagement in the project of his or her life. One need only consider *Medea* to see the point of this. The word used in the acknowledgment of heroic character is *agathos* (Good/Great!), for example, "*Achilles agathos!*" In later tragic literature, a similar meaning is invested in praising great passion at the heart of some courageous or memorable action. So even if one agrees to the conceptual limits of *pathos* as "passive," the active and generative passion of the heroic requires an accounting. The passion of virtue can be alternatively framed in the language of the times, for example, as a divine energy that flows through the actions of the hero—that is, that the heroic action is magnified through the invasive and compelling will of the gods. Once the gods drop out of moral life, however, we must continue to account for passion as formative in the excellence of action and discernible in the judgment of that character.

Although *Arete* was a female *daimon*—the spirit of virtue, excellence, goodness, and valor—the word *arête*/virtue is related to the Greek god of War, Ares. This is partly explained in that virtue was first associated with a warrior culture. This odd masculine/feminine conceptual confluence of *arête* attests to the complexity of the Homeric concept of virtue, but even so, it is a difficult fit. Ares, as the god of war, is attended by Terror and served by *Eris*/Strife. His character is decisive but impulsive, fearless but combative, determined but bloodthirsty. The Homeric *arête*—virtue understood in this range of excellence—is a far stretch from the later period of Hellenic philosophy in which virtue or excellence is limited to *arête* that is more and more comparative and descriptive in its valuative use. Indeed, one seemingly can speak equally of the virtue of a man (the comparative and functional excellence of *sophrosyne*, good judgment) or of the virtue of a knife (the comparative and functional excellence of good cutting.)

In terms of moral life, one may wonder what may be lost in moving to this latter and now common functional domestication of the concept of virtue. My concern here is to restore a broader and more complex idea of the excellence of character that is manifest throughout the world of literature. What I have in mind is suggested in the following comment from Nietzsche:

It is not in satiety that desire shall grow silent and be submerged, but in beauty. Gracefulness is part of the graciousness of the great-souled.... There is nobody from whom I want beauty as much as from you who are powerful: let your kindness be your final self-conquest. Of all evil I deem you capable: therefore I want the good from you. Verily I have often laughed at the weaklings who thought themselves good because they had no claws. Nietzsche, "On those who are sublime," from *Thus Spake Zarathustra*)

This angular concept of excellence/virtue in literature finds expression well beyond the range of tragic heroes and Nietzschean *Übermenschen*, for example, in the following ordinary of the Elizabethan sonnet:

> They that have power to hurt and will do none,
> They rightly do inherit heaven's graces
> ...
> They are the lords and owners of their faces,
> Others, but stewards of their excellence.
> Shakespeare, from *Sonnet* XCIV

II

In opposition to the standard view that character is formed through the rational constraint and domestication of passion, I will try to show how the poetic imagination in Western literature transcends the ethics of the disjunction of passion and reason in its examination of moral life, which in turn will show an essential connection between passion and virtue.

Although some modern naturalist views tend to locate virtue in feeling, with rational reflection as a developmental addendum, the division of passion and reason invariably reasserts itself in favor of reason when general rules of valuation are formed and virtues normatized. However, it can be argued that virtue itself is an expression and modality of passion even within the foundational Greek and Judeo-Christian traditions. The importance of this recognition of a fundamental and essential connection between passion and virtue is that it provides the imagination with a poetics of moral sensibility independent of the inhibitions and prohibitions of custom and free of social embarrassment or excuse for public sanction.

The first expressions of virtue in Western literature—that is, of the excellence of character distinct from praise in honor of the attributes of the gods—is found in the heroic literature of the archaic Greeks. Recent scholarship suggests that Greek literature is not independent of ties to the Levant, however, and so its substance and form have elements of even earlier oral traditions. For example, the epic of *Gilgamesh* may be argued as a formative model for part of the language and structure of the Homeric epic. Should this be so, and some aspect of it is surely so, then Greek literature and the language of passion and virtue that we discover in the Greek world bridge earlier cultures, and associative expression extends back into the Sumerian mists of oral culture and story telling. At the very least, this line of research reconnects the sometimes hermetically sealed literatures of Hebraic and Hellenic cultures.

Within the Greek literature available to us, virtue only later in the classical period of philosophy came to be analytically classified as commonly normative, a matter of public *ethos* (character) and social *mores* (customs). Earlier, however, virtue is expressed in the epic literature of the *Iliad* in uncommonly singular terms: The virtue of the hero, whether Archive or Trojan—swift-footed Achilles or man-slaying Hector—is embodied and recognized in the unique character of his passion: Achilles *agathos*; Hector *agathos*. The expression here is an affirmation in praise of unique stature. The *virtue* of Achilles is of a piece, the whole of his character embodied in the passion of its expression. Nietzsche famously laments the reframing (and defanging) of the *agathos* of warrior culture into the rationalized *arête* of the classical *polis*, where the emphasis is on the civil virtues of harmony and justice in human community (the meaning of *polis*) rather than the unique character of heroism that distinguished the individual warrior. But even this reconstituting of virtue—of *agathos* into the civilizing *arête* of political life—is arguably a matter of transformed, not mitigated, passion. The ironic voice of Socrates, the censorious preclusions of Plato, the therapeutic revisions of Aristotle all attest to a shift in which the collective and distributive passions of political life displaced the bellicose passions that once rose above the sound and fury of the killing fields. Even so, the bond of virtue and passion common to both cultures—albeit transformed—is preserved. The resolute courage of the embattled statesman is not the sustaining courage of the embattled warrior, but the excellence of virtue in both is manifest in the different passions of their engagement.

Virtue/*arête* in the Classical Greek world is most often referenced by the "cardinal virtues" of wisdom, courage, moderation, and justice. It is significant, of course, that these are virtues attributable to the male citizen of the *polis*—a woman's *arête*, for example in Aristotle's account, is to observe the decorum of obedience. The cardinal virtues are familiar to us through Plato's analysis in the *Republic*, where he aligns each virtue as the excellence of that activity natural and appropriate to defining aspects of the individual as well as the sustaining resources of the state. Recall that in the individual the virtue of intellect is wisdom, the virtue of will is courage, and the virtue of appetite or desire is moderation, and each has an analogue within the organic totality of the State. Justice, finally, is a comprehensive virtue that ensures the harmony and health of the individual and the State by giving each functioning part its "just" due. On this reading of Plato, the virtue of justice is not simply that of rational constraint, but rather an active ordering of the passions as well as the faculties of intellect, spirit, and appetite.

It requires little argument to show that wisdom is a virtue: excellence in the exercise of intellect. It is only slightly more of a task to show that wisdom is equally a *passion*—an expression of the aspiration, in Plato's terms, to *understand* what it is we already in some sense *know*—to transform knowledge into understanding—to make knowledge part of our very being. This is the rationale of Plato's claim that Virtue is Knowledge. Knowledge is only Virtue, however, when it becomes embodied in character. Aristotle later provides just this rule: that some subjects (ethics, politics) can be understood only by being made part of the learner's very nature, and, he adds, this takes time. Much the same can be argued of courage. The virtue of courage is manifest in the passion of engagement in the face of fear. Courage must become a disposition to act, that is, be made an indelible feature of character; but we must be *moved* to act, and reason alone, as Hume has persuasively argued, is insufficient to move us to action. Courage consists precisely in the passionate conviction that one must act notwithstanding a cognitive awareness of danger.

The critical culture of modern ethics began with Descartes' attempt to demonstrate that Man exists as a thinking being, such that will or volition functions only as an on–off switch, an executive "yea" or "nay" to the rational cognition of clear and distinct ideas. This skeptical turn helped further to divide reason and passion and conceptually divest virtue of the energy needed to realize action. Hume's corrective reminder that Man is not only a thinking being, but also a feeling and deciding agent and that passion is required as a motive to action served to conceptually reconnect passion and virtue in the ordinary of moral life.

In this light, virtue is portrayed and explored in literature in terms of the full and variegated passion of human beings. It thus provides a field of meaning within which the moral character of virtue and passion is mutually and fully developed. Virtues expressed in the context and time of their portrayal in drama or the novel make no specific claim on our allegiance, but appeal rather to a critical range of imagination and understanding. Achilles remains *agathos* in all his tent-hiding, backsliding resentment no less than in taking up arms in personal vengeance and desecrating the body of noble Hector. We are not invited to judge nor are we inclined simply to admonish Achilles, and so his actions remain full bodied and fully articulate in their human expression. Literature rarely is saddled with sorting between virtues and vices. The passions that engage human beings in life as they are expressed through literature are allowed a depth of expression in which we recognize that excellence may be overdetermined and other directed, that virtue may turn vicious in the energy of its excess. The lesson of literature (beyond the domain of morals and legislation) is that there is a continuum in the energies of passion such that "virtues" become "vices" and vice versa: Both can contribute to, without diminishing the excellence of, character.

III

One way to approach the great history of Western literature from the epics of *Gilgamesh* and the *Iliad*, from tragic and comic drama, through medieval passion plays to the pulp novels and popular theatre of today is to note that human beings have grown no new emotions since coming out of Eden (or down from the trees.) This is part of the explanation of how it is we can respond to literature written thousands of years ago, yet we will not pick up, much less read, a computer software book a year after its publication. We find ourselves responsive to the outrageous courage of Gilgamesh whatever its excess and arrogance, and we are drawn into the great wrath of Achilles however irrational its provocation. In each case, we are moved by archaic passions that still haunt the human heart and mind and so find resonance with the literature of its expression. However one defines the virtues—as human excellences of mind and spirit that variously inform and direct—the response of action is inclusive of the divergent energies that contend with the order of our individual and communal lives.

I noted that the originating discourse about virtues in the archaic Greek period developed into the Classical ideal of the four cardinal virtues, which in turn and in one or another way find a place within the expanded empire of the Roman World. At the advent of Christianity, however, a dramatic and creative break occurs in the relocation of passion and virtue. Christianity, which brought Judaism directly into contact with Classical Greek thought, proclaims a different spiritual sense of passion and transforms the cultural expression of moral life into new and very different virtues under the aspect of a very different deity. The generative Christian virtues of Faith, Hope, and Love include others equally divergent from the cardinal virtues of the Classical Greeks. The Christian virtue of *humility*, for example, makes the Greek virtue of *pride* into a vice. In general, Christian virtues have the effect of turning away from public disclosure (a primary element in the cardinal virtues), and so the discourse of passion turns intimately inward to a concern for the secret soul.

This exchange of gods and the transformation of the passions of virtue also breeds a change in and of literature. One is no longer living a public life disclosed in the free and open venue of the *polis*, where actions are to be judged and character assessed under penalty of utter visibility, nor morally ordered within the vast space of the Roman Empire, where prudence is the common coin of virtue. Rather, in Christian community one lives the private life of the soul, whose secrets only God can know. In this new moral scheme, the pain of viciousness is not from the shame of public disclosure or from stoic disharmony from nature, but from an absolute alienation from God, the source of all value and life. The difference between Hellenic and Hebraic cultures is usually indexed in terms of "shame culture" (Greek) and "guilt culture" (Hebrew). Arguably, the Christian synthesis incorporates both, so that the individual is now subject to cycles of guilt and shame—guilt for what one has done; shame for what one has become in the doing (no longer that of public disclosure, but, as it were, naked before God.)

The relational convergence of passion and virtue is in some ways clarified in this transition from the cardinal virtues of Hellenic culture to the ordinal virtues of Judeo-Christian culture—from the Classical imperatives of Wisdom, Courage, Temperance, and Justice to the Christian commandments of Faith, Hope, and Love. It is clear in context that the latter are not to be understood as feelings, but as passions, not descriptions on what to feel, but prescriptions on how to live, and as such they constitute an order of virtue in the passionate resolution of commitment. Conceptually, the way has already been prepared in the religious expression of the Passion of Christ, understood not merely as a passive suffering, but as a willful offering that confronts the violence of office with the charity of forgiveness. It is in that symbolic event that the passional virtues of Faith, Hope, and Charity find completion. In each tradition—profane and political versus religious and scriptural—the excellence of life, although differently construed in emphasis, requires the passion of virtue for its realization.

The truncated scheme I have presented so far concerning the historical foundations of Western cultural values should at least suggest that guilt and shame are two sides of the same coin in the critical framing of human passion. Clearly, guilt frames the actions of Achilles dragging the dead body of great Hector around again and again before the walls of Ilium venting his rage, exulting in the blood lust of victory, although it is shame and a concern for honor that will move him later to relent and give over the warrior's body to his father, Priam. This is a complex scene in which one might argue that Achilles' action is less one of compassion for Priam than it is a recollection of his own father—that is, that this whole issue remains one about Achilles.

Passions of vengeance and rage—the reflective guilt of excess and the shame that attends dishonoring another—is presented in the *Iliad* in a way that exemplifies rather than undermines the virtue of Achilles. Moreover, this paradoxical expression of virtue is recognized and understood through the timeless quality of its passion. In literature, a response of approbation or disapprobation remains much the same however much the particular historical priorities of virtue are altered or realigned. That the virtue of pride is given one valuation in the warrior cult of Greek culture and the virtue of humility, its seeming opposite, is valued above or in place of it in Christian culture does nothing to affect the force of the expression of both in world literature.

Aristotle's familiar classification in the *Poetics* that determines the genres of literature in how characters are depicted—as superior, equal to, or inferior to nature or to ourselves—is still broadly accepted. This classification makes it possible after more than two thousand years to continue to discuss virtue and passion appropriate to and expressed in each genre from epic literature to tragic and comic drama. Nietzsche makes use of Aristotle's categories in a parallel account in the *Birth of Tragedy,* and Northrop Frye's contemporary explication of "fictional modes" in *Anatomy of Criticism* directly mirrors Aristotle's description. Whatever historical emphasis may be accorded the value of virtues, they remain within the literary constants of Aristotle's relational description.

Although it is true that archaic passions remain at the heart of what is moving in literature, and the virtues that refine the passions remain similarly accessible to ancient or modern literature and life, inversions and distortions occur as well. It is a familiar feature of literary criticism to contrast the classical idea and ideal of the heroic with the ironic expression of the antihero in contemporary literature, although clearly there are strands of irony already in the work of Euripides, in which the focus becomes more one of psychological than spiritual analysis. In any event, the great deeds of warriors unique in their attributes no longer frequent the battlefields of our age; they are replaced by soldiers in uniform functioning as replaceable parts in an indifferent machine that mass produces death and destruction. Even so, we still speak of courage in the face of fear, of loyalty to comrades standing in the ranks of death, and of honoring those who died however unwilling in service to a cause however meaningless. But *Walkuries* no longer ride out to carry the fallen dead to *Walhalla*; in our time, there are only weary death details that toe-tag naked remains for the body bags that mark the effluence of war. Thus it is hardly surprising that a later literature, accustomed to peace and aware of the mindless destruction and the anonymity of its victims, finds the passions of war and the romance of victory less inspiring to virtue. It is only within a sustained and brittle, sometimes bitter irony that such virtues find a voice. Compare only the opening lines of the *Iliad*, "Sing, Muse, of the wrath of Achilles...," with the closing lines of Hemingway's *A Farewell to Arms*: "the words 'honor', 'courage'... became meaningless and profane... only the names of places had any meaning...." Or compare the dramatic intensity of Hamlet's engaged deliberation with the wages of life and death—whether 'tis nobler to take up arms against a sea of troubles... or turn those arms against oneself and end it—with the ironic meditation of J. Alfred Prufrock's disengaged contemplation of a life measured out in coffee spoons: 'No I am not Prince Hamlet, nor was meant to be....' I have already noted the remove from the ancient warrior in armor to the modern soldier in uniform; consider the further remove from the immortality of remembered heroes of the *Iliad* to the mortality and anonymity commemorated in the tomb of the Unknown Soldier, and the even further remove to Auden's ironic depiction of the Unknown Citizen. But with all the revisions, revaluations, and reversioning of virtue, the passion of literature in the expression of these values and virtues remains intact. The virtues and passions of Hamlet are not those of Prufrock; the moral exhaustion of Hemingway's soldier is not the moral exhilaration of Homer's warrior; each man on the battlefield of Ilium is not the Everyman of *Pilgrim's*

Progress, much less the Anyman of Auden's citizen. But the passion of their expressions in literature gives voice to the character of an age and forms the substance of our moral heritage as human beings.

IV

Man is an adverbial creature in the sense that his defining activities are valued in terms of how they are done. Well or ill, courageously or cowardly, wisely or foolishly, justly or unjustly, gracefully or crudely, courteously or rudely, viciously and cruelly, or gently and graciously. We speak casually of *"the virtues"* or conversely of *"the seven deadly sins,"* but of course there are no such things. Such words are linguistic reminders about human activities; in refinement, they function in the valuation of human action.

Virtue, first analyzed in Classical Greek philosophy as an excellence of the human mind and spirit, is not that which sets the animal man apart from other animals—the possession of *logos* (language, reason) already does that—but rather that which attests to the possibilities of greatness in human kind. When Homer earlier remarks that of one race are gods and men, he has in mind those characteristics of spirit in action that mark the possibility of transcendence of the commonplace. Shakespeare speaks to the point in a similar way in Hamlet's memorable declension of "this paragon of animals":

What a piece of work is man: How noble in reason! how infinite in faculties! in form and moving how express and admirable! in action how like an angel! in apprehension, how like a god! the beauty of the world! And yet... this quintessence of dust.
Hamlet II, ii, (115–117)

It is a mistake to think that virtue has to do only with "the good" in the sense of respectable or allowable, and that a check list can be made of the virtues to measure the acceptability of character, much less the depth of the human soul. There are two primary sources for this mistake—rational philosophy and Biblical scripture. In the pre-judicial analysis of Greek philosophy, the bifurcation and preference for reason over passion insisted on rational moderation as the defining feature of virtue. Scripture, on the other hand, requires obedience to God in place of or in addition to reason, which makes the good life one sanctioned by divine will. So the "good life" is marked out in both Hellenic philosophy and Hebraic scripture as one of rationality and obedience. I have insisted that Greek literature, in contrast with Classical Greek philosophy, shows a preference for passion over reason as a defining feature of moral life. In a similar fashion, the flesh and blood characters of the Old Testament, in contrast with the purities of Hebrew law, and exceeding the pieties of the New Testament, provide additional cultural testimony that the depth and worth of life is fully understood only within the reach and extremes of human passion.

In fact, any and every human activity can be done well or not. The remarkable and distinctive genius of world literature is its capacity to demonstrate the full expression of human excellence in conception, resolution, and action. We may find admirable and feel resonance with the actions and personalities of the most demonic of creatures: with the fallen Angel who proclaims that it is better to reign in hell than serve in heaven; with the misshapen form of a King whose winter of discontent is turned glorious summer only in the contrivance of malice; with the sea captain whose life becomes an obsession with vengeance; and with the savage genius of an ivory hunter who can embrace the heart of darkness and pronounce judgment.

Literature, broadly speaking, is an investigation of the moral life of human beings, where "moral life" is understood to encompass all activities of consequence to human beings—a use of "moral" familiar to the eighteenth century Enlightenment. Virtue, portrayed in literature as the excellence of action and character, examines the depths of moral life found in the passions at the heart of human aspiration—whether they be for good or ill, whether generated by an overweening pride and ambition or by humility and reciprocity, whether motivated by lust and greed or intended with benevolence and generosity. In the world of great literature, there are no simple bifurcations of vice and virtue, of good and evil. Acknowledging with St. Augustine that all being is good, literature proceeds without the Augustinian apologetics that evil exists only as an absence of good. Both good and evil exist fully in the world of literature as positive forces and not necessarily in opposition. That is to say, the moral interest of literature is not normatively prescriptive. The insight as well as the attraction of literary expression is discovered more often in the exception than the rule. Heroic character, for example, is embodied in an excess that violates the norm of expectations, whether in terms of nobility or villainy. The exemplary figures in literature from Greek myth, Classical epic, and tragic literature, and from Biblical scripture through fairy tales to modern fiction, are notable *not* for their "moral goodness" but for the exceptional passion of their projects. Consider the history of this assemblage in ancient myth and literature: the fateful "parricides" of Ouranos and Kronos, the arbitrary injustices of the Olympians, the thieving of Prometheus, the ecstasies of Dionysos, the wrath of Achilles, the connivings of Odysseus, the audacities of Agamemnon, Orestes, Oedipus, and Antigone.... It is much the same with the principals of Hebrew literature and scripture, from the first rebellion of Satan and the disobediences of Adam and Eve, through the treacheries of Cain and the ensuing events east of Eden. It is not that evil is more attractive or exciting than good, it is that good and evil are not opposites but are inclusive if sometimes limiting concepts that constitute the moral lives of human beings. Both are requisite to a creature who must find a resource of energy in the full scope of human possibility.

There is arguably a learning factor that contributes to the human interest in exception. Whether or not exception proves the rule, those things learned as exceptional are indelibly imprinted in ways that routine occurrences are not. Tolstoy makes this point memorably in the opening lines from *Anna Karenina* that every happy family is happy in much the same way, whereas every unhappy family has an unhappiness all its own. Paradoxically, what we learn most and best about ourselves through literature comes through an embodiment of the exception, for it is the intensity of difference that imprints the virtue of passion on consciousness.

V

It may be useful, in discussing virtue in the context of moral life, to distinguish between passion and emotion in terms of both degree and kind. Ethics is prescriptive of normalcy and as such it focuses on obligation, on what binds action to a rule. Emotions present a problem in that they are variable and not subject to rule, hence the contrast of emotion and reason, the latter being the predictable domain of moral deliberation. Occasionally there are forceful counterarguments presented against this configuration, which reject reason as definitive of morals. The most persuasively famous is that of Hume, who suggested rather that reason is a slave to the passions, and who argues that reason has no moral force, and so locates moral life and sense in feelings.

Hume made the point that if we do not respond sympathetically to the pain of another person, no amount of reason will move us to care about their plight. But having said this, we are a long way from understanding the passion of virtue. Feeling, emotion (*pathe*), has as its central meaning something endured or something that happens to one. It is, if not negative or neutral, then reactive to some event or situation. Aristotle remarks relative to this point that one cannot be blamed for feelings, only for actions. Even Aristotle, however, insisted that emotions themselves must become rational in the well-tempered soul, which indicates that reason is not an independent faculty, or at least that emotions somehow partake in and are not simply subject to reason.

The point here is that even in its philosophical framing, passion (*pathos*) has an active connotation—a positive energy that is not merely reactive.

This suggests, for example, that the essential difference between anger and wrath is one of kind, not degree. The wrath of Achilles with which the *Iliad* begins is anything but passive or merely reactive; passion here is not limited to a sense of offense, but marks a positive and generative force only occasioned by that offense. It is this passion that is the source of the judgment or acclimation "*Achilles agathos!*"; passion is the way in which Achilles proclaims himself, the measure of his character. It is here and in this sense that passion and virtue converge. In the milder culture of later times, virtue is more generally recognized, for example, in the passion for justice. Finally, in its most comprehensive and universal sense, the virtue of humanity is realized in the passion for life.

Plato famously distrusted and devalued passion, particularly in its characteristic poetic expression, which he nonetheless credited as a kind of divine madness. But in *Symposium* Plato dialectically develops the journey of the philosophical spirit toward the beauty of truth, in which *Eros*, desire, remains at the root of what moves and provides the energy of that spiritual quest. In this context, *philein sophian*—the love and pursuit of wisdom that defines philosophy for Plato—serves to qualify his earlier rejection of passion and existentially anchor wisdom in *pathos*. It is passion for the beauty in life that leads to the love of wisdom and the truth of understanding—to the *eidos* of the Good, which in turn is the source both of enlightenment and the virtue of a fully *human* life. So understood, the *quadrivium* of excellence in the classical world—wisdom, courage, temperance, justice—owe their existence and force in the life of individual and community to *pathos* (passion) no less than *logos* (reason).

Whether one aspires to a greatness of soul (the tragic hero) or only to the excellence of a particular spiritual endowment (the range of humanity), movement only begins in the passion of that commitment. Justice in the state or in the soul of the individual is never realized without such commitment. The road to virtue, to the excellence of character in action, whether for the tragic hero or the stoic everyman, must overcome obstacles, excuses, occasions, and all the other roadside distractions that imagination can invent. The world of literature is a collected canon of investigations of the lateral movements of human passion, a comprehensive and dynamic manifold of heroic achievement and ironic failures in the human aspiration to virtue. In its positive form, however, passion attests to that most common and ordinary virtue that defines humanity—a tenacity of spirit and resolve that affirms the beauty of life in the face of inevitable defeat.

It would be appropriate for my point to quote the whole of William Faulkner's memorable remarks on his acceptance of the Nobel Prize for literature. He ends with this:

> I believe that man will not merely endure: he will prevail. He is immortal, not because he alone among creatures has an inexhaustible voice, but because he has a soul, a spirit capable of compassion and sacrifice and endurance. The poet's, the writer's, duty is to write about these things. It is his privilege to help man endure by lifting his heart, by reminding him of the courage and honor and hope and pride and compassion and pity and sacrifice which have been the glory of his past.

If the rational imperative of *logos* in philosophy is "Only connect!" its mirror image in literature is the imperative of *pathos* in poetry: "Always affirm!" However tragic the realization of the hero, the anguish of his or her cry is still an affirmation of the beauty and sublimity of life. The classical Greek insistence on this point is confirmed in the practice of ending the trilogy of each tragic drama during the festival of Dionysos with a Satyr play in which life is again affirmed in all its primal and libidinal passion. The contrast in the modern ironic turn of culture and literature is only apparent in this context. In *The Heart of Darkness*, for example, in which the tragic and the ironic are contrasted in the characters of Kurtz and Marlowe—two faces of the human spirit: participant and spectator—the tragic affirmation of Kurtz, "The Horror!" is followed by the ironic commentary of Marlowe on his own confrontation with the heart of darkness "Droll thing life is...." But Conrad finds poetic affirmation in both characters: The virtue of passion is discovered both in action and reflection, in the character of the tragic figure who can look into the heart of darkness with complete conviction, and in the ironic figure who can only go on to tell the story. It is arguably a further remove from the classical passion of the tragic hero to the ironic antihero of modern poetic fiction—from Prometheus to Prufrock—but the passion of virtue is found still, if only in the ironic beauty of its expression.

Even in the most despairing moments of tragic drama in which man but frets and struts his hour upon the stage in a life full of sound and fury there is no remorse in the journey that has led to this revelation. Even in the recognition that all our yesterdays have but lighted fools the way to dusty death, there are still no vapid regrets or recriminations. This, simply, is how it is with humankind. But in the interim between birth and death the human spirit has been shown to reach beyond its limits to rival the gods, and in this recognition is an affirmation of the passion of human virtue. The gods have no need to try and fail, to live and die—indeed they lack the capacity to do so. The passions of the timeless gods are pale by comparison to those of a creature caught in the ravages of time, in which passion is all that sustains him. The gods are without virtue, not because they lack restraint, but because only human beings must risk and suffer and fail in aspiring to become what they can only imagine.

The tragic and comic masks of dramatic literature serve finally as expressions of the conflicting and inclusive faces of humanity. As a poetic prism of the human condition, literature embodies an affirmation of passion, an expression of that singular virtue that ennobles the character of the human spirit.

Trinity University

SECTION I

HISTORICAL AND CONTEMPORARY VIRTUES AS REFLECTED IN CHINESE LITERATURE

I

In view of the fact that today the Chinese comprise the largest section of mankind, questions of the persistence of their way of life and the longevity of their culture merit exploration. If virtue can be defined as the principle by which the Chinese have guided their behaviors and beliefs, as a foundation for living and creating individual lives and shaping the collective whole, then it is important to examine how virtue is expressed in Chinese literature. Literature is an invaluable source of historical and contemporary virtues prevalent in Chinese society. The most authoritative Chinese literature throughout the centuries provides relevant data and insights into patterns of behavior and their role in building a foundation for the future.

II

Confucian virtues have been predominantly, if not exclusively, molded by the Confucian perception of what it is to be a human being and how one should behave to fulfill the meaning of life. Confucius, it is said, propounded these precepts in response to his students' questions, which are recorded in *Analects* (*Lu Yu*), the most authoritative notes his students recorded of Confucius' teachings. Confucius purported not to be a genius, but only to have studied very hard to acquire his knowledge. At the age of fifteen, he made up his mind to pursue learning and felt he knew no more than others. He disdained the views of revelation or the existence of a "messenger of God" and refrained from engaging in discussions about topics such as miracles, myths, ghosts, and supernatural phenomena (*Ze bu yu quail luan sheng*). In Confucius' view, knowledge, as such, is the product of the human mind operating in a continually evolving process with no permanence or limit. As one discovered unknown aspects in the pursuit of learning and knowledge, one demonstrated that even the unknown is knowledge (*bu zhi yi zhe yi*). Although human beings are endowed with creative minds, the learning process enhances the mind's creativity, leading it to achieve its potential. Thus, Confucians considered learning as an essential virtue. It is not static but requires interaction with others, most notably the teacher or expert. There is a Chinese saying: Parents give you life, teachers make you into a human being. In *The Great Learning* (*Da Xue*), another Confucian classic, the first sentence states that the virtue of learning is to reach the ultimate goodness. Learning is a lifelong process. Taoists, centuries ago, even advocated that the process began the moment a child is conceived (*tai jiao*) because the fetus perceived experiences of its world through interactions with its mother in the womb.

In reality, what Confucius defined as what it was to be a human being (*Ren*) was humanity (*Ren zhi ren yi*). The character for "*Ren*" consists of two people interacting. The exposition of this concept takes center place in *Analects*. The character "*Ren*" appears 105 times in this work. The manifestation of this fundamental human quality is, in Confucius' perspective, the outpouring of the sentiment of love, particularly parental love. Mencius, the great defender of Confucius, contended in the work *Mencius* that humans differ little from animals except that human beings are born with a sense of empathy, a sense of right and wrong, a sense of shame, and a sense of propriety and that it is best to act with the greater good of humanity in mind rather than that of the individual. Thus, in the practice of *Ren*, one must not only establish oneself, but also help others to survive. If one desires to live well, one must see to it that others accomplish the same (*jun ze cheng ren zhi mei*). Mencius pointed out that because people are not born equal, it is the duty of those who have become enlightened to enlighten those less fortunate (*xien zhi jiao he zhi*). Furthermore, Confucius stated, "What I do not wish others to do to me, I wish not to do the same to them" (*Analects*, Book V, Chapter XI). According to Confucius, depriving others of their livelihood to enrich oneself violates the principle of *Ren*.

Since Confucians upheld the conviction that the survival of mankind as a whole is of primary importance, the union of marriage is of fundamental importance, preceded only by the necessity to eat. Mencius argued that to act against this natural impulse would invite disaster (*Ni fu xing za bi dei fe sheng*). Therefore, the institution of marriage in Chinese culture is all-important. Confucius stressed that it signified the beginning of moral action and the foundation of civilization (*Jun ze zhi dao cai duan hu fe fu*). In traditional Chinese society, one must get married and produce progeny. Allowing the discontinuation of the family line violates the basic Confucian virtue of filial piety. The *Classic of Filial Piety* clearly states that a bachelor who does not marry is a disgrace not only to his family, but also to the community as a whole. Consequently, "go-betweens," or matchmakers, achieved professional status. Maintaining and fostering the institution of marriage was the responsibility of the ruler and partly became the function of the government and can even be seen today in Singapore. Long before Confucius, the Chinese recognized the relationship between genetic defects and consanguineous marriage. One of the founders of the Zhou Dynasty, the Duke of Zhou, Ji Dan (1115–1108 BC), issued a decree forbidding it. From then on, a man with the family name of, say, Wang was not allowed marry a young woman by the name of Wang. Recent studies showed that of one billion, three hundred million Chinese, there are no more than 4,102 family names (*The People's Daily*, January 13, 2006); 100 of these predominate. The impact of this traditional practice on Chinese population development is difficult to assess. The overwhelming majority of Chinese today identify themselves as Han Chinese, based more on the cultural and historical identity of the Han Dynasty (206 BC–220 AD) than racial origins.

Confucians contended that for human beings to survive, life must be sustainable, enjoyable, and have a sense of meaning or purpose. It was believed that the harmonious union of man and woman begetting a family was a primary source of happiness and provided the core meaning of life. The story of Adam and Eve and the suffering their existence reflected runs counter to these beliefs. In Chinese literature, the expression of the feeling of love between man and woman and among the family is abundant. For example, among the earliest Chinese poetry, the *Book of Songs* (Shi Jing), allegedly edited by Confucius, vividly portrays these sentiments. Verses about courtship and marriage receive prominent exposition.

Verse 137 (*Mao Shi*) says

> The elms of the eastern gate
> Oaks of the hollow mound—
> The sons of the Ze-Zhong
> Trip and sway beneath them
> It is a lucky morning, hurrah;
> The Yuan girls from the southern side
> Instead of twisting their hemp
> In the market trip and sway.
> It is a fine morning at last;
> Let us go off to join the throng.
> You are as lovely as the mallow.
> Then give me a pepper-seed.

The poems of the Tang period (618–907) have been acclaimed as the pinnacle of literary achievement. Among the most popular and authoritative anthologies even today, *Three Hundred Tang Poems* includes 85 poems that encompass the theme of courtship and marriage. "The Golden Threaded Gown" ("*Jin Lu Yi*") by the female poet Du Qiy-niang is an example:

> I urge you not to cherish the golden threaded gown
> But the time of your youth
> When there is a flower to which you can pluck
> Do it right away, don't wait for it to become an empty branch

III

Confucius idealized this universal human instinct of love to define the moral principle of humanity (*Zen*). He also did not deny that human beings were capable of hate. In an effort to resolve the dilemma of the duality of love and hate, Confucius instructed his students to love those who acted in accordance to the principle of *Zen*, humanity, and to despise or hate those who did not. But human nature revealed that the pairing of man and woman is not always ideal, and one can experience the pain of rejection. In this situation, rejection may not necessarily be wrong or immoral. In the cycle of life, death comes to all. Yet, no one wants to die, and with it comes suffering and sadness. If this cycle falls out of balance, survival of the human race would be precarious. No scientific explanation yet fully addresses the endless array of questions regarding this balance of the creation of life and death. Many see it as a blessing of God. The early Chinese, most likely through the observation of the most fundamental dichotomies—day and night, summer and winter, love and hate, hunger and satiation—envisioned a twofold structure interacting in a contradictory yet complementary balance. This harmonious balance became the guiding principle for all behavior and was crystallized as *Zhong*.

In the *Book of Changes* (*I-Jing*), Yin and Yang, a virtual formula of an interacting succession of 64 primordial pairings, was created to foretell the fortune or misfortune of one's actions. Confucius attributed its inception to King Wen, the founder of the Zhou Dynasty (1122–221 BC) and humbly expressed his hope of living longer to study it. Among the 64 hexagrams, the idea of harmonious balance plays a central role 53 times. Confucius adopted it as the kernel of his vision of virtue. In the *Doctrine of the Mean* (the standard translation of *Zhong Yun*), Confucius extrapolated it to *Zhong He*, stating

> While there are no stirrings of pleasure, anger, sorrow or joy, the mind may be said to be in the state of balance, or equilibrium; when those feelings have been stirred, and they act in their due degree, these ensues what may be called the state of harmony. This equilibrium is the great root from which grow all the human activity in the world, and this harmony is the universal path which they all should pursue. (J. Legge translation)

This concept of *Zhong* is incorporated into China's state name today (*Zhong Guo*), which is somewhat misused because of its literal translation.

Historically, Confucius' concept of virtues did not reach its ascendancy until the Han Dynasty, when Emperor Wu (140–87 BC) acted upon the advice of Dong Zhong-shu, a follower of Confucius, and proclaimed Confucianism the state doctrine, which remained until 1949, when the People's Republic of China was formed. In his work *Luxuriant Dews of Spring and Autumn* (*Chun-qiu Fan Lu*), Dong developed his theory of the five elements: metal, wood, water, fire and earth. These elements support the principle of the primordial pair—Ying and Yang. The elements interact in contradictory and complementary ways to maintain a harmonious balance assuring change in the world and perpetuating its existence. In view of the advances of quantum mechanics, this proto-scientific rationale has provided an enormously important tool with which the Chinese and others have studied nature and human events. For example, acupuncture is based on this idea, as explained in the *Yellow Emperor's Internal Medicine* (*Huang Di Su Wen*).

Yin-Yang has permeated every aspect of Chinese life and has almost become a seamless pattern of thinking. In Arnold Toynbee's estimation, the Chinese have a Yin-Yang culture. For instance, calligraphic landscape painting created by Chinese scholars, which is considered to be a unique and significant contribution to the arts, can be translated as mountain and water paintings. A solid, strong, motionless state interacts with a soft, fluid state in constant motion to attain a harmonious balance, from which a sense of beauty and meaning can be drawn. In fact, it is a virtual reality rendered by the artist or scholar to express a philosophy of life or world view, which is also conveyed through a classical poem written at the top of the painting. Without a certain degree of proficiency in classical Chinese, it is difficult to appreciate this art form because the picture is an idealized representation of a poem rather than simply a depiction.

Chinese literary forms, the rigid poem, rhyming prose, and even essays are created to express ideas and feelings. Even the tonal nature of the Chinese language has shaped these literary expressions. There is a balance and counterbalance between the characters and a point and counterpoint between the high-pitch (*ping*) and low-pitch (*ze*) tones of the characters. This sing-song effect is derived to enhance the harmonious balance of the piece. One of the more popular forms of poetry, *Lu Shi*, or rigid poem, has four lines containing five or seven characters. Take "In the Quiet Night" by Li Ba, one of China's preeminent classical poets from the Tang period, as an example:

> *Chuang qian Ming Yue Guang* (A gleaming moonlight lies at the head of my bed)
> [*Ping Ping Ze Ze Ping*]
> *Yi Shi De Shang Shaung* (Could it be frost on the land?)
> [*Ze Ze Ping Ping Ze*]
> *Ju Tou Wang Ming Yue* (Lifting my head to look, it is moonlight)
> [*Ping Ping Ping Ze Ze*]
> *Di Tou Si Gu Xiang* (Lowering my head, I am thinking of my home town)
> [*Ze Ze Ze Ping Ping*]

Not only has attention been paid to achieving a tonal harmonious balance, but also note that there is a balance between the actions of the subject's head rising and lowering. Some say entertainers in the teahouses, where these poems were often presented, used these techniques simply to amuse the audience, yet the overall effect is significant. Take another example for illustration. The most popular Chinese couplet, which is used to adorn the front door to welcome in the new year, follows that same rhythm:

Bao Zhu Yi Sheng Chu Jiu (One explosion of firecrackers gets rid of the past)
[*Ze Ze Ping Ping Ze Ze*]
Tao Fu Wan Hu Geng Xin (Arrival of a peaceful rally of thousands of families heralds a fresh start)
[*Ping Ping Ze Ze Ping Ping*]

Attention is given to harmonious balance in other types of literature as well, among them the novel, drama, folksongs, and ballads. For example, the popular novel *The Journey to the West* (*Xi You Ji*) by Wu Cheng-en (1500–1582), written during the Ming dynasty, portrays an intelligent monkey attempting to enlighten an ignorant pig. The monkey, able to comprehend the emptiness in life, gives the pig eight warnings as it tries to enlighten the pig and confer the ultimate liberation from suffering by attaining Nirvana. Through the use of satire, a harmonious balance is skillfully maintained by the animals' master, the monk Xuan Zhuangl, as they attempt to reach their goal of enlightenment while seeking truths from Buddhism and India, its source of origin.

IV

In the final analysis, the idea of harmonious balance as the ultimate virtue calls for the correct proportions interacting in the primordial pairs to sustain the existence of and changes in all things and events in the world. It does not mean precisely equal parts. Literally, the Chinese phrase, for harmonious balance of Yin-Yang is "*xie huo*" or "*he*." The character "*xie*" is composed with three forces in the unity of one heart. It suggests three people coordinating or cooperating wholeheartedly to achieve a common goal. How these ideal proportions exhibited by these primordial pairs are attained poses a tremendous challenge to human action. It is no surprise that in the *Doctrine of the Mean* (Chapter 3), Confucius laments that while harmonious balance constitutes the ultimate goodness in life and fosters survivability, it is very difficult to pursue successfully and then to maintain (*Zhong yong zhi wei de, qu zhi yi hu, min xian neng jiu yi*).

What historical experience of this practice has been revealed or reflected in Chinese literature? The *Book of Changes*, for instance, points out that what appears to have sustained the world and its harmonious balance is the incessant rebirth of the primordial pair, Yin-Yang. The human species, as well, through the joining of Yin and Yang has perpetuated. Throughout China, Yang is viewed as symbolically male and Yin as symbolically female. Dong Zhon-shu institutionalized these beliefs in a system of three cardinal rules and five constants. The three cardinal rules are: King rules over subjects, father rules over sons, and husband rules over wife. The five constants of morality are humanity (*Ren*), righteousness (*Yi*), propriety (*Li*), wisdom (*Zhi*), and sincerity (*Xing*).

The renowned poetess and historian Ban Zhao (40–120) described the relationship of husband and wife in her work *Lessons for Women* (*Nu Zai*), Chapter 2. She stated, "Yin and Yang are not of the same nature.... The most distinctive quality of Yang is rigidity; the function of Yin is yielding; Man is honored of strength, while woman is beautiful on account of her gentleness." Consequently, it is difficult to sustain harmonious balance in a family relationship under this interpretation. No doubt, this assertion promoted population growth and could be viewed positively from that perspective. Yet, the subjugation and discrimination against women that it promoted was unfortunate. Women were excluded from getting an education or claiming an inheritance, were deprived of social status, and even were victims of foot-binding as a symbol of perfection and also forced into polygamy as a status symbol.

Moreover, the enforcement of filial piety as a cardinal rule further aggravated the situation. Arranged marriages flourished, and, at times, even were contracted before a daughter was born (*Zhi fu wei hun*). Two outstanding and extraordinarily popular literary works vividly portray the torment and conflicts brought about by filial piety and underscored their didactic purpose. The first is *The Dream of the Western Chamber* (*Xi Xiang Ji*) by Wang Shih-fu and possibly Guan Han-qing during the time of the Yuan (1260–1368 AD). The second is *The Dream of the Red Chamber* (*Hong Lou Meng*), a novel by Cao Xue-qin from the early Qing (1644–1911) period. It portrays a promising young scholar, idealized in a society that reveres education, who falls in love with a beautiful woman. Even though he has a certain status for being a scholar, he is unable to escape his domineering mother, who interferes with the marriage by allowing the couple to marry but forcing them to live separately. While this is essentially a love story, it is nowhere near as erotic as *The Golden Lotus* (*Jin Ping Me*), which depicts a spoiled scion who recklessly pursues women in his family compound where five generations live. It is a Confucian ideal to keep family property intact, explaining why all five generations live together. Rather than reviving the family fortune, he squanders it.

In addition, he detests formal learning, refusing to be a faithful Confucian scholar even though he successfully negotiates the examination system and acquires a degree. Eventually, he recognizes that life is illusory and becomes a Buddhist monk.

Since Confucius purported that learning enables a person to realize his ultimate goodness as recorded in the *Great Learning*, the institution of education became the most important undertaking in Confucian society. The Imperial College (Tai Xue) was established during the Han dynasty not only for ordinary subjects, for but also for the imperial family. Lasting until the Tang dynasty, it oversaw an examination system that administered a proto-civil service test. Those who achieved the highest scores in the metropolitan or imperial level received extremely significant opportunities. The top three often married into the imperial family and served as the prime minister, imperial tutor, or other ministers. There was a saying China in those days, "Early in the morning one is a rural boy; in the evening he enters the imperial palace." High scorers not in the top three were appointed regional governors and on down to magistrates, who enforced the criminal code. Civil disputes were resolved through arbitration controlled by Confucian scholars. The opportunities bestowed upon these successful scholars caused many families to center all their attention on fostering education among their children. Yet, in reality, did harmonious balance exist in such a system?

During the Ming and Qing dynasties, the examination system, originally created to foster Confucian virtues, deteriorated into an arduous and capricious memorization contest, which came to be called the "eight-legged contest." It stipulated that the tests and their answers be exclusively written in original Confucian sentences. The end result of this sterile examination system was that it froze creativity, the opposite of what Confucius had called for with daily renovation. Consequently, the examination system may have contributed to China's problems in matching the rise of industrialized Western countries. The novel *The Scholars* (*Ru Lin Wai Shi*) by Wu Jing-zi of the early Qing dynasty attacked the absurdities of the examination system in an extraordinarily satirical style, skillfully pointing out that the attainment of true virtue may not be related to learning the classics and pure memorization. However, Wu remained conservative in questioning the basic Confucian virtues and, in particular, the family institution as it existed.

Blunt exposure of the suffering and disharmony caused by adhering rigidly to these Confucian family virtues and the superficiality they wrought did not appear in literature until recently. The first such novel of note was *Family* (*Jia*) by Ba Jin. The second, *A Madman's Diary* by Lu Xun, under the penname of Zhou Shu-ren (1881–1936), presented a tale that implied that some Confucian virtues could induce man to devour man. The principal character suffers from a persecution complex and was afraid of being eaten by his family members. Ironically, Lu raised the question of whether a son should cut off part of his body for his parents' medical needs, fulfilling the role of filial piety. The question is also surprisingly relevant today worldwide in regards to organ donation and stem cell research. Is this filial piety?

Buddhism and Taoism were also popular throughout China during this time and brought with them different kinds of morality tales. Chinese literature typically avoided supernatural phenomena or ghost figures, but *Strange Stories in the Chatting Room* (*Liao Zhai Zhi Yi*) by Pu Sun-Lin effectively incorporated ghosts, spirits, and animals in a morally uplifting story. The novel implied that divine retribution will be visited upon evil-doers. It was based on the assumption that the world contains a variety of unseen, unexpected, and unpredictable ghosts and spirits who dispense justice with rewards and punishments. Pu appears to have incorporated the Buddhist concept of predetermination along with the Taoist presentation of a twofold soul: the "*hun*," which dissipates upon death, and the "*po*," which becomes a ghost after death, interacting with others to bring fortune and misfortune to other living beings as they deserve it.

In the *Analects* (Book XII, Chapter 5), Confucius pronounced that "all within the four seas are brothers" and "a virtuous person wishes to establish oneself seeking to establish others too." Thus, promoting brotherhood has been a Confucian motto for centuries. However, different interpretations are inevitable as circumstances change. Maintaining a harmonious balance in personal conduct while promoting brotherhood is indeed a challenge. Two popular novels from the time of the Yuan dynasty exemplify this issue.

The Romance of Three Kingdoms (*San Guo Yen Yi*) by Luo Guan-zhong (1330–1400) is a historical novel depicting the collapse of the Han empire during the Three Kingdoms period (220–589). Three brothers pledge to devote their lives to restoring the Han empire. Two of them sharply differ in temperament, although not quite as dramatically as the monkey and the pig in the *Journey of the West*. One brother, Zhng Fei, is a marshal who is impulsively ready to fight using his physical presence and valor to his advantage. The other, Commander Guan Yu, is calculating and skillful tactician, who is later worshipped as a deity of good fortune. The third character is the clever elder brother, Liu Bi, who is skilled at maintaining a harmonious balance between his brothers with the assistance of a scholar, Zhu Ge-liang. Zhu's devotion to Liu became legendary, while Liu eventually defeated a talented general from northern China and a warlord from southern China to establish his own kingdom in western China, although he never succeeded in unifying China.

The second novel, *Men from the Marshes* (*Shu Hu*), is by She Nei-an. In it, a band of brigands embarks in subtle underground resistance against Mongol rule. While they may have been seen as "robbing Peter to pay Paul," the sense of trust among their brotherhood was stronger than that among ordinary people. In addition, there is a saying in China, "Gangsters have their own rules of ethics though their principles may not be conventional." This effort to combat injustice and the corruption of society somehow counterbalanced their other questionable methods, leading to this novel being widely circulated and still popular today.

V

As has been said, the past is a prelude to the future. What Confucians perceived as the ultimate virtue—harmonious balance—is reflected throughout Chinese literature. The twofold primordial structure represented by Yin and Yang is embodied in all literature cultivating harmonious balance and assuring existence and change in the world. In a sense, harmonious balance calls for the most beneficial proportions of Yin and Yang to foster progress and achievement in a process the *Book of Changes* calls continuous rebirth in cyclical progression (*Sheng sheng zhi wei yi*). Historical practice in China has showed that the practice of harmonious balance through a continually cyclical progression of rebirth is difficult to attain. Only timely change can facilitate the path, whereas exclusivity and extremism can only lead to mutual destruction. The principle of quantum mechanics resonates with this Confucian concept of relational duality. The world has entered a new era of the information age and further globalization. The Confucian experience of virtues and brotherhood as it has been depicted throughout the centuries may serve as reference for the world as it moves into the future.

Emeritus, Florida Atlantic University, Boca Raton, Florida

BIBLIOGRAPHY

Analects [Confucian text].
Ba Jin. *Family* [in Chinese].
Ban Zhao. *Lessons for Women*. In: Lynn H. Nelson. *Classics of Eastern Thought*. New York: Harcourt, Brace Jovanovich, 1991.
Book of Changes [Confucian text].
Book of Songs [Confucian text].
Cao Xue-qin. *The Dream of the Red Chamber* [in Chinese].
Classic of Filial Piety [Confucian text].

Doctrine of the Mean [Confucian text].
Dong Zhong-shu. *Chu-qiu Fan Lu* (*Luxuriant Dews of Spring and Autumn*). Guangyi, Shanghai, China.
Du Qiy-niang. "The Golden Threaded Gown" [in Chinese].
Golden Lotus [in Chinese].
Great Learning [Confucian text].
Legge, James, transl. *The Four Books*. New York: Paragon, 1966.
Li Ba. "The Quiet Night" [in Chinese].
Lu Xun. *A Madman's Diary* [in Chinese].
Luo Guan-zhong. *The Romance of Three Kingdoms* [in Chinese].
Mencius [Confucian text].
Pu Sun-Lin. *Strange Stories of the Chatting Room* [in Chinese].
She Nei-an. *Men From the Marshes* [in Chinese].
Shi Ji. *Three Hundred Tang Poems* [in Chinese], Singapore.
The People's Daily (Beijing). January 3, 2006.
Toynbee, Arthur, J. *A Study of History*. Oxford: Oxford University Press, 1969, p. 51.
Wang Shih-fu. *The Dream of the Western Chamber* [in Chinese].
Wu Cheng-en. *The Journey to the West* [in Chinese].
Wu Jing-zi. *The Scholars* [in Chinese].
Yellow Emperor's Internal Medicine [in Chinese].
Yi Wen. *Thirteen Classics* [in Chinese]. Taipei.

BERNARD MICALLEF

REVISITING THE TRADITIONAL VIRTUES OF THE HERO

A Phenomenological Study of Wilfred Owen's Disabled Soldier

THE LITERARY ENTITY WITHIN A NARRATED WORLD

Thanks to critics like Roman Ingarden and Wolfgang Iser, we treat the literary object as a phenomenon actualized and then maintained in being through the reader's effort in realizing the poem, that is, only through irony, paradox, metaphor, metonymy, and other aesthetic techniques that perform the text as a portrayed world. Real external entities, such as a disabled war victim, attain to a poetic existence, such as Wilfred Owen's mutilated soldier in the poem "Disabled," by virtue of this aesthetic effort, fulfilled each time literary comprehension is felt to have reached beyond a previous inadequate degree of realization.

The reader's effort, however, cannot lie outside his lived-world (in the Husserlian sense of the *Lebenswelt*). Any literary enlargement of meaning is primarily registered in terms of alterations to the reader's background knowledge, which cannot therefore be excluded from the process of original meaning. One recurring point in this study will be that the *Lebenswelt* is preserved and accessed as a *narrated* world, composed out of mythical, religious, literary, historical and other shorter narratives, say, fables and parables, the unfolding nature of which has long provided us with predictable roles. Even less desirable narratives such as TV commercials continue to narrate our world, providing its entities with conceivable sequences of events, accustomed roles, and stereotyped culminations. The reader is born into this world of articulated challenges, responses, and destinies, all of which precede his literary interpretation with familiar patterns of behaviour and expected outcomes. Each and every unfamiliar experience is thus first engaged within a familiar narrative, which is activated at the same instant that it is modified to accommodate the new experience. Iser approaches such a notion of prescribed phenomena when defining the world as composed of systems that stabilize certain expectations while deactivating certain possibilities, thereby reducing a contingent reality into a predictable frame of reference.[1] For Iser, literature neither copies nor discards the world's systemic nature, but infiltrates and then complements its inadequate articulation by activating its neutralized possibilities: "the text must [...] implicitly contain the basic framework of the [world's] system," he says, but this happens only in order that literary devices enable us to "reconstruct whatever was concealed or ignored by the philosophy or ideology of the day."[2] Thus, it can never be said that normative assumptions do not play a significant part in transforming the reader's narrated world. Penetrating and modifying their familiar structure (or paradigm) is the very process whereby literary objects emerge as original and significant articulations.

Ingarden had earlier stressed the self-sufficient reality of the literary work, whose phenomena are simply correlates of corresponding sentences (for instance, a problem is the correlate of a question rather than an independent, external entity). But for Ingarden, too, the reader must realize the various stages of the aesthetically constructed object "under the aspect of the image of the world which he has constructed for himself in the course of his life."[3] Owen's poem "Disabled" exemplifies this interplay of the familiar and the unfamiliar through its subtle interweaving of the narrated world of the hero and a war victim. Owen's disabled soldier *is understood only in the process of transforming the narrative texture of heroic virtue already in place.* In Heideggerian and Gadamerian terms, the hero has come down to us in the form of linguistic preservation, which has sedimented his virtues and made this foreknowledge available to further linguistic mediums that continue to unravel and weave further on its inherited tapestry. Heidegger, in particular, enlightens us with an approach that is simultaneously a destruction and a reconstruction of phenomena embedded in language, a process which may degenerate into idle talk (or simplified assumptions) as well as rise to the status of a revelation about Being.

There are different linguistic mediums of preservation, just as there are of innovation. Mythical and historical texts purport to retrieve phenomena in their original state, although to different ends and degrees. Poetry, on the other hand, functions as a deliberately transformative and inferential engagement with traditional phenomena. The poem "Disabled" exemplifies what is characteristic of most poetry: it contains aesthetic devices merging within a highly condensed structure and projecting their composite object through a close interaction of perspectives. This contrasts with the generally successive stages of realization encountered in other literary forms, such as the novel. The closing lines of Owen's poem may provide an initial example. Here, the narrator's voice (which narrates in the third person) blends with the disabled soldier's inner bitterness of tone, which protests against the cold and against not having been put to bed, a piteous appeal that at the same time reverses the heroic virtue of mental and physical fortitude:

> How cold and late it is! Why don't they come
> And put him into bed? Why don't they come?

This ambiguous attribution of voice allows a glimpse into the soldier's inner distress while assuming a detached narrative of his broken spirit by a separate narrator. The personal, detached, pathetic, and narrative shifts of this voice testify to the fact that Owen's disabled soldier is poetically realized by multiple conflicting viewpoints, ultimately capable of inserting an ironic reversal of heroic virtue (that is, a despairing voice) into a seemingly uninvolved narrative. Once revealed as an unstable complex of irreconcilable elements, the aesthetic object becomes the very endeavour to negotiate the widening distances between its disparate and mutually questioning components. It henceforth endures as a constructive effort to connect viewpoints, reconcile emerging differences, and negotiate blank spaces, in a bid to keep its overall configuration intact. This poetic demand for reconstruction also sets in motion a wider conflict between the aesthetic object as an evolving construct and the narrated world of the hero as a previously established realm of archetypes predetermining the reader's response. The poetic experience thus reactivates the reader's constructive faculties within a narrated world of the hero, which is evoked through ironic discrepancy. For even as the inner conflicts of the aesthetic object are resolved into a new configuration, new distances start to emerge between this novel configuration and the pre-established constructs of the heroic world.

As will be argued in the second part of this study, new depths of insight are achieved within the evolving phenomenon of the disabled soldier through its predominant schema of ironic reversal, that is, its recurring inversion of the familiar paradigm of the hero and thus its primary mode of merging with the narrated world of heroism. Other mutually questioning perspectives within Owen's disabled soldier find their meaningful place within this evolving pattern of irony, whose configuration creates an alternative impression of depth and reality in a world of flat stereotypes. The qualitative performance of this poetically constructed reality replaces the quantitative force with which traditional narratives have long established phenomena like the hero as real and immutable entities. If the reader cannot stand outside his narrated world of the hero, the poetic experience at least provides him with some significant options as to the way (insightful, interrogative, liberating, distorting) he might profitably stand within it, thereby generating the unfamiliar within the boundaries of the familiar. The poetic experience demands of the reader what Hans-Georg Gadamer says of tradition in general: "To be situated within a tradition does not limit the freedom of knowledge but makes it possible."[4] All the interpreter needs is a tactful, strategic way of belonging to the "continuing effect of the tradition in which he himself has his historical reality."[5]

OWEN'S DISABLED SOLDIER AS AN AESTHETICALLY UNFOLDING ENTITY

In realizing a tenable correlation between the disparate components of the disabled soldier, irony suggests itself as the pattern of aesthetic response that will sustain the aesthetic object through an alternative mode of combination. The third stanza of the poem "Disabled" will serve to illustrate how this *modus operandi* of irony can be extended to other poetic elements, which are made significant within its evolving pattern. Here, two contrasting images of drawn blood emerge. First, in order of reading, comes the image of "the hot race / And leap of purple" blood "spurted" from the soldier's thigh and "poured [...] down shell-holes." Then there is the soldier's flashback to the image of "a bloodsmear" down his leg, endured as a mark of athletic prowess at a game prior to the war, an occasion he now recollects only as a war victim. The bloodsmear of an athletic hero is, therefore, exploded into a wartime scene of mutilation and bloodshed even before it is poetically conveyed. The whole relevant piece reads

> He's lost his colour very far from here,
> Poured it down shell-holes till the veins ran dry,
> And half his lifetime lapsed in the hot race
> And leap of purple spurted from his thigh.
> One time he liked a bloodsmear down his leg,
> After the matches, carried shoulder-high.

Apart from constructing the aesthetic object, irony here infiltrates and loosens the conventional structure of the athletic hero, bringing the unrealized possibilities of this heroic paradigm to light. For instance, besides the glaring disproportion of bloodshed between the trivial "bloodsmear" of a sports event and the hyperbolic pouring of blood "down shell-holes till the veins ran dry," there is also the antithesis between the local crowd that cheers the athletic hero and the desolate scene of war "far from here." There is, furthermore, the contrast between the implicitly flushed complexion of the athletic hero and his having "lost his colour" in war (which is also, of course, a metonymy for the soldier's loss of blood). Finally, there is the obvious antithesis in terms of height between the experience of being "carried shoulder-high" and the humbled state of lying wounded in a shell-hole. The overall schema of irony is thus corroborated at the very instant when these additional contrasts are validated by its postulated predominance in the poem. But also, in combining the disparate components of the war victim, irony starts to mediate between the archaic structure of the hero and the deviant configuration of the war victim, becoming a distinct performance due to its contrastive paradigm within the larger narrated world of the hero. If the bloodsmear down the athlete's thigh evokes the traditional initiation rite of the hero, the ironic amplification of this bloodsmear into the bloodshed of the Western Front, where the true ordeal of mutilation replaces the mere ritual of bloodletting, realizes a novel way of belonging to this evoked world of heroism.

Let us recall that in ancient ritual the hero's symbolic death is customarily reversed by resurrection, unless substituted with an animal's sacrificial blood. In "Disabled," on the other hand, the pouring of blood "down shellholes" neither wholly sacrifices nor allows any ritualistic substitution for the disabled soldier: it denotes an extreme mutilation depriving him of both active life and death, and thus of the possibility of resurrection, deification, and immortality—the usual course of events in ancient myth. The ritualistic bloodshed traditionally providing the hero with a passage through death and back to a revered life is thus inverted: an actual bloodletting that confines the protagonist to an anonymous life within an institute, a life that is essentially dead. Articulating a war victim through such inversions of ancient ritual can be accomplished, however, only because the past ritual of bloodletting has long prepared the ground for its reversal. There is both a long mythical and religious history of the hero's deification through mutilation and a long-standing scholarly examination of it. Suffice it to mention Lewis Richard Farnell's *Greek Hero Cults and Ideas of Immortality*, which at one point examines the ancient practice of "paying posthumous worship to the human being that had been offered to the deity in sacrifice."[6] Whether this sacrifice then involves periodic revival as in the mythical figure of Persephone, or the dismemberment of a hero partly consumed and then rejoined by the gods themselves as in Pelops (son of Tantalus), or the sacramental sacrifice of an animal (such as the lamb) offered and consumed as a surrogate of the resurrected hero, these ancient rituals of bloodshed have long prescribed the path through death to revered immortality. In Owen's disabled soldier, however, vestiges of this Dionysiac rebirth themselves are torn to pieces; the components of the myth of eternal renewal are scattered, and start to suggest a powerful reversal: mutilation as death in life, a perpetual dismemberment of heroic elements experienced by the disabled soldier.

In "To a Comrade in Flanders," a poem Owen wrote prior to his first experience of combat, soldiers envisage themselves as godlike, for their death is not a "sev'rance" from loved ones, but a cause of "rev'rance."[7] Moreover, the "rough knees of boys shall ache" in adoration upon the death of these soldiers, who in their living voice also assert that "girls' breasts are the clear white Acropole / Where our own mothers' tears shall heal us whole." This envisaged rebirth through the ultimate sacrifice (blending the archaic notion of resurrection with the loving and immortalizing memory of the living) illustrates the mythical paradigm that must have governed some of Owen's presuppositions about war and that would eventually be ironically reformulated after his first experience of combat. In another untitled poem of the same period, Owen mingles a wartime fatality with an evocation of myth, whose archaic power of sacred suggestion already appears to have dwindled. Thus, the poet witnesses a "Smile, / Faint as a wan, worn myth, / [...] On a boy's murdered mouth."[8] By interweaving the alluring beauty of the smile, its oneness with a "murdered mouth," and the resemblance between this hybrid countenance and a pale, exhausted myth, Owen subordinates myth to the actual decay of war and yet allows a vestige of mythical beauty or glory in the alluring smile. Such examples point the way to the subtler vestiges of myth incorporated into the play of irony in the poem "Disabled."

The phenomenon of the soldier in this poem is, in fact, a literary object sustained in being through significant accretions to this ironic schema, the initial field of poetic comprehension within which other poetic features gain their aesthetic validity. For instance, the reader now accustomed to the ironic reversal of heroic virtues will notice that "the hot race / And leap of purple" referring to the soldier's blood "poured [...] down shell-holes" actually employs athletic terms (that is, "race" and "leap") robbed from the immediately following athletic scene. In contrast to being a defining quality of the athletic hero, the agile qualities of racing and leaping are here metonymically transferred to the opposing outcome of physical deterioration ("half his lifetime lapsed in the hot race / And leap of purple spurted from his thigh"). This poignant relocation of athletic terms within the opposing image of mutilation illustrates how the components of the narrated world of the hero are never actually lost in poetic modes such as irony, a device that evokes similarities as much as it juxtaposes incongruences between athletic hero and war victim. The narrated world of the hero remains, therefore, a cognitive prerequisite that is revived at the same instant that it is questioned, corrected, and remoulded by the ironic unfolding of the disabled soldier. As an interpretative performance of a war victim, irony must constantly include traditional heroic traits as material for differentiation. The ironic image, in other words, is derived as much as it is created, for the ironically unfolding phenomenon still mobilizes the causes and stimuli of ancient heroic narratives, albeit towards a different end. This is why the literary experience entails an artistic mediation between the reader's construction of a new entity and the dominant figures of a narrated world.

Reader-response critics like Ingarden and Iser speak of literature in terms of insightful accretions to our lived-world, whose total dismantling would amount to having no horizon of understanding. Ingarden, for instance, speaks of the aesthetically unfolding entity as an object that appears not "to belong to our life," yet "enriches it in an unsuspected way and gives it a new, often very deep, meaning."[9] Iser, for his part, speaks of a prevailing repertoire of social, cultural, and literary norms, which is corrected by the actual event of literary comprehension that accesses it. The repertoire serves as the indispensable background whose correction puts in relief new literary insights emerging against it. "In this way," he points out, "traditional schemata are rearranged to communicate a new picture."[10] One such traditional schema responsible for a major preconception about the Great War itself was, in fact, that of a game. Paul Fussell, in *The Great War and Modern Memory*, observes that the feeling of a sporting spirit just prior to the start of hostilities made the initial perception of the Great War similar to that of a sporting contest, even to the extent of judging the progress of the war in terms of the competitive spirit expected to be displayed in a game of football.[11] More importantly, Fussell's underlying thesis is that certain events of the war became memorable in their literary portrayal due, not to their scale of horror, but to *their embodiment of the ironic discrepancy between such preceding paradigms of how the war should be successfully conducted and the later actual disasters or disillusions of trench warfare.*[12] Since the discrepancy between preceding formulas of bravado and shocking devastation was realistically lived by soldiers at the Western Front, it seems natural that irony should become the preferred cognitive mode for representing trench warfare. Irony allows preconceived heroism and unexpected horror to mingle in its cognitive process of inserting differences amid similarities. Owen's disabled soldier *is a hero in this aesthetically qualified sense*: his heroism is to endure and embody this ironic equation generated by the war itself, namely, the mingling of mythical expectations with human fragility, initiation with mutilation.

If near immortality and superhuman strength continue to prescribe the classical paradigm of heroic virtues, as embodied in Achilles and Hercules, later literatures only resort to this orthodox paradigm through their own progressive application of heroic ordeals. The play on words constantly employed in Joyce's *Ulysses* exemplifies the way modern literature loosens the fixed platitudes of the narrated world of heroism and yet expands our everyday world, such as a modern day in Dublin, to heroic and mythical proportions that somehow remain effective. The modern literary hero has thus emerged out of a transformative interaction with mythically prescribed virtues, and in many cases this has led to refined adaptations of long-standing heroic attributes. For instance, being the novel's or the poem's protagonist, regardless of outcome, has become a modern adaptation of the challenges of the classical hero in many literary minds, but only because our daily preoccupations have convincingly adopted the proportions of dramatic ordeals faced by earlier heroic types. Morton W. Bloomfield argues that if the word "hero" has become a synonym for protagonist in literature and literary criticism, it still "often carries with it a penumbra, if not more, of its earlier meaning of a superior human being."[13] This penumbra of superiority can be variously remoulded and applied. It can incorporate the seemingly trivial chores of everyday life, or it can involve a whole new religious outlook as its heroic quest. Bernard F. Huppé, for instance, observes that in Medieval literature "the imagination of an audience brought up on heroic poetry" of an earlier heathen type was remoulded by Christian writers intent on forging a whole new paradigm of Christian heroism out of it.[14] Even the epic poem *Beowulf*, Huppé points out, is a transformative engagement with a pre-existent heroic language, aiming to show the limits of its heathen ways while remoulding its virtues into the new sensibility of a Christian hero.[15]

In his book *The Literature of War: Five Studies in Heroic Virtue*, Andrew Rutherford analyses five heroic types that constitute a continuum along which each later type betrays a subtle development or sophistication upon the preceding. Rutherford's book is expedient for this phenomenological study of Owen's soldier, for his evolving types suggest a heroic tradition that constantly assimilates subtle modifications, thereby extending the boundaries of its familiar realm along its historical evolution. Rudyard Kipling's hero, for instance, no longer simply promotes imperial civilization in foreign lands of supposedly inferior moral and civil qualities—the quest of an earlier heroic formula. Rather, Kipling's protagonist adopts the heroic stance of the common soldier maintaining "courage, endurance, loyalty, friendship, honour, [and a] sense of duty" under a dubious authority, cold-blooded and inhuman.[16] And Kipling's obedient hero is himself superseded by Thomas Edward Lawrence's (Lawrence of Arabia's) intellectual type of hero, who combines this readiness for action with the "sensitive, scholarly, self-analytical and self-tormenting" qualities of the questioning self.[17] The combination of these two virtues— action and reflection—takes the new heroic paradigm a step beyond Kipling's merely obedient soldier. Lawrence's heroic type now questions the wisdom of the action he still carries out, in an anguished consciousness that must combine the analysis and the execution of war and that can criticize a previously unquestioned authority. In effect, Rutherford's five types show the hero prevailing through a progressive refinement of his increasingly complex consciousness, which steadily becomes his most interesting aspect, usurping even the predominance of heroic action itself. They illustrate the *eidos* of the hero maintained through ever more sophisticated variants of his self-conscious becoming, a heroic identity sustained through revisions that, as relevant responses to its inherited structure, accrue to its understanding.

Such investigations should induce the reader to re-examine the traditional narratives themselves, and realize that such classical tragic heroes as Oedipus and Renaissance models like Hamlet are, in fact, anything but purely virtuous figures. To be sure, these last two examples still belong to Northrop Frye's high mimetic mode, a heroic type that, although fallible due to faults like self-blindness or hesitation, still surpasses ordinary men in its heroic qualities of "authority, passion, and power of expression."[18] Nevertheless, Oedipus and Hamlet exemplify traditional models of the hero whose complex natures hardly evoke unquestioned admiration and imitation. Frye's five heroic modes, too, demonstrate an overall phenomenon of the hero subsisting through a wide range of phenomenological adaptations, all of which somehow continue to assert its *eidos* or essential idea. This has also supplied later literatures with more than one heroic variant as their point of departure. Literary performance thus makes us conscious of a frequently forgotten cultural factor: that the heroic *eidos* cannot be adopted as an immutable figure or a fixed point of departure, but rather is reopened as a complex of perspectives taken up at some point of cultural or literary extension.

In his book *The Hero: A Study in Tradition, Myth, and Drama*, Lord Raglan distinguishes the traditional hero from the historical hero precisely on the basis of this accumulation of narratives from many ages and places. The hero of tradition is an intertextual and multicultural product, a hybrid of narrative sources joined anachronistically. The numerous versions of his life emerge from the ritualistic adaptations carried out by the different communities adopting him as their ancestor. For Lord Raglan, "the story of the hero of tradition [...] is the story of his ritual progress."[19] The overwhelming vastness of this precursor heroic lore, I suggest, is grasped within a new manageable frame of interpretation afforded by the poetic event, which reopens the traditional discourse of the hero by means of an aesthetic performance carried out by the reader under literary instruction. This aesthetic performance achieves a sense of closure only through a significant level of realization or play. Poetic devices fail to exhaust traditional phenomena like the hero, but their purpose in the first place is hardly to do so. It is, rather, to enable the reader *to stand within traditional narratives with a new performative strategy*, allowing him to bracket certain clichéd aspects of the traditional phenomenon while executing significant accretions to its less pronounced possibilities. This is how the hero can be realized through a significant becoming (or adaptation) of his precursory presentations. If tradition prescribes archaic phenomena, the reader's application of poetic devices allows his own insights and novel reintegrations to be inscribed into their significant rehearsal and presentation. This reciprocity of memory and extension compels Iser to state that the literary phenomenon "has no existence of its own," and only comes into being by an interplay of retrospection and projection,[20] which in our case happens through the play of irony.

The whole process can be exemplified by the way Owen's ironic schema reopens another traditional heroic virtue, namely, his reputed possession of a wisdom superior to that of other men. This platitude is, of course, already seriously questioned in such literary figures as Faust, whose intellectual superiority derives from a contract with evil, and ultimately disrupts a papal and imperial world in Marlowe's drama. Closer to our day, there is, of course, the gothic hero Victor Frankenstein, whose superior scientific faculty is quite literally embodied in a monstrous shape, a knowledge incarnated out of hideously joined limbs plundered from graveyards. Even earlier classical models are not exempt from such unwelcoming relationships between hero and superior wisdom. Consider Oedipus, who, despite his promising solution of the sphinx's riddle and his initial deliverance of Thebes, is actually constituted out of recurring instances of failed awareness: he lacks the fundamental awareness of his origins, parentage, and actual actions (that is, patricide and incest). And he also fails to interpret the surrounding portents of his wrongdoing. Oedipus's bewildering accumulation of failed perceptions makes the audience of Sophocles's drama constantly more knowledgeable of the hero's fate than he himself is. Owen's disabled soldier entails a vestige of this dramatic irony, and reopens the unresolved enigma of the hero's intellectual superiority. Somewhat like Oedipus, he displays a constant lack of perception during his recruitment, allowing the reader's comprehension of the Western Front to surpass his trivial motives for joining up, namely, looking smart and impressing his girl:

> He thought he'd better join. — He wonders why.
> Someone had said he'd look a god in kilts,
> That's why; and maybe, too, to please his Meg,
> Aye, that was it, to please the giddy jilts
> He asked to join. [...]

However, classical dramatic irony is here complicated by the fact that now, while recollecting his own recruitment, the disabled soldier embodies the very tragic fate ignored by his earlier self. His recollected ignorance of tragic fate co-exists with his present awareness (and actual embodiment) of it. This is, of course, in keeping with his ironic constitution, which mingles mythical expectations with tragic fate. Evidently, the classical formula of dramatic irony is here revived with poignant adaptations required by the highly ironic phenomenon of a disabled soldier. But a subtler irony obtains in the recollected image of the recruit himself. The traditional hero, observes Lord Raglan, gains his "victory over the elements and over man" through possessing a "power [...] conferred by divine descent and the absorption of divine wisdom."[21] The youthful recruit, on the other hand, tries to attain to a divine status *by simply looking like* "a god in kilts" at the same instant when he ironically lacks even fundamental, let alone divine, wisdom (regarding the eventual demands of war). With an eye for this subtler irony, the reader can observe that the appearance of a god here substitutes true wisdom, rather than heralds it in accordance with ancient myth. Divine manifestation here becomes a mere outer ritual, a deification "in kilts" that replaces, rather than accompanies, a corresponding growth in awareness. The classical heroic virtue of divine wisdom is thus separated into mutually exclusive opposites: during the Great War, to look divine was to lack a true awareness of the atrocities that lay ahead. Such a negative attribute of the war hero, once again, tallies with frequent reports of the shock undergone by recruits after their first experience of combat.[22] They met mutilation where they had expected mythical resurrection, glory, and deification. War poetry conveyed the distinctive ironies of the Great War through infiltrating and reworking those narrative elements of the hero that had hitherto served to predetermine the way war itself was initially defined and approached.

In his extended flashback, Owen's soldier also recalls that he knew neither enemy nor "fears / Of fear" while joining up. As in the preceding quotation, the young recruit had been distracted from knowing these heroic essentials by the lure of outward appearance—his aspiration to military dress, behaviour, and ethos:

> Germans he scarcely thought of; all their guilt,
> And Austria's, did not move him. And no fears
> Of Fear came yet. He thought of jewelled hilts
> For daggers in plaid socks; of smart salutes;
> And care of arms; and leave; and pay arrears;
> *Esprit de corps*; and hints for young recruits.

Traditionally, the hero is expected to overcome fear prior to embarking upon a clearly envisaged quest. Franklin D. Roosevelt's modern dictum that "The only thing to fear is fear itself" is, in fact, pre-dated by many ancient rituals, which treated fear as a primal force to be reckoned with, reifying it as the physical endurance of injury during initiation rites. Owen's recruit, however, stands oblivious to fear, due to recruiting authorities intent on obscuring this essential heroic trait. The "hints for young recruits" of the recruiting authorities suggest a deliberately misplaced emphasis on military trappings, and is a stark reminder that the instituted propaganda was merely another linguistic medium vying with the literary in a bid to infiltrate and manipulate the narrated world of the hero, if only for its own military ends. Appropriating the semiotic possibilities of the heroic narrative, war propaganda intended to promote the hollow gestures of military drill and dress over other heroic virtues whose physical and mental demands might well have been beyond the common recruit's endurance. Nonetheless, not all essential traits of the hero could be omitted if the heroic *eidos* was to be evoked. Thus, the "*Esprit de corps*" listed as part of this misleading ritual is, in fact, a heroic trait that has received sophisticated development in the literature of the Great War, being one of the distinguished human responses to the Western Front. Rutherford points out that comradeship (another term for "*Esprit de corps*") became a chief moral value generated by a war otherwise evoking "bitter moral condemnation."[23] A wholly condemned war at least offered this modestly consoling possibility of reaching heroic stature by sacrificing oneself for one's comrades.

Once again, therefore, we see the heroic paradigm itself adopted with a veritable interplay between its derived and potential elements, its residual and emergent aspects. Owen's disabled soldier thus emerges not from a flat denial or an unquestioned adoption of heroic virtues, but from assimilated supplements, crafty shifts of emphasis, and rearranged correlations realized within the heroic paradigm itself. As the recruiting authorities demonstrate with their propaganda machine, there can be a rhetorical entry into this heroic model that plays down fear, obscures motive, and promotes trivial heroic aspects. On the other hand, there can also be a poetic infiltration activating the reader's ironic reworking of the heroic phenomenon in a way that ultimately makes trench warfare more effectively represented. A literary phenomenon *stands out* only because of the way its poetic realization *stands within* its inherited tradition, and an ironic play with the familiar (perhaps trivialized) attributes of heroism is one such significant way of inhabiting precursory narratives. If we cannot shed tradition, or the way its prejudices have moulded our understanding, through art we can at least choose a style or method of enlarging its possibilities from within.

This productive infiltration into the dynamics of heroism is evident in yet another poignant antithesis in Owen's soldier, namely, his abrupt transition from immature looks (suggested by a face "younger than his youth") to his present mien of old age:

> There was an artist silly for his face,
> For it was younger than his youth, last year.
> Now, he is old; his back will never brace;
> [...]

This implies, of course, that the soldier's true adolescent age was never actually lived. His adolescent years were missed in the immediate leap from immature youth to an overly mature adulthood. The simple utterance "Now, he is old" makes the recruit's sudden maturity paradoxical: it is a premature arrival of old age, yet it still arrives too late to avoid his tragic disablement. In archaic heroic depictions, wisdom is a slowly acquired virtue resulting from a sequence of trials, unless it is already a precocious quality of the youthful hero or a supernaturally bestowed faculty. As Gwyn Jones puts it,

> wisdom, in the formal statements of the heroic age, was an embracing quality in which were subsumed education and training in the young and a wealth of digested experience in the old, observation of events and the power to draw general conclusions from them, insight into character and the ponderables of human nature, and an unfailing awareness of the personal, social, and national [...] rights and duties, ties and acceptances, which alone made life meaningful and alone could make it good.[24]

The sudden onset of adulthood in Owen's soldier is, on the contrary, full of conflicting interactions with this paradigm: it is an adulthood that literally takes no time; it is belated in relation to event but early in relation to age; it is an adulthood without any clear memory of the causes of its predicament ("He thought he'd better join. — He wonders why"), and thus an adulthood without experience. The disappearance of adolescence between immaturity and insubstantial maturity—both out of keeping with the victim's true age— is made still more poignant by the use of pictorial terms. The "artist silly for his face" recalls the image of the youthful recruit as a former model, an image that is then abruptly dissolved by the disabled soldier's subsequent inability even to sit upright, in the rhyming utterance "his back will never brace." The whole verse, "Now, he is old; his back will never brace," triggers the customary connection between old age and physical debility, craftily conjuring the unexpected image of an aged man unable to stand firmly and straight. As such, it cleverly summons the concrete image of old age as an abrupt change from youth, intensifying the paradox of a sudden adulthood without experience. In poignant contrast to the archetypal hero accompanied by a wise old man, the young disabled soldier *incorporates* old age without its correlative experience and wisdom.

In Gadamer's terms, only because the anticipated meaning of the hero is lost, only because we lose harmony with our foreknowledge of heroic virtue, is there need for interpretation, for a renewed understanding of the heroic archetype as provoked by Owen's disabled soldier.[25] The ironic portrayal of the hero in "Disabled" reminds us of the Gadamerian notion that interpretation is not *reproductive* of tradition, but *constantly productive* of traditionally preserved phenomena. While it is only through traditional accounts of the hero that we can first put in relief the ironic portrayal of Owen's disabled soldier, it is the actual play of irony (irony as an aesthetic game) that provides the channel for appropriating past heroic accounts with progressive insight. Gadamer argues that *"understanding is to be thought of less as a subjective act than as participating in an event of tradition, a process of transmission in which past and present are constantly mediated."*[26] In the case of Owen's ironic mediation between past and present, a past heroic lore converges with an actual poetic phenomenon in the process of evoking similarities and unexpected differentiations between the two. From the point of view of studies of heroism, much the same point is suggested by Lord Raglan, who observes that heroic accounts are not pure invention, "not the faculty of making something out of nothing, but that of using, in a more or less different form, material already present in the mind."[27]

This is, after all, how the traditional hero has absorbed mythical, ritualistic, and historical material into his complex narrative constitution. As a result of this traditional evolution, Northrop Frye is able to give us a whole typology of heroic types, which in turn refines our expectations concerning the modern literary hero. For instance, Frye's basic distinction between the tragic hero, isolated from his society (or pantheon if he is a god), and the comic hero, incorporated into society,[28] helps us define Owen's disabled soldier in terms of tragic isolation: he is isolated both in the field of battle "very far from here," and in the institute: from boys playing in the park, from friends and crowds who had once cheered his athletic prowess, from girls whose slim waist "he will never feel again," and even from an erstwhile "artist silly for his face." Again, Frye's more sophisticated distinction of the low mimetic mode of hero, who transforms tragic pity into pathos, due mostly to his "defective intelligence" and his exclusion "from a social group to which he is trying to belong,"[29] gives us a refined insight into the plight of Owen's disabled soldier. He, too, evokes pathos through isolation incurred by his "defective intelligence." What is strikingly relevant in Frye's study is that, rather than a hero, he presents a heroic system in which different types are mutually defining and emerge through a reciprocal highlighting of attributes within a growing heroic tradition. The contrasts and similarities between Frye's heroic types provide highly evolved differentiations, implying that only as the reader becomes more versed in heroic nuances will he perceive and activate later ironic extensions of the heroic figure. Understanding the significant evolution of Owen's literary phenomenon of a war victim is, thus, belonging to a heroic tradition through ever more sophisticated enrichments of its heritage.

This can be exemplified by further reference to Frye, who ultimately presents an ironic hero emerging from adjustments to the low mimetic mode. For Frye, the ironic hero separates two inseparable qualities of the tragic hero: inevitable fate and innocence. Christ, the archetype of this ironic mode, is "the perfectly innocent victim" who faces an inevitable fate.[30] More importantly, if this ironic hero begins in the "realism and dispassionate observation" of the low mimetic mode, it nevertheless moves back "towards myth, and dim outlines of sacrificial rituals and dying gods begin to reappear in it. Our five modes," continues Frye, "evidently go around in a circle."[31] If Owen's disabled soldier lies within the ironic mode, as my choice of ironic devices suggests, then this explains why he is constructed out of a discrepancy between inevitable fate and innocent enrolment, and why this ironic equation (fate and innocence) evokes the "dim outlines of sacrificial rituals and dying gods" in the poetic image of bloodletting, as well as in the recruit's godlike appearance in kilts.

Frye's evolving schema of heroic types in fact testifies to Iser's phenomenological principle that the aesthetic object emerges from an *interplay* between a familiar schema and its correction, or a conventional model and adjustments to it. According to Iser,

The correction can therefore only take place through the restructuring of points of *significance* in the schemata. [...] The aesthetic object signalizes its presence through the deformations of the schemata, and the reader, in recognizing these deformations, is stimulated into giving the aesthetic object its shape.[32]

But if Owen's soldier is the result of reacting to our own previous creations and reinterpretations of the hero, thereby enabling us to articulate our immediate concerns about twentieth-century warfare through a transformative encounter with an archetypal figure, then there is a curious consequence for the literary phenomenon. This phenomenon is made perceptible *only during a discernible growth in our anticipated knowledge of it*. In other words, in literature we understand neither old nor entirely new phenomena; rather, we *discern the significant extension of our own presuppositions*. This is why the disabled soldier is neither a neutral nor an immediate phenomenon, but a growth in heroic understanding, or, as Gadamer would put it, a participation in the effective history of the hero. We understand the disabled soldier only at the instant when the tradition of the hero is becoming something more significant than it had conventionally been for us, when the archetype it evokes starts including our mediating performance of ironic reversal and differentiation because it has, in the first place, not sufficiently encompassed our apprehension of victims of the Great War.

The ironic relocation of a mythical god in the mere manifestation of kilts, the coincidence of divine manifestation and innocence during the youth's enrolment, the tragic transformation of a ritualistic bloodsmear into true bloodshed, the sophisticated play on the hero's defective intelligence, and the uncanny leap from immaturity to old age all belong to the *eidos* of the hero as meaningful transformations. They are an interpretative activity of the reader that belongs not to the way the hero is, but to the way the hero might significantly become more than he has conventionally been in relation to the Western Front. This is why I maintain that in literature we experience not the actual being of traditional phenomena such as the hero, but *their significant becoming in the mediating event of reading the poem.* And the mediating discourse responsible for this significant becoming, that is, the mythical and ritualistic inferences and ironies indicated above, are none other than the open-ended but regulated performance of poetry.

In terms of Husserlian phenomenology, the reader of poetry first puts aside seemingly realistic assumptions about the hero, which is the reduction of the natural attitude (the *epoché*); then he reduces the phenomenon of the hero to its essential idea or *eidos*, which is the eidetic reduction, lying beyond that of the natural attitude. This second reduction simplifies the phenomenon into an essential notion of heroism, but does so only in readiness for the assimilation of new perspectives and applications. It is this eidetic reduction that provokes an inquiring re-entry into the dynamics of the hero, where ironic reversals and shifts of emphasis start to dissolve its more rigid parts and to stress new areas of integration. The phenomenological reduction of the hero can be compared to Heidegger's notion of public talk, the inauthentic and conventional mode of articulating a phenomenon that maintains it as a daily function in a pragmatic and immediate world. This public talk is responsible for our shared preconceptions about what a hero should be. But the literary reader is hardly ever after this common understanding, and often reads poetry as an event, that is, an experience whose outcome cannot be known in its entirety in advance. For him, the poetic experience starts where the prejudice of idle talk is brought up short, because its pragmatic and communal uses fail to satisfy his recognition that a tremendous occurrence, such as the Great War, has surpassed most of his conventional methods of depiction. This is where historical event and poetic event coincide: they both demand that our understanding be re-actualized through a new interpretative encounter with tradition.

Against this approach to Owen's poem, there is, of course, the claim that the Western Front was too unprecedented and overwhelming an affair to be conveyed through an artful mediation of heroic myth and legend. In the next section, I will take up this issue of the war as a harsh external reality demanding poetic immediacy to historical situation, rather than a mediated heroism.

THE POEM'S REFERENCE TO AN EXTERNAL OCCASION

Owen was killed while the German army was on retreat, a mere few days before the Armistice on 11 November. On this latter momentous date, a telegram received by his father and mother announced his death, presumably amid the triumphant ringing of bells.[33] As tragic and ironic in itself as any compelling piece of war literature might be, this biographical detail epitomizes a war whose daily reversals of fate and unending ironies outnumbered those recorded by its artistic portrayal. The war's gargantuan, though largely pointless, sacrifice of limb and life (a crucial thematic element in "Disabled") is uncannily embodied in the poet's own untimely death.

The poem "Disabled" itself draws constant attention to those outrageous practices and occurrences of the Great War whose cynical and ironic potential was simply greater than anything produced by literary imagination alone. One exemplary case is incorporated in Owen's representation of the deliberate enrolment of recruits younger than the required age (that is, nineteen), a blatant practice conveyed with matching levity in the poet's respective verses:

> [...]
> He asked to join. He didn't have to beg;
> Smiling they wrote his lie: aged nineteen years.

The tacit knowledge of the recruiting authorities—whose "smiling" features betray both arrogance and illicit gain—is a well-known fact. John Purkis cites the typical account of one recruit who, upon giving away his true age ("sixteen years and seven months"), was brazenly asked by the recruiting sergeant to return on the next day, when perhaps he might turn nineteen.[34] The death of boy soldiers as young as fourteen in the trenches, together with such cases as the sentencing to death of Herbert Burden, aged seventeen, for desertion, provoked indignant protests even in Parliament at the time, yet to little avail. The enrolment of underage recruits remained rampant, and was aggravated when recruiting sergeants, desperate to fill the dwindling ranks at the front, resorted to accosting and harassing young men in public, even where the latter protested they had not yet reached the required age. Such irregular measures would seem to define the ironic perversion of heroic virtue as an integral, and thus non-literary, aspect of wartime practices, with the risk that artistic mediation might then seem superfluous and dispensable. Fussell, in fact, calls the Great War a "war where irony was a staple,"[35] and argues that the predominance of irony in modern understanding originated "largely in the application of mind and memory to the events of the Great War."[36] To many, the war in itself must have seemed an event too atrociously aberrant and viciously bizarre to be in any way enhanced or bettered by artistic sensibility. To hold such a view is, of course, to argue that the enduring appeal of war poetry resides simply in its having candidly recorded an unprecedented degree of suffering in an unrivalled moment of human history.

There is, in fact, ample proof of the realistic derivation of several of the poetic images in "Disabled." Likewise, there can be little doubt that various other poems by Owen—amongst which "The Sentry" is perhaps outstanding in this regard—originated from singular wartime events he literally played a leading role in. That Owen does not abstract from the particulars of trench warfare, that he does not easily shift his attention from a real local trauma to some idle generalization of military conflict, and that his focus on minute details results from the lasting impact of their true occurrence on his wartime sensibility—these qualities characterize much of his best poetry. In "Disabled," the portrayal of permanent mental and physical scars borne by the war victim is fraught with subtle linguistic and aesthetic features that evidently abridge Owen's own first-hand experience in Craiglockhart War Hospital in Edinburgh. Consider the following lines from the last stanza, in which poetic devices seem so subservient to the poet's own historical experience:

> Now, he will spend a few sick years in institutes,
> And do what things the rules consider wise,
> And take whatever pity they may dole.

Owen's relocation from a Casualty Clearing Station to Craiglockhart as a victim of shell shock (considered at the time a euphemism for nervous breakdown)[37] may well have prompted the grammatical and poetic features employed here. For instance, the slow process of relocation all the way to Craiglockhart seems to stand behind his grammatical choice of plural nouns in "a few sick years in institutes," with the obvious understatement "few." Furthermore, the disciplined regime that would have prevailed somewhat at Craiglockhart can be speculated as the cause behind Owen's choice of "rules" as the impersonal agent running the institute with "wise" decisions. This metonymic shift from human management to dehumanized "rules" gains a special proximity to Owen's wartime experience when one considers that he wrote these lines while recovering at the war hospital.[38] Finally, in the last quoted line, what is rationed out in small quantities (due suggestively to its short supply) is "pity." This metonymic shift from rationed food, the customary object of "dole," to rationed pity once again testifies to Owen's immediate outlook on the war hospital, conceivably sparing in its compassion due to its more essential need of clinical efficiency.

Concurrent with this personal involvement in historical events was another motivation towards realistic portrayal: that of countering the false image of war implanted in the civilian mind. The war poet's willingness to give first-hand accounts of trench warfare was, in fact, constantly fuelled by his need to correct the romanticized picture of it produced by the instituted propaganda, a picture often taken in by an unsuspecting civilian population. The distorted image of conditions at the Western Front provided by the contemporary press, as well as the use of poetry itself to arouse the patriotic sentiment,[39] would have further provoked the war poet's resolve to adhere to lurid individual details in order both to respond to false public convictions and to remedy the impersonal generalization of the conflict. It is not to be denied, either, that the sufferings, the large-scale disasters, and the minor triumphs peculiar to each battlefield held their own distinctive appeal for direct graphic depiction. The captivating individuality of each battlefield can be clearly demonstrated by the remote (and thus exceptionally illustrative) case of the theatre of war depicted in Lawrence's *Seven Pillars of Wisdom*. This epic account, Rutherford points out, is not a stylized anachronism intended to romanticize the desert war. It is rather the result of a truly lived type of twentieth-century warfare that produced a matching style of literature. Lawrence's Arabian adventure necessarily has a more epic quality than literature depicting the Western Front since "the exotic setting, the blend of the primitive and civilised in Bedouin life, the acknowledged status of great [Arab] warriors [...], the willing endurance of arduous conditions," and other lingering classical and medieval traits were realistic elements of the "picturesque, adventurous quality of this desert war."[40] Likewise, the singular setting of each battlefield at the Western Front, including its unprecedented conditions and unequalled disasters, held their own special appeal for realistic portrayal.

While it cannot be denied that war poetry has this strong referential element, readers still productively responding to it testify to anything but a referential whole. Some light can be shed on this paradox by Iser's argument that literature *provides the reader with instructions for building a situation* rather than with the external situation itself, ready-made and complete. The reader can bring "his own faculties into play"[41] only because the literary state of affairs, built as it is from instructions implemented during the act of reading, is *an aesthetically unfolding situation*. The literary situation is thereby "depragmatized," the loss of its "familiar surroundings" releasing its "hitherto unseen possibilities."[42] This occurs to such an extent that its object can never henceforth be equated either with the reader's own initial disposition or with the text itself, or, for that matter, with any single one of its constituent perspectives. Rather, the literary object is maintained by the very interaction between text and reader, and along accumulating perspectives that it continually transcends as their overall product. One might add that Iser's aesthetically unfolding object constantly progresses towards a new cognitive event: a resumed intensity of contrasting viewpoints; a deeper scrutiny of marginalized aspects; an extended association of ideas; or a refined judgement. Iser would simply define these cognitive events as higher-order *gestalts*, that is, successive configurations each of which gains its apparent fullness only in relation to the comparative failure of some preceding assumption of wholeness. If literary reference obtains only during such transitions between earlier and later *gestalts*, then any initial similarity to an external object gives way to the latter's unforeseeable becoming, a process that yields the object as an innovative experience while revealing the conditions of its composition. The literary field of execution becomes the object's active frame of reference, and any habitual response to it predetermined by the real world is replaced by what Steven Mailloux sums up as the temporal process of reading: "making and revising judgments, solving mysteries and puzzles, experiencing attitudes, taking on and rejecting perspectives, discovering sequential structures of similarity and contrast, formulating questions and answers, making and correcting mistakes."[43] The literary object can never be identified with its external reality precisely because its cumulative experience "tells us something [more] about reality."[44]

The mechanical functioning of our institutionalized systems and daily routines makes the pragmatic composition of everyday objects both automatic and economical. Aesthetic accomplishment, on the other hand, demands "aesthetically relevant features" that, while filling in the successive concretizations of an "aesthetically receptive attitude,"[45] prolong and complicate the object's literary mode of becoming. It follows that any external object evoked by the literary text is recognized (that is, cognized anew) through the intervening experience of aesthetic composition, which supplements the prevalent system of reality with a *cumulative recollection of the object*. To be sure, in "Disabled," both the cultural conventions of the hero and the historical context of the war victim, however transformed by the operative field of irony, are in themselves more complex than the pragmatic composition of everyday objects. As such, they make extensive provision for their ironic reversal. Nonetheless, when the poem's ironic schema makes incompatible what is traditionally associated (hero-god) and compatible what is customarily distanced (hero-disability), the transformative power of its cumulative recollection becomes manifest.

Further insight into this notion of a cumulative recollection can be gained by focusing on its underlying concept of experience. Fundamentally, experience is the ability to master any unfolding situation through the adaptive growth of one's past knowledge, thereby grasping the unknown through a corresponding extension of the known. The essential quality of the experienced person, observes Gadamer, is the very ability to be open to a novel experience "made possible by experience itself."[46] In the poem "Disabled," the ironic novelty of the war victim is made possible by the reader's prior experience of heroic virtue, which is confronted, relativized, and polemicized in the process. The Great War, too, proved an outstanding historical experience through the extent to which it modified hitherto accepted notions of doing battle. Its historical significance lies primarily in the momentous scale to which it reworked previous experiences of warfare. Whether literary or historical, significant events are first registered through an adaptive growth in one's foreknowledge, which acts as the primary evidence of their newly unfolding situation. While this process invariably results in transforming one's narrated world, the extent to which this takes place is nonetheless determined by the different spheres of operation in which the unfolding novelty is accomplished. Whereas an increased military efficiency may prove to be an acceptable accomplishment for the historically unfolding situation of modern warfare, only those literary factors optimizing "the aesthetic 'impression'"[47] can lead to an aesthetic fulfilment. Determined as it is by the range of operations demarcating and identifying the sphere of performance itself, our foreknowledge is subject to varying standards of transformation.

Owen's disabled soldier is therefore sustained both through a modification of the inadequate models (or foreknowledge) of the hero and through a constant effort to reach his aesthetic synthesis in a poetically adequate manner. Ironic distance from precursory models prevents heroic traits from simply falling into their familiar paradigm. This is made evident when the recruitment of Owen's soldier turns out to be a hollow deification, his initiation an eventual disability (or death in life), his sudden maturity paradoxically destitute of all experience. Such contrasts with traditional heroic configurations make room for the alternative and more problematic state of affairs unfolding through the act of reading the poem "Disabled." This entails the ironic progression of interwoven opposites: divine manifestation and human fragility, initiation into life and disability for life, extreme innocence and premature old age, artistic beauty and revolting mutilation, cheering crowds and secluded hospitalization.

Such an evolving play of contrasts, however, only insinuates its self-regulating schema of irony, its alternative performance and adequacy, into the hero's evoked tradition, thereby restoring the quality of a significant experience to the hidden potentialities of the heroic archetype. It is thus that the evoked archetype can speak to us again, as a memory endowed with an unexpected range of operations.

Gadamer constantly alludes to this reciprocity between memory and novelty as the essential dynamics of all experience. While memory explains "the lasting meaning that an experience has for a person who has it," the other contrastive, yet equally essential, quality of experience is the "definite immediacy" through which it "eludes every opinion about its meaning."[48] These two elements merge in the inexhaustible nature of a meaningful experience: a memorable acquaintance that is yet unfolding beyond its accepted opinions, being able to enlighten us anew through the latest contexts and applications in which its memorable aspect is revitalized. Experience thus grasps the unfolding uniqueness of life that in turn heightens and extends its initial sphere of acquaintance. In reading "Disabled," this same reciprocity of memory and extension is made evident when the immediacy of the poetic performance, while eluding accepted opinions about the hero, nonetheless retrieves *possibilities long embedded within the progressive history of the heroic phenomenon*. In the preceding sections, the aesthetically reworked notions of ritual mutilation, divine manifestation, and celebrated athleticism have clearly demonstrated that, rather than being discarded, potentialities intrinsic to the mythical hero are recalled and relived through their aesthetic admixture with human weakness and disability. Constructed well in advance of war poetry, the mythical identity of the hero has long contained such implicit possibilities of becoming. Consider the age-old mutilation-resurrection motif, which is not a fixed archaic structure, but rather an inbuilt potential of the hero for metamorphosis between human fragility and divine status. This metamorphosis can be worked in both directions: either towards an ultimate apotheosis of the hero or towards his nemesis (a thwarting of his hubristic presumption of equalling the gods). Husserl's notion that the "*intending-beyond-itself*" of the consciousness of something is "an essential moment of it," or "a 'meaning more' of the Same,"[49] is a crucial insight into this notion of engaging tradition as a preserved capability for more meaning. It indicates how the heroic phenomenon already contains possibilities of becoming that an aesthetically adequate engagement can both disclose and activate.

The poetic unfolding of Owen's war victim reawakens the latent dynamics of the mythical hero to a performative degree that accommodates the novel ironies of the Great War. In the process, the war's historically concluded event enters a familiar play of heroic possibilities now subject to an aesthetic mode of execution and projection. The extraliterary event thus acquires the two essential elements of experience: it moves backwards, towards a naturalizing memory, and forwards, towards an ironic performance able to accommodate the absurdities and paradoxes of the Great War through its self-regulating novelty. The whole process ensures the significant becoming of the extraliterary event, whose primary assignment to memory subsequently expands with relevancies generated between aesthetic configurations. The only further significance to be gained by this aesthetically unfolding situation is through further productive responses to its earlier poetic syntheses, a meaningful becoming of what the reader has formulated up to a previous point of aesthetic performance. The end of performance (whether in dramatic play, match, dance, poetry, or any other field) is not a final structure, but the outstanding realization of a pre-established plot, set of rules, choreography, or archetype. However consummate the individual performance, its sense of completion lies in restoring the immediacy of the act to the memory of the game, that is, in reasserting the identity of the game by excelling all its previous realizations. Likewise, the context of modern warfare in "Disabled" is not captured by a fixed heroic structure, such as the commonplace of physical ability and fortitude, but through a continued realization of endured opposites (deification and fragility, ritual and true bloodletting, beauty and mutilation, and so on) whose resumed play with heroic potentialities continues to articulate an otherwise irrational war.

The fact that the war itself was predetermined by various cultural and narrative texts of armed conflict facilitates this aesthetic appropriation of the conflict. So powerful were the antecedent narratives of conflict in 1914 that they proved responsible for the obsolete mode of doing battle applied at the Western Front. "There are," Fussell remarks insightfully, "conventions and styles in Orders of the Day just as for any literary documents."[50] Only against the background of such outmoded articulations of war could the new trench warfare be foregrounded as a distinctly ironic way of doing battle, with its own specific demands on human endurance and fortitude. Accordingly, it is not only Owen's reader who comes to poetry with preconceptions of heroic virtue; but humanity at large that embarks upon actual war governed by instructive myths and archetypes (primary amongst which stands the heroic archetype itself). Here, too, a historical event merits being called of epical proportions, or unprecedented in its dramatic consequences, because it redraws the boundaries of the myths and archetypes that naïvely introduce it. By reopening the traditional discourse of the hero, the poem "Disabled" already, in a very essential way, reveals the revisable myths of war itself. For if the traditional hero's fundamental activity is that he must do battle, this heroic activity is as open to significant reconstruction as is the hero himself. One critic illustrates the point by observing that from the ancient hero's virtue of doing battle there emerges the later Christian hero who does spiritual battle with his own conscience, thereby revising the very notion of violent conflict into a self-questioning consciousness.[51] In "Disabled" the hero's inner conflict between mythical and human dimensions can be seen as one such possible extension of this revisable narrative of conflict itself.

That the Great War was especially prone to revisable mythical and legendary narratives is an extensively recorded fact, and attests to the force of cultural texts even in overwhelming historical events. Fussell gives a detailed account of how this war was particularly mythologized, calling it a "myth-ridden world" articulated in terms of the ancient rituals of resurrection and metamorphosis.[52] It was also a war fictionalized by legend and fable, inhabited by widely acknowledged ghosts, and believed to have been partly carried out by ancestral warriors. One outstanding example is the myth of the angels of Mons—ancient English bowmen believed to have risen to defend the British during their retreat from this location—a myth that originated from a short story entitled "The Bowmen" published by the journalist Arthur Machen on 29 September 1914.[53] Even though Bernard Bergonzi speaks of the Great War as an ultimately demythologizing experience, he still recounts this and other such instances of mythmaking to illustrate the "mythopoeic imagination of the public" at the time, a mentality that in the case of the angels of Mons would reject even the journalist's own "energetic assertion that his story was pure invention."[54] "In one sense," observes Fussell, "the movement [of the war] was towards myth, towards a revival of the cultic, the mystical, the sacrificial, the prophetic, the sacramental, and the universally significant. In short, towards fiction."[55] This demanded of war poetry a constant negotiation between evoked myth and actual horror. And where myth failed to fill the role of recollection, other literary conventions stepped in. When the poet William Noel Hodgson blended the Georgian convention of a red sunset with the actual redness of bloodshed in one of his poems, comments Fussell, he exemplified how war poetry typically "caught [literary conventions] in the act of turning literal."[56] By negotiating the distance threatening to grow between traditional models of representation and the unprecedented atrocities of modern conflict, war poetry could thus articulate an immediate context already considerably dependent on literary precedents and ancient ritual. Unable to shed the literary and mythical conventions governing its unforeseeable development, the actuality of war demanded an intervening aesthetic performance to recapture their hidden potentialities and proceed meaningfully beyond their accepted structures.

This function of the literary experience as a mediation between retention and protension is, of course, Iser's whole point when he speaks of literature in terms of transformed memories interacting with the modified expectations that emerge from them.[57] Accordingly, Owen's ironic hero obliges the reader to stand between a revised mythical discourse and a refined anticipation of what heroic virtue might consist of in future conflicts. This explains why it has been said, even of earlier heroic types like the romantic hero, that his enigmatic being is experienced through a hermeneutical distance.[58] Distance will inevitably grow between our normalized preconceptions of the hero and the renewed actuality of heroic action. Threatening to make the old heroic paradigm irrelevant and the actual world incomprehensible, this growing distance could only be covered with ever more sophisticated negotiations between memory and expectation, which become mutually transformative in the process. Ultimately, such a process accounts for the effective history of the hero, as well as the ability of a poem like "Disabled" to register the new complexity of trench warfare through the novel application of heroic rituals. Irony is an apt device in this regard. Intervening between what is mythically said and what should be additionally understood about the hero, irony effects, in the words of Linda Hutcheon, a "rubbing together" of "the said and the plural unsaid."[59] The device of irony relies on similarities in order to expose incongruities, becoming complicitous in what it ultimately surpasses by alternative suggestion.[60] Instead of merely excluding archetypal heroic virtues, therefore, the ironic schema of "Disabled" includes them in a differential equation, an exercise in divergence. Here lies the reason why the mutilation of Owen's soldier, as well as his defective knowledge and his ultimate seclusion, are significant: they are not the mutilation, ignorance, and seclusion of a common man, but of a would-be god. They are disfigurement, inferiority, and solitude inextricably interwoven with the age-old figure of a godlike youth, a virtual deity whose ritual has gone horribly wrong. They are the unexpected potentialities of a familiar archetype.

The situation of war could become "available for interpretation," says Fussell, only because its "unprecedented meaning" found "precedent motifs and images" that could be adopted and adapted through novel application.[61] This implies that the distance between precursory models and the extraliterary situation could only be bridged each time our narrated world regained the status of a meaningful experience, a singular extension of memory. In Owen's poetry, this process of restoring experience to a narrated world is enhanced by the poet's own habit of reacting to literary images, metaphors, and diction already established by earlier and contemporary writers. It has been amply demonstrated by Stallworthy that Owen's poetic inventiveness was accomplished through repeated borrowings and ironic reworkings of rival literary and mythical images,[62] implying that his work, at once derived and innovative, was frequently a negotiated distance between some dominant literary image and a projected otherness. When passed on to the reader, this play of receptive and creative faculties leads to another question, namely, whether there can ever be a final synthesis of the literary phenomenon. It is to this question that I turn in the final section of this study.

IS THERE A FINAL SYNTHESIS OF THE WAR HERO?

Iser draws our attention to the reader's "wandering viewpoint," which "travels along *inside*" the literary phenomenon that the reader constructs out of various intersecting (and possibly conflicting) perspectives.[63] The first point made in this study—that poetry compresses multiple perspectives, which then interact, put each other in relief, and demand that the literary object be significantly reconstructed—reveals the origin of the wandering viewpoint. In "Disabled," the reader's wandering viewpoint is first activated by a collision of aspects pertaining to the war victim. These loosened aspects then relate to each other through the alternative schema of irony. However, the wandering viewpoint does not end here, at the interplay between mythical residues and human limitations; it also brings about a process capable of questioning and reformulating itself through its "ever-expanding network of connections."[64] One of its features is that newly emerging gaps are inevitably brought to light with every effort towards a definitive synthesis between its disparate perspectives. Another is that in filling out these gaps with new combinations, the reader would also bring to light aspects that normally remain hidden in any directly perceived object but that are now made the very focus of the sophisticated assembly of perspectives making the poetic image possible.[65] Accordingly, the poetic image of Owen's war victim always exists through assimilating new aspects demanded by the very need to bridge its intrinsically evolving gaps. This self-regulating process removes the distinction between the memory of the literary entity and its last projected aspect, its retained identity and its prospective being.

The foregoing process can be illustrated with a further gap made noticeable in the construction of Owen's war victim only now, that is, after the open-ended schema of his ironic being is well in place. This gap concerns the fact that, despite his highly individualized irony of divine manifestation blending with human fragility, Owen's soldier remains anonymous throughout the poem. The missing name of his exceptionally personal agony (his tragedy greatly individualizes myth, and his distressed voice can be heard through the narrating voice) stands out as the blank space that calls for further synthesis within the ironic schema, and thus as a need for further interpretation. Such a need may simply prolong the orientation of the ironic schema, by providing a further contrast with heroic virtues. In this case, the soldier's anonymity would simply feature as a contradiction to the heroic convention of accumulating various exploits under a famous name, which signifies a "unified and integral being."[66] As Gwyn Jones points out, "love of fame" in the traditional hero is not a crude vanity, but the very essential heroic trait of being recognized as an immortal identity.[67] As stated above, even the sacrificial death of the classical hero reinforces this immortalized identity, since it posthumously absorbs supernatural deeds from various cultures under a mythical or legendary name. Yet this classical ascendancy of the hero's immortalized name had already been subjected to ironic treatment in past literature. Bloomfield, for instance, discusses how in the Middle Ages the hero's good name becomes only one end of the "polarity between fame and conscience."[68] Inspired by Augustine's notion of *conscientia*, the Middle Ages became steadily more aware that "fame is the approval of men, whereas conscience is the approval of God," making the former subservient to the latter.[69] A new self-questioning conscience—one performing inner action for God in preference to outer action for men—thus led to a weakening of the hero's celebrated individuality, and an eventual splitting of heroic virtues "among several men."[70] Walter L. Reed likewise observes how the integrated identity of the later Romantic hero is split into the hero and his alter-ego, if not fragmented into a multiplicity of roles that destroy his "unifying power of personality."[71]

This literary history of a split heroic personality already implicates the hero as the inner struggle between the lure of fame and the prick of conscience, the making of a name and the breaking of identity. Owen's soldier is, in fact, shifted to the side of a troubled conscience, as illustrated by his inner torment about disability and seclusion. His obscurity within an institute goes further than being a direct result of his physical inability to maintain athletic celebrity. It also represents a deeper schizophrenic nature: namely, a conscience doing battle with itself, and therefore unable to integrate its mythical aspirations and bodily mutilation under a single name. The soldier's anonymity can, in this respect, be treated as the outer sign of an inner failure of unity, a symbol of the contradictory components that allow no unifying name, let alone a celebrated personality, to emerge. Yet the blank space opened up by the soldier's anonymity also allows a more significant combination of perspectives to take place, thereby gaining a further impression of depth.

This can be readily demonstrated with the following inversion: whereas the athlete's fame results from physically playing the game of football, his later obscurity results from the ironic play of mythical and human elements in the more serious game of warfare. The loss of the hero's unifying identity, his anonymity, thus exposes the tragic result of a misguided shift of the heroic game, its transfer from the athletic field to the battlefield. This transfer shatters the athlete's fame by separating the mythical and the human into irreconcilable elements, making their future connection possible only through the ironic game of an anonymous hero.

The notion of a heroic game is definitely not foreign to the poem "Disabled," which clearly evokes its image with terms like "ran," "hot race," "leap," "matches," "carried shoulder-high," and "football." Nevertheless, after the athletic hero conveys these play elements to the trenches, in accordance with the semiotic practice of the time, his athletic virtues mingle with mutilation ("the hot race / And leap of purple [blood that] spurted from his thigh"). As a result, athletic celebrity dissolves into obscurity, fame into seclusion. When the athletic components—racing and leaping—are relocated in a situation of bloodletting and sacrifice, the soldier seems closer than ever to a name of mythical stature, yet his resultant mutilation paradoxically eliminates the very possibility of a physically conducted game, let alone a celebrated or immortalized identity. The transposition of the heroic game to warfare, in fact, makes for a more serious game of mythical and human contrasts, the outcome of which is a nameless ironic hero. No longer able to be physically carried out, the heroic game henceforth depends on the reader's ironic shifts and interacting perspectives within the poetic event. For it is only the reader's engaged faculties that enable the heroic game to go on being skilfully executed, although as a literary performance leading to the agonizing realization of a nameless victim. Literature "conserves and recycles" products like the hero, says John Leyerle, by setting up their "structure of [...] play" as a pattern whose rules only the reader's further individual implementation can carry out.[72] With reference to *Sir Gawain and the Green Knight*, the fourteenth-century romance full of play elements undertaken by its knight hero, Leyerle makes an important observation: what starts out to be a heroic game *within* the text in fact becomes a literary game, one in which symbols must be deciphered and action appropriately taken not only by the knight himself, but also by the very act of literary composition. Literary phenomena like Owen's ironic hero can reach unprecedented levels of performance because literary play replaces other, less versatile and less far-reaching applications of the heroic game. This is why it can be said that the poem "Disabled" departs from a familiar heroic game towards an ever more sophisticated ironic fashion of playing it. The blank space opened up by the soldier's anonymity is, in fact, the site where a momentous performance of the heroic game can take place. While renouncing the mythical claims of immortal fame, this ironic play utilizes none other than the virtues of the immortal hero. It transforms the traditional hero's name, made immortal through ritual sacrifice, into the soldier's unknown name, made anonymous through the war's pointless sacrifice.

The last, concluding comment must therefore be that, rather than a final synthesis of Owen's disabled soldier, there is a memory of the hero's traditional components realized only through further performance, a belonging to the constituent narratives of the hero registered through significant potentialities discovered in his typical game. Owen's reader cannot stand outside the constraining framework of a recognizable world of heroism if his interpretative moves are to make any difference and their significance to emerge against a familiar background. As stated above, the ironic performance of Owen's disabled soldier *stands out only through the novel way it stands within the narrated world of the hero*, which is to say that rather than dispense with the literary object or simply possess it as a fixed structure, the reader inhabits its pre-established game with outstanding and skilful adaptations that better satisfy his own experience of a lived world. The heroic game is thus broadened with literary possibilities first realized within its own boundaries, ensuring that the process never dissolves into a meaningless practice, and that each move remains an efficacious part of an evolving whole. In this way, the literary reader masters the very game whose structure had first constrained his moves, using techniques (such as irony) that extend it by revealing the hitherto unrealized possibilities of its tradition. In Owen's poem "Disabled," the significant becoming of the hero is just this skilful merging of the traditional rules of the heroic game and the ironic possibilities emerging in the act of playing it.

University of Malta

NOTES

[1] Wolfgang Iser, *The Act of Reading: A Theory of Aesthetic Response* (Baltimore: Johns Hopkins University Press, 1978), 71.
[2] Iser 72–73.
[3] Roman Ingarden, *The Cognition of the Literary Work of Art*, trans. Ruth Ann Crowley and Kenneth R. Olson (Evanston, IL: Northwestern University Press, 1973), 58.
[4] Hans-Georg Gadamer, *Truth and Method*, trans. Joel Weinsheimer and Donald G. Marshall, 2nd ed. (London: Sheed and Ward, 1989), 361.

[5] Gadamer 359. Gadamer is not speaking of a literary reader, but of the general understanding of tradition by any "historically effected consciousness" that engages it in the form of a dialogue. Nevertheless, his observation includes the literary reader as one example of this "historically effected consciousness."

[6] Lewis Richard Farnell, *Greek Hero Cults and Ideas of Immortality* (London: Oxford University Press, 1921), 18.

[7] Jon Stallworthy, *Wilfred Owen* (London: Oxford University Press, 1974), 140.

[8] Stallworthy 141. That Owen never abandoned this strong mythopoeic inclination, even after combat, is evident in both his poetry and his letters. His draft of the unfinished poem "The Wrestlers," which deals with the mythical combat between Heracles and Antaeas, was written during his recovery in Craiglockhart. Stallworthy 195–197. In *Heroes' Twilight: A Study of the Literature of the Great War* (New York: Coward-McCann, 1965), 131–132, Bernard Bergonzi quotes a letter written by Owen to Osbert Sitwell in 1918 that exemplifies the poet's ironic re-enactment of religious ritual, vividly recounting details of the passion of Christ as relived by the men under his command. Bergonzi, for whom the "retreat [from actuality] into myth" diminished the authenticity and realism of some of the war poems, still admits that "It is the sense of the war as a ritual sacrifice, in which he was involved as both priest and victim, that gives Owen's finest poems their particular quality, far transcending the simple protest and rebellion of Sassoon (or some of his own less ambitious pieces)." Bergonzi 67, 132.

[9] Ingarden 188.

[10] Iser 80.

[11] Paul Fussell, *The Great War and Modern Memory* (New York: Oxford University Press, 1975), 25–27. So dominant was this preconception of war as a game that one assault on the German trenches started by kicking balls towards their line and attempting to dribble them the rest of the way. In actual action, as by convention, war was taken to be a game.

[12] Fussell 31–32.

[13] Morton W. Bloomfield, "The Problem of the Hero in the Later Medieval Period," in *Concepts of the Hero in the Middle Ages and the Renaissance*, eds. Norman T. Burns and Christopher J. Reagan (Albany, NY: State University of New York Press, 1975), 28. Bloomfield adds the following: "The fact that a word originally meaning a semi-divine creature has come, in one of its senses, to mean the protagonist in literature, does not tell us a good deal about how we conceived the chief personage in literary works from the seventeenth century onwards." There has developed, in fact, a proliferation of literary types of hero: "There are the epic hero, the romantic hero, the dramatic hero, the tragic hero, the ironic hero, the realistic hero, and even the comic hero and anti-hero." Bloomfield 29.

[14] Bernard F. Huppé, "The Concept of the Hero in the Early Middle Ages," in *Concepts of the Hero in the Middle Ages and the Renaissance*, eds. Norman T. Burns and Christopher J. Reagan (Albany, NY: State University of New York Press, 1975), 7–8.

[15] Huppé 19.

[16] Andrew Rutherford, *The Literature of War: Five Studies in Heroic Virtue* (London: Macmillan, 1978), 33.

[17] Rutherford 39.

[18] Northrop Frye, *Anatomy of Criticism*, 2nd ed. (London: Penguin, 1990), 33–34.

[19] Raglan, 4th Baron of (Fitzroy Richard Somerset), *The Hero: A Study in Tradition, Myth, and Drama*, reprint (Westport, CT: Greenwood Press, 1975), 189.

[20] Iser 113.

[21] Raglan 192.

[22] This abrupt shift from a glorifying to a realistic portrayal of the soldier's lot, brought about by real combat at the front, is starkly exemplified by Owen himself. In the space of sixteen

days, Owen describes his war experience first as "perfect spirits" and then as "seventh hell" in two letters sent to his mother one before and the other after his first combat experience. Fussell argues that this dichotomy of before and after resulted (along with other common polarizations of thought) from the instantaneous transformation of outlook exacted by the war. Fussell 81.

[23] Rutherford 70.
[24] Gwyn Jones, *Kings Beasts and Heroes* (London: Oxford University Press, 1972), 45.
[25] Gadamer 294.
[26] Gadamer 290.
[27] Raglan 208.
[28] Frye 35–36.
[29] Frye 38–39.
[30] Frye 42.
[31] Frye 42.
[32] Iser 92.
[33] Stallworthy 286.
[34] John Purkis, *A Preface to Wilfred Owen* (London: Longman, 1999), 45.
[35] Fussell 16. Consider, also, the observation that "Every war is ironic because every war is worse than expected. Every war constitutes an irony of situation because its means are so melodramatically disproportionate to its presumed ends." Fussell 7.
[36] Fussell 35.
[37] Purkis 27, 36.
[38] Stallworthy 223–226. Owen showed the first draft of "Disabled" to Siegfried Sassoon and Robert Graves at Craiglockhart.
[39] Purkis 65–66.
[40] Rutherford 47.
[41] Iser 108.
[42] Iser 184.
[43] Steven Mailloux, *Interpretive Conventions: The Reader in the Study of American Fiction* (Ithaca, NY: Cornell University Press, 1982), 70–71. As do most other reader-response critics, Mailloux applies his observations to narrative texts rather than poetry. Nevertheless, his sequential model of reading serves to explain why the poetic object and situation are cumulative.
[44] Iser 54.
[45] Ingarden 48.
[46] Gadamer 355.
[47] Ingarden 182.
[48] Gadamer 66–67. In his discussion of the concept of *erlebniskunst*, originally meaning "that art comes *from* experience and is an expression of experience," Gadamer shows how this concept was "then used for art that is intended *to be* aesthetically experienced"; this prompts him to argue that "the significance of that whose being consists in expressing an experience cannot be grasped except through an experience." Gadamer 70. It is this supplementary experience of poetic realization that restores eventfulness to textual, cultural, and institutional phenomena derived from the reader's narrated world.
[49] Edmund Husserl, *Cartesian Meditations: An Introduction to Phenomenology*, trans. Dorion Cairns (Dordrecht: Kluwer Academic Press, 1999), 46.
[50] Fussell 17.
[51] Huppé observes how the literary task undertaken by early medieval Christian poets was to weave the heathen heroic virtue of doing battle with the Christian doctrine of *imitatio Christi*, the resultant hybrid being the notion of a soldierly striving for Christian virtues such as compassion.

The new Christian hero emerging out of this dialectic with the old heathen hero was a moral requirement of the time. Huppé 8–10.

[52] Fussell 114–115.
[53] Bergonzi 35.
[54] Bergonzi 36.
[55] Fussell 131.
[56] Fussell 61.
[57] Iser 111.
[58] Walter L. Reed, *Meditations on the Hero: A Study of the Romantic Hero in Nineteenth-Century Fiction* (New Haven, CT: Yale University Press, 1974), 18.
[59] Linda Hutcheon, *Irony's Edge: The Theory and Politics of Irony* (London: Routledge, 1995), 19.
[60] Hutcheon 23–27 *passim*.
[61] Fussell 138–139.
[62] Stallworthy 226–249 *passim*.
[63] Iser 109.
[64] Iser 116.
[65] Iser 137.
[66] Reed 28.
[67] Jones 48.
[68] Bloomfield 42.
[69] Bloomfield 43.
[70] Bloomfield 44.
[71] Reed 29.
[72] John Leyerle, "The Game and Play of Hero," in *Concepts of the Hero in the Middle Ages and the Renaissance*, eds. Norman T. Burns and Christopher J. Reagan (Albany, NY: State University of New York Press, 1975), 74–75.

BIBLIOGRAPHY

Bergonzi, Bernard. *Heroes' Twilight: A Study of the Literature of the Great War*. New York: Coward-McCann, 1965.

Burns, Norman T., and Christopher J. Reagan, eds. *Concepts of the Hero in the Middle Ages and the Renaissance*. Albany, NY: State University of New York Press, 1975.

Farnell, Lewis Richard. *Greek Hero Cults and Ideas of Immortality*. London: Oxford University Press, 1921.

Frye, Northrop. *Anatomy of Criticism,* 2nd ed. London: Penguin, 1990.

Fussell, Paul. *The Great War and Modern Memory*. New York: Oxford University Press, 1975.

Gadamer, Hans-Georg. *Truth and Method*. Trans. J. Weinsheimer and D. G. Marshall. London: Sheed and Ward, 1989.

Hibberd, Dominic. *Wilfred Owen: A New Biography*. Chicago: Ivan R. Dee, 2003.

Husserl, Edmund. *Cartesian Meditations: An Introduction to Phenomenology*. Trans. Dorion Cairns. Dordrecht: Kluwer Academic Press, 1999.

Hutcheon, Linda. *Irony's Edge: The Theory and Politics of Irony*. London: Routledge, 1995.

Ingarden, Roman. *The Cognition of the Literary Work of Art*. Trans. Ruth Ann Crowley and Kenneth R. Olson. Evanston, IL: Northwestern University Press, 1973.

Iser, Wolfgang. *The Act of Reading: A Theory of Aesthetic Response*. Baltimore: Johns Hopkins University Press, 1978.

Jones, Gwyn. *Kings Beasts and Heroes*. London: Oxford University Press, 1972.
Kerényi, Carl. *The Heroes of the Greeks*. Trans. H. J. Rose. London: Thames and Hudson, 1959.
Mailloux, Steven. *Interpretive Conventions: The Reader in the Study of American Fiction*. Ithaca, NY: Cornell University Press, 1982.
Moran, Dermot. *Introduction to Phenomenology*. London: Routledge, 2000.
Purkis, John. *A Preface to Wilfred Owen*. London: Longman, 1999.
Raglan, 4th Baron of (Fitzroy Richard Somerset). *The Hero: A Study in Tradition, Myth, and Drama*. Reprint. Westport, CT: Greenwood Press, 1975.
Reed, Walter L. *Meditations on the Hero: A Study of the Romantic Hero in Nineteenth-Century Fiction*. New Haven, CT: Yale University Press, 1974.
Rutherford, Andrew. *The Literature of War: Five Studies in Heroic Virtue*. London: Macmillan, 1978.
Silkin, Jon. *Out of Battle: The Poetry of the Great War*. London: Oxford University Press, 1972.
Stallworthy, Jon. *Wilfred Owen*. London: Oxford University Press, 1974.

VICTOR GERALD RIVAS

BEAUTY, TASTE, AND ENLIGHTENMENT IN HUME'S AESTHETIC THOUGHT

L'homme accompli doit employer sa vie à faire du bien, à cultiver les arts, à pénétrer les secrets de la nature, à perfectionner son être.

Voltaire, *La Princesse de Babylone*, IV.

The aim of this essay is to unfold the logical unity of the concepts mentioned in the title. It is divided into two sections: In the first, I review the historical setting of the unity at issue in the light of the modern subjectivism wherein Hume was formed as a philosopher, so as to understand why it was incompatible with the metaphysical transcendence of beauty that ancient philosophy upheld; in the second, I account for how Hume connected the problem of beauty with the problem of the personal fulfilment of humanity. Finally, in a brief coda, I reflect upon the topicality of these considerations.

I

The identification of "beauty" and "taste," two concepts that have almost been indistinguishable from the eighteenth century onwards, is far from being comprehensible by itself, although it has become a platitude both for the intellectual discourse and the sociocultural relations that stem from the idea that beauty hinges upon taste, which in plain language means that something is beautiful when someone perceives it so and not because of a quality inherent to it (whether this is metaphysical or physical). This is especially so when the beauty in question is human, whose plurality and relativity have during the second half of the twentieth century been universally postulated to such a point that it is considered natural that someone's beauty relies utterly on factors as aleatory as the society or the culture wherein the individual who assesses it has been educated or also on the psychological framework that is supposed to make everyone beautiful or not to others and to himself. This has fostered, on one hand, a raw individualism that has unrestrainedly triumphed all over social links (in the sense that everyone can claim that others are as he perceives them) and, on the other, the odd disappearance of beauty both from the social idealization of personal features (wherein it has been reduced to mere attractiveness, if not to so-called "sex appeal") and from all the fields of creation, especially from the plastic arts, where it has turned into a sidetrack, more adequate for interiors design than for creation as such (which is doubtlessly due to the relevance of the psychological approach to the matter and the concomitant search for sundry emotions and feelings experienced by everyone beyond the harmony and stillness that were the metaphysical elements of beauty). Indeed, whereas Hegel upheld that the greatest achievements of Hellenic antiquity in sculpture endeavor to express the perfect beauty that was simultaneously the perfect human way of being ("the human bodily form, then, is employed in the classical type of art not as purely sensuous existence, but exclusively as the existence and natural shape appropriate to mind"),[1] the creations of the current day leave aside both beauty and human ideality and whenever they deal with them, appeal either to irony or to open criticism, whereof the best instances would very likely be the series of portraits of Marilyn Monroe by Andy Warhol.[2]

I am not so sure that this triple nexus of the reduction of human beauty to psychological appreciation, the loss of social ideality, and the disappearance of a standard of artistic perfection has been examined as much as it deserves to be, and although I will not dwell upon it either, it was necessary to mention it as the general background of my true aim, which lies in appreciating that the unity of beauty and taste is by no means natural or evident and stems from the interests and problems that accrue from the subjective framework of modernity, which is more blatant when it is contrasted with the ancient philosophical tradition that instead of linking the two concepts, beauty and taste, kept them in different realms of reality and human activities. According to this tradition, the essence of beauty had to be set out together with the metaphysical framework of reality (which was expressed by the concept of "cosmos"),[3] whereas taste was a merely individual phenomenon unworthy of attention for the wise man inasmuch as it just stood for how someone perceived things or for his particular penchants, which had nothing to do with what they were by themselves (*stricto sensu*, taste was not even mentioned by ancient philosophers, at least not with the meaning that it has for modernity). Still more, the ontological difference between reality and opinion supplied the fulcrum for the further development of the metaphysical unity of beauty and human ideality, inasmuch as it took for granted the correspondence between a cosmic and a personal quality, a correspondence that was accountable by philosophical reflection. Appealing to a basic metaphysical dualism between being and becoming in order to overcome the sophist reduction of knowledge to opinion, Plato upheld that beauty belonged to the world of transcendence whereas taste—or rather passion[4]—belonged to the world of becoming, which made it impossible to peruse them in unity, as the philosopher pointed out in the *Phaedrus* (246a ff.). After describing how the human soul has accidentally fallen from heaven and become incarnate while it participates in a cosmic cycle wherein the souls both of gods and the rest of the living beings rise into the heavens towards the top of the celestial vault, where they behold "the very being wherewith true knowledge is concerned" (247c–d), Plato adds that this "colourless, formless, intangible essence" is remembered thanks to beauty, which works as a universal nexus between the soul and the reality to which it belongs, which is hidden by the sensitive perceptions and the bodily drives that prevent soul from recollecting its true nature:

> Few only retain an adequate remembrance of [the celestial reality]; and they, when they behold here any image of that other world, are rapt in amazement; but they are ignorant of what this rapture means, because they do not clearly perceive. For there is no light of justice or temperance or any of the higher ideas which are precious to souls in the earthly copies of them; they are seen through a glass dimly; and there are few who, going to the images, behold in them the realities, and these only with difficulty [...] But of beauty, I repeat again that we saw her there shining in company with the celestial forms; and coming to earth we find her here too, shining in clearness through the clearest aperture of sense. For sight is the most piercing of our bodily senses; though not by that is wisdom seen; her loveliness would have been transporting if there had been a visible image of her, and the other ideas, if they had visible counterparts, would be equally lovely. But this is the privilege of beauty, that being the loveliest she is also the most palpable to sight. (250a–d)[5]

The conceptual framework of this passage and of the cultural and philosophical tradition that started with it does not include taste: Beauty is set out in regard to the transcendent essence of reality, and instead of relying on the individual that beholds it, it determines his existence throughout, whereby the concept that agrees with it is not "taste" but "love," which, for its part, has to be differentiated from the passions or penchants of the individual, who is, as it were, subject to a "want of being"[6] that compels him to search for beauty in order to overcome the trials that body imposes over soul, the worst of which is blindness to its heavenly origin; thus, overwhelmed by wants and shattered by drives utterly alien to it, soul becomes corrupted and loses its opportunity to rejoin the cosmic cycle after the death of the individual, which shows that it was perfectly possible for ancient tradition to explain the nature of beauty and to postulate a social and cultural archetype in accordance with it without requiring at all the mediation of taste, which, as I said, was rather identified with those evil strengths that have to be avoided or checked so as to allow soul to be released from body.

How, then, was beauty linked with taste? The answer to this question compels us to make a digression, for it is understandable only in the light of the axial transformation of thought that took place during the second half of the seventeenth century and from which modernity stemmed. In essence, this transformation lay in the substitution of the metaphysical framework of reality by the rational determination of subjectivity. Taking into account that this last concept was defined from Descartes onwards as the only reliable ground from which to methodically determine reality or, more concretely, the qualities and function of whatever element thereof—whether by pure reason or by experience, which is unimportant for this discussion—the elucidation of the relation that in accordance with Antiquity existed between the world of essences and the world of appearances was substituted by the demand for a clear understanding of the unity of the sundry faculties of the subject and of the respective way of achieving a model of knowledge that was no longer aimed at the revelation of the beyond but at the transformation of immanence, which, of course, does not entail that reflection on God or on the *post mortem* destiny of the human soul were set aside; on the contrary, these themes were pursued more eagerly than before, although from a utterly different standpoint, for they were no longer set out in accordance with the would-be nature of things but with the mental or rational constitution of subjectivity that was represented by ideas of all kinds and cogency; this means that the philosophy of the time strove for making out the rise and meaning of every idea in knowledge and also in behavior in order to get a universal system of representations that encompassed rationally everything, including those manifestations of the subject that seemed at first sight irreducible to a clear determination, which was the case of the phenomena that were included in the hardly definable field of sensibility, which all of a sudden acquired a relevance and rather a specificity unimaginable until then, considering that subjectivity, instead of the almost ineffable being with which Plato and Antiquity dealt, was not simple but complex.[7] Furthermore, the importance of Descartes and, in general, of rationalism, in the genesis of Aesthetics is notable, for notwithstanding Cartesianism's rejection of the value of the senses in the determination of reality, the systematization that it upheld implied the necessity of defining the part that sensibility played in subjectivity. Thus, inasmuch as subjectivity was supposed to work in accordance with rules whose sense and reach were—at least theoretically—clear and based on an intuition that was original and evident for everyone (according to the Cartesian conception of the *cogito*), it was necessary to determine the formal unity of its faculties and operations, which demanded overcoming the problematic difference of two imports of the concept that have nothing to do each other: the logical or formal and the psychological or material one. "Subjectivity" was indeed originally equivocal, since it stood both for the "universal determination of reason" and for the "spontaneous expression" according to which everyone perceived and projected everything in accordance with his own sensibility, an ambiguity that spread over the rationalist and the empiricist field alike (which is evidenced by Descartes and Locke).[8] In other words, subjectivity was understood as a framework or, contrariwise, as an individual in the flesh, and since it lacked the ontological simplicity whereby the transcendent Being had rightly or wrongly been conceived by ancient tradition, the main task of modern metaphysics after Descartes and until Kant had been to show how, despite whatever ambiguity was entailed, knowledge and science relied on a logical ground that allowed them to order jointly the processes of transformation of nature, regulation of society, and self-knowledge of each individual.

This triple aim would be unattainable, however, on the plane of the individual life if the difference of the two senses of subjectivity were absolute, for then everyone would be constrained by a rational framework alien to his sensitive projections or would be carried away by a mental stream that would doom him to a solipsistic reality bordering on outlandishness or rather on madness (which is brutally exemplified by Sade's characters). To avoid that, it was necessary to forge a link that ensured the unity of subjectivity in the absence of an all-embracing metaphysical principle such as the one on which ancient tradition was based and beyond the determinations pertaining directly to theoretical and scientific knowledge. That link was provided by the vast field of sensibility and, concretely, of taste, a concept that stood, first, for one of the senses; second, for the formative experience that everyone shared with others, thanks to which the organic sense turned into the ground of coexistence and self-formation; and, third, for the way everyone felt and imagined himself and the rest of reality, which was by principle only his and could not be mistaken for someone else's.[9] The interaction of these planes was widely analyzed throughout the eighteenth century, for it embraced organic, social, and personal dispositions that accounted for the identity of "taste" as such with "fine taste," that is, with the unity of a biological function with a cultural integration. This was emphasized by Joseph Addison, a man of letters who wrote one of the most influential works of the time, a series of articles that were compiled under the title of "The Pleasures of the Imagination,"[10] in which he says

A man of fine taste in writing will discern after the same manner, not only the general beauties and imperfections of an author, but discover the several ways of thinking and expressing himself, which diversify him from all other authors, with the several foreign infusions of thought and language, and the particular authors from whom they were borrowed.[11]

As we see, "taste" and "fine taste" were just the extremes of the process of integrating an individual into a sociocultural world in which he could express himself freely and originally but not necessarily outlandishly, flippantly, or vulgarly; that is to say, the community of meaning of both concepts implicated an ideality and an objective reference that prevented them from being the mere expression of an irrational drive or want (insofar as they evinced the unity of sensibility and the formative action of the sociocultural environment), and simultaneously included an element irreducible to experience, which could even be made out either as the organic constitution of everyone or as the unaccountable particularity of the individual at issue (insofar as this or that feature had been manifest from the onset and had resisted all steps taken to modify or avoid it, which was the situation for all those individuals that stood out from others, whether in a positive or in a negative way, for instance, by their creativeness—as in the case of the artists—or by his thought—as in the case of the philosophers, who were very meaningfully also called "libertines"). At any rate, taste implied that the difference between the formal and the material or psychological planes of subjectivity was not absolute and that it was rather the possibility of partaking intensely but not blindly in a social life ruled by true conventions or absurdities that, although they hardly made room for true originality, were not tantamount to either shallowness or bathos. Indeed, taste allowed the learned individual to integrate into the social bustle and follow the whims of fashion like anyone else but without his feeling perfunctory since he endeavored to identify universal participation and individual originality, which was feasible by means of sharing a way of feeling that was, I repeat, certainly ideal although it could not be postulated as the laws of reason. Thus, taste was neither an objective law nor an operative rule, let alone an ideal before which one's own will should bow, but a standard whereto everyone should appeal in accordance with his sensibility, his culture, and his knowledge, which is what Hume put forward in one of his most celebrated works, *Of the Standard of Taste*, published in 1757.[12]

II

It is very meaningful that the starting point of this work is precisely the "great inconsistency and contrariety" of taste, whether among individuals or among cultures throughout history. Independently of their common education, people show utterly opposite penchants and preferences that are praised or blamed according to criteria that are hardly justifiable although very effective, for notwithstanding that no one knows for certain how to differentiate smartness from outlandishness or affectation, the fact is that everyone perceives the difference, which contrasts with the situation prevailing in the field of knowledge, where contradictions or problems are solved by means of arguments and proofs that everyone handles in accordance with concepts whose meaning is clear and can at best be mathematically expressed.[13] As we see, Hume focuses the question by principle from the modern logical distinction of sensibility and understanding (which culminated with Kant)[14] and from the modern conception of society as a whole whose elements interact in accordance with a multiplicity of interests and dispositions while they must obey a common order; nevertheless, Hume does not dwell upon this issue but on the singular, intuitive unanimity manifested through it, for although diversity and even opposition exist, they go hand in hand with an acknowledgment that spans the ages and cultures and is decisive for morals, as he notes in a remark on the singular universality that morals evinces despite any other difference. Peoples or individuals that have nothing to do one with another appeal, however, to the elemental notions of morals such as "justice" and "virtue," and although they mean by those terms very dissimilar things or deeds, the fact is that their behavior shows a universal tendency that is usually linked to reason but that Hume accounts for the "very nature of language," that is to say, for the imaginative plane wherein conceptions evolve thanks to the multivocal and figurative sense of language, which is, on the other hand, the cause of misunderstandings and conflicts because what was supposed to be perfectly clear is not, which is evident as soon as it is necessary to settle a disagreement or a conflict. This shows that sociocultural life and concretely moral ideals do not hinge upon rational principles but upon common sense and the sundry feelings that allow people to go on together despite their endless disagreements. That is what Hume means by seeking "a Standard of Taste; a rule, by which the various sentiments of men may be reconciled; at least, a decision, afforded, confirming one sentiment and condemning another."[15]

It was before said that the notion of "standard" is different both from that of "law" and that of "ideal" inasmuch as it does neither implies logical principles and procedures nor transcendence, for although it evinces a sui generis constant, its ground is the similarity of sense furnished by language and imagination and not the would-be nature of things; furthermore, it does not mean reality as such or objectively, but the way everyone feels in accordance with imagination, whereby its use is practically unrestricted and encompasses the whole of culture, morals included, whereof Hume makes the most in order to span the traditional opposition of philosophy and common sense, on the one hand, and, on the other, to solve the problem raised by the relativity of morals, which would lead to the most selfish drives as the pessimists and skeptics claimed. Now, notwithstanding the impossibility of relying on rational principles to lay the foundations of a universal moral, Hume argues that there is a principle very superior to reason for the same aim: experience.

Taking advantage of the historical constants with regard to virtue or vice, he upholds that there is a universality of feeling that provides us with some principles that are much more effective than the abstract precepts of reason. Furthermore, it would be absurd to reduce these principles to reason, for then they would lack the emotional strength by which they order social and individual life and foster creativity in the field of art, above all because their lack of a rational formulation does not mean either that they are imprecise; on the contrary, they are unmistakable and regulate behavior with an effectiveness that a rational rule never gets,[16] which has, however, mostly been passed over by thinkers and moralists because they are wont to appeal to rules that are alien to the diversity and the complexity of feelings and also of circumstances, a point that Hume emphasizes so as to avoid the simplifications of skeptics (who cling to the incidental to deny that there is a possibility of arriving at a set of moral rules) or the claims of rationalists (who start from a too abstract conception of life).[17] This allows Hume to show that the moral utility of taste is not attainable when the individual is not up to the unity of experience, intention, and potency, which is tantamount to beauty:

> A perfect serenity of mind, a recollection of thought, a due attention to the object; if any of these circumstances be wanting, our experiment will be fallacious, and we shall be unable to judge of the catholic and universal beauty. The relation, which nature has placed between the form and the sentiment, with at least be more obscure; and it will require greater accuracy to trace and discern it. We shall be able to ascertain its influence not so much from the operation of each particular beauty, as from the durable admiration, which attends those works that have survive all the caprices of mode and fashion, all the mistakes of ignorance and envy.[18]

Hume reinterprets in this passage the universal reach of beauty that the ancient tradition upheld beyond the relativity of the so-called "world of appearances." Just as Plato had discerned a celestial beauty from an earthly one (*Symposium* 180d–e) and had linked the former to wisdom and social order and the latter to debauchery and political upheaval, Hume discerns the balanced unity of the subjectivity faculties (which he calls "universal beauty") from the prevalence of one of them over the others (which he calls "particular beauty"), which evinces that beauty relies utterly on the harmony of the individual subject and has nothing to do with any characteristic of things, whether metaphysical or not. Now, what is meaningful here is that whereas Plato sets out the issue in qualitative terms (transcendence and immanence), Hume appeals to quantitative ones (universality and particularity), a difference accountable for the general aim of his essay, which lies in showing that the multiplicity of cultural and historic viewpoints does not belie the unity of the individual subjectivity because everyone can reshape it thanks to taste and to the universality of feeling, that is, beauty. At any rate, this is not objectively furnished, as it were, and everyone must endeavor to get it; thus, the quantitative distinction of universal and particular beauty aims at bottom to establish the standard required to measure the integration of the individual into a cultural world that is his insofar as it is everyone's. Thus, the universality of beauty is simultaneously the fulfilment of humanity, which is emphasized by Hume by praising, at the onset of the passage just quoted, a series of intellectual conditions that are not, however, joined by a rational principle but by the aspiration to judge or, rather, to embody beauty, which means that the ancient identity of beauty and good remains, although changed into a subjective endeavor that works in the absence of the would-be metaphysical essence of beauty because this is incompatible with the systematic order of knowledge and experience. It is absurd to try to figure out what beauty is—as ancient metaphysics foolishly did—because what is important here is just how to get it, and the best expedient for that lies in the cultural tradition, whose formative influence is determinant to harmonize the sundry faculties or features of the individual subject, who, instead of actualizing a prenatal vision of celestial beauty, lays the foundations of a personal accomplishment that serves as the standard to measure everyone else's, which requires a temporal and spatial distance to work well. In other words, it is very easy for someone to miss the target when he assesses something under the platitudes that rule his age or under the influence of local habits, whereas he will very likely be successful if he does it under ideals and works that have prevailed over the corrosive strength of time and cultural differences, which shows that the effectiveness of the standard of taste hinges to a great extent or rather utterly upon the distance that one keeps with regard to one's contemporaries, which, as it has already been said, requires the concourse of mental balance, bounty, and sensibility, that is to say, of beauty.

Beauty is thus a form or rather a value whose universality relies upon everyone's capacity for transcending the viewpoints imposed by his circumstances and not upon the nature of reality, contrary to what ancient metaphysics upheld, which means that instead of being an ontological framework prior to experience, beauty stems from the latter as a psychological achievement that becomes a new way of coexisting. Still more, it is not an outcome among others, for it is the standard of taste as such, which, however, seems to raise a problem, for it is at variance with the regulative function and with the would-be universality of the same standard, given that this last is the outcome of a process that it should instead frame, and, on the other hand, that it is linked to a series of factors and conditions that are very hard to find in an individual, above all because their fulfilment is at first sight almost based on a standpoint (the original penchants of the individual), which implies that everyone could claim that this or that is beautiful if he feels that it is so or even it he wants it to be so, which would make the standard of taste as useless as the rules by which reason intends to order behavior.

To overcome this double objection, Hume introduces the concept of the "delicacy of imagination" or, as he also calls it, "delicacy of taste," which means that independently of the differences in the way of feeling that organic constitution and/or education have caused among individuals, there is an average sensibility that allows everyone to perceive some objective qualities and features that agree with an ideal standard of taste, whose ground is cultural tradition and experience:

> Here then the general rules of beauty are of use; being drawn from established models, and from the observation of what pleases or displeases, when presented singly and in a high degree. And if the same qualities, in a continued composition and in a smaller degree, affect not the organs with a sensible delight or uneasiness, we exclude the person from all pretensions to this delicacy.[19]

Thus, the delicacy at issue is by no means identifiable with weakness, let alone with sloppiness, because it goes hand in hand with intellectual formation and objective knowledge; instead of furthering abstract individualism (which is linked with the tendency to cling stubbornly to one's opinions and emotions), it compels everyone to be disposed to learn and enjoy the sundry manifestations of culture through the average sensibility that has just been mentioned; otherwise, the individual will have to acknowledge that, if he cannot revel in what others can (provided that it had been sanctioned through history and that it is not only a momentary fashion that unlettered people follow, which a fine taste should rather reject), it is because "he wants the delicacy, which is requisite to make him sensible of every beauty and every blemish, in any composition or discourse."[20] Thus, without requiring another's assistance or censure, everyone must regulate his own preferences, and measure, as it were, his advancement with regard to the ideal universality of taste, whose fulfilment is psychological and cultural, yes, but whose soundness is utterly moral, that is, it must be presupposed at least as "a decision" that everyone must make against his own selfishness and also, on the other hand, against what is in vogue, for this is more proper to the taste that has not received the influence of learning and education and remains within the narrow limits of its own time. Thus, the self-excelling and the critical link with culture are the two factors that allow the individual to share the human perfection that Hume and his contemporaries called meaningfully "enlightenment," which, contrary to the pre-modern metaphysical ideals (such as those of the Renaissance), does not implicate the revelation of a transcendent archetype but the accomplishment of an immanent type, which is no other than the utter formation of everyone that is identical to the unity of taste, beauty, and personality, in accord, of course, with cultural tradition and social coexistence: "I must depart from [the platitudes and prejudices of my environment] and considering myself as a man in general, forget, if possible, my individual being and my peculiar circumstances."[21]

Hume emphasizes that the greatest hurdle against fulfilling such an ideal is prejudice, which has a pernicious effect on understanding and taste alike, for when someone does not reason properly, he is unable to appreciate beauty, which, as has already been shown, harms the character of the individual and unbalances him. In other words (and contrary to what the rationalist philosophers upheld), a man whose taste has not been formed or whose sensibility has been distorted so as to make him a prey of platitudes and fashions cannot be a rational individual, and, although he can stand out from others with regard to circumscribed or second-rate intellectual tasks, he will lack the capacity to link the field of knowledge with culture and society in general, and above all with art, which demands both intelligence and sensibility to be understood and enjoyed. Thus,

The same excellence of faculties which contributes to the improvement of reason, the same clearness of conception, the same exactness of distinction, the same vivacity of apprehension, are essential to the operations of true taste, and are its infallible concomitants. It seldom, or never happens [...] to meet with a man who has a just taste without a sound understanding.[22]

In short, a man like the one of whom Hume speaks will be one of those individuals that have at best specialized in a certain subject or matter but are at bottom alien to the very essence of enlightenment, which is to form persons with a critical consciousness of society and culture, which is the basis of a really moral conception of life.

This leads to the issue of the difficulty or almost impossibility of finding such an accomplished individual. As a matter of fact, finding him seems to be as hard as reifying a metaphysical ideal. For although this type is supposed to agree with anyone and does not imply substantial transcendence but sociocultural and historical integration, it seems that this is only a mystification unsuitable for the formation of taste. Hume, who heeds the point very carefully, considers that, in fact, the standard will seldom or never be applicable to specific circumstances without raising disputes and disagreements; however, he adds straightaway, the standard is not supposed to be a panacea, much less to solve all the differences, but rather to furnish a ground so that people can reason about their preferences and come to agreement, which is perfectly possible because it must be carried out through imagination and does not require theoretical or moral statements. Moreover, the standard will foster interaction and coexistence because its application will give rise to reflection and allow everyone to be aware of his penchants and also of those of others, which plays an axial part in any society whose members must not bow to alien standpoints or preferences. Thus, the aim of the standard is not to impose a rule or an ideal over everyone, but to guide everyone to the fulfilment of his own taste, which entails (we recall) understanding, self-consciousness, and something more, which the upholders of the abstract individualism that borders on solipsism are wont to pass over very easily: that no human being is utterly alien to others, let alone in matters concerning sensibility, where the structural condition of personality is more evident than in what concerns knowledge, to the point that it can perfectly be upheld that there is a historical transcendence of certain ways of feeling that are doubtlessly what allows everyone to share the conflicts that are set out in works of other epochs and identify with them:

> Nothing has been experienced more liable to the revolutions of chance and fashion than [the] pretended decisions of science. The case is not the same with the beauties of eloquence and poetry. Just expressions of passion and nature are sure, after a little time, to gain public applause, which they maintain forever. Aristotle, and Plato, and Epicurus, and Descartes, may successively yield to each other: but Terence and Virgil maintain a universal, undisputed empire over the minds of men. The abstract philosophy of Cicero has lost its credit; the vehemence of his oratory is still the object of our admiration.[23]

Thus, the continuity of tradition goes hand in hand with its inevitable transformation, just as the formation of a person is inseparable from the strengthening of his sensibility. The standard, it has already been said, cannot be an ideal in the proper meaning of the concept, at least neither a metaphysical nor a natural one,[24] because it does not stand for anything else but the spontaneous expression of an individual before the contents of culture and their social dynamism, which always must be considered universal precisely because it has been formed through experience and learning, the double touchstones of enlightenment. Therefore, the standard also must work as a retaining wall against the bigotry and the superstition that most religions further among their adepts (which reflects the jingoism and false community spirit that most governments instill into their citizenry), which are so contrary to fine taste that they must be set aside even in artworks so as not to mar our pleasure in them. In other words, each character or aspect of the work has to be assessed and enjoyed by the imaginative drive that they convey, provided that it has previously been formed, and not by the ideas that they stand for, by which the spectator will preserve his freedom of taste and will enjoy the cultural world wherein he partakes, and be more able to consider the ideas at issue: in short, he will embody the fullness that everyone can get if he endeavors to. *Vale.*

CODA

On reading Voltaire's spirited passage that appears as the epigraph to this essay, one cannot but wonder what current individualism owes to the enlightened thinkers that were supposedly its forerunners, in particular to Hume, whose philosophy is so characterized by the unique identity of skepticism and eagerness to live that also was axial for so many romantics. For if philosophy is first and foremost a kind of thought based on the intuition that every man possesses the capacity of knowing reality, Hume's is distinguished from others because it joins a sui generis appeal to reason with a very personal expression (which borders on confession more than once), which, as far as I know, is only perceptible in Descartes, Locke and Rousseau.[25] Thus, Hume has to be considered one of the most cogent influences on the romantic exaltation of genial individuality, however much romanticism disavowed the enlightenment approach to subjectivity, which it branded shallow and alien to the deepest wants of man, which is, very meaningfully, a feature that it shares with the present-day criticism against the so-called tyranny of reason (which should rather be aimed against the omnipresence of technology). Now, precisely because I started this paper by pointing out that the disappearance of the triple nexus of beauty, sociability, and creativity is the most important token of current times and because these times brag of their fostering vitality and individuality as no other epoch before, they seem to be the final point of a process whose onset was contemporary to Hume and whose strength has been nurtured time and time again both by his vindication of critical individuality and by the romantic vindication of life over reason.

Is this, however, true? Is our present era, notwithstanding its contradictions and aberrations, a consequence of eighteenth-century individualism and, more particularly, Hume's? I do not think so. Why? Because what present thought and culture want is the subjective unity of reason and experience, which, as we have seen, was tantamount for Hume and his contemporaries to taste. As a matter of fact, taste was the solution to the philosophical and sociohistorical problem of how anyone could overcome the opposition of the universality that reason demanded and the singularity that life imposed, an opposition that would inexorably have led to the split or literal alienation of the individual subject if he had not had the possibility of participating consciously in the process of his self-formation through an experience that was simultaneously the perfect reflection of coexistence, which is what "taste" or rather "fine taste" stood for and what the present time has set aside due to the lack of a philosophical bond among art, individuality, and beauty, which is, on the other hand, a feature by no means as recent as might first seem, considering that it can be traceable at least to Nietzsche's vindication of Dionysus (although without the philosophical and the historical background that this last implies).

Another aspect that must be emphasized is that in the absence of a theoretical framework for personal formation, this last becomes the spontaneous or rather thoughtless expression of an individuality that does not even need to probe its would-be talent, which is why it has so repeatedly been proclaimed during the last half century that art does not require other feature than imagination and that technical skillfulness or cultural formation are equally irrelevant or even harmful to authentic creativity, which accounts for why beauty has for the last several decades been branded an anachronism in the field of creation and of social relations and why it has been reduced to the realm of advertisement, entertainment, and fashion, where, nevertheless, there is neither essence to reveal nor desire to arouse and where everything is labeled with that disgusting value (sorry for the oxymoron) of "look," which prevents differences from being conceptualized and allows everyone to get simply carried away by his impulses, the most potent of which is, of course, the one to consume and spend. Thus, whereas beauty implied for philosophical and cultural tradition an unforgettable memory, an unquenchable desire, and a conscious formation, the odd, almost inexpressible thing that "look" stands for does not imply anything but instant oblivion, tediousness, and bathos.

This leads to the third aspect of the question that I wanted to emphasize, which has been pursued exhaustively in the most diverse fields of knowledge: the monstrous disarticulation and meaninglessness of verbal language and logical thought. Language has become for us nothing more than conventionalism, on the one hand, and image, desire, or want, on the other, and because of that literature is despised while slang is lauded, a situation that spreads over social life and over intellectual discourse alike, to the extreme that the latter emulates more and more the perfunctoriness of journalism. From a diametrically opposed standpoint, Hume and his contemporaries (following a secular tradition that had begun with Western thought itself) considered language the common ground of personal imagination and of creativity, for no one could show his would-be inward hoards if he did not master a language that allowed others to understand, admire and, why not, take him as a model. Still more, these thinkers and artists considered that language furthered the same ambiguity and sociability because when an expression is hard to understand, it must be analyzed and commented on with others, whereas everyone uses language nowadays as if words were simply particles with which an image could be traced. Thereby, the present triumph of the image in language does not lead to conceptions but to gibberish.

Lastly, the feature by which Hume's foundation of a standard of taste shows the utter difference between the Enlightenment's trust in individual sensibility and the current vindication of an undifferentiated "creativeness" and "spontaneity" is the thesis that there is a cultural and, above all, moral transcendence of feelings and emotions that allows anyone to identify with the characters of the literary masterworks of tradition and with the conflicts they face, which supplies the learned individual with the elements of a sentimental education indispensable to leading a beautiful life both in the social and moral sense of the expression, which aims at the fulfilment of everyone's potencies and preferences in accordance with and in favor of others, which is very similar to what the ancient conception of morals upheld concerning the supremacy of public accomplishment over individual satisfaction, although it had resorted to a metaphysical ground, whereas Hume resorted to a cultural and aesthetic one.[26] Instead, inasmuch as everyone claims nowadays that his "ideas" (whatever this means) are his and no one else's and that his feelings are equally or more original and only stand for his inward primeness, the thesis at issue ends up being practicably unintelligible for us and must be substituted by the platitude that what one can share is not his feelings as such but the experience of them, that is, that happiness, pleasure, love, sadness, and so on cannot be mutual because they spring from one's inner movements, which entails that instead of participating in a common reality, each individual expresses his sensations and reactions, whereby mutual comprehension is impossible, which shows that the main difference between Hume's standard and the current proliferation of preferences and lifestyles lies in the conception of subjectivity, which has stopped being the ground of a conscious sociability and has become an absolute by itself, practically a parody of the metaphysical idea of soul in an odd mixture with the most perfunctory image of the individual, which is evident particularly in the fall of whatever social paradigm of behavior and creativeness, that is, of the unity of beauty, individual life, and personal performance, of which the best proof is the decadence (or rather death) of art and the transformation thereof in one of the most successful kinds of investment.

    This does not mean at all that the enterprise of enlightenment and individual harmony that Hume and his contemporaries lauded has historically failed, because it was neither devised to rule society from top to bottom, as it were, nor to provide a recipe within everyone's reach, but to help whoever wanted to get a fuller existence with the cultural and sensitive unity that would allow him to do it. Thus, despite the sloppiness and coarseness whereby our time has been branded a new dark age, enlightenment is still a possibility at hand for whoever is lucid enough to see beyond the present. *Iterum vale.*

Meritorious University of Puebla, Mexico

NOTES

[1] G. W. F. Hegel, "The Philosophy of Fine Art" (abridged), transl. F. P. B. Osmaston, in *Philosophies of Art and Beauty. Selected Readings in Aesthetics from Plato to Heidegger*, eds. Albert Hofstadter and Richard Kuhns (Chicago: University of Chicago Press, 1976), p. 433.

[2] On this point, see Jacques Aumont, *De l'esthétique au présent* (Brussels, Boeck et Larcier, 1998), Chapter IV.

[3] Of course, this identification by no means implied that the cosmos lacked ugliness, but, rather, that it integrated organically any deformity in such a way that the superior unity was equivalent to beauty. See, for instance, the fragments 54 ("to delight in the mire") and 61 ("To God all things are fair and good and right, but men hold some things wrong and some right") of Heraclitus (according to the arrangement of Bywater and the translation of Burnet, available at http://plato.evansville.edu/public/burnet/ch3a.htm).

[4] This point must be heeded so as to grasp the difference between the ancient and the modern approaches to the matter: Taste means a subjective perception and does not imply perforce a moral connotation, which is instead axial to the concept of passion.

[5] Plato, *Phaedrus*, transl. Benjamin Jowett, in *Philosophies of Art and Beauty. Selected Readings in Aesthetics from Plato to Heidegger*, eds. Albert Hofstadter and Richard Kuhns, (Chicago: University of Chicago Press, 1976).

[6] This concept will provide the argumentative thread of Socrates' discourse in the *Symposium* (201c and ff.), where it is directly linked to the cosmic cycle of the soul and the possibility to escape the worldly condition.

[7] Marc Jimenez says, regarding this question: "The aesthetic reflection begins when it is possible to establish a link between what is agreeable to sense and what is pleasurable to soul, between the sensitive pleasure and the intelligible pleasure or, in other words, between perception and judgement, or rather (in order to remain in the Cartesian universe) between body and soul" [*Quest-ce que l'Esthétique?* (Paris: Gallimard, 1997), p. 56].

[8] I mean concretely the unjustifiable inclusion of sensitive functions in the formal framework of the *cogito*: "What am I then? A thinking thing. What is that? It is a thing that doubts, that knows, that states, that denies, that wants, that does not want, that also imagines and feels" [R. Descartes, *Metaphysical Meditations*, II, in *Oeuvres*, eds. C. Adam and P. Tannery (Paris: Vrin, 1964–1974), Vol. IX, p. 22]. If the self-consciousness must be prior to the consciousness of bodily existence (so as to guarantee the rational dualism between soul and body), functions such as imagination and desire should not be included in the *cogito*. On the other hand, with regard to Locke, it is obvious that he too accounts for the framework of experience that furnishes all of the contents of the human mind from the viewpoint of a psychological subject that is sometimes identified with the philosopher himself (which prevents him from achieving the universality required to put the foundations of experience beyond any question raised by the psychological sense of subjectivity). Thus, Locke rejects the Cartesian argument of the existence of the *cogito* with the following words: "I confess myself, to have one of those dull souls, that doth not perceive itself always to contemplate ideas, nor can conceive it any more necessary

for the soul always to think, than for the body always to move" [*An Essay Concerning Human Understanding*, ed. Roger Woolhouse (London: Penguin, 1997), Book II, Chapter 1, Paragraph 9, p. 112].

9 In addition to the classic work by Galvano della Volpe, *Schizzo di una Storia del Gusto* (Rome: Riuniti, 1971), see, regarding the concept taste, the excellent book by Luc Ferry, *Homo Aestheticus. L'Invention du Gôut à l Âge Dèmocratique* (Paris: Grasset Fasquelle, 1990).

10 J. Addison, "The Pleasures of the Imagination," in *Eighteenth-Century British Aesthetics*, ed. Dabney Townsend (Amityville, NY: Baywood, 1999), pp. 107–136.

11 Ibid., p. 108.

12 Ibid., pp. 230–241.

13 Which agrees with the Cartesian project of a *mathesis universalis* that furnishes the ground for the idea of the systematic order of scientific knowledge.

14 Kant's greatest achievement (as set out in the *Critique of Pure Reason*) was to overcome the ambiguity inherent to subjectivity thanks to the development of a purely transcendental conception thereof that set aside the metaphysically problematic assumptions of rationalism and the equally problematic psychological generalizations of empiricism.

15 D. Hume, in *Eighteenth-Century British Aesthetics*, ed. Dabney Townsend (Amityville, NY: Baywood, 1999), p. 231.

16 Which is stressed in the following passage of the *Treatise of Human Nature*: "It is impossible that the distinction betwixt moral good and evil can be made by reason; since that distinction has an influence upon our actions, of which reason alone is incapable. Reason and judgement may, indeed, be the mediate cause of an action, by prompting, or by directing a passion. But it is not pretended that a judgement of this kind, either in its truth or falsehood, is attended with virtue or vice. And as to the judgements, which are caused by our actions, they can still less bestow those moral qualities on the actions, which are their causes" [3.1.1] [D. Hume, *Treatise of Human Nature*, David Fate Norton and Mary J. Norton, eds. (New York: Oxford University Press, 2001), p. 298].

17 It is interesting that if Hume rebuffs so earnestly any attempt to base morals on reason it is because his concept of the former is utterly contrary to dogmatic metaphysics (wherein he includes the thought of the rationalist philosophers), whereas an author such as Spinoza upholds their identity precisely because he takes for granted the primacy of reason over experience.

18 D. Hume, in *Eighteenth-Century British Aesthetics*, ed. Dabney Townsend (Amityville, NY: Baywood, 1999), p. 233.

19 Ibid., p. 235.

20 Ibid.,

21 Ibid., p. 237.

22 Ibid., p. 238.

23 Ibid., p. 239.

24 I am aware that the notion of a "natural ideal" seems to be a *contradictio in terminis*, considering that, on one hand, modern rationality has rebuffed from the beginning the thesis that there is a formal superiority of some species with regard to others (which also has amply been confirmed by the theory of evolution) and, on the other, the multiplicity of nature goes against the idea of a hierarchical disposition of living beings. However, there is an undeniable affinity between man and some natural forms, while some others are, as it were, naturally contrary to sensibility, which is what Kant explains in one of the most complex and deep sections of the *Critique of Judgement* (A33ff.). Also see Eva Schaper, *Studies in Kant's Aesthetics* (Edinburgh: Edinburgh University Press, 1979), Part I. Then, on speaking of a natural ideal I just mean the spontaneous affinity with the image of a being or of a natural form.

[25] One can immediately think of Pascal, Schopenhauer, and Nietzsche as great modern philosophers (so as not to speak of any ancient ones) that share the double condition that I just mentioned; however, in all of them the expression goes hand in hand with some kind either of pessimism or of irrationalism or of both, whereas in the former four (even in Hume), optimism and trust in reason and are one and the same.

[26] I know that there are deep differences between, for instance, Plato's and Aristotle's conceptions of ethics (not to mention their forerunners or further philosophers), but I think that the idea of the accomplished man that is set out both in Plato's *Republic* and in Aristotle's *Nicomachean Ethics* agrees perfectly with my interpretation. See Alasdair MacIntyre, *A Short History of Ethics* (Notre Dame, Indiana: Notre Dame University Press, 1998), Sections 5 and 7.

SECTION II

EVGENIA V. CHERKASOVA

VIRTUES OF THE HEART
Feodor Dostoevsky and the Ethic of Love

I. INTRODUCTION

A number of twentieth-century studies in phenomenology, philosophy of emotions, and psychology have spoken of the necessity to reconsider the role of feelings and emotions in the contemporary philosophical discourse. In the realm of ethics in particular, these studies have marked a departure from overly rationalist morality; instead, they have proposed to focus on the training of the emotions as an essential part of moral education and to explore the unique role of feelings, intuition, imagination, and creativity in our conception of the good life. However different their goals and methods, these studies belong to a philosophical tradition that acknowledges the centrality of "virtues of the heart" and encourages corresponding practices that have as their end the harmony, balance, and emotional equilibrium of a person and his/her community.

This essay on Dostoevsky's "ethic of the heart" stands within these lineages. Following Dostoevsky, I propose to leave behind the archaic distinction between the allegedly superior powers of reason and inferior primal emotional energies; instead, I suggest that the emphasis must be shifted to the interplay between reason and the heart, both understood in all their subtlety and richness. "If one day the heart could have been opposed to reason," writes Paul Ricoeur, "it was not because it was irrational—according to Pascal, the heart even apprehends the first principles—but because it does not proceed by means of analysis and argument, rising as it does from the depth of life toward the absolute pole in a single movement." It is precisely with this movement of the heart, vividly presented in Dostoevsky's stories and novels, that this essay is concerned. I begin with the following "groundwork" questions: What is the heart as an ethical phenomenon? What role does it play in Dostoevsky's novels? What kind of ethic can be built on such an illusive phenomenon?

THE HEART

What is the heart as an ethical and artistic symbol? It seems odd that although the most fundamental philosophical terms such as "reason," "spirit," "mind," and "soul" are no less obscure than the idea of the heart, their usage does not cause bewilderment. Moreover, it is interesting that Western philosophers mention the heart here and there, but they very rarely (Rousseau, Pascal, and Kierkegaard are the few exceptions) treat this phenomenon as seriously and with the same philosophical attentiveness as they treat reason or spirit. Does this mean that the heart cannot be considered as a philosophical category?

Perhaps the heart cannot be categorized; however, it can be spoken of. The heart is central to the mysticism, the religion, and the poetry of all nations. Odysseus made his decisions "in the heart." The Stoics proclaimed the heart to be the governing source (*hegemonikon*) of a human being. In Latin, a clever, smart person is called *homo cordatus*. Indian mystics believed that the heart, not the head, is the locus of the self—*Atman*. Chinese sages spoke of "middle-heartedness" and believed that heart and mind are inseparable. According to the Christian tradition, conscience is the "law written on the heart." "The hand and the heart" are joined when two people are united in marriage. Knowledge of the heart is the sacred knowledge of what is most intimate in human nature. We say "he has a heart of gold," "she cried her heart out," "he speaks from the bottom of his heart," "she waits with a sinking heart," "her heart bleeds," "his heart is broken," and so on; sometimes we have a change of heart, a heart-to-heart talk; we learn "by heart" and carry the most precious thoughts and memories in "our heart of hearts." We speak of the heart as if it were the deepest depth of all our thoughts, desires, feelings, and emotions. In addition, the heart is also a bodily organ and the symbol of life; it organically joins the psychological and the physical phenomena of human existence.

Although we may not be able to depict the enigmatic nature of the heart directly, we may be able to do so indirectly by asking what the heart does. Its most mysterious, and at the same time its most recognized, ability is the ability to love. Love is born and dwells "in the heart." Self-transcendence and self-sacrifice are associated with the heart, while the heart is also something that brings us back to ourselves, back home, to the people and the things we love. Reflecting both the transitory and the transcendent dimensions of human experience "the heart" embraces a whole spectrum of possible meanings, from the bodily organ to the haven of love.

It seems almost impossible to search for the identity of the heart in the boundless region of meanings that people ascribe to it. Yet "the heart" is more than a figure of speech or a poetic image. The notion of the heart resists clear-cut distinctions and definitions; but in all cultures the rhetoric of the heart engenders intuitive impulses, indefinable, yet communicable. Moreover, the variety and richness of connotations associated with "the heart" makes it possible to describe the depth of a person's inner life without violating its transcendent, enigmatic nature. That is why when it comes to speaking about the inscrutable in human nature, or the immediacy of moral experience, or the role of intuition and imagination, philosophers and mystics resort to the powerful symbolism of the heart. That is why in the world's great literature and poetry the most intense, emotionally charged moments are often marked by a metaphorical portrayal of the hero's heart.

THE WAYS OF THE LIVING LIFE: DOSTOEVSKY'S ETHIC OF THE HEART

The complex rhetoric of the heart has deep roots in Russian religious tradition: it descends from the earliest writings of the Greek and Orthodox church fathers and was embraced with enthusiasm by Russian theologians of the eighteenth century, specifically by religious elders (*startzy*)[1]; it was also elaborated by the nineteenth-century philosophers and employed artistically by Russian writers, notably by Dostoevsky and Tolstoy.[2]

To a significant degree, the Russian religious and philosophical tradition is the "tradition of the heart," and Dostoevsky is undoubtedly one of its creative expressions. He acknowledges the primary role of the heart in man's moral conduct, expresses skepticism concerning the moral worth of speculative reason, and passionately searches for the harmonious communion of human hearts flourishing in love. But Dostoevsky's rhetoric of the heart is not a repetition of a certain religious creed or philosophical theory; rather, it is an artistic fusion of the most cherished convictions of the Orthodox spiritual tradition within the rich texture of the novelist's own intellectual and life experience. And it is to this unique artistic vision of the heart and its ethical implications that I now turn.

The incarnations of the heart in Dostoevsky's writings are virtually endless. They range from the very straightforward ("frantically beating heart") to the highly metaphorical ("the human heart is a battleground where God and the Devil struggle for mastery"). In addition, the allegorical and physiological images often merge when Dostoevsky speaks about the heart. In *Notes from Underground*, we see how the protagonist's unbearable humiliation induces "convulsive pains" in his heart and heat in his back. In *Crime and Punishment*, Raskolnikov, after having a prophetic dream about the beating to death of a horse, feels as though "the sore that has festered in his heart for a month has burst at last." The numerous faces of the heart, both literal and figurative, perpetually mirroring one another, form a unique psycho-physical picture that brings the reader to the undiscovered blood-level depth of human existence.

Crime and Punishment is replete with the startling images of the murderer's heart "rising," "jumping," and "banging so hard it is difficult to breathe." In the ugly scene of the murder, the real physical presence of the painfully and loudly beating heart intensifies Raskolnikov's suffering and horror. Climbing upstairs to the old woman's apartment, he has to "hold his heart"—so violently does it beat. Before ringing the bell, he waits until his heart stops its feverish cacophony, but, alas, the heart does not stop.

Throughout the novel, Raskolnikov's spiritual torment always goes hand in hand with the physical suffering. He "wanders around like a drunkard," stumbles, feels nauseated, struggles for breath, and constantly experiences fits of emptiness and paralysis of the heart. At the same time, the heart emerges metaphorically as a core of his moral awareness: Raskolnikov is frightened by "the vileness his heart seems to be capable of," confesses to Sonya that he has "an evil heart," and constantly tries to fight "old, sore questions, lacerating his heart."

In Dostoevsky's writings, the corrupted heart is often linked allegorically to the feelings of suffocation, darkness, noise, and lack of space, while the heart seeking purification and spiritual freedom is accompanied by the lively images of clear water, fresh air, light, and tranquility. Both biologically and spiritually, the human heart is a conduit for mysterious life-giving forces, which sustain a person's vital connections to his loved ones, the world, the earth, and all nature. *The heart appears simultaneously as a giver and a receiver of life.*

One of the distinctive features of Eastern Orthodox spirituality is its focus on the preservation of the unity of nature and grace.[3] According to the Orthodox patristic teaching, a man coming to God does not turn his back on nature because "God is the reality that sustains both man and nature." This theme is not only embedded in Dostoevsky's vision of the heart, but it also is carried further to suggest that if the person renounces his belonging to the earth, other people, and nature, his heart "grows dim" and inevitably becomes more and more susceptible to evil. At the same time the opposite movement, toward openness to the "living life" (*zhivaya zhizn'*) exhibits an immense spiritual power to heal the sores of the heart. Let us recall the detective's advice to Raskolnikov:

> don't be too clever about it, just give yourself directly to life, without reasoning; don't worry – it will carry you straight to the shore and set you on your feet.... Be of great heart, and fear less.... I know you don't believe it, but, by God, life will carry you.... All you need is air now – air, air![4]

The detective urges the murderer to choose life unconditionally, without deliberation and doubt, to make the ethical choice of being alive.

It takes Raskolnikov a very long time to appreciate the meaning of this prophetic saying. According to Dostoevsky's design, he who "kills life" by committing a murder has to go through a grandiose torment before he can "come back to life." The reader witnesses how, during the painful process of purification, Raskolnikov's contaminated heart simultaneously resists "the living life" and is drawn to its salutary sources; step by step, diffidently, his sense of belonging is restored.

Guiding currents of life that he tries to ignore very often reach his heart through irresistibly physical encounters; thus, when the little girl Polechka spontaneously hugs and kisses Raskolnikov, he feels "as if he were on the moon and came back to people." "What happened?" asks Dostoevsky in one of the notes for the novel; he answers: "Nothing more than a sense of life. It is possible to live, then, live the same life as others live, live for others and with others."[5] This and numerous other flashes of life gradually lead Raskolnikov through the murk of his cultivated separation to the very end, where he suddenly finds himself at Sonya's feet, his heart overflowing with love.[6] They are both triumphantly raised from the dead and "the heart of each [holds] infinite sources of life for the heart of the other."[7]

The "living life" theme is one of Dostoevsky's favorites and extends all the way through his post-Siberian novels. The underground man praises life but is terrified by its persistent claims. Raskolnikov eventually comes to terms with life, but not until his heart passes through all the circles of spiritual and physical agony. In *The Brothers Karamazov*, Dostoevsky devotes much care to developing this theme in a still broader context. Here the dynamic of the human heart and its organic receptivity to the living life evolves on many different levels: personal and communal, religious and secular. Moreover, the heart emerges as a unique symbol of life, which embraces irreconcilable contradictions and mysteries. "There still an awful lot of centripetal force on our planet, Alyosha," confesses Ivan Karamazov to his younger brother,

I want to live, and I do live, even if it be against logic. Though I do not believe in the order of things, still the sticky little leaves that come out in the spring are dear to me, the blue sky is dear to me, some people are dear to me, whom one loves sometimes, would you believe it, without even knowing why; some human deeds are dear to me, which one has perhaps long ceased believing in, but still honors with one's heart, out of old habit. . . . Such things you love not with your mind, not with logic, but with your insides, your guts, you love your first young strength.[8]

It is in this confession that Alyosha hears the strongest signals of Ivan's future redemption: "I'm terribly glad that you want so much to live. I think that everyone should love life before everything else in the world."[9] The appeal to the life affirmation appears again in the next chapter, when Alyosha, frightened by Ivan's rebellion against God's world, exclaims,

And the sticky little leaves, and the precious graves, and the blue sky, and the woman you love! How will you live, what will you love them with? Is it possible, with such hell in your heart and in your head?[10]

Ivan's verbal disclosure, as well as Alyosha's desperate questioning, immediately reveal the dynamic, reciprocal relations of life and heart. By virtue of its ability to love, the human heart becomes an inexhaustible source of life; at the same time, because of its organic attunement to the living life, the heart is capable of loving. Alyosha senses that the beginning of Ivan's salvation is his love of life. This reflects one of Dostoevsky's most treasured beliefs: for him, an individual's redemption is always manifested in love, whereas the inability to experience love is indissolubly linked to evil.

CAN REASON UNDERSTAND THE "REASONS OF THE HEART"?

If a devout rationalist were to give a definition of the heart, he would most likely characterize it in terms of feelings and inclinations. Immanuel Kant, perhaps the most famous proponent of unconditional ethics based on "reason and reason alone," ceaselessly emphasized that moral duty involves absolute necessity, to which the movements of the heart (Kant mentions grace, compassion, and love) "stand in direct contradiction."[11] By contrast, Dostoevsky's ethics focuses on the virtue of vital, active love and of trust, free from both utilitarian appeals and constraints of rationality. "Ethic of the heart" is unconditional, but not because it is universal and rational, or because it is detached from nature, the human body, and emotions, as is the case with Kant's duty theory. Instead, for Dostoevsky, moral duty and virtues refer to the entire person in the midst of the "living life": in the living heart they are born and through the work of the heart, of active, humbling love, they are realized. Moreover, it is precisely in the absence of love that Dostoevsky perceives the devastating flaw of any ethic based solely on reason. Dostoevsky's polemical stance should not be interpreted as anti-rationalism, however (a characterization common among both Russian and Western commentators). The novelist does not oppose reason as such, but simply refuses to accept the hegemony of detached reasoning (or what he would call the "three-dimensional, Euclidean mind") that reduces all the paradoxes and controversies of human existence to the laws of necessity and universality.[12]

Dostoevsky holds that because of reason's strong orientation toward certainty, necessity, and determinism, reason should not be considered a governor in the moral realm. An ethical decision must be blessed by the heart; otherwise, it is a mere idea, however "sensible," intellectually sophisticated, or tempting it may be. Moreover, heartless ideas are often immoral: they bring with them destructiveness, nihilism, and death. Exploring the phenomenon of moral indifference and corruption, Dostoevsky appears to be asking: "What if reason takes the side of evil?" "What if evil is done for the sake of Good?" For the novelist, at the point where reasons for good and reasons for evil clash, the ultimate verdict can only come from the heart: recall Raskolnikov's thoroughly rational speculations that justify the murder of the "ugly old hag," or the Grand Inquisitor's brilliant totalitarian arguments. Not until Raskolnikov goes through all the torment of his heart does he become free from the "deadly temptation." Likewise, Christ's silent kiss that "glows in the Grand Inquisitor's heart" is the only response equal in power to the Inquisitor's monologue.

Let us look again at the dialogue between Ivan and Alyosha, in which the complex dynamic of reason and the heart unfolds. The two brothers have their first heart-to-heart talk in the tavern, and they "get to know each other" by discussing "the eternal questions": the existence of God, His creation, immortality, freedom, the suffering of the innocent. "I humbly confess," says Ivan to Alyosha,

that I do not have any ability to resolve such questions, I have a Euclidean mind, an earthly mind.... And I advise you never to think about it, Alyosha, my friend, and most especially about whether God exists or not. All such questions are completely unsuitable to a mind created with a concept of only three dimensions.[13]

Advising Alyosha to stay away from thinking about "the whole offensive comedy of human contradictions," Ivan himself is very deeply engaged in it; he even says that being concerned with these "cursed questions" about divine purpose, human suffering, immortality, and the existence of God is his very essence—it makes him "the sort of man he is."

Ivan is not a disinterested spectator of the "comedy"—indeed, these unresolved questions bring him to despair. He is tormented, but not because his "Euclidean mind" finds his rebellion against God's creation self-contradictory; the pain comes from his heart, which is capable of superior spiritual torment[14] and cannot live in peace with the destructive conclusions of his mind. Ivan claims that he *chooses* not to listen to his heart, whose "child-like convictions" of universal harmony do not make sense in the "three-dimensional" world of his mind. Even if, he says,

the suffering will be healed and smoothed over, [if] the whole offensive comedy of human contradictions will disappear like a pitiful mirage, a vile concoction of man's Euclidean mind, feeble and puny as an atom, and [if] ultimately, at the world's finale, in the moment of eternal harmony, there will occur and be revealed something so precious that it will suffice for all hearts, to allay all indignation, to redeem all human villainy, all bloodshed; it will suffice not only to make forgiveness possible, but also to justify everything that has happened with men—let this, let all of this come true and be revealed, but I do not accept it and do not want to accept it! Let the parallel lines even meet before my own eyes: I shall look and say, yes, they meet, and still I will not accept it. That is my essence, Alyosha, that is my thesis.[15]

Ivan's idea to set the limits within which his Euclidean mind can legitimately work and his *choice* to live by these limits sound very Kantian. No wonder his dream is to go to Europe to weep over the stones of "the precious dead," one of whom must be the sage of Königsberg, Immanuel Kant.[16] Yet Kant, as we know, chose to deny knowledge in order to make room for faith.[17] By contrast, Ivan actively rejects any leap of faith and decides to stick with what he can know.

It seems that on a merely empirical or logical ground an attempt to justify the world and the necessity of moral choice leads to the complete victory of the "three-dimensional mind" over the convictions of the heart. Dostoevsky is very well aware of this difficulty. In one of his letters he expresses uneasiness about his reply to Ivan's arguments, which "was not presented point by point, but as an artistic picture." If the heart and empirically oriented reason speak two different languages, there is always the danger that they will never be able to communicate; perhaps Pascal was right: the heart has its reasons that reason cannot (and we can add "*does not want to*") understand.

Yet Dostoevsky believes that some communication is possible, if not at the level of understanding, then on the level of heart-felt conviction. As elder Zosima says at the beginning of the novel, "one cannot prove anything here, but it is possible to be convinced." How? Through the work of the heart, active vital love, answers the elder. He speaks:

Brothers, do not be afraid of man's sin, love man also in his sin, for this likeness of God's love is the height of love on earth. Love all of God's creation, both the whole of it and every grain of sand. Love every leaf, every ray of God's light. Love animals, love plants, love each thing. If you love each thing you will perceive the mystery of God in things. Once you have perceived it, you will begin tirelessly to perceive more and more of it every day. And you will come at last to love the whole world with an entire, universal love.[18]

To a skeptical reader, Zosima's message may sound as another exalted utopia, overly naive and sentimental. However, we have to keep in mind that Dostoevsky does not answer the skeptic, either in his reader or in his characters, by constructing a "point-by-point" argument; rather, he calls upon the hagiographic tradition of recounting a *life (zhitiye)*. Zosima's word is "*zhitiynoye slovo*"—a word that arises from the depth of his life. Both literally and allegorically, Zosima's speech bears witness to his life and the lives of those who contributed to the conception of *the word* in his heart (his brother Markel, his servant, and the "mysterious visitor"). The reader receives the word from

Alyosha, Zosima's "dear, quiet boy," who does not simply record the teaching of the *starets*, but bears witness to his love. In one of his letters, Dostoevsky predicts that some people would shout at Zosima's words and call them "absurd, since too elated." But, he continues, "they are of course absurd in the everyday sense, but in another inner sense, they seem justified."[19] And they are indeed internally justified, for they are the living words of love, the testimony of one's heart.

There are perhaps some melodramatic and sentimental motifs in Zosima's speech, but the love of life, people, and all nature of which he speaks are not merely matters of sentiment. They represent the unconditional values every human heart must strive for. This is not an easy path, and one must be ready for the hard work of the heart. Zosima describes active love as a harsh and fearful thing; unlike love in dreams, which "thirsts for immediate action, quickly performed, and with everyone watching," active humbling love requires "labor and perseverance, and for some people, perhaps, a whole science."[20] Love is also a teacher, but

one must know how to acquire it, for it is difficult to acquire, it is dearly bought, by long work over a long time, for one ought to love not for a chance moment but for all time. Because anyone, even a wicked man, can love by chance.[21]

Zosima urges his followers to recognize love as a precious gift, but more than that, he insists that a warm and vital commandment to love is the core of all human responsibility; it is the highest expression of what it means to be human and fully alive. *This implies that as ethical creatures, human beings are under an obligation to love.*

DUTY TO LOVE: ABSURDITY OR A VIABLE ETHICAL POSITION?

Indeed, strictly speaking, is not a duty to love internally contradictory? Dostoevsky's famous philosophical interlocutor, Immanuel Kant, put this problem in a straightforward way: "*Love* is a matter of *feeling*, not of willing, and I cannot love because I *will* to, still less because I *ought* to (I cannot be constrained to love); so a *duty to love* is an absurdity."[22] Ivan Karamazov would applaud this statement and append to it a further empirical observation: not only is the imperative to love theoretically self-contradictory, it is practically hopeless:

I never could understand how it's possible to love one's neighbors. In my opinion, it is precisely one's neighbors that one cannot possibly love. I read some time, somewhere about "John the Merciful" (some saint) that when a hungry and frozen passerby came to him and asked to be made warm, he lay down with him in bed, embraced him, and began breathing into his mouth, which was foul and festering with some terrible disease. I'm convinced that he did it with the strain of a lie, out of love enforced by duty, out of self-imposed penance. If we're to come to love a man, the man himself should stay hidden, because as soon as he shows his face—love vanishes.[23]

In response to this radical statement, Alyosha, who was listening carefully to his brother's confession, remarks that Ivan was speaking as yet "inexperienced in love." Alyosha mentions that for people like Ivan, a man's face (or any other unappealing features he may possess) often prevents the inexperienced from loving him. Alyosha says that he knows that there is still much love in mankind "almost like Christ's love," but Ivan cuts him off: "Well, I don't know it yet." Both brothers speak from experience; however, Alyosha speaks of something he has witnessed, while Ivan makes a negative statement: "I don't see it and therefore it does not exist." Although Ivan stresses that he is the kind of man who always sticks to the facts—and he indeed has an overwhelming collection of facts that allegedly prove the absence of active love and sincere forgiveness in the world—even he seems vaguely aware that this "empirical evidence" need have no bearing on the question of whether human beings must try to be loving. The ethic of the heart precludes rational and empirical justification, but—we remember—it is possible to be convinced. And it is the intricacies of choosing active love and gradually becoming convinced that Dostoevsky struggles to communicate. Thus, according to his design, Ivan's empirical realism is destined to surrender to the no less *real* spiritual experience of active love.

For Ivan, such transformation is a possibility partly because he is not a complete stranger to love, as is his half- brother Smerdiakov, who had never loved and had never been loved by anyone. Ivan experiences a love of life, loves his younger brother, and perhaps remembers his mother's meek and loving image.[24] What he is lacking is ethical resolution to follow the commandment of love. This brings us back to the Kantian question, namely, "How is a duty to love possible if it is not a matter of willing?" True, nobody can force another person to love. Yet love is a matter of choice. Choosing here does not mean meticulous rational deliberation, sticking to the facts or weighing the consequences; choosing love is choosing to learn the language of the heart, to be receptive to its expressions—that is, it is a choice to develop virtues of the heart.

It is Ivan's conscious choice to listen only to his "three-dimensional Euclidean mind" and remain deaf to the voice of his heart, whose "child-like convictions" cannot be rationally verified. According to Dostoevsky, Ivan's most profound tragedy and his deepest personal fault lies in neglecting the stirring of his heart while being perfectly aware of it. Consequently, the only responsibilities that Ivan assumes with respect to himself and other people are formal, rationally or legally relevant. He says that if Dmitry bursts into the house and tries to kill old Karamazov, he will try to stop him. In the realm of his thoughts and aspirations, however, he reserves the absolute freedom to wish that Dmitry and his father would "eat each other alive."

For Dostoevsky, this understanding of responsibility is not just limited; it does not deserve the name of an ethical commitment at all. By choosing not to fight his hatred and inner repulsion toward his father, Ivan inspires Smerdyakov, a monster who kills the old man. When this happens, the son has no choice but to accept full responsibility for his corrupted thoughts. He sincerely recognizes the destructive implications of his programmatic statement, "everything is permitted," and even calls himself a murderer. And this recognition is a cathartic moment for Ivan's heart that awakes him to a new ethical receptivity.

The crowning theme of Dostoevsky's *Brothers Karamazov*, "each is guilty for all," is also fleshed out through the dynamic symbol of the heart, which is both a center of an individual and a carrier of a transpersonal ethical relations. Each human heart is a part of the circulatory system of life, a denizen of community of the living hearts. Our thoughts, words, and actions pass through the arteries of this system and often exhibit a tremendous power to injure or heal, degrade or nourish other people's hearts. A call to take responsibility for this power that we always already possess can be heard in Zosima's message, which also, in a highly concentrated form contains the whole problematic of the *Brothers Karamazov*—mutual responsibility of fathers and sons, brother for brother, and ultimately everyone for everyone else:

See, here you have passed by a small child, passed by in anger, with a foul word, with a wrathful soul; you perhaps did not notice the child, but he saw you, and your unsightly and impious image has remained in his defenseless heart. You did not know it, but you may thereby have planted a bad seed in him, and it may grow, and all because you did not restrain yourself before the child, because you did not nurture in yourself a heedful, active love.[25]

For Dostoevsky it is our duty to take care of our hearts; that is, to nurture an active love, to learn how to be attentive to our inner life and that of other people; how to live with others and have trust in them; how to listen to the summons of the living life and develop a sense of belonging to the world. These obligations are unconditional, they do not depend on one's situation, and do not guarantee any gratification. We must only remember that it is where the heart's life-giving sources are contaminated, where its essential bonds to the hearts of other human beings are ignored, where love is forgotten—evil dwells and flourishes.

II. CONCLUSION

In the post-modern world, an attempt to reintroduce an unconditional ethic may be perceived as old-fashioned and naïve at best and retrograde at worst. In this essay I have tried to show that Dostoevsky's far-reaching psychological and philosophical insights point to a new way of thinking about the unconditional. By emphasizing "virtues of the heart"—unconditional love, patience, compassion, trust, self-sacrifice—Dostoevsky's writings provide a unique perspective on moral commitment. Without any recourse to rational necessity and universality, his ethic of the heart emphasizes the interplay between reason and the heart, taking into account the dark and destructive, as well as the creative, traits of human character; it celebrates the ideal of "wholeheartedness" and views a person, *qua* moral agent, as irreducible to the sum of his or her social, historical, and physiological factors; finally, it defends a phenomenological account of an individual as a shared self, embodied and rooted in his or her community, and thus offers a viable alternative to individualistic and utilitarian approaches to ethics.

Department of Philosophy, Suffolk University, Boston

NOTES

[1] Thus, in the classic writings of Byzantine theologians, one often finds the elaboration of the New Testament's appreciation of the heart as "the main organ of psychic and spiritual life, the place in man at which God bears witness to Himself." According to St. Makary of Egypt (301–391), the heart is an expression of the "inner person" as well as the center of one's "wise (or reasonable) essence" (*umnaya sooshshnost'*). And this phrase is not accidental: it is a reflection of an Orthodox ideal of human perfection as an attunement of the mind to the heart. This ideal was articulated by both the Eastern Fathers and later by Russian religious elders as the maxim "One must stand with the mind in the heart." Similarly, the unity of the mind and the heart finds its expression in the art of so-called "wise prayer" (*umnaya molitva*). Throughout Russian history, the heart is also described as a center of a person's moral life and a guide in the process of moral development. See George Fedotov, *The Saints of Ancient Russia of 10–17 Centuries* (New York, 1959), pp. 154–163; George Fedotov, *The Russian Religious Mind* (Belmont, Massachusetts: Nordland, 1975), Vol. 4, p. 269; George Fedotov, *A Treasury of Russian Spirituality* (Gloucester, Massachusetts: Peter Smith, 1969). Also see *The Works of Our Father Among the Saints, Tikhon of Zadonsk*, reprinted from the St. Petersburg 1912 edition, with a new introduction by Nadejda Gorodetzky, in two volumes (Westmead, England: Gregg International Publishers, 1970), Vol. 1, pp. 137–150; and John B. Dunlop, *Staretz Amvrosy, Model for Dostoevsky's Staretz Zossima* (Belmont, Massachusetts: Nordland, 1972).

[2] On the heart in nineteenth-century Russian philosophy and theology, see, for example, P. Yurkevich, "The Heart and its Significance in Man's Life in Accordance with the Word of God," in *Philosophical Writings* (Moscow: Pravda, 1990), pp. 86–91; B. Vysheslavstev, *The Heart in Christian and Indian Mysticism* (Paris, 1929). On the contributions of Florensky, Il'in,

and Frank to the theme of the heart in Russian philosophy, see N. K. Gavryushin, "B. P. Vysheslavtsev and His Philosophy of the Heart," *Voprosi Filosofii*, No. 4 (1990):59–60.

[3] See, for example, Sergei Hackel, "The Religious Dimension: Vision or Evasion? Zosima's Discourse in *The Brothers Karamazov*," in *New Essays on Dostoevsky*, Malcolm V. Jones and Garth M. Terry, eds. (Cambridge: Cambridge University Press, 1983), p. 146.

[4] Fyodor Dostoevsky, *Crime and Punishment*, translated and annotated by Richard Pevear and Larissa Volokhonsky (New York: Alfred A. Knopf, 1992), p. 460.

[5] The translation of this passage is mine, from the Moscow edition of the *Notebooks to Crime and Punishment* (Moscow: Nauka, 1970), p. 619n.

[6] I do not wish to engage in the scholarly discussion about the credibility of Raskolnikov's moral resurrection in the Epilogue. Whether we believe Dostoevsky or not, his moral message is clear (and he states this explicitly in the letter to Katkov, where he outlines the pivotal conflict of the novel): Truth and justice are the matters of the heart, and they claim their rights, so that the criminal himself accepts suffering in order to atone for his deed. See K. Mochulsky, *Dostoevsky: His Life and Work* (Princeton, NJ: Princeton University Press, 1971), pp. 272–273.

[7] *Crime and Punishment*, p. 549.

[8] *The Brothers Karamazov*, translated and annotated by Richard Pevear and Larissa Volokhonsky (New York: Alfred A. Knopf, 1992), p. 230.

[9] Ibid., p. 231.

[10] Ibid., p. 263.

[11] *Groundwork of the Metaphysics of Morals*, p. 55, and *The Metaphysics of Morals*, pp. 568–571, in Immanuel Kant, *Practical Philosophy*. See also I. Kant, *Religion within the Limits of Reason Alone* (New York: Harper, 1960), p. 19.

[12] For example, James Scanlan, in his article "Dostoevsky's Arguments for Immortality" (*Russian Review*, Vol. 59, No.1, January 2000), notes that Dostoevsky himself uses rational arguments to defend his belief in the immortality of the soul: "[Dostoevsky] recognized, as logicians have for centuries, that an argument need not yield deductively necessary or indubitable conclusions in order to have force. Inductive conclusions and explanatory hypotheses, though always open to question, may be based on solid evidence. Dostoevsky thought that "there were reasonable arguments in favor of immortality, and he presented them in several of his writings, speaking either in his own voice or in that of a fictional character" (p. 9).

[13] *The Brothers Karamazov*, p. 235.

[14] Recall elder Zosima's prophetic words about Ivan's predicament: "For the time being you, too, are toying, out of despair, with your magazine articles and drawing-room discussions, without believing in your own dialectic and smirking at them with your heart aching inside you.... But thank the Creator that has given you a lofty heart, capable of being tormented by such torment." *The Brothers Karamazov*, p. 70.

[15] Ibid., pp. 235–236.

[16] We can add that Dostoevsky would share Ivan's passion toward Europe and its geniuses, among whom the novelist mentions Aristotle, Bacon, Newton, and Kant. See *A Writer's Diary*, pp. 1067, 1372. Moreover, it is well known that Kant's *Critique of Pure Reason* was one of the first books Dostoevsky ordered immediately after his return from prison.

[17] *Critique of Pure Reason*, translated by Norman Kemp Smith (New York: St. Martin's Press, 1965), p. 29.

[18] *The Brothers Karamazov*, pp. 318–19.

[19] Letter to Pobedonostsev of August 24, 1879, PSS (1988): vol.30.I, p.122.

[20] *The Brothers Karamazov*, p.58.

[21] Ibid., p. 319.

[22] *The Metaphysics of Morals*, p. 530.
[23] *The Brothers Karamazov*, pp. 236–237.
[24] Dostoevsky does not offer an explicit indication that Ivan has any recollection of his mother. However, the reader knows that she died when Ivan was seven years old and Alyosha was only four. Alyosha's vivid childhood memories constitute a significant part of his psychological make-up. Thus, one can assume that Ivan must have had an even clearer memories of a loving mother than Alyosha, even if suppressed. See F. F. Seeley, "Ivan Karamazov," in *New Essays on Dostoevsky* (Cambridge: Cambridge University Press, 1983), pp. 115–136.
[25] *The Brothers Karamazov*, p. 319.

BRUCE ROSS

THE WILLING SUBJECT AND THE NON-WILLING SUBJECT IN THE *TAO TE CHING* AND NIETZSCHE'S *HYPERBOREAN*

Taoist and Deconstructive Challenges to the Idea of Virtue

Art marks the Sabbath from the penal servitude of willing.

Schopenhauer

Skepticism regarding morality is what is decisive. The end of the moral interpretation of the world, which no longer has any sanction after it has tried escape into some beyond, leads to nihilism.

Nietzsche, *The Will to Power*[1]

Hence when the Tao was lost there was virtue.

Tao Te Ching, XXXVIII

What are we without some form of intention? Some glorified version of the vegetative soul or, in its modern version, the id, or, in a postmodern version, the desiring natal state without a center. Would the world then be a projection of our unrelenting will? Would the willing subject be fated to this monomaniac pursuit, reprieved perhaps by the Schopenhauerian creative act? A critique of some fundamental points in our understanding of consciousness, will, and understanding would elucidate the ground of these questions. The Nietzschean project to undermine the then-understood realm of morals and his solution in the hyperborean's higher subject may be critiqued by the *Tao Te Ching*. The nihilism of an empty moralized universe (restated in Pascal's infinity or the expanses of geologic time) is seen in Taoism as a natural progression when a phenomenological break with the presiding life force Tao was made. Without an understanding of the life force, a resultant fear and nihilism, and moralism, is made manifest, excising, however, projects in pure faith. The Nietzschean solution is the hyperborean elevated consciousness. If the so-called "postmodern condition" has produced Heidegger's "homeless men" and deconstruction has undermined the nature of logos, the hyperborean subject, like a logos that "glides over its own groundlessness," could institute a true establishment of virtue in transcending the consumptive willing for "facts," for materiality, for identity.[2] There is a kind of "unwilling" in the hyperborean subject and a kind of "non-understanding" that might be elucidated by non-Western thought. Thus Ying-An advises: "Do not try to predefine understanding, and do not make a principle out of non-understanding." In a Zen context, Morimoto Roshi places consciousness into a phenomenological grounding: "There's no point in translating all of the old Chinese texts—not if you're serious about understanding Zen. The sound of the rain needs no translation." In an Eastern Wisdom context, G. I. Gurdjieff uses the same metaphor: "[Gurdjieff] only wished to return [humanity] to something as manifestly real as 'the rain making the pavement wet.' "[3] These metaphors of consciousness are reflective of the Taoist way of non-contentious willing and non-conceptual understanding in connection with the idea and practice of virtue.

In a booklet accompanying a recent art installation at The Institute of Contemporary Art in Boston, Marcus Steinweg, a teacher at the Hochschule fur Bildende Künste Braunschweig and the installation artist's favorite philosopher, offers a meditation called "Worldplay" upon Nietzsche's elevated being, the hyperborean, in the context of deconstructionist thought. Steinweg connects the "higher good" of Antigone's disregard of civil law with Nietzsche's "hyperborean subject... the hyperbolic subject of love and truth. It loves, it asserts and it defends a truth which destabilizes its objective (sociopolitical, cultural, etc.) identity."[4] Antigone is in the realm of the gods, so to speak, irrespective of civil law. She becomes a metaphor as a holy outcast for a "higher mode of being." Steinweg uses quasi-spiritual language and the existential rubric that existence precedes essence to ruminate over the hyperborean. He quotes from Heidegger's *On the Essence of Ground* to this extent: "to 'be' a subject means to be a being in and as transcendence.' "[5] The hyperborean thus exists in a space of "higher ontology" that is more "being" than willing.

The world the hyperborean exists in is "Chaos... the lack of ground or the abyss. It is the dimension which forever precedes the 'Logos,' reason, language and communication."[6] This space is the "experience of nonidentity, of incommensurability, of pre-ontological chaos."[7] This space is juxtaposed to the world of facts, identity in its broadest sense, and the "higher human," "the human of knowledge, of duty and humanity."[8] Such humanity prefers "facts" rather than the hyperborean's "possible truths."[9] The hyperborean is groundless and doesn't rely on what Steinweg calls the "idealism of facts."[10] Rather, the "hyperborean subject inhabits the universe of facts without assimilating itself... to the order of facts."[11] The hyperborean is in a "'strange zone' alienated from any dialectic."[12]

The hyperborean subject is what Steinweg calls "headless." It is without identity in the normal sense and not grounded by facts. The hyperborean is in a different mode of epistemology from that of the "idealism of facts": "A thinking without a subject would no longer be any thinking. It would be nothing other than the unwitnessed wave motion of nothingness."[13]

Yet this formidable existence is the "real world": The hyperboreans are "subjects of the real, subjects that have fallen out of reality or evaded it from the outset, that inhabit its impossibility as the condition of possibility of their freedom and responsibility."[14] This freedom is predicated on the infinite nature of the "strange zone,"[15] but what determines responsibility in this infinitude is infinitude itself: "The essence of freedom...consists in being inexhaustible, infinite, eternal. This infinitude is what makes the subject's subjectivity so difficult, because infinite freedom constitutes an infinitely lonely, an infinitely responsible subject."[16] Yamada Roshi expresses this in a Zen context: "The mind is empty infinity, infinite emptiness, full of possibilities." Exactly how this Western philosophic tradition of "infinitely lonely" space can produce "responsibility" can be elucidated in Eastern, and particularly Taoist, philosophy.

The *Tao Te Ching* (*The Book of the Way of Virtue*), a manual for establishing correct leadership, like the hyperborean model, elucidates a program to become "headless," the *wu-wei* (non-action) of Taoism, in order to apprehend true virtue. Just as, in a deconstructionist context, the hyperborean subject engages the "strange zone" to establish a higher model of ontology and virtue, the leader, following the *Tao Te Ching*, will follow the Tao, the formlessness that inhabits all things, and establish a more perfect state.

The nature of the "elevated" Taoist subject, the leader, is introduced in the first chapter of the *Tao Te Ching*. If one is motivated by desires, in effect being grounded by manifestation and the hyperborean's rejected identity and factuality, one is bound by the "named," but if one is not motivated by desires, one becomes connected to the "nameless" or Tao. The formless Tao that existed before the created universe is present in all manifestation, the "ten thousand things."[17] To be aligned with the Tao is to be in connection with the fundamental Virtue (*Te*) of reality. As a student of Gurdjieff puts it, "we see only 'good' and 'evil,' and not the Tao flowing through positive and negative [the yin and yang that constitute manifestation] to generate the whole."[18] The *Tao Te Ching* accordingly states "Is there much difference between yes and no? Is there much distance between good and evil¿'[19] The answer to these questions from the "elevated" subject would be "no." This subject, one might say, is, like the hyperborean, beyond good and evil.

This subject practices *wu-wei*, a state of non-action. If the subject becomes accordingly empty of will and desire, the Tao will take over and the subject will be on the path of Virtue, the "virtue of non-action."[20] The *Tao Te Ching* offers this paradox: "In pursuit of the Tao one does less everyday until one does nothing at all and then nothing is left undone."[21] What this observation suggests is that the leader achieves a "headless" state through practice. If this state is achieved, then, according to the *Tao Te Ching*, the world will be at peace[22] and the "ten thousand things" will be likewise transformed.[23]

Thus through non-action or not forcing things, the leader precipitates world order. In Taoist terms, the desired balance of yin and yang will have been achieved in whatever matters arise. Yet, here virtue is connected to an internal process of transformation. The *Tao Te Ching* suggests that if the leader follows the correct path, Tao, there will be universal virtue, *Te*, and a reconnection with the universal Tao.[24] This *Te* or "virtue" is what constitutes a Taoist's daily existence. In an essay on global ecology, Zhang Jiyu notes, accordingly, "A Daoist believes in Dao, relies upon Dao, cultivates Dao, and practices Dao. *De* refers to the particular conduct of the believer as ... [he or she practices] Dao."[25] Zhang cites here a reference to Chapter 51 of the *Tao Te Ching*, which distinguishes between the Tao that gives birth to things and the *Te* that fosters things. However, this lowercase *te*, this commonplace adjustment of worldly matters, not, perhaps, unlike the "higher human" who the hyperborean "rises above," may be contrasted to the program of the Taoist leader who fosters the uppercase *Te*.

Moreover, there are hints that the leader's procedure of non-willing is precipitated by actual meditative and alchemical procedures, such as breathing techniques, emptying the mind of "thought," creating a "higher" psychic self, and so forth.[26] These activities, which are available to any practitioner, are usually centered on non-conceptual states and silence. The first chapter of the *Tao Te Ching* thus defines the Tao metaphorically in language suggestive of such activities in which the "Tao that can be verbalized is not the Tao"[27] and one must "eliminate desires to experience the Tao."[28] In a political sense, the recommendation of the *Tao Te Ching* "to be silent rather than to talk" is a useful tactic.[29] However, the presiding Taoist saying "Enter stillness" refers to the meditative connection with the Tao and is embedded in this political wisdom.

In comparing Steinweg's deconstructionist meditation on the Nietzschean hyperborean model with the Taoist representation in the *Tao Te Ching* of the ideal leader model, one wonders if the willing subject in both cases is separated from the idea of virtue. At its simplest, the hyperborean is in a "headless" and presumably unwilled state divorced from any idea of virtue floating in some vast psychic space; the Taoist leader is advised to connect virtue (*Te*) with the Tao that infuses all things. We might set up a schema of how the "higher" and "lower" humans in each model are thought to function. In terms of "mind": the hyperborean is in the empty but infinite, "headless" state, while the "higher human" is filled with facts; the Taoist leader is in a state of Zen no-mind in communion with the Tao, while the "lower" human is filled with daily activities. In each case, the higher being has an "elevated" empty mind and the respective "lower" fellow humans have minds filled with ordinary reality. In terms of ordinary "will": the hyperborean is in the "headless" but unwilled and responsible state, while the "higher human" is "headed" and actively willed; the Taoist leader is bound by non-action and aligned with the Tao, while the "lower" human is filled with activity. In each case, the higher being's will is bound to a limitless higher ground and the respective "lower" fellow humans are "headed" and full of activity. In terms of ordinary "desire": the hyperborean has no desire, while the "higher human" desires identity; the Taoist leader has no desire, while the "lower" human is filled with desire. In each case, the higher beings are without desire, and their respective "lower" fellow humans are filled with desire.

In terms of "virtue": the hyperborean assumes responsibility in its state of infinite freedom and idealized virtue, while the "higher human" distinguishes between good and evil; the Taoist leader aligns with the *Te* that is connected to and predicated upon the Tao,[30] while the "lower" human is bound by a lowercase *te* based on yin and yang. In each case, the higher beings are connected to a "higher" level of virtue, and their respective "lower" fellow humans are governed by a definite polarity of good and evil. In terms of "Ground": the hyperborean is grounded in infinite chaos, while the "higher human" is grounded in facts; the Taoist leader is grounded in the Tao, while the "lower" human is grounded in the "ten thousand things." In each case, the higher being is grounded in an infinite primordial space and the respective "lower" fellow humans are grounded in the manifested world. Finally, in terms of "Will": the hyperborean is willed by infinite responsibility without desire, while the "higher human" is willed by desire in its normal sense; the Taoist leader is willed by a lack of desire in non-action, while the "lower" human is motivated by desire in its normal sense. In each case, the higher beings are determined by a lack of desire, and their respective "lower" fellow humans are grounded in desire.

Thus we find that both "higher" beings, the hyperborean and the Taoist leader, are passive and non-contentious in will but are privy to a "higher" morality predicated on a connection with an infinite grounding. Their grounding, Chaos and Tao, could easily be misconstrued as God in a theological sense, although the analogy would hold. In the case of the hyperborean, the ground is an infinite psychological space. In the case of the Taoist leader, the ground is the fundamental phenomenological support of all being, the so-called "web without a weaver." In both cases, Virtue, whether responsibility or *Te*, is clearly based on an alignment with an expansive ground, whether Chaos or Tao. Likewise, the "lower" humans' virtue, whether good and evil or yin and yang, is based on an alignment with ordinary reality, whether facts or the "ten thousand things." This designation of the Nietzschean postmodern and Taoist nature of Virtue is imperative and is elucidated by G. I. Gurdjieff's apparent thought on "conscience." According to his biographer, Gurdjieff "doesn't mean merely a little prod of guilt that warns us, now and then, but a state of being, a function of higher consciousness."[31] Thus, this "higher consciousness" is purportedly real and part of us and not merely a mechanical super-ego based on some static formulation of good and evil. Nor is it some antinomianism that would reduce conscience to an idea. It may, moreover, even be the still, small voice of the Western Wisdom tradition.

Nietzsche stated "In the end one only experiences oneself." This bow to the creation of the idea of "self" in the Western philosophic tradition and its correlative investigation of souls may be related to that small voice. It may be also related to the Eastern tradition of consciousness as in this Zen *koan*: "I have something. When you look at it, it's there, but when you look for it, it's not. What is it?" If the modern Western philosophic and psychological programs posit various identities for this human awareness, whether consciousness, will, super-ego, and the like, there seems over long periods of historical time a worldwide reckoning with and dependency upon this awareness, particularly in what might be termed the spiritual program. In the Taoist program the metaphysical concept of Tao, which is thought to be both immanence and transcendence, becomes the equivalent of God within the organized Taoist religion. Borrowing from Nietzsche, perhaps, the postmodern program deflects any final equivalent of God, which, in the written expressions of historical time, in the deconstructive context, becomes an endlessly deferred search for authentic meaning, not unlike Beckett's characters waiting for the symbolic god that never arrives. Or, in Steinweg's Nietzschean terms, the state of Chaos.

Thomas Hirschhorn's installation "Utopia, Utopia = One World, One War, One Army, One Dress" is a reflection of the postmodern condition. Its central metaphor is the appropriation of the camouflage design throughout world culture, from military functionality to high fashion. Within this disturbing montage of mannequins, photographs, videos, toys, clothing, and the like, Hirschhorn placed snippets of Steinweg's philosophic essay to reference the postmodern condition and, particularly, deconstruction. Here was a good correlative for that Chaos here presented for its intellectual, if not artistic, affect.

What is the relationship of the so-called metaphysical world and the so-called real world? Discontent with something in the latter has frequently formulated the inadequacy of what is basically a polarity of good and evil. A "something higher" is seen as a corrective space, whether of a "higher" order or of a primal "higher" Chaos. Yet one Eastern religious teacher cautions "Far too many Westerners seem to equate metaphysical progress with withdrawal from the contamination of the world. You need not be contaminated by the world provided you adhere to certain basic values and beliefs."[32] Like the hyperborean gliding over the Logos, he advises one to "be in the world and yet not of the world."[33] Perhaps such a wise impulse motivated the Lutheran pastor Dietrich Bonhoeffer to construct his model of Christian ethics upon engagement with the secular world.[34]

In that secular world, as they say, humans will be humans. The question here is what constitutes authority and what is the effect of that authority. The *Tao Te Ching* puts it satirically: "The more laws there are, the more criminals there are."[35] It likewise notes "The Tao takes from what is excessive and gives to what is deficient; humanity takes from what is deficient and gives to what is excessive."[36]

The Persian poet Rumi, in a contemporary retelling, perhaps resolves some of the grounding issues of willing and virtue by placing this grounding again within the self: "[First humanity] worships humans, stones, money or the elements, secondly [humanity] worships God, and thirdly [humanity] does not say 'I worship' or 'I do not worship.' "[37] Rumi is speaking of the mystical state from which he often wrote. By extension, one might see the "elevated" beings, the Nietzschean hyperborean and the Taoist leader here.

Moreover, just as Nietzsche and Steinweg connect the model of the hyperborean with their respective intellectual contexts, the philosophic questioning of Western theology and its attendant ethics in the one case and the postmodern condition and deconstructive projects that reflect the failure of modernism and traditional ethics in the other, Lao Tzu's *Tao Te Ching* connects the "Way of Virtue" with then contemporary philosophic contexts, the "godless" *yin-yang wu-hsing* "five-element" system in which Tao is the metaphysical ground and *Te* or virtue is the continuous balancing of yin and yang. Why in each case "will" as it is ordinarily understood becomes an impediment to true virtue is the real question here.

Hampden, Maine

NOTES

[1] Walter Kaufman, ed., *Existentialism from Dostoevsky to Sartre* (New York: World Publishing, 1956), p. 110.
[2] Marcus Steinweg, "Worldplay," in Thomas Hirschhorn, ed., *Utopia, Utopia = One World, One War, One Army, One Dress* (Boston: Institute of Contemporary Art, 2005), p. 34.
[3] John Shirley, *Gurdjieff, An Introduction to His Life and Ideas* (New York: Jeremy P. Turcher/Penguin, 2004), p. 63.
[4] Steinweg, p. 34. The actual installation addressed the ubiquitous appropriation of camouflage design through various aspects of worldwide culture. The artist placed fragments of Steinweg's meditation throughout the installation, thus reinforcing the deconstructionist bent of the installation and the meditation.
[5] Steinweg, p. 27.
[6] Steinweg, p. 25.
[7] Steinweg, p. 28.
[8] Steinweg, p. 27.
[9] Steinweg, p. 28.
[10] Steinweg, p. 47.
[11] Steinweg, p. 25.
[12] Steinweg, p. 36.
[13] Steinweg, p. 47.
[14] Steinweg, p. 29.
[15] Steinweg, p. 51.
[16] Steinweg, p. 16.
[17] *Tao Te Ching*, XXXIX.85.
[18] Shirley, p. 236.
[19] *Tao Te Ching*, XX.45. My translation here and in all citations.
[20] *Tao Te Ching*, LXVIII.166a.
[21] *Tao Te Ching*, XLVIII.108.
[22] *Tao Te Ching*, III.10.
[23] *Tao Te Ching*, XXXVII.
[24] *Tao Te Ching*, XXVIII.63.
[25] Zhang Jiyu, "A Declaration of the Chinese Daoist Association on Global Ecology," trans. David Yu, in N. J. Girardot, James Miller, and Liu Xiaogan, eds., *Daoism and Ecology, Ways within a Cosmic Landscape* (Cambridge, Mass.: Harvard University Press, 2001), p. 362.
[26] See *Tao Te Ching*, Chapter X, and the footnotes to Chapter X in Lao Tzu, *Tao Te Ching*, trans. D. C. Lau (London: Penguin, 1963), p. 66, and Hua Hu Ching, *The Unknown Teachings of Lau Tzu*, trans. Brian Walker (San Francisco: Harper, 1992), Chapters 42 and 66, among others.
[27] *Tao Te Ching*, I.1.
[28] *Tao Te Ching*, I.3.
[29] *Tao Te Ching*, V.16 and LVI.128.
[30] See *Tao Te Ching*, LI.114, where the "Tao produces all life and the Te sustains all life." Also see LI.114a, where an according reverence for the Tao and the Te is a natural expression and not dictated by authority.
[31] Shirley, p. 58.
[32] Rafael Lefort, *The Teachers of Gurdjieff* (Cambridge, Mass.: Malor Books, 1998), p. 91.

[33] Lefort, p. 91.
[34] See Dietrich Bonhoeffer, *Ethics* (New York: Macmillan, 1965).
[35] *Tao Te Ching*, LVII.32.
[36] *Tao Te Ching*, LXXVII.184a.
[37] Lefort, p. 70.

REBECCA M. PAINTER

VIRTUE IN MARILYNNE ROBINSON'S *GILEAD*

A thing I have always loved about writing, or even simply intending to write, is that it makes attentiveness a habit of mind.... I do feel that writing is like praying. I think that in both, if they are to be authentic, grace and truth must discipline thought.

Marilynne Robinson[1]

Where Shall Wisdom Be Found? Harold Bloom takes Ecclesiastes' question as his title for a book that attempts to answer it by identifying the greatest concepts of what he calls the wisdom tradition in literature and philosophy.[2] This reflection, Bloom explains, arose out of personal need, as he sought solace to face the traumas of aging, recovery from grave illness, and grief at the loss of beloved friends. "The mind always returns to its needs for beauty, truth, and insight. Mortality hovers, and all of us learn the triumph of time" (1).

For Bloom and perhaps most of us, "the deepest motive for reading has to be the quest for wisdom" (101). After a lifetime spent in literary appreciation and teaching, he concludes he'd rather be a version of Falstaff or Sancho Panza than a Hamlet or Don Quixote, "because growing old and ill teaches [him] that being matters more than knowing" (97–98). Bloom endorses Montaigne's view: "There is nothing so beautiful and legitimate as to play the man well and properly, no knowledge so hard to acquire as the knowledge of how to live life well and naturally; and the most barbarous of our maladies is to despise our being" (137). The most difficult task of great literature may be to portray the wisdom of a life lived well and naturally, showing us how to overcome the human predilection to despise our own lives for our humiliating subjection to universal suffering, which we have secretly assumed would mostly afflict others.

Such a life and earned wisdom is convincingly evoked in Marilynne Robinson's long-awaited second novel. *Gilead*[3] is remarkable—beyond its almost biblical poetic power—for daring to focus on the interior life and spirituality of a presumably dull literary figure, a man of virtue. Even riskier was making her protagonist a clergyman, and a third generation one at that. She accomplished this feat well enough to win the first-ever Grawemeyer Award for Religion for a novel—as well as the 2005 Pulitzer Prize.

In the 25 years between her first and second novels, Robinson proved an intrepid essayist and critic of contemporary political and popular culture.

Mother Country (1989) is a well-researched escoriation of British policies that permit and conceal the radioactive pollution of England's revered Lake District. Though a finalist for the U.S. National Book Award, it remains banned in Great Britain. Her collection *The Death of Adam* (1998)[4] won a PEN essay award, and should eventually be granted a place alongside works of wisdom writers such as Plato, Montaigne, Samuel Johnson, Goethe, Emerson, Kierkegaard, Freud, Nietzsche, Jung, and some spiritual authors unmentioned in Harold Bloom's selection of wisdom writers: Karl Barth, Dietrich Bonhoeffer, Simone Weil, Thomas Merton, and the Dalai Lama.

If Robinson had her druthers, more readers would acquaint themselves with the legendary but seldom-read theologian John Calvin, whom she prefers to call by his native French name, Jean Cauvin. She claims he is no longer given due credit for his nonhierarchical metaphysics, "based on the splendors of individual human consciousness," whose impact on the development of the modern West included universal education for boys and girls, the common people's justification for both the American and French Revolutions, and the belief that the sacred has no boundaries.[5] Perhaps in tribute to Cauvin, Robinson has written a gravely beautiful novel whose main character also lost his wife and baby in childbirth, and continued his ministry as a widower for many years.

One sees the impetus behind *Gilead* in a passage from *The Death of Adam:*

> lacking curiosity and the habit of study and any general grasp of history, we have entered a period of nostalgia and reaction.... We feel we have lost our way. Most of us know that religion was once very important to our national life, and believe, whether we ourselves are religious or not, that we were much the better for its influence.... Our ignorant parody of history affirms our ignorant parody of religious or "traditional" values. This matters, because history is precedent and permission, and in this important instance, as in many others, we have lost plain accuracy, not to speak of complexity, substance, and human inflection. (206)

Gilead characterizes a time when religion was a vital factor in people's lives. The narrative takes the form of a long letter written in 1956 in the dignified prose of 76-year-old Reverend John Ames, whose heart is failing and who is concerned that his son, turning seven, the gift of a late marriage equally unexpected and blessed, will not grow up knowing his father. Addressing the man his child will become, Ames challenges himself to set an example of complete honesty, not only to record his son's "begats," but also to confide his deepest feelings about the trials and joys of his life and faith.

These "begats" cast light on a key swath of the American past from the time of the Abolitionists through the Civil War and its painful unresolved aftermath in the lives of people who had put their faith into actions that cost them dearly. Rev. Ames' father emerged from the Civil War as a fierce pacifist, who clashed irreconcilably with his Abolitionist father, the narrator's grandfather, who had fought with the rebel Abolitionist John Brown and had most probably killed a Union soldier to protect Brown's escape. This took place in the hardscrabble fictional town of Gilead, Iowa, across the border from bloody Kansas, so named because it was fought over by those who wanted to extend slavery into the West and those who vehemently opposed it. The three generations of Ames clergy represent a span of American history when people believed in putting into practice their understanding of Biblical virtues. Through Ames, Robinson displays for contemporary readers the now countercultural tendency to look inward for spiritual accountability. His overt war is with his sorrow at having to leave a beloved much younger wife and the jewel of his old age, his young son. A more covert conflict and test of personal virtue is waged with his conscience. Here a man of faith cannot bring himself to forgive his godson and namesake for disgracing his name and the family of his closest friend, Reverend Boughton, a Presbyterian minister.[6] Yet for one so knowledgeable of the tenets of his faith, the refusal to forgive is so serious as to threatens one's personal salvation.

The dramatic tension of the novel builds within the heart and mind of its central character, who turns the act of writing into a prayer of self-scrutiny and this letter into a time capsule of fatherly upbringing. It can be seen as a novelized treatise on the difficulty of lived virtue, in a narrative form that illustrates the phenomenology of virtue perhaps better than most moral philosophy because it focuses our attention on moral consciousness itself. It may also be seen as a religious epistle, in the lineage of Paul's letters, a distinctly American contribution to modern theology. Robinson has spoken of theology as "the level at which the highest inquiry into meaning and ethics and beauty coincides with the largest-scale imagination of the nature of reality itself... it is thinking that is invested with meaning in a humanly evocative form."[7] *Gilead* is in this sense a theological novel, in which Rev. Ames takes stock of the historical American values he would like to pass on to his son, who, coincidentally, would now be the age of current or prospective leaders of this country. We could look upon the novel as a modern parable in a bottle, dated 1956, but meant for our troubled times.

The plot in Rev. Ames' book-length letter to his young son is presaged in a scenario Robinson sets forth in the essay "Family." Loyalty, always, is the only antidote to fear, distrust, and self-interest, she declares. It is "the balm for failure or weakness, or even for disloyalty," and is no better expressed than in family loyalty, when someone disgraced and failed returns to his family and they grieve with him, take on his sadness, and ponder together "the deep mysteries of human life." "Maybe," she suggests, "the saddest family, properly understood, is a miracle of solace." The novel *Gilead* offers balm for the failure, weakness, and disloyalty of Jack, Ames' godson. Old and dying, Ames elucidates Robinson's statement that loyalty should matter especially when we age, and founder, but that in our time it means so little and contributes "enormously to the sadness so many of us feel at the heart of contemporary society" (*The Death of Adam*, 89–90). The qualities that Robinson feels have passed out of our culture, changing it invisibly and absolutely, are the very qualities infusing her novel: humor, courage, dignity, graciousness, learnedness, fair-mindedness, loyalty, respect, and good faith. These qualities, she observes, only exist in behavior (*The Death of Adam*, 106). It is in the behavior, internal and external, that Rev. Ames inscribes for his soon-to-be-fatherless son that these qualities take on substance and significance.

Ames' account of the standoff between his father and grandfather resonates with the fierce political animosity of present times. His zealous Abolitionist grandfather had preached the men of his congregation into fighting for the Union cause, which they did devotedly and disastrously, decimating the old preacher's congregation. The senior Rev. Ames went with them as a chaplain, losing an eye in the conflict but not his restless zealotry. His son, the narrator's father, also served as a union chaplain but came back intensely opposed to warfare in any form. After the war, the two exercised grim restraint to remain civil to one another.

Things came to a head when the retired older preacher, who normally attended his son's services, walked out one Sunday in search of less passive preaching at the nearby Negro church. Afterward, when asked if he'd found what he'd sought, the old man shrugged. The sermon he'd heard had been about loving one's enemies. Ames recalls the ensuing conversation:

> My father said, "You sound disappointed, Reverend."
>
> My grandfather put his head in his hands. He said, "Reverend, no words could be bitter enough.... There is just no end to it. Disappointment. I eat it and drink it. I wake and sleep it."
>
> My father's lips were white. He said, "Well, Reverend, I know you placed great hope in that war. My hopes are in peace, and I am not disappointed.... Peace is its own justification."
>
> My grandfather said, "And that's just what kills my heart, Reverend. That the Lord never came to you. That the seraphim never touched a coal to your lips—"
>
> My father stood up from his chair. He said, "I remember when you walked to the pulpit in that shot-up bloody shirt with that pistol in your belt. And I had a thought as powerful and clear as any revelation. And it was, This has *nothing* to do with Jesus. Nothing. Nothing. And I was, and am, as certain of that as anyone could ever be of any so-called vision. I defer to no one in this. Not to you, not to Paul the Apostle, not to John the Divine. Reverend."

My grandfather [who, unlike his son, had experienced numerous spiritual visions] said, "So-called vision. The Lord, standing there beside me had one hundred times the reality for me that you have standing here now!"

After a minute my father said, "No one would doubt that, Reverend."

And that was when a chasm truly opened. Not long afterward my grandfather was gone. He left a note lying on the kitchen table which said:

No good has come, no evil is ended.

That is your peace.

Without vision the people perish.

The Lord bless you and keep you.

Ames saved his grandfather's note in his Bible. His grandfather headed off to Kansas where he died. His son and grandson later made a belated and arduous pilgrimage to his rough-hewn grave. "I think that fierce anger against him was one of the things my father felt he truly had to repent of," Ames writes. Nevertheless, the Civil War had so convinced his father of war's futility that he nearly died of rage and exasperation in 1914 when Americans were celebrating their entry into world war I with parades and marching bands, when "we already knew what a miserable thing it was we were sending our troops off to" (86).

There is no taking of sides in this narrative between those who would fight and those who refuse to on principle—just respect and compassion for both. Still, Ames saved his grandfather's parting message, that people perish for lack of vision. His grandfather's bitterness arose from the lingering injustice of racism, the repudiation of the Abolitionists' victory. Robinson's novel calls readers to figure if what we stand for as a nation may perish for the lack of a timely vision of justice and that which defeats it.

Central to Ames' epistle is his distress over the return of a latter day Prodigal Son, welcomed by his own father but not by his godfather, who shares responsibility for his spiritual direction. Jack is a soul Rev. Ames simply could not get himself to like, let alone love. This namesake gave him nothing but embarrassment upon seeing his full name, John Ames Boughton, appear in local papers for one trespass after another. The worst of these Ames describes in cringing detail: Jack's youthful fathering of a child by a poor unprotected girl who lived outside town in a ramshackle house with a pack of mean dogs under the porch and a yard littered with broken glass. Though Jack would have nothing to do with his child or its mother, his parents offered to adopt it and were refused, so they brought the child whatever the mother's family would accept, including shoes. These, if they had been worn by the toddler and not saved for special occasions, might have spared the child from death by tetanus. Jack's parents were devastated; their son simply took off for parts unknown. Or that's how Rev. Ames records it.

Critics who feel shortchanged that the novel's narrator is so essentially good, preferring "a bit more malice, avarice, or lust—or just an intriguing unreliability,"[8] or claim that the novel's "controlling perspective,... for a non-Christian,... is impossible to share" and may arouse readers' longing for something ironic and urbane[9], should take special note of Ames' struggle with his tendency to condemn his faithless, renegade namesake. Though a man of the cloth, he is repelled where his godson is concerned from practicing what he has no doubt preached. But because he struggles to be honest with himself and his son, Ames continues to question the fixity of his judgments. Because he addresses the generation of our current leaders and mature adults, through him Robinson challenges us to question our own and our nation's assumption of the moral high ground.

A subtle example arises when Ames describes a visit by Jack shortly after his homecoming, looking for a game of catch with Ames' son. He declines an invitation to dinner, which disappoints both the boy and his mother. Ames notes merely that Jack "was sunburned from working in the garden. It gave him a healthy, honest look" (119). With acidic reserve, he writes,

> You and your mother still regard him as a fairly wonderful surprise, this John Ames Boughton with his quiet voice and his preacherly manner, which, by the way, he has done nothing to earn, or to deserve. To the best of my knowledge, at any rate. He had it even as a child, and I always found that disturbing. Maybe it's something he isn't conscious of, growing up the way he did. But it seems to me sometimes that there's an element of parody in it. (120)

Ames' dilemma is not limited neither to a Christian belief system. He is, quite simply, prejudiced against Jack Boughton. Repulsed by Jack's manner of expressing himself similarly to his father and godfather, Ames has misinterpreted Jack's childhood pranks as attempts to fluster and annoy him. Readers easily perceive them as the actions of an isolated and lonely boy who was trying to get his godfather's attention when his father was unavailable for companionship. Did Jack need to attend seminary to earn or deserve a manner of speaking that he would have acquired by growing up in the presence of two preachers? The Reverend provides a lucid example of an uncharitable mindset, Christian or otherwise.

Ames barely manages to check himself: "I hope there's some special providence in his turning up just when I have so many other things to deal with, because he is a considerable disruption when peace would have been especially appreciated. I'm not complaining. Or I ought not to be."

Contemplating Jack's past transgressions in quasi-humility, he emerges with a shard of wisdom: "Transgression.... There is never just one transgression. There is a wound in the flesh of human life that scars when it heals and often enough seems never to heal at all. Avoid transgression. How's that for advice" (122).

High moral tone, even with humility about for the depth of transgression, does not deter the dark intention of the Reverend's heart: to warn his son and wife against Jack Boughton. Though he states forthright that he is fallible and cannot trust his own feelings on the matter, he forges on: "Jack is not a man of the highest character. Be wary of him" (125). Surely not by accident, Ames shortly thereafter reflects on the most vexing to him of the Ten Commandments:

> I believe the sin of covetise is that pang of resentment you may feel when even the people you love best have what you want and don't have. From the point of view of loving your neighbor as yourself (Leviticus 19:18), there is nothing that makes a person's fallenness more undeniable than covetise—you feel it right in your heart, in your bones. In that way it is instructive. I have never really succeeded in obeying that Commandment, Thou shalt not covet. I avoided the experience of disobeying by keeping to myself a good deal. (134)

This keeping to himself refers to the many years he lived alone, a widower, while his friend Rev. Boughton enjoyed a loving marriage and many fine children. Boughton named his last and favorite child after Ames in hopes of sharing his own abundance and filling some of the void of his friend's childlessness. Ames' paradoxical aversion to his namesake was something he kept scrupulously hidden from his best friend.

The self-questioning progresses as Ames records a dialogue he had with two sides of himself. He asks, "What is it you fear most, Moriturus [Latin for soon-to-be-dead]?" Moriturus answers, "Leaving my wife and child unknowingly in the sway of a man of extremely questionable character." Then he asks, "What makes you think his contact with them or his influence upon them will be considerable enough to be damaging to them?" (140). Moriturus admits that his evidence of Jack's ill intent is paltry. Jack has only come by the house a few times and attended his church once. So he has to dig for a more honest answer, for his son and for himself:

> The truth is, as I stood there in the pulpit, looking down on the three of you, you looked to me like a handsome young family, and my evil old heart rose within me, the old covetise I have mentioned elsewhere came over me, and I felt the way I used to feel when the beauty of other lives was a misery and an offense to me. And I felt as if I were looking back from the grave.

If there is anything Rev. Ames does not wish for himself, it is to die inside before his brief remaining time is up. What is more, he confesses,

> I don't want to be old. And I certainly don't want to be dead. I don't want to be the tremulous coot you barely remember. I bitterly wish you could know me as a young man, and not really so young, either, necessarily. I was trim and fit into my sixties.... Even now, if I could trust my heart, there's a lot I could do. (p. 141)

Here, finally, we recognize one of the commonest unspoken and shame-filled forms of human misery: the ugly and humiliating envy of the young experienced by practically all of the aging—saints perhaps excepted. Still, Ames forgives himself a little, acknowledging that even Jesus wept on the night before his crucifixion. But to most readers, at least older ones, this confession might have a liberating quality. Though not consoling, it frees us from a false sense of singularity in our envious regret to be shuffling ever nearer our exit from the mortal coil. Call it the communion of non-saints.

Robinson places the narrative in a larger phenomenological perspective when she has Ames attack, shortly afterward, "two insidious notions, from the point of view of Christianity in the modern world." The first Ames identifies as coming from atheists such as Feuerbach and Freud: that "religion and religious experience are illusions of some sort." The second he thinks is more insidious, that "religion itself is real, but *your* belief that *you* participate in it is an illusion." Ames believes, as does the author, that "it is religious experience above all that authenticates religion, for the purposes of the individual believer" (145). This novel allows us to witness an arduously achieved personal virtue that is made possible or at least strengthened by religious faith. The narrative can be experienced as a transmogrified sermon. What makes it worth listening to is its representation of the phenomenology of human experience as virtue, reflected in the spiritual honesty of Reverend Ames.

Candid self-scrutiny makes Ames' story virtuous from both a religious and a secular perspective. It is virtuous because it is self-questioning, continually seeking a ground of honesty to personal experience. In phenomenological terms, the process of scrutinizing one's experience and feelings for their truthfulness, and the exercise of constant vigilance it requires, is about as close as one can get to a phenomenology of virtue. One might say, in phenomenological terms, that there can be no virtue that is not based on awareness of experience. From another angle, we could posit that in the absence of truth-seeking attentiveness, the ground of experience becomes fertile for evil in thought and action.[10]

Robinson and Ames are well aware of the hypocrisy and pettiness of much that calls itself religion in this world. Ames ruminates,

But if the awkwardness and falseness and failure of religion are interpreted to mean there is no core of truth in it... then people are disabled from trusting their thoughts, their expressions of belief, and their understanding, and even from believing in the essential dignity of their and their neighbor's endlessly flawed experience of belief. It seems to me there is less meanness in atheism, by a good measure.

The Reverend notes of the "destructive potency of religious self-righteousness" (146), a factor that takes on crucial proportions in Jack's story.

Robinson saves the crisis of atheism versus belief for the confrontation that ensues between Ames and his namesake. Though at first he is perceived by Ames as up to the annoying tricks of his youth, it becomes clear that Jack is actually a weary middle-aged man, heart-broken and despairing, earnestly if awkwardly seeking the balm of family succor and guidance. He has sought, though never received, the gift of faith, and has therefore felt alienated from his father, godfather, and other family members since childhood. Old Boughton is dying more quickly than Ames, and Jack cannot bring himself to tell his father what has happened to him in the 20-plus years he's been away, for fear the knowledge would kill him.

Gradually we realize that, more than for any other reason, Jack's desperate situation has resulted from the religious exclusivism and self-righteousness of others.

"I would like your help with this, Reverend," Ames recalls Jack saying, "so seriously that I began to think he might be serious." He had assumed Jack was merely "bedeviling" him.

Jack persists. "I assume predestination does not, in your understanding, mean that a good person will go to hell simply because he was consigned to hell from the beginning."

Ames explained his belief that no person who is good in any meaningful sense can also be consigned to perdition, and the same goes for a sinful person, with Scripture supporting both cases.

Jack narrows things down to himself. "But are there people who are simply born evil, live evil lives, and then go to hell?"

"On that point," Ames said, "Scripture is not so clear." He grants that human behavior can change, but whether "their nature changes or that another aspect of it becomes visible is hard to say."

Exasperated, Jack observes, "For a man of the cloth, you're pretty cagey."

His father laughs and says, "You should have seen him thirty years ago" (150–151).

It takes Ames' little-educated but intelligent wife, who has been listening intently to this exchange—whose face, Ames noted earlier to his son, reflects a life of unspoken sadness before they met, a history of sorrow he respectfully never asked her to reveal to him—to end the stalemate. She declares shyly but firmly, "A person can change. Everything can change." Jack says, "Thanks. That's all I wanted to know" (153).

Walking home, Mrs. Ames tells her husband, "He was only asking a question," which Ames wonders could be a rebuke. "Maybe some people aren't so comfortable with themselves," she adds. "Now, that *was* a rebuke," he writes, admitting she was right. "Often enough," he muses, "when we think we are protecting ourselves, we are struggling against our rescuer," though he acknowledges not knowing "how to live by it for even a day, or an hour" (154). The best he can do is remind himself, and his son, that "the grace of God is sufficient to any transgression, and that to judge is wrong, the origin and essence of much error and cruelty" (155). Statements like those between Ames and Jack beg to be tested, and Robinson's narrative does not disappoint.

Ames eventually renders in detail Jack's youthful transgression against the young girl, whose family situation was "desolate, even squalid,"

> She enjoyed none of the protections a young girl needs. And there he was with his college airs and his letter sweater and that Plymouth convertible he got somewhere for a song, he said.... Jack Boughton had no business in the world involving himself with that girl. It was something no honorable man would have done.

On that none would disagree. But his next statement bears the rub:

> Sinners are not all dishonorable people, not by any means. But those who are dishonorable never really repent and never really reform. Now, I may be wrong here. No such distinction occurs in Scripture. And repentance and reformation are matters of the soul which only the Lord can judge. But, in my experience, dishonor is recalcitrant. When I see it, my heart sinks, because I feel I have no help to offer a dishonorable person. I know the deficiency may be my own altogether. (156–157)

His wife has not been reading his words to their son, but she participated decisively in the discussion of predestination. On the pretext that he spare himself time to write more to their child by reusing past sermons, she locates one he had given on forgiveness in June 1947. Ames guesses that he could have been thinking about the Marshall Plan. The connection, however, between personal and international forgiveness appears elsewhere in Robinson's writings.

In an essay in *The Death of God* on the Lutheran theologian Dietrich Bonhoeffer—who was murdered by the Nazis a few months before the end of World War II—Robinson praises Bonhoeffer's critique of the self-defeating exclusivism of the official church. He had preferred a church without boundaries, and predicted the eventual disappearance of religion in Europe if existing boundaries remained in place. Referring to the war's aftermath, but not limited to it, Robinson remarks that "we have not learned the heroic art of forgiveness, which may have been the one thing needful" (111).

Recalling that the boy's mother would have heard this sermon, Ames launches into his most favorite memory, the day she first attended his church, on Pentecost. On the day Ames' future wife appeared he was 67, though he did not feel old. He writes his son,

> I wish I could leave you certain of the images in my mind, because they are so beautiful that I hate to think they will be extinguished when I am.... And memory is not strictly mortal in its nature, either. It is a strange thing, after all, to be able to return to a moment, when it can hardly be said to have any reality at all, even in its passing. A moment is such a slight thing, I mean, that its abiding is a most gracious reprieve. (162)

This might seem irrelevant to the topic of forgiveness, given the Reverend's memory of seeing his beloved second wife for the first time. His tenderness, however, contrasts sharply with his notation soon after, that "remembering and forgiving can be contrary things." Referring to the loss of his first wife and child, he adds, darkly,

> It is not for me to forgive Jack Boughton.... That one man should lose his child and the next man should just squander his fatherhood as if it were nothing—well, that does not mean that the second man has transgressed against the first. I don't forgive him. I wouldn't know where to begin. (164)

It does not occur to Rev. Ames that young Jack might have been genuinely interested in overhearing his conversations with his father, ineptly trying to establish some kind of bond with him, when he describes going over to Rev. Boughton's place to borrow a book during the time a photo of his wife was missing. Ames recalls the boy listening to every word as his father and Ames talked on the porch and from time to time, and from time to time he would look up at me and smile, as if we were in on a joke together, some interesting conspiracy. I found that extremely irritating.... Maybe you can see why, when the business with the young girl came up, I was chiefly struck by the meanness of it. (184)

Even though he concludes this recollection by admitting that Jack was always a mystery, so he cannot judge him, readers are immersed in an attitude that precludes compassion and fair judgment. Ames asserts, "I can't assign a moral valuation to his behavior. He's just mean." To many readers, pronouncing Jack "mean" would amount to a moral judgment on his entire character, never mind his behavior.

No sooner than Ames digs this hole for himself, basic decency and religious scruples prompt him to pull back:

Well, I don't know that that is true of him now. But I do see what he might injure.... While I was standing there in the pulpit, the thought came to me that I was looking back from the grave and there he was, sitting beside you, grinning up at me—This is not doing me any good at all. I'd better pray. (184–185)

Ames steps back from the abyss of condemnatory self-righteousness into prayer. What is virtuous is that he steps back to avoid distorted thinking; what is spiritual, of course, is that he prays.

Surely in any bitter divorce proceeding, partisan animosity, business rivalry, family feud, or sectarian strife verging upon civil war, there are feelings this intense or more. But too rarely there is a stepping back, whether to pray or to refrain from condemnation or violence. *Gilead*'s narrator embodies virtue as spiritual honesty, self-questioning, and reluctance to render final judgment when it begins to resemble condemnation. How badly do contemporary decision-makers need this example? Rev. Ames' story compellingly expresses that before a mutual peace and blessing can occur, each side, particularly the side more capable of self-discernment, needs to reexamine old conceptions of reality. Before Ames hears what Jack has experienced in the last 20 years, he has to purify his consciousness of the bitterness he has felt about having been Jack's namesake.

Revisiting this memory marks the turning point of the narrative.

Ames recalls how he had been asked to baptize and christen Rev. Boughton's youngest son and was told that the infant would be named after a preacher Ames' grandfather had greatly admired. But in the ceremony itself, when he asked Boughton what name he wished the child to be called, he was shocked to hear "John Ames." There was weeping in the pews and tears streaming down Boughton's face, but Rev. Ames confesses that his own heart froze. It seems to have been the only time in his life that he did not feel the tender blessing of baptism, an experience he had described as one of the greatest joys of his ministry, beginning with a childhood urge to baptize a litter of kittens.

Though Ames' reaction seemed paradoxical, one has to admire the painful honesty behind his slantwise explanation: "I thought, This is *not* my child—which I truly had never thought of any child before. I don't know exactly what covetise is, but in my experience it is not so much desiring someone else's virtue or happiness as rejecting it, taking offense at the beauty of it".

He admits he was distracted by his own miserable thoughts, having lost his first wife and child. Here was his best friend offering to share a son with him and have the child carry his name, people were weeping at the beauty of the moment, but in his envy of their virtue and generosity he could only take offense. Yet such honesty is oddly liberating. At once he takes a mental breath: "That's interesting. There is certainly a sermon there." The dispassionate clergyman takes note: " 'Blessed is he who takes no offense at me.' That would be the primary text. I hope I have time to think it through" (188). Actually, the primary text in his case happens to be the entire narrative of *Gilead*.

"I do wish I could christen him again, for my sake," Ames resolves. "John Ames Boughton is my son.... By 'my son' I mean another self, a more cherished self. That language isn't sufficient, but for the moment it is the best I can do" (189). Later Jack comes over for a visit, and Ames tells him he's impressed to learn that Jack has been reading Karl Barth. "Oh," Jack said. "From time to time I still try to crack the code." At 43, Jack is still not blessed with the gift of faith, but Ames now has the compassion to admire his tenacity (196). After Jack leaves, Ames sits in the dark and wishes he "could forget all the tedious particulars and just feel the presence of his mortal and immortal being," to "sit at the feet of that eternal soul and learn." Jack seemed to him at that moment

the angel of himself, brooding over the mysteries his mortal life describes, the deep things of man. And of course that is exactly what he is. "For who among men knoweth the things of a man, save the spirit of the man, which is in him?" (197)

Emmanuel Levinas could not have expressed it better. Ames hits upon the very essence of Levinas' concept of full respect for unknowable spirit of the Other, whether enemy or friend, whom either chance or Providence puts among us as our neighbor.

One might think that the Reverend is now ready to hear Jack's heartrending story and be ready to offer this prodigal, unbelieving, suffering, and martyred son his blessing. But it is key to Robinson's narrative that, before readers witness this climactic conferral, Ames inscribes for his own son the intensely humbling and death-resembling passion that overcame him when he fell in love with the boy's mother at 67:

If I had had this experience earlier in life, I would have been much wiser, much more compassionate. I really didn't understand what it was that made people who came to me so indifferent to good judgment, to common sense.... And I know now that it is passion that moves them to their prodigal renunciations. I might seem to be comparing something great and holy with a minor and ordinary thing, that is, love of God with mortal love. But I just don't see them as separate things at all. If we can be divinely fed with a morsel and divinely blessed with a touch, then the terrible pleasure we find in a particular face can certainly instruct us in the nature of the very grandest love.
[She had appeared one Sunday in his church.]... [N]othing had prepared me to find myself thinking day and night about a complete stranger, a woman much too young, probably a married woman—that was the first time in my life I ever felt I could be snatched out of my character, my calling, my reputation, as if they could just fall away like a dry husk.... [I]t was a foretaste

of death.... And why should that seem strange? "Passion" is the word we use, after all.... I felt so ridiculous. But I would speak to the Lord about it just the same, asking Him to strengthen me in exercising my pastoral responsibilities, and not a word I said was true, because I was really just a foolish old man asking the Almighty to indulge his foolishness and I knew it at the time. And my prayers were answered, beyond anything I could have thought to ask. A wife, and a child. I would never have believed it. (204–205)

This recognition of the power and mystery of passion, as Robinson puts before us in this fictionalized sermon, is what makes forgiveness possible. It is a profound illumination of the necessity to stand back from assuming that we can know the contents of another's heart. Respect for the mystery of passion, the author urges, should spur us to forbear passing judgment on others' extreme transgressions.

Compassion, the beneficent cohort of passion, seems to spring from appreciation of shared suffering as well as joy. Mrs. Ames, because of her unexplored sad past, is able to converse comfortably with Jack. He and she concur, for example, that St. Louis is a terrible place to be broke in, laughing together when she says, "If there's a good place to broke, I sure never found it. And I tried 'em all" (200). It becomes clear that Jack Boughton, Rev. Ames, and his wife Lila (whose name we hear only once, when Jack addresses her), have each experienced abject loneliness, having been on the outside looking in on comfortable homes and families: Ames in his widowhood, Lila in her poverty and lack of a family, and Jack in his exile of shame. They have each tasted love's deep reciprocal passion.

It takes the length of this novel for an essentially kind and devout man to reevaluate his prejudice against a person who could have been relieved of some of his loneliness, whose transgressions might have been mitigated by a more loving acceptance from his godfather rather than pained toleration based solely on regard for Jack's father. Yet if Ames were not so intent on honesty and setting a moral example as well as a fatherly history for his young son, we would not have such an intimate phenomenology of virtue in action. The thorniest virtue may be that of forgiveness, being so hard won.

Jack finally reveals to his godfather that he has a wife and child, a son nearly the age of Ames' boy, and that he too has experienced a loving marriage, though due to unjust outside factors, not a stable one. "In the eyes of God," as Jack puts it, "we have been man and wife for about eight years." Because he had trouble finding work enough to support a family, and had to hide their union from laws against interracial cohabitation, they lived together only "seventeen months, two weeks, and a day" (220). His wife Della is a black schoolteacher whose father is also a minister. He met her in St. Louis at a low point in his life, he explains, and her friendship and the respect she showed him meant a great deal. Her family did not accept him, however, *not because he is white but because he is without faith.* Though Della seemed willing to endure any hardship to stay with him, her imposing father convinced Jack that he should tell Della to go home where her family would be able to care for her. To his shame, and her obvious disappointment, he was relieved to do so, fearing that something would go wrong with the baby and—as in his youth—he would be blamed for it.

Jack explained that he borrowed money from his father, got another job, and eventually was able to purchase a house in a mixed neighborhood and live with his wife and child for a few months, until they were spotted together by his employer, who promptly fired him. Jack then sent Della and the child back to Memphis, where they stayed with her family while he returned to Gilead to investigate the possibility of relocating, since Iowa had no laws against interracial marriage. Afraid that his father was too frail to hear his story, Jack asked his godfather how his father might react, tactlessly mentioning that Rev. Ames knew something about being the object of scandal, being "unequally yoked and so on," adding that "Della is an educated woman." Ames, whose wife was not formally educated, again misreads Jack's attempt to reach out to him:

> Now, that was just like him. That meanness.... I never felt there was anything the least bit scandalous about my marriage. In her own way, your mother is a woman of great refinement. If a few people did make remarks, I just forgave them so fast it was as if I never heard them, because it was wrong of them to judge ... and they should have known it.
>
> But then that look of utter weariness came over him and he covered his face with his hands. And I could only forgive him.

Then it was Ames' turn to put foot into mouth:

> I said, "I would love to know the child. Especially if you explained everything to me the way you just did." And then I said, "[Your father] certainly took to that other child."
>
> Young Boughton gave me such a look as I have never seen in my life before. He went stark white....
>
> I said, "You have to forgive me for that. That was such a foolish thing to say. I'm tired. I'm old."
>
> "Yes," he said, and his voice was very controlled. "And I have taken far too much of your time. Thank you. I know I can trust your pastoral discretion." (230–231)

Ames in his weariness tries to salvage the situation, putting his arms around Jack and saying he's a good man. Jack laughs and says there are worse, then asks what would happen if he brought his family to Gilead to be married and live. "You have influence here," he suggests. But Ames can't promise to live long enough to make much use of it. "No matter, Papa," Jack says, "I believe I've lost them, anyway." He expects, correctly, that Della has finally succumbed to pressure from her family to marry a black man of the same faith who promised to adopt the child. It is clear that Jack's loving marriage "in the eyes of God"—in painful contrast to Rev. Ames' equally loving but more acceptable marriage—had been made unsustainable by racist laws *and* by the religious exclusivity of Della's family, who could accept a white man in their midst but drew the line at a non-believer even one who read Karl Barth to try to "break the code."

Ames writes to his son that he was overlooking pastoral discretion to divulge Jack's story. "I just don't know another way to let you see the beauty there is in him." Readers share Ames' sense of wonder as he declares that the next Sunday, looking out on the congregation and seeing Jack sitting next to his wife and their son, he was amazed to find himself wishing there actually were grounds for his old dread: "I felt as if I'd have bequeathed him wife and child if I could to supply the loss of his own" (p. 233).

The narrative is filled with eloquent passages, so I will not linger over Robinson's evocation of the fictional Gilead as "a place John Brown and Jim Lane could fall back on when they needed to heal and rest," and whose "urgency... is all forgotten now, and their littleness and their shabbiness, which was the measure of the courage and passion that went into the making of them, now just look awkward" (234), except to say that the balm of a symbolic Gilead invoked here may well be the shabby but surviving potential for our society to reacquaint itself with courage and passion.

When Ames explains how his father moved away to Florida, assuring him that he did not have to remain in such a small town founded upon "notions that were very old and even very local," as if to excuse his son from loyalty to him and the ministry he was vacating, he writes that the very suggestion made him feel homesick for the place he'd never left (235). Even casual readers could perceive this as a call to old virtues in current times. Though Ames' long letter to his son closes with his prayer that the child will "grow up a brave man in a brave country... [and] find a way to be useful" (247), the author delivers this parting shot a glancing blow. Patriotic rhetoric would not be given the time of day by the ironic cognoscenti of our day, but Rev. Ames' final benediction of the desolate Jack Boughton probably would. We much more readily accept the plight of those who are emotionally bereft and unable to experience the possibility of faith.

The prodigal son of Robinson's narrative leaves his family's loving embrace, just as his older brothers and sisters are returning with their fine children from their successful lives elsewhere to gather around their father's deathbed. It is an unthinkable abandonment, but Rev. Ames now feels he understands Jack's heart, as readers are meant to.

The house will fill up with those estimable people and their husbands and wives and their pretty children. How could he be there in the midst of it all with that sad and splendid treasure in his heart?—I also have a wife and a child.

I can tell you this, that if I'd married some rosy dame and she had given me ten children and they had each given me ten grandchildren, I'd leave them all, on Christmas Eve, on the coldest night of the world, and walk a thousand miles just for the sight of your face, your mother's face. And if I never found you, my comfort would be in that hope, my lonely and singular hope, which could not exist in the whole of Creation except in my heart and in the heart of the Lord ... [Jack] would utterly and bitterly prefer what he had lost to everything they had.

Ames understands his own passion and Jack's. He also feels certain that his old friend Boughton

would abandon all those handsome children of his ... and follow after that one son whom he has never known, whom he has favored as one does a wound, and he would protect him as a father cannot, ... [and] would utterly pardon every transgression, past, present, and to come, whether or not it was a transgression in fact or his to pardon. (237–238)

It is a biblical kind of compassion, strongly reflecting the Christian parable in Luke 15 that illustrates a loving father's all-forgiving love for a wayward child who has returned having squandered his material inheritance. Robinson's novel is also the confession of a man whose honesty about his own capacity for mistaken judgment has rendered him capable of taking on the role of the forgiving father, the honest judge. Only this time the need for forgiveness extends to the one who has denied this child his nurturing attention and moral support, a moral authority who has not shown true family loyalty.

Speaking as a good son who never left his father's house, even when his own father left it, Ames admits that he is one of the righteous "for whom the rejoicing in heaven will be comparatively restrained." Despite these credentials, he declares,

There is no justice in love, no proportion in it, and there need not be, because ... it is only a glimpse or parable of an embracing, incomprehensible reality ... the eternal breaking in on the temporal. So how could it subordinate itself to cause or consequence? (238)

Some commentators have remarked that the foregoing sentiments are not exactly Christian in their favoritism. It is hard to concur when one considers the parable that Robinson seems to be illustrating. In it there is an older brother who resents the father's magnanimity toward his younger sibling and clearly would not have welcomed him home if he were in charge of the family domain. One could say that before Ames hears all of Jack's story and recognizes in it the unbounded passion he has for his own wife and child, he was of that disapproving brother's purview. In Jesus' parable of God's boundless parental love for the wayward, forgiveness is subsumed within the father's celebration of the Prodigal Son's return. But in Robinson's novel, the pathway to the most difficult-to-achieve forgiveness is painstakingly explored in terms of self-questioning and rigorous honesty.

Jack is distressed that once again he is doing the worst thing, leaving at such a time—his "masterpiece," in the eyes of his incredulous oldest sister. Ames writes, "It was the kind of thing only his father would forgive him for"—and his Father, as this modern parable implies, and as a result of Robinson's artistry, the readers of this story. Ames tells Jack that he advised his sister "not to judge, that there might be something more to the situation," and Jack thanks him. Reassuring Jack that he truly does understand why he has to leave, the Reverend writes that it was as true a thing as he has ever said. In that moment, amazingly, he felt grateful for all his "old bitterness of heart" (240).

While this seems fairly miraculous in itself, the most profound moment comes when Ames asks Jack if he will allow him to bless him—placing his hands on the man's forehead in a gesture similar to the baptism and christening that long ago he had performed with an impure heart. Jack readily agrees, the paradoxical gesture of a man who may not believe in God but values his godfather's blessing. Rev. Ames says an ancient prayer asking the Lord to be gracious unto him and give him peace. When Jack leaves his head resting on Ames' hand, the Reverend asks also that Jack be blessed as a "beloved son and brother and husband and father" (241). It is an honor to bless him, he tells Jack. He writes to his son that he would have gone through seminary and ordination and all his years of ministry for that one moment.

Jack boards the bus, doffing his hat, leaving the impression that he will never return. Ames goes to his church to rest, imagining how his old friend Boughton would envy him for the way Jack received his blessing. It is a moment that obliterates his old sin of covetise that Ames had confessed when describing the baptism and christening of his namesake. He imagines his friend Boughton "beyond the world, looking back at me with an amazement of realization—'This is why we have lived this life!' There are a thousand reasons to live this life," he asserts, "every one of them sufficient" (243). But this example of gradually becoming able to bless those who have caused us long-galling bitterness is perhaps more sufficient to our contemporary world. It may even be our most crucial virtue.

We finish Robinson's novel with the image of old Reverend Ames, having finally blessed— re-baptized—his namesake and godson, who is setting out for a life bereft of those he loves, while Ames is about to leave the world and family he loves. Both have participated in the healing balm of Gilead. But the man without faith has met far greater injustice and sorrow, pointing to the kind of iniquities a society must seek to eradicate. There should be no doubt about the significance of the little fictional outpost on the prairie, that bedraggled place that looks "like whatever hope becomes after it begins to weary a little, then [wearies] a little more. But hope deferred is still hope." It is a town, and a state of mind, that Ames loves so much he considers that being buried in its soil will be his "last wild gesture of love" (247). It is a Gilead meant for a nation and a people perilously lacking in hope.

In *The Death of Adam* Robinson defines morality as a covenant that can only be imposed and enforced by oneself: "Society can honor these covenants or not.... The great antidote to morality is cynicism, which is nothing more than an understanding of how arbitrary morality is, how unpredictable and unenforceable, how insecurely grounded in self-interest" (170). This cynicism should not be allowed to devolve into nihilism. "The human condition," Robinson notes, "has an amazing wrongness about it. But if it is agreed we are in this respect mysterious, then we should certainly abandon easy formulas of judgment" (171). As readers of *Gilead* are rendered incapable of judging Jack Boughton's conduct, we are precluded from abandoning the hope of forgiveness, healing, and deconstructing the wrongness of the world. As Rev. Ames prayed for his child, we must be brave, and useful. Brave enough to scrutinize ourselves, to be vigilant in honesty. These are phenomenological virtues, and they are useful.

Marymount Manhattan College

NOTES

[1] Robinson, Marilynne. Interview, The *New Yorker Online Only* 2004-09-06. Available at http://www.newyorker.com/printables/online/040913on_onlineonly01; accessed December 8, 2005.
[2] Bloom, Harold, *Where Shall Wisdom Be Found?* (New York: Riverhead/Penguin, 2004).
[3] Robinson, Marilynne, *Gilead* (New York: Farrar, Strauss and Giroux, 2004).
[4] Robinson, Marilynne, *The Death of Adam: Essays on Modern Thought* (New York: Houghton Mifflin, 2000 [1998]).
[5] Robinson, Interview, *op. cit.*
[6] Robinson was raised Presbyterian and became a Congregationalist, serving a term as deacon in her church, where she has been called upon to deliver sermons.
[7] Robinson. Interview, *Religion and Ethics Newsweekly*, March 18, 2005, Episode 829. Available at http://pbs.org/wnet/religionandethics/week829/p-interview.html; accessed December 8, 2005.
[8] Woods, James. Review, *The New York Times*, November 28, 2004. Available at http://query.nytimes.com/gst/fullpage.html?res=9E004DC103FF93BA15752C1A92629C8....; accessed December 7, 2005.

[9] Siegel, Lee. *New York Magazine Book Review*, December 7, 2005. Available at http://www.newyorkmetro.com/nymetro/arts/books/reviews/10525.

[10] See my related articles, "Fiction and the Growth of Moral Consciousness: Attention and Evil," in *Analecta Husserliana XCII* (Springer, 2005), pp. 235–257; and "Literature and the Play of Attention: A New/Ancient Look at the Roots of Evil," in *Analecta Husserliana LXXXV* (Springer, 2005), pp. 655–674.

SECTION III

ALIRA ASHVO-MUÑOZ

INHERENT AND INTENTIONAL INQUIRIES ON VIRTUES

In the short narrative "Like the Night" by Alejo Carpentier, written in 1958, the text questions and investigates differing and conflicting possibilities that allow the reader to interpret and authenticate intentions and virtues such as faithfulness, honesty, and personal responsibilities. The main character, a soldier, constantly reflects on the situations he has to confront, which permits the differentiation of truth from falsity based on his intentionality and virtuosity. The narrative, divided in five parts or cantos, covers the history of literature in Western culture. It begins with *The Iliad* and follows a continuum until the fourth canto; then, in the fifth, it regresses to Classical Greece and mixes both time frames, contemporary and Classical, in a perfect temporal circularity.

The second canto also begins with a voyage, this time of Spaniards sailing to the Americas in their vessel, *La Gallarda,* to spread their religious ideology and gain economically from its natural resources. The soldier explains,

We should win thousands of souls to our holy religion and carry out Christ's commandments to the Apostles. We were soldiers of God as well as soldiers of the King, and by baptizing the Indians and freeing them from their barbarous superstitions our nation would win imperishable glory and greater happiness, prosperity, and power than all the Kingdoms of Europe. (Carpentier, 1970, 142)

The third canto continues a century later with a similar maritime enterprise during the eighteenth century, this time in the name of the King of France, and uses for its argument textual references from Montaigne's *Essais*:

Last night, with her eyes inflamed with weeping, her anxiety to know something about the world across the sea to which I was going had driven her to pick up Montaigne's *Essais* and read everything to do with America in the chapter on Coaches. There she had learned about the treachery of the Spaniards, and... (Carpentier, 1970, 144–145)

The *Essais* (1575) of Michel de Montaigne serve as a pedagogical guide through the main philosophical inquiries of the era. Existence is not a predicate; statements of existence are predications on concepts. The form of reasoning in Carpentier's text refers to the skepticism that appears in Montaigne's work, who lived a life of excess but ended his life in contemplation. The *Essais* contain essays very pertinent to this narrative, such as

VII, "Of Age"; IX, "Of Glory"; X, "Of Presumption"; XVII, "That to Study Philosophy is to Learn to Die"; XVIII "Of Vanity"; and XXI, "Of Experience." This compendium of twenty-one essays is a study of mankind and how it is not as great as it seems. Montaigne presents evidence of how this is the case and illustrates the value of knowing our faults and incapacities. Perceptions in the Aristotelian sense provide the foundations of the logic and syntax within a given statement. One finds in this canto a very different view than that of the previous one. Here the woman is the one who initiates the philosophical discussion and the one who confronts her mate, the soldier, with these issues. She tries to make him reason according to the premises in the *Essais* and analyze causes and future consequences. The author may be acknowledging this woman's power of persuasion or that she is particularly enlightened for her time, 1575.

The forth canto, a very short one, is concerned with preparations before a battle at a harbor reminiscent of the first canto, but this time in German lands and again centering on male–female relations. In the fifth canto, the plot returns to Troy and takes a new, postmodern direction in a setting that reflects an altered temporality including the classical perspective on our values, difficulties, and current philosophical inquiries. Time is circular in this narrative, which takes a universal premise, belonging to all times and places.

The beginning, in the first canto, occurs when King Agamemnon sends fifty vessels for the soldiers who will engage in the war against Troy. The central character of this saga is always an unnamed soldier who participates in the five different conflicts, presumably in temporal progression to the nineteen fifties, when the narrative was written, 1953. One sees in the central character, the soldier, a singular identity at different times; he remains the same while being different, a single character in a time continuum.

Throughout the five episodes, the virtues in question are personal as well as historical, with literary texts as points of references, even though they are basically the same premise with slight variations due to differential historical and cultural circumstances. All of them relate to circumstances and thoughts that sprout from someone's responsibilities in time of war. We have not change much, as Harold Pinter mentioned in his acceptance speech for the Wilfred Owen Award: "Yet we have learnt nothing" (Pinter, 2005, p. 1).

In each of the five cantos, the unnamed soldier tries to maintain personal integrity in spite of countless difficulties and occasional doubts. As time progresses toward the modern period, what change are the perceptions of others important to him—parents, lover, colleagues, and friends. Here one finds summarized references to literary texts concerning crucial historical moments in Western civilization. We as readers are unable to distinguish its verisimilitude from the literature and may differ on whether people in general have altered their feelings about war, but it seems odd that in Classical Greece everyone supported the enterprise. Maybe this oddness is a result of postmodernity, where dissent is common. Nevertheless, is clear that the soldier's engagement results from a sense of national responsibility and was not taken lightly, and that before he arrived at his commitment, he questioned in depth the endeavor and the many possible circumstances that might arise. While he thought that he was prepared for war, certain issues were beyond the scope of his imagination:

a manly understanding and the supreme triumph of a war that would give us prosperity, happiness, and pride in ourselves forever. I took a deep breath of the breeze blowing from the olive covered hillside and thought how splendid it would be to die in such a conflict, the cause of Reason itself. (Carpentier, 1970, p. 138)

The nameless soldier, despite adversities remains virtuous, fulfilling his duties, a demonstration of the importance of virtue in personal integrity. However, there are instances where the young, inexperienced soldier does not fully understand the nature of the enterprise. War is one of the most difficult human enterprises and requires a great deal of abnegation, maturity, and wisdom. It is contradictory that the less experienced are selected to carry out these plans. Enmeshed in this reality is a sense of adventure, which these men might not even recognize for what it is. In addition, pride is united with duty, which cannot be separated in many cases, establishing a conflict between ego and responsibility. Adding to the conflicting situations the unnamed character faces and is clearly unprepared for or never had imagined is the necessity for immediate reaction to the events that unfold. A distinction arises in certain circumstances that go from personal gains to responsibility. The text establishes a differentiation from a soldier to a commander. Virtue takes precedence because the unnamed soldier follows his true nature with little time for reasoning. As time evolves into the present, the reader perceives a pattern: in the classical era, literature captures the troops' credulity, but later this decreases. Those affected by the war—soldiers and families—question its cost. War here is a result of diplomatic failure. The end approaches as in quasi cynical mode when those close to him, including his commanders, benefit economically and covertly from the war, which at first makes him doubt the validity of what he committed himself to; after philosophical inquiries, however, he continues acting the same, never hesitates, and obeys orders even after he verifies that some of the commanders are corrupt, understanding that some do not represent all. Interestingly, at this time a change in parental attitude occurs, from their being proud to having more concern for their children's safety; some remained fearful, while others oppose war. Meanwhile the women they love show a varied range of feelings, going from praised to scorn. "She more than once called me a 'hero' as if she knew how cruelly her flattery contrasted with my sweetheart's unjust remarks" (Carpentier, 1970, p. 149).

Many women feel abandonment at their lover's departure, while others express a sense of betrayal, as their lives are altered irremediably when in most instances they have no say in the matter:

Before I could stop her, she had jumped out the window. I saw her running away as fast as she could among the olives, and I realized in that instant that it would be easier for me to enter the city of Troy without a scratch that to regain what I had lost. (Carpentier, 1970, p. 153)

These men seem to engage in little dialogue with their loved ones before deciding to go to war; if they are married, the women will not be able to overcome the pressures and difficulties that will arise without family support, and in case of the man's death, their children's lives will be altered forever. In the second canto, the Spanish episode, they cannot remarry. Constant internal monologues are forums for questioning personal behavior in war and in relation to war, which equally affects the lives of those who participate, their families, and their lovers. *The Iliad* does not address these conflicts. With the Age of Enlightenment and the *Essais*, these issues, values, and judgments of the participants begin to be considered, and as the narrative progresses into the twentieth century, the ambiguities are increasingly noted, especially after World War I, the "war to end all wars." As Pinter notes: "He [Wilfred Owen] articulated the tragedy, the horror, indeed the pity of war.... Yet we have learnt nothing" (Pinter, 2005, p. 1).

Humankind seems to continue engaging in war, but support for it varies according to each specific circumstance. All of the cantos show family members profoundly affected by the very nature of war as their children's lives become more precious than the cause the nation chooses to be involved in. The unnamed soldier is concerned with the philosophical and economic issues war creates. The essential function of the historical consciousness follows the call of these philosophical questionings, which permits an idealist presupposition of the power of reflective consciousness in personal experience. This demonstrates a method toward hermeneutic truth. The questioning is concerned with Husserl's concept of evidence: "Truth is an idea, whose particular case is an actual experience in the inwardly evident judgment" (Husserl, 1970, Vol. I, pp. 194–195).

This concept maintains the phenomenological maxim of inquiry through concealments brought about by traditional and historical interpretations, opposing argumentative attempts to create solutions by opposing the actual content (*Sachgehalt*) of the problem itself. The basic transcendental question concerns the possibility of having objective knowledge neither questioned nor answered in the analysis of actual knowledge-relation, an intentional investigation of the ontic experience in relationship to intentional and constitutive analyses; it demonstrates internal coherence in individual intentions; intentionality and meaning are internalized, a necessary transformation as part of a development of the transcendental-phenomenological. Is an inner finality easier to explain considering the resulting external influences; however, these questions cannot be answered by the analysis of the factual knowledge-relation between object and subject. The answer results when the knowledge relation is traced back to the presuppositions that created it and question the objective validity of the knowledge being discussed.

The question of transcendental idealism is comprehensible within its empirical reality as in his sacrifice in the name of the nation:

At this distance, it was impossible to tell women from men in the evening mist. Yet it was in order that this crowd of unknown human beings should go on existing that I was due to make my way to the ships soon after dawn. I should plow the stormy ocean during the winter months and land on a remote shore under attack from steel and fire, in defense of my countrymen's principles. (Carpentier, 1970, pp. 149–150)

His reflection is idealistic, which includes *Sinn* over *Sein*. He is doing this for his countrymen's principles, as he understands them. The perception is that this will be the last conflict, the battle for peace that many have been mentioned multiple times, as Pinter says, "Yet we have learnt nothing." Fluctuations, vacillations, and oppositions result from the critical or dogmatic motives he encounters; his critical determination undergoes intuitionistic-ontologistic reinterpretations as he faces the value and virtue of his actions and the war when he sees behind the expressions of idealism of his superiors an obscure materialistic bent profiting from the enterprise:

In fact behind the enterprise and the noble ideals it had set up as screen, a great many aims were concealed which would not benefit the combatants in the very least: above all, so the old soldier said, to sell more pottery, more cloth, more vases decorated with scenes from chariot races, and to open new ways of access to Asia, whose peoples had a passion for barter, and so put an end once and for all to Trojan competition. (Carpentier, 1970, pp. 154–155)

Disregarding these findings, the soldier remains firm as an idealist, knowing the sacrifices he will face. These passages question the transcendental ego as Husserl explains it: an individual existing ego, nonempirical, belonging to the nonontological subject, *Zocher*, where inner experience plays an empirical role and the transcendental ego is ontic. Various monologues show inner and outer perceptions related to immanent acts of subjective experience, transcendent objects of intentional forms of meaning. The soldier's actions are criticized and clarified by his actions in the historical intention. His experiences examine with self-clarity and evidential references through the historical, the literary, and the temporal while foregoing inherent and intentional inquiries on virtue. In the intention of consciousness, a critique forgoes a development of practices leading to free actions, casting light in his virtue. In order to carry out his duties, he ignores the criticism of others. His acts have to be carried out practically while his life is at risk; in desperation, he reacts with tears:

> Too heavily loaded with flour and men, the ship responded slowly to the oars. I gazed for a long time at the sunlit houses of my native town. I was nearly in tears. I took off my helmet and hid my eyes behind its crest. (Carpentier, 1970, p. 155)

This sense of sorrow and pity is an outcome he never prepared himself for. The arguments he heard could have changed his ideas and he could have become pragmatic, but in actuality he arrived at a deeper understanding, revealing to us a self-legitimization that shows his virtue in spite of the sad occurrences and distorted perceptions others might have had. He cries when others have become hardened and critical. The image of the soldier has undergone drastic changes from hero to antihero, culminating in a combination of both. New alignments or interests have taken place that question selfless behavior, others are practical, cynical, critical, and egotistic, creating the impossibility to accept selflessness. The world is like a carnival where enjoyment is prioritized over responsibility, the pursuit of happiness has been taken out of its proper context: "I realized that the display, excesses, and feasting that precede the departure of soldiers to the battlefield were now over" (Carpentier, 1970, p. 154).

He is unable to explain the reasoning behind his actions and sacrifices and of those like him; here the narrative reflects internal conflicts between mundane and transcendental meaning. The true nature of sacrifice lies in selflessness, his great virtue. The narrative deals with components and possibilities in dependent and independent fragments grounded in a unity, commentaries on literature and history that presuppose the inseparability of essence and facts. These relations constitute the foundation of the plot and gives value to its philosophical inquiries. At the end, he has undergone a complete transformation from an inexperienced young man to a mature wise man with a deeper sense of purpose than his contemporaries. War made him wiser, an experience theoretically valid within a correlative relationship to a pre-objective content based on transcendental conditions by the acquisition of personal experiences.

The speculative nature of the text aids the reader to question the consequences of a phenomenological intuitionist bias and the reciprocal nature of thoughts with actions, construed by his persona. The conclusion is not a critique of his actions but reassures values, virtues, and intentions; it shows true virtuosity based on selflessness. Criticism clarifies decisions in transcendental presuppositions; his true nature is better understood by unjust criticism. The realism intended is of an individual engaged in war and the process undergone in acquiring virtue through personal experiences in the worst circumstances, implying metaphysical idealism. Language, in the internal monologues, is a bearer of ideality in each specific inquiry; the intention being dealt with reactivates them by what was self-evident through his experiential sense. He does not easily become misdirected nor feels victimized since his virtues and sense experience are primordial to his character. Consciousness is not a hermeneutically sealed realm, is open in terms of its relation to other things and does not transcend the categorically structured field of knowledge in Kantian terms (Kant, 1958), the basis of Husserl's realism.

Truth is an investigation in process that shifts in the summary of perceptions, the soldier, his family, loved ones, commanders, the others (Derrida, 1967) and does not solely come from personal judgment. The plot goes in crescendo as the intensity of the questioning increases, and the last, fifth, canto is a *ritorno* (return), with the original premise in the *Iliad* seen as part of our postmodern reality comparing the intended and given: "I grew more and more angry at having exhausted my strength in all-too-familiar coupling, in the absurd belief that I was ensuring a future serenity by means of present excesses" (Carpentier, 1970, p. 152).

The narrative constitutes a judgment on intention of virtue and in its assertions, in statements that make truths assert more than its content.

Temple University, Philadelphia

BIBLIOGRAPHY

Arpaly, Nomy, *Unprincipled Virtue*, Oxford University Press, Oxford, 2004.
Bauman, Zygmunt, *Globalization, the Human Consequences*, Columbia University Press, New York, 1998.
Brainard, Marcus, *Belief and Its Neutralization, Husserl's System of Phenomenology in Ideas I*, State of University of New York, Albany, 2002.
Byers, Damian, *Intentionality and Transcendence. Closure and Openness in Husserl's Phenomenology*, University of Wisconsin Press/Noesis Press, Madison, Wisconsin, 2002.
Calhoun, Craig, ed., *Habermas and the Public Sphere*, MIT Press, Cambridge, Massachusetts, 1992.
Camps, Victoria, *La imaginación ética*, Seix Barral, Barcelona, 1983.
Carpentier, Alejo, "Like the Night" [original publication, 1958], in *War of Time*, Alfred A. Knopf, New York, 1970.

Coundouriotis, Eleni, *Claiming History*, Columbia University Press, New York, 1999.
Derrida, Jacques, *La Voix et le Phénomène*, Presses Universitaires de France, Paris, 1967.
Elveton, R.O., *Phenomenology of Husserl, Selected Critical Readings*, Quadrangle Books, Chicago, 1970.
Font, María Cecilia, *Mito y realidad en Alejo Carpentier*, Editorial Rodolfo Alonso, Madrid, 1984.
Habermas, Jürgen, *Moral Consciousness and communicative Action*, MIT Press, Cambridge, Massachusetts, 1990.
Husserl, Edmund, *Logical Investigations*, Volumes I, II, Humanities Press, New York, 1970.
Johnson, Barbara, *The Critical Difference, Essays in Contemporary Rhetoric of Reading*, Johns Hopkins University Press, Baltimore, 1985.
Kant, Immanuel, *Critique of Pure Reason*, Macmillan, London, 1958.
Levinas, Emanuel, *Existance and Existents*, Kluwer, Dordrecht, 1988.
Lynch, Michael P., *Truth in Context: An Essay on Pluralism and Objectivity*, MIT Press, Cambridge, Massachusetts, 1998.
McGinn, Colin, *The Problem of Consciousness: Essays Toward Resolution*, Blackwell Press, Oxford, 1993.
Merleau-Ponty, Maurice, *Le visible et l' invisible*, Gallimard, Paris, 1964.
Merleau-Ponty, Maurice, *Husserl and the Limits of Phenomenology*, Northwestern University Press, Evanston, Illinois, 2002.
Norris, Christopher, *What's Wrong With Postmodernism*, Johns Hopkins University Press, Baltimore, 1990.
Pinter, Harold, *Death etc.*, Grove Press, New York, 2005.
Tito, Johanna Maria, *Logic in the Husserlian Context*, Northwestern University Press, Evanston, Illinois, 2002.
Wegner, Daniel M., *The Illusions of Conscious Will*, MIT Press, Cambridge, Massachusetts, 2002.

RAYMOND J. WILSON III

STRIVING AND ACCEPTING LIMITS AS COMPETING META-VIRTUES

Goethe's *Faust* and Ibsen's *The Wild Duck*

What if a man with an ax in his hand and evil in his expression demands to know where your friend is? Do you tell the truth or tell a lie? This poses an ethical dilemma to someone who believes in always telling the truth. In Goethe's *Faust* and Ibsen's *The Wild Duck*, two great writers challenge any simplistic analysis of virtue. Phenomenology, a complex conceptual framework, can deal with the complexity of the ethical choices made in these two plays.

Hubert Dreyfus cites a striking example from Immanuel Kant that ethics cannot be a simple matter of following rules such as "never lie": "Faced with the dilemma posed by Kant—an avowed killer asking the whereabouts of the child's friend—the child might tell the truth." Dreyfus (1989) continues, "After experiencing regret and guilt over the death of the friend, however, the child would move toward the realization that the rule, 'Never lie,' ... needs to be contextualized" (p. 8). Kant draws his example from the profound end of the spectrum of possibilities; near the other end of the spectrum of possible issues of lying, we find answers to such questions as, "How do you like my new hat or haircut?" in which it would be ridiculous to insist on following the rule "never lie." A move to a higher level of conceptualization is needed to guide us as to when it is ethical to lie and when it is necessary to tell the truth. In *The Foundations of the Metaphysics of Morals*, Kant suggests a three-step procedure: (1) forming maxims such as "Never lie except when an innocent person will be harmed by the truth," (2) transforming the maxim into a universal law, and (3) following the law only in the cases in which it contains no logical contradiction and we can logically will that the law be applied universally. However, Dreyfus points out that the maxim also "will, under some circumstances, lead to regret." Therefore, he claims, "Finally, with enough experience, the ethical expert would learn to tell the truth or lie, depending upon the situation, without appeal to rules and maxims" (p. 9).

Dreyfus reaches these ideas by following three "methodological precautions":

1. We should begin by describing our everyday, ongoing ethical coping.
2. We should determine under which conditions deliberation and choice appear.
3. We should beware of making the typical philosophical mistake of reading the structure of deliberation and choice back into our account of everyday coping. (p. 3)

Relying on these guidelines, Dreyfus says that he "will lay out a phenomenological description of five stages in the development of expertise, using driving and chess as examples" (p. 3). In this essay, I will limit the examples to driving and refer the reader directly to Dreyfus' article for the parallel chess-learning examples. Using the driving example, Dreyfus develops what he calls "A Phenomenology of Skill Acquisition" (p. 3). This can then be applied to the acquisition of ethical expertise. I will supply examples from literature that, I hope, make Dreyfus's point specific.

Dreyfus's five stages are as follows.

In stage 1, "Novice," the "student automobile driver learns to recognize such interpretation-free features as speed (indicated by his speedometer). Timing of gear shifts is specified in terms of speed" (p. 3). The person follows rules, such as shift to second gear at five miles per hour, to third gear at fifteen miles per hour, and so on. We can see a literary example of stage 1 thinking in William Golding's *Lord of the Flies*. Here a group of boys crash land on an island with no adults and make their own rules. The first is that no one can speak at the assembly unless he is holding the conch, a shell that a boy named Ralph had used as a trumpet to call the other boys to a gathering. Another boy, Jack, "was on his feet. 'We'll have rules!' he cried excitedly. 'Lots of rules!'" (Golding, 1997, pp. 32–33). Although Golding presents an example of communal rule creation, the example externalizes the internal situation of a person beginning to develop a self-governing ethical system. The novel depicts what happens when even this elementary ethical system breaks down. Toward the end, a boy called Piggy asks "Which is better—to have rules and agree, or to hunt and kill" (p. 208). "Which is better, law and rescue, or hunting and breaking things up?" (p. 208). Roger gives the answer of the wild pack of boys. He rolls a boulder down a hill and kills Piggy.

In stage 2, "Advanced Beginner," the person progresses from following strict rules to forming "situational maxims" for herself—learning, for example, to "shift up when the motor sounds like it is racing and down when it sounds like it is straining" (Dreyfus, 1989, p. 4). In Ibsen's *A Doll's House*, for example, Nora reveals a "when x happens, I will do y" strategy that is analogous to what I take Dreyfus to be describing. Nora tells Christine that she will help her old friend get a job in the bank where Nora's husband will soon manage: "Just leave it to me; I will broach the subject very cleverly—I will think of something that will please him very much. It will make me so happy to be of some use to you" (Ibsen, 1879, p. 19). Putting this into the form of a maxim, it would be, "when I want to help a friend in need, and the help requires my husband to take action, I will do something to please my husband and put him in a good mood, and while he is in the mood, I will ask him to help my friend." In this way, Nora remains within the virtue of being a submissive wife and can still help her friend. According to Dreyfus, "Familiar situations begin to be accompanied by emotions such as hope, fear, etc." (p. 5). Of course, such feelings form the essence of drama.

In stage 3, "Competence," Dreyfus points out that with "increasing experience," the person "learns to adopt a hierarchical view of decision-making" (p. 4). Approaching a steep curve in the rain, for example, a competent driver "has to decide whether to let up on the accelerator, remove his foot altogether, or step on the brake. He is relieved when he gets through the curve without mishap and shaken if he begins to go into a skid" (p. 4). Ibsen's *A Doll's House* illustrates Nora's progress from advanced beginner to competent; she moves away from rule-following duty to a higher level of judgment. Her husband evokes the rules of duty when he says, "It's shocking. This is how you would neglect your most sacred duties" (Ibsen, 1879, p. 69).

To advance to stage 4, "Proficiency," the "competent performer stops reflecting on problematic situations as a detached observer, and stops looking for principles to guide his actions" (Dreyfus, 1989, p. 6); "No longer is the spell of involvement broken by detached conscious planning" (Dreyfus, 1989, p. 6). Nora seems to be in this zone when she announces her departure: "I know only that it is necessary for me" (Ibsen, 1879, p. 69).

While the "proficient performer, immersed in the world of skillful activity, sees what needs to be done, but must decide how to do it," in stage 5, "Expertise," the driver advances to a new way of proceeding. The "expert driver" simply does what must be done "generally without any attention" (Dreyfus, 1989, p. 6). Something similar happens when Huck Finn paddles off from the raft "all in a sweat to tell on" Jim. However, when he meets "a skiff with two men in it, with guns," men who are by coincidence searching for escaped slaves, Huck finds he cannot tell on Jim and instead scares the men off. He tells a lie that his family members on the raft are sick, and tricks them into believing that the family members have smallpox (Twain, 1885, p. 74). Thus, without reflection, Huck simply acts the ethically correct way—he tells a lie!

Dreyfus summarizes:

It seems that beginners make judgments using strict rules and features, but that with talent and a great deal of involved experience the beginner develops into an expert who sees intuitively what to do without applying rules and making judgments at all. The intellectualist tradition has given an accurate description of the beginner and of the expert facing an unfamiliar situation, but normally an expert does not deliberate. He does not reason. He does not even act deliberately. He simply spontaneously does what has normally worked and, naturally, it normally works. (Dreyfus, 1989, p. 7)

Literary works sometimes present what I will call meta-virtues; these are not principles under which all actions can be judged, but statements that attempt to identify the automatic actions of ethical experts. Two competing meta-virtues are striving and accepting limits. To illustrate: if striving is accepted as the meta-virtue, actions normally considered unethical, such as lying, would be accepted as ethical if they are part of a pattern of striving. The conflict between striving and accepting limits is played out in the "Prelude on Stage" in Goethe's *Faust*, in a conversation among three characters: a poet, a director, and a clown. The striving poet wants to make art that will bring him renown in posterity. The director, accepting the limits imposed by the needs of a typical playgoer, wants something "lively," "novel," "pleasant," and full of "action." Of course, the play must be "not meaningless" (Goethe, 1970, p. 3), but the poet must keep the limitations of the audience members in mind: one audience member "comes because he's bored and another comes from gorging at the dinner table"; others come out of "curiosity"; ladies come to show off "their finery" (p. 4). These conditions create the limits under which the writer must work if the play is to be a success: "coarse, cold-hearted people" are "hard to please" (p. 4). People can only understand "in snatches," anyway, so if "you present them an artistic whole," you're wasting your time. They are looking for entertainment, not art. Coming to the support of the director's desire to accept limits, the clown says to forget "posterity." If poets think only about future generations singing their praises, "who would amuse the people now?" And "don't forget, there has to be some clowning, too" (p. 3). The poet tells them to "get someone else to do your dirty work" (p. 4). He wants, "driving passions—the deep happiness that hurts, the force of hate, the power of love." He calls on the experience of creation to "make me young again" (p. 5). Thus, Goethe has put the appreciation of striving in contention with the view that the greatest virtue is that of accepting limits. A second prologue further specifies the conflict.

In the "Prologue in Heaven," Mephistopheles suggests to God that God has made a mistake in creating humanity. "It would be better for them if you hadn't given them the light of heaven. They call it their reason and all they use it for is to make themselves more bestial than the beasts"; humans "bury their noses in all the dirt they find" (p. 6). "Men's lives are so miserable I'm sorry for them" (p. 6). To this implication that God, despite claiming to be all-knowing and perfect, has, in fact, made a mistake, the Lord asks, "Do you know Faust?" (p. 6). The devil scoffs, but the Lord insists that, even though Faust is striving in "darkness," his striving justifies all he does (p. 7).

Goethe's striving is the meta-virtue by which we can judge if an action is ethical or not. His play *Faust* then illustrates this principle. By having the Lord refer to the generic "man" rather than always saying "this man Faust," Goethe generalizes his point and makes Faust a symbol for all humanity. As long as humanity strives, it will eventually be saved. Only if humanity stops striving is it damned. Mephistopheles offers to bet that, given a free hand by God, Mephistopheles can offer Faust enough to satisfy Faust (and all humanity by implication) and make him stop striving, and says, "I'm not afraid of losing my bet" (p. 7). However, a close reading reveals that God never accepts the bet; he merely says, "I give you complete freedom as I always have" (p. 7). Beings such as Mephistopheles prod humanity into action and promote striving. The scene is an exact evocation of the book of Job, with the difference that in Job, God gives Satan a free hand to harm Job as much as he wishes to see if Job will curse God, while in *Faust*, God gives Mephistopheles a free hand to help Faust as much as possible to see if the devil can make Faust sufficiently satisfied to induce him to stop striving. The underlying assumption is implied: most humans do not know it, but they are striving to reach God. As long as they continue to strive, they will some day reach Him. Such a meta-virtue principle will tell us when it is ethical to lie and when to tell the truth.

In the play itself, beyond the two prologues, we find Faust in a similar situation with Marlowe's Dr. Faustus: Faust says, "I've worked right through philosophy, right through medicine and jurisprudence, as they call it, and that wretched theology too" (p. 8). But because he sees "plainly that we don't and can't know anything," he has "lost all joy in life" (p. 8). He has turned to magic to "discover, it may be, what it is that holds the world together, behold with my own eyes its innermost workings, and stop all this fooling with words" (p. 8).

When Mephistopheles appears to Faust, he identifies himself: "I am the spirit that always negates, and rightly so, since everything that comes into existence is only fit to go out of existence" (p. 21). Unlike Marlowe's Dr. Faustus, who signed a contract with the devil, selling his soul for twenty-four years to have Mephistopheles as his servant, Goethe's Faust makes a bet with the devil:

> If ever I lie down in idleness and contentment, let that be the end of me, let that be final. If you can delude me into feeling pleased with myself, if your good things ever get the better of me, then may that day be my last day. This is my wager. (p. 25)

The famous phrases follow in Faust's next sentences: "If ever the passing moment is such that I wish it not to pass and I say to it 'You are beautiful, stay a while,' then let that be the finish" (p. 25).

Faust states his goal:

> All that is given to humanity, total humanity, to experience I desire to experience in my own person, the heights and the depths of it, the weal and the woe, to enlarge myself in this way to humanity's size, and to smash up with the rest of humanity in the end. (p. 26)

Throughout the play, Faust commits many actions that break moral rules like the Kantian example, "Never lie." In Act One, Faust seduces and impregnates Gretchen, a simple teenaged girl, and abandons her after killing her brother. Faust has gone on to more interesting pursuits, striving to understand the occult through participating in Walpurgis Night on the Brocken Mountain. Sensing, probably, that he was losing his bet, Mephistopheles had tried to lure him back, hoping that Faust will be happy with Gretchen, that he would be enticed into contentment at the image of happiness with a loving wife and perfect child, within the enclosure of the bourgeois home. Then, Faust might say to the passing moment, "You are beautiful, stay a while." That is why Mephistopheles got her for him. But Faust had seen the feminine ideal through Gretchen, and that is why he wanted her. That is also why he is unsatisfied when he has her. He has the real girl. That is not what he was striving for. He strove for the ideal that Faust saw through her. Based on the "Prologue in Heaven," we can assume that the ideal of feminine beauty is not the ultimate. Behind it is a larger ideal of beauty itself, and behind that is the source of all beauty, God. Not finding in Gretchen what he sought, Faust drifts on, away from her. Alone, Gretchen hides her pregnancy and drowns the baby after its birth to avoid shame. Caught, she is condemned to death. Faust does try to rescue her after learning of her situation, but she chooses death as the expiation of her crime, and a voice from above says she is saved.

The striving continues: Faust strives, but does not know what he seeks. In a later episode, Faust sees a vision of Helen. He goes to the underworld and rescues her; he woos and wins her. He still is not satisfied because, although she is an earthly beauty over whom whole nations had battled for ten years, he discovers that she is not the ideal of the feminine toward which he is striving. When their child dies, she fades back into the underworld. Yet, if we take the words of God in the "Prologue in Heaven" seriously as Goethe's intent, the feminine ideal is not the ultimate. Faust—that is, humanity—will never be satisfied by anything short of God. Faust is thrashing around "in the dark" and, without knowing it, is striving to reach the light.

Throughout the play, Faust continues striving through many adventures, until, in the last act, he has created his own kingdom. Faust uses devils as pirates to bring in treasure to finance his project of adding to his kingdom by reclaiming land from the sea. He sends his devils to evict an old couple from the only land in his domain that he does not own. Mephistopheles says, "What we're doing is an old story. Naboth's vineyard all over again" (p. 192). The reference is to I Kings 21, in which King Ahab coveted Naboth's vineyard. Naboth's wife Jezebel ordered Naboth to be falsely accused and killed and his land seized for the king. Similarly, the two people in Goethe's *Faust* resist, and Faust's agents kill them. Shortly afterward, Faust renounces the devil's aid and suddenly becomes a 100-year-old dying man. An allegorical messenger suggests that he repent, but he decides not to do so: "I've just raced through the world, seizing what I fancied," Faust says. He says a man should "find his pleasure and his pain in moving on and on, knowing he'll never be satisfied" (p. 195). Faust does not say he calculated and decided that his actions are ethical. He reports that he just acted and reacted like the ethical expert in Dreyfus's analysis: "normally an expert does not deliberate. He does not reason. He does not even act deliberately. He simply spontaneously does what has normally worked and, naturally, it normally works" (Dreyfus, 1989, p. 7).

Let us further dramatize Goethe's point by following out the comparison to the biblical reference. In the Bible story, the Prophet Elijah demands that Ahab repent, and Ahab humbles himself; "because he humbleth himself before me," God says to Elijah, "I will not bring evil in his days" (I Kings 21, 29). In having Faust refuse to repent and humble himself, Goethe specifically reverses the biblical situation near the end of the play, just as he had reversed the Job story near the beginning. Even a king so famous for arrogance that his name became a literary icon for obsession (as Herman Melville's later use of it for his obsessed captain in *Moby Dick* illustrates) had repented and humbled himself. Faust, however, in the parallel situation with the biblical Ahab, refused to abandon his striving way of thought.

The play's ending further supports the position that Goethe is justifying all of Faust's actions as part of his striving. Faust hears the devils digging his grave and thinks it is his men expanding his kingdom "opening up living space for millions" (Goethe, 1970, p. 196). "Oh how I'd love to see that lusty throng and stand on a free soil with a free people" (p. 197). Imagining that his striving has set off a process that will continue for hundreds of years, he says, "Now I could almost say to the passing moment: Stay, oh stay a while, you are beautiful" (p. 197). The devil, hearing the words of forfeit, insists he's won the bet, but angels come and escort Faust's soul to heaven. "Angels," carrying Faust's soul, say, "This noble member of the spirit-world is saved from evil. *He who strives and ever strives, him we can redeem*" (p. 201, my italics).[1] Goethe thus reverses Marlowe's Dr. Faustus, who declined to repent and went to hell, if the overt interpretation stands. If Marlowe did covertly open the door for an interpretation that Faustus might have been spared, he had to do so covertly, and even if it is true, Marlowe's Dr. Faustus could only have been saved if he repented.

Goethe has Faust commit one last crime, stealing the land from the elderly couple and indirectly causing their deaths. Like Don Giovanni in the opera of Mozart and Da Porte, Faust refuses to repent when ordered to do so by a supernatural, probably allegorical figure. But unlike Mozart, who had Don Giovanni dragged down to hell, Goethe has Faust escorted by angels to heaven, where it is announced that he will be reunited with Gretchen.

The explanation that makes sense of the play's actions is that Goethe sets up "striving" as a meta-virtue by which to measure the ethicality of actions. Even murder is acceptable to the striver, just as lying is acceptable for the little boy in the example given by Kant. In setting up striving as the meta-virtue, Goethe implies that seducing and abandoning a clueless girl, piracy, stealing land and causing the deaths of its owners, along with any lies Faust might have told are all justified in their circumstances because Faust is striving. Goethe thus makes striving a meta-virtue.

Many years later, Klaus Mann wrote a novel called *Mephisto* in which an actor who is famous for playing Mephistopheles in Goethe's *Faust* joins the Nazis in order to keep performing in Germany after they come to power. In Klaus Mann's *Mephisto*, a character called "the Prime Minister," a uniformed fat man, loves the actor's portrayal of Mephisto:

"You're the first person to make me understand this character," said the general. "He really is splendid! And isn't there a little of him in us all? I mean, hidden in every real German isn't there a bit of Mephistopheles, a bit of the rascal and the ruffian? If we had nothing but the soul of Faust, what would become of us? It would be a pushover for our many enemies! No, no—Mephisto, too, is a German national hero. But it's better not go around telling people that." (Mann, 1977, p. 189).

The Nazis, by implication, take for themselves the task of bringing out the Mephisto in the soul of the German people. Symbolically, Mann makes the Nazis the Mephistopheles to the Faust of the German people. Mann wrote *Mephisto* in 1936, but given the record of the Nazis in history, he obviously discredits Goethe's position that striving is a virtue that makes all of a person's otherwise unethical actions into ethical ones.

Not surprisingly, an answer had already been made to Goethe's glorification of striving as the meta-virtue, an answer given by Henrik Ibsen. Ibsen started out writing in Goethe's mode. *The Pretenders*, an early play, was one of countless plays in European languages that echoed Goethe's *Gotz von Berlichingen*, and even contemporaries, such as the German critic Eugene Zabel, noticed that "both *Brand* and *Peer Gynt* had much in common with Goethe's *Faust*," as Michael Meyer (1985, p. 497) points out. Both are verse dramas that ignore any restrictions imposed by the supposed economics of production and abolish the distinction between the natural and the supernatural. Plot elements support the idea of similarity. In *Brand*, Ibsen reproduces the "Helen" episode of *Faust*; in both plays, a child dies and the mother dies in grief, launching the grieving husband on a search for the transcendent. In *Peer Gynt*, the title character seduces a young woman and abandons her, goes forth to a life of questing adventure, and is reunited to her in what might be an after-death experience. "Like Goethe's Faust, Peer, too, is saved in the end, although we are apt to wonder why," says Raymond Canon, Peer "having been saved by what many have considered as a too apparent *deus ex machina*," also a similarity to the ending of Goethe's *Faust* (Canon, 1967, p. 7). Bernard Shaw said, "Peer Gynt will finally smash anti-Ibsenism in Europe, because Peer is everybody's hero. He has the same effect on the imagination that Hamlet, Faust, and Mozart's Don Juan have had" (quoted in Meyer, 1985, pp. 779–780). However, in Ibsen's later life, as Meyer tells us, "when anyone spoke, as Germans often did, of Goethe's *grosse, reine Liebe* (great, pure love), Ibsen would laconically comment, 'That damned old goat!' ' (p. 487). By then, Ibsen had made a radical departure from the Goethean mode. He had become a realist to express what he wanted to say about his society.

One of his great realist plays, *The Wild Duck*, pits the concept of striving ironically up against that of accepting limits. Gregers Werle represents the idea of striving as the meta-virtue. He presents the "claim of the ideal"; the metaphor is of a bill collector who presents the claim of the creditor and demands payment. The payment he demands is that the person to whom he submits the claim must strive to reach the ideal and not be satisfied with the ordinary. Dr. Relling represents the concept that accepting limits is the meta-virtue. Relling no longer practices as a regular doctor. Long ago, he noticed that most of the ills of his patients came from self-loathing. The reader thinks of suicidal depression, drug addiction, and alcoholism, all derived from seeing one's self not measuring up to high expectations. Relling figures out and offers his "patients" a life-lie: "Rob the average man of his life-lie, and you rob him of his happiness at the same stroke," says Relling. Without their life-lie, most people "would have succumbed to self-contempt and despair many a long year ago" (Act Five). This fits neatly with Kant's example, detailed earlier in this essay, that in some circumstances, telling a lie might be the ethically correct action.

Gregers and Dr. Relling contend for the life of Hialmar Ekdal. Gregers—the advocate of striving—says, "Dr. Relling, I shall not give up the struggle until I have rescued Hialmar from your clutches!" (Act Five). Relling has given Hialmar the life-lie that he is a great inventor. Believing this, Hialmar can live with the disgrace and loss of status resulting from his father's serving a prison term for fraud. He can believe not only that he is no ordinary shopkeeper who is married to a former servant woman, but also that he will some day soon be able to demand respect for himself, his father, and his wife. Gregers has discovered that Hialmar's wife Gina was once the mistress of Gregers's father Old Werle, who may even be the father of Gina's daughter Hedvig. Old Werle had set Hialmar up in his photography business and enabled him to marry Gina. Gregers informs Hialmar that Gina was once another man's mistress, expecting him to answer the call of the ideal and build a perfect marriage on the basis of "truth." The result is disaster.

Hialmar says he will leave forever. Gina, knowing he loves to dramatize himself with high-sounding speeches, plays along, expecting that her husband will not leave or that he will soon be back. Events indicate that she has read her husband correctly, for at Gina's suggestion, he stays one extra day. He even agrees to Gina packing a lunch for him to take with him. Meanwhile, Hialmar tells Hedvig that he would like to wring the neck of her pet wild duck because they got the duck from Old Werle, his wife's former lover; "I ought not to tolerate under my roof a creature that has been through those hands," he says in Act Four. When eventually Hialmar realizes that Hedvig is probably not his daughter as he has believed for her entire life, he tells the thirteen-year-old girl: "Don't come near me, Hedvig! Keep far away. I cannot bear to see you," (Act Four). Although Hedvig can't understand the adult facts, she guesses that "Perhaps I'm not really father's child." When Gregers asks uneasily, "How could that be?" Hedvig suggests that "Mother might have found me. And perhaps father has just got to know it; I've read of such things" (Act Four). Hialmar states in Hedvig's presence that he cannot live in this house while Hedvig is present. Every time he sees her, the daughter of another man whom he had been tricked into believing to be his own child, he is he is reminded of his humiliation. He leaves.

Gregers now presents the claim of the ideal to Hedvig, asking her to shoot the wild duck: "Suppose you were to make a free-will offering, for his sake, of the dearest treasure you have in the world!" Then, Gregers assures Hedvig, her father would love her again. When Hedvig admits the next day that she has not shot the wild duck, Gregers tells her that her father will return if she does so: "Oh, if only your eyes had been opened to that which gives life its value—if you possessed the true, joyous, fearless spirit of sacrifice, you would soon see how he would come up to you.—But I believe in you still, Hedvig" (Act Five).

Hedvig, perhaps, sees the parallel: they got the wild duck from Werle, and they got her from Werle. With that and her love for her pet, Hedvig decides to shoot herself instead. Having pitted the call of the ideal (the meta-virtue of striving) against the meta-virtue of accepting limits, Ibsen demonstrates that in this instance striving leads to tragedy.

But is Ibsen on the side of the force that drives the play to a tragic conclusion, or against it? The fact that a tragic death occurs near the end does not, in itself, mean that the author opposes the reasoning that led to it. Sophocles, for example, may have been more in favor of Antigone's position than of Creon. If so, Antigone's death stands as a glorification of her view and a condemnation of Creon's. If the play ended with Hedvig's death, the answer might be undecipherable.

However, Ibsen gives us a clue by continuing the play long enough for Gregers and Dr. Relling to debate her death's significance. Gregers claims that "Hedvig has not died in vain. Did you not see how sorrow set free what is noble in him?" Relling answers, "Most people are ennobled by the actual presence of death. But how long do you suppose this nobility will last in him?"

We will talk of this again, when the grass has first withered on her grave. Then you'll hear him spouting about 'the child too early torn from her father's heart;' then you'll see him steep himself in a syrup of sentiment and self-admiration and self-pity. Just you wait! (Act Five)

Gregers answers, "If you are right and I am wrong, then life is not worth living." Relling replies in the bill-collecting metaphor that Gregers created: "Oh, life would be quite tolerable, after all, if only we could be rid of the confounded duns that keep on pestering us, in our poverty, with the claim of the ideal." Relling lies to people, and he induces them to accept a life-lie about themselves that enables them to live happily within the limits that life puts upon them. Thus, I believe, Ibsen tips the scale against the idea that striving for the ideal justifies actions. The scale tips in favor of accepting limits as a meta-virtue that justifies Relling's lies and any other questionable act that helps people accept limits and live happily. In doing so, Ibsen refutes the theme of Goethe's *Faust*, just as Ibsen had abandoned Goethe's mode of writing that had inspired him in his youth, enabling Ibsen to become a creator of realistic drama, and it helps explain why Ibsen had taken to calling Goethe an "old goat."

Department of Language and Literature, Loras College
Dubuque, Iowa

NOTE

[1] The next line introduces a possibility of an interpretation—with which I disagree—that softens Goethe's apparent conflict with Christianity: "And if love from on high is also his, the angels welcome him" (p. 201). Although Gretchen is not mentioned in Act Five until after Faust reaches heaven, it is possible to interpret that the "love from on high" is hers, that perhaps he is saved by her prayers. The straightforward assumption, however, is that the love from above is God's love, that of the Lord in the "Prologue in Heaven" whose claim that Faust is striving to reach Him set up the entire sequence of actions in the play. The Lord does not say that Faust can be saved despite his bad behavior if a soul in Heaven prays for him. For the "saved-by-Gretchen's-prayers" interpretation, there is a type of "back-door" support: "roses of love" were used to distract the devils when they saved Faust from them; an angel reveals that the roses came from the "penitent women"; and Gretchen is subsequently identified as a member of this chorus. However, such an interpretation would change the play's theme. It would now be that if a man seduces and abandons a woman who dies as an indirect result of his indifference to her, and her soul in heaven still loves him enough to pray that he be saved despite his lack of repentance, then he goes to heaven. That would mean that all of Faust's striving would not have justified him except for the fact that, with the devil's help, he had aroused love in Gretchen that no behavior of his, no matter how bad, could discourage. This strikes me as unlikely to be the import of the play's full text.

REFERENCES

Dreyfus, Hubert. "What is Moral Maturity? A Phenomenological Account of the Development of Ethical Expertise" (1989). Available at http://www.berkeley.edu. See Departments, P, Philosophy, Hubert Dreyfus, Home Page, Selected Papers.
Goethe, Johann von. *Goethe's Faust* [1832]. Translated by Barker Fairley. Toronto: University of Toronto Press, 1970.
Golding, William. *Lord of the Flies* [1954]. New York: Penguin, 1997.
Henrik Ibsen (1879). *A Doll's House. Four Major Plays*. New York: Airmont, 1966: pp. 11–72.
Ibsen, Henrik. *The Wild Duck* [1884]. New York: Boni and Liveright. Loras College Library On-line Books Page.
Mann, Klaus. *Mephisto* (1936). Translated by Robin Smith. New York, Penguin, 1977.
Meyer, Michael. *Ibsen* [1967]. Abridged by the author. New York: Penguin, 1985.
Twain, Mark. *The Adventures of Huckleberry Finn* [1885]. New York: Norton, 1960.
Raymond Canon (1967). "Introduction" to Henrik Ibsen, *Peer Gynt* (1867)., New York: Airmont, pp. 3–8.

PETER WEIGEL

HAPPINESS, DIVISION, AND ILLUSIONS OF THE SELF IN PLATO'S *SYMPOSIUM*

Plato's *Symposium* understands love (*eros*) as a force both dividing and integrating the self in its search for happiness (*eudaimonia*). The good life involves love as a harmonizing force in the psyche that brings together elements of the self that are normally in opposition.[1] The work also explores how a person can fail to unite these elements and instead live according to illusory views of the self and the world. Plato shows that happiness is not possible in these circumstances.

The *Symposium* prominently features the theme of things "splitting" into opposing elements. These elements in opposition call for proper integration in view of a larger whole. The person is divided into a body and soul, each with its corresponding type of *eros*. The self is divided from others, and the individual from the polity. The human world and divine order are separate. The changing physical world is separate from the spiritual order and its eternal, unchanging Platonic forms. Similarly, Plato divides love, beauty, and the good into higher and lower kinds. The *Symposium* ties the good life and the completion of the self to integrating these paired opposites in due proportion to their value. The self must do so in relation to time and in light of its own mortality. An illusory and incomplete self emerges from one of these opposites being denied or diminished, and the self cannot grasp its relation to time.

My approach in this essay is more exploratory than exhaustive and keeps the nonexpert in view. By keeping mostly to the *Symposium*, I aim for brevity and a strong focus, although I note some parallels with other dialogues. Section I examines the dialogue's setting. Section II sees the speech of Phaedrus as introducing some major themes. Section III examines Pausanias and Eryximachus effecting a doubling of *eros* and a lowering of spiritual *eros* to the bodily plain. Section IV considers Aristophanes's attempt to heal the division of *eros* and place the happiness of the self in romantic love. Section V looks at Agathon's aestheticism as a foil to Socrates's philosophical life. Section VI treats the climactic speech of Socrates and Section VII the significance of Alcibiades's intrusion. Section VIII briefly draws some conclusions.

I. THE SETTING

The setting introduces the theme of opposition and splitting, as well as the notion of temporality, as a backdrop in the speeches. It does this by underscoring a layering of temporal periods as well as of narrative accounts of the party. The setting also alludes to the destructive potential of *eros* for the individual and the polis. It suggests the philosophical channeling of *eros* to offset its chaotic potential.

The opening finds Apollodorus relating the events of the dinner party to an anonymous Friend. It is sometime between 406 and 400 BC and is likely within a few years of Socrates's execution in 399.[2] Apollodorus tells the Friend "just the other day" he gave an account to Glaucon (172a), who could be Plato's brother in the *Republic*. The dialogue then briefly relates Apollodorus's meeting with Glaucon. This constitutes a doubling of the narrative setting. The setting also contains the further setting of the dinner party for the speeches.

The setting showcases a division of temporal periods. The dinner is set on a night in January of 416 BC, celebrating Agathon's first victory for his tragedy. Glaucon is oddly confused that the celebration might be for a more recent event, even though Apollodorus notes that Glaucon must realize that Agathon moved from Athens many years previously (172c). Plato is composing the dialogue in middle age, after 385 BC. The *Symposium* appears to postdate the *Phaedrus* and to be more or less contemporaneous with the *Republic*. The reader is looking back on Plato and his immortalization of the dinner and its characters by way of an exchange some years afterward. Both the setting and the dinner point toward the time of Socrates's execution. The dialogue thus underscores the fleetingness of important people and events. The narrative and the events of the dinner described in it point beyond their own temporality and immediate historical circumstances.

Paralleling the divisions of temporal periods is a layering of various accounts of the dinner. Apollodorus tells his story twice, first to Glaucon and then to the Friend. Glaucon hears it twice (the first account is weaker than the second). He heard it first from another unnamed man before finding Apollodorus. Aristodemus, who was present at the dinner, is the common source of both narrative lines. Aristodemus told Apollodorus and also separately told Phoenix, who then told Glaucon's unnamed source. The proliferation of narrative copies of the events prefigures in Diotima's account of love the ascent to absolute beauty through various imitative levels. Similarly, the search for philosophical truth demands the comparison of the varying accounts of love for their quality and accuracy. Sorting through the confusing temporal and narrative strands in the setting parallels the way the speakers on love have us peel away outward appearances. The distinctive elements of a whole must be separated and analyzed before they are recombined into a larger picture. (The varying accounts also allow Plato the license to supply his own fictional details of the dinner and the speech. It is not known if the dinner actually occurred, although the main speakers appear to have been historical figures.)

Finally, the setting also introduces the separation of properly ordered *eros* from its chaotic and darker side. The dialogue explores the connection of *eros* with enmity or strife (*eris*). The setting has us consider three erratic personalities who are lovers of Socrates—Alcibiades, Aristodemus, and Apollodorus. Plato presents the latter two as almost complementary selves of Socrates. (Alcibiades by the end of the dialogue is virtually his complementary half.) Apollodorus is a self-described "maniac" who "makes it his business to know everything Socrates says and does everyday" (172e). Hard on himself and on everyone else, except for Socrates, he wallows in his self-condemnation, as will Alcibiades in his speech later. Aristodemus is a small, barefoot shadow of Socrates, who comes to the party uninvited. His name is a play on the word for strife (*eris*). The goddess Eris came uninvited to the marriage celebration of Peleus and the goddess Thetis, the mother of Achilles.[3] Eris tosses an apple marked for "the most beautiful" among Hera, Aphrodite, and Athena. Zeus has Paris settle the dispute among the three. His choice of Athena fuels the Trojan War. Socrates, the lover of wisdom, is tailed by a pair of dolorous and obsessive lovers, Apollodorus and Aristodemus. They are pathetic copies of Socrates's original and more dangerous lover, Alcibiades.

On the way to the party, Socrates splits off from Aristodemus to stand in motionless contemplation on a neighbor's porch. He enters the world of timeless contemplation, separating himself from all concern for the physical and everyday world. Unconcerned with courtesy or convention, Socrates arrives halfway through dinner. Taking the other side of a double coach with Agathon, whose name in Greek means "Goodman," Socrates promptly insults the host when Agathon speaks of absorbing some of Socrates's wisdom. Of course, the contention that wisdom cannot travel from teacher to pupil by osmosis will be part of Socrates's downfall. A similar request for wisdom from Alcibiades is also accorded an ironic and highly cutting rebuff. Plato might be inviting us to consider the larger effects of a habitual irony and distance toward people. The low estimation of Agathon's wisdom also anticipates the contest later in the dialogue between respective claims of poetic and philosophical wisdom. There is the odd contrast of Agathon's physical beauty and showy literary renown next to the inner virtue of Socrates, who was never good-looking and is now past his prime.

Erixymachus's proposal to put aside deep drinking for formal speechmaking suggests that Apollo will initially preside at the party instead of Dionysius, two antipodes of human nature. The flute-girl (a symbol of sexuality) is sent away. The harmonious effects of reason and eloquent conversation associated with Apollo will dominate. Put to one side is the god of wine, revelry, and the savage disorder of the passions when reason sleeps. The somewhat nobler side of Dionysius is represented by the dramatic talents of Agathon and Aristophanes. (Athens celebrated the festival of Dionysius—the Greater Dionysia—with public drunkenness and drama; it served as a venue for the comedies of Aristophanes and the tragedies of Aeschylus, Sophocles, and Euripides.) The rougher side of Dionysius of course reasserts itself at the end when Alcibiades and later a final wave of revelers break into the party.

The dinner party signifies a protective sphere of reason and ordered harmony in the face of darker entropic forces closing in on the society and the speakers. The two lovers central to the dialogue, Socrates and Alcibiades, are central to the fate of Athens. Both will succumb to politically motivated murder. The party occurs in the year prior to the ill-fated Sicilian expedition. Alcibiades is called back from it to face charges of instigating the mutilation of Hermae in Athens and of mocking the Eleusinian mysteries. He will betray Athens for Sparta and later be assassinated. The Athenians will interpret the mutilation as a tyrannical conspiracy and execute Athenians on questionable evidence, after suspending the normal legal standards and procedures.[4] The Peloponnesian War with Sparta will combine with political infighting to divide and deplete the culture. The dialogue and its historical allusions raise the question of whether the harmony of reason can prevail in the polity over the forces of chaos and individual selfishness. In a dialogue on *eros*, Plato is suggesting that *eris* will in great measure have the last word in Athens, despite the final image of a clear-headed Socrates ambling off into the Apollonian sunrise. The dialogue is a calm, Socratic oasis for modeling the proper role and nature of eros, in contrast to its destructive mishandling in the surrounding society.

II. PHAEDRUS

Phaedrus is the first to speak. The first half of his speech establishes romantic love between males as the preferred paradigm for *eros*. His underlying idea is that the lover loves an idealized image of the self. The second part discusses examples of lovers who sacrificed themselves. The speech raises the problem of how love rewards the lover, often despite appearances. Love promises plenitude and self-fulfillment for the lover. It also asks that the lover give himself over to something greater than the self. Can love be altruistic, or is it fundamentally only about the self? Plato will view the dichotomy as somewhat falsely conceived. It will be left to Diotima to consider how altruistic and self-regarding motives are related to each other in matters of love.

Phaedrus downplays love's connection with strife, particularly in discussing the god's origins. He assures the party that love always engenders noble acts, as a great god "wonderful in many ways to gods and men," and the god "gives to us the greatest goods" (178b–c). He suppresses any hint of trouble or misery arising from love and its desires. His appropriation of Hesiod's *Theogony* suppresses Hesiod's reference to the shadowy underworld depths of Tartaros being paired with Earth. His account could be interpreted as saying that love technically has no parents. Love triumphs over time, causation, and death. We see little reference to pain, strife, or division.

The noblest kind of love is that between an older male lover (*erastes*) and his beloved younger boy (*eromenos*), "what greater good there is for a young boy than a gentle lover, or a lover for a boy to love" (178c). This and his proposals for a great polis or an unstoppable army of male lovers establish the superior position accorded to males and male homosexuality in other speeches, a pattern that Aristophanes will begin to break and that Diotima will overturn. The paradigm of the noble lover and his younger, beautiful beloved implicitly separates beauty from goodness. Beauty is accorded the beloved; the lover is good. The dialogue will have to work out how the beautiful stands in relation to the good, and the core of each has to be discerned from its lesser manifestations and appearances.

The emphasis on the lover as being motivated by honor suggests that *eros* is motivated primarily by the lover's desire to regard himself in a certain way. A student of the Sophist Hippias, Phaedrus counsels, "nothing imparts this guidance [in life] as well as love. And what do I mean? I mean a sense of shame at acting shamefully, and a sense of pride in acting well" (178d). Love motivates virtuous behavior, but with the end in view being the regard of others and how this reflects on the self:

if a man is found doing something shameful, or accepting shameful treatment... then nothing would give him more pain than being seen by the boy he loves.... We see the same thing also in the boy he loves.... [a city or army of lovers] would be the best possible system of society, for they would hold back from all that is shameful, and seek honor in each other's eyes (178e–179a).

The completion of the self (and happiness) lies in being able to regard itself well. This is largely a reflection of how the self is regarded by others. Phaedrus's lover loves an ideal image of himself projected into the future (possibly post mortem).

The tripartite psyche of the *Republic* (reason, passion, and lower desires) sees reason desiring the pleasures of wisdom and understanding, the passions desiring public honor and inner self-regard, and the lower desires proximate to the body wanting nourishment, sex, and money to gratify the sensate pleasures (435c–445c). Courage is less physical courage (as it is for Phaedrus) than a calm inner disposition of the psyche, which resists inordinate passion from skewing right reason.

The psyche and polis of Phaedrus are timocratic, or honor-loving. Individual self-regard effects a harmonization of inner desires with the common good. The city benefits from prudent initiative and occasional bravery, while the individual is well-remembered for his noble deeds. The limitation is that the lover really loves an imagined idea of himself. Human relations and society become mirrors of the self. A cagey and sophistically trained individualist can gratify himself and be honored as much for the appearance of excellence as for the reality. The self-sacrifice of the lover hints at love being ordered to something transcending the self, yet what it is, is not quite articulated.

Phaedrus considers the self-sacrificial aspect of love in the examples of Alcestis, Orpheus, and Achilles. To be beloved is nobler than to be the lover, but "no one will die for you but a lover, and a lover will do this even if she is a woman" (179b). Alcestis agrees to take the place of her husband in the underworld and unexpectedly gets her life back as well, which suggests that love means valuing one's self less than one's beloved. Real fulfillment is in giving up the self to another or to something greater. In return, we receive a higher self, symbolized in the return of Alcestis's life along with her husband. Love's benefits to the self need not conflict with its properly other-directed nature; Socrates's speech will develop this.

Orpheus sought his beloved Euridice in Hades but "he did not dare to die like Alcestis for Love's sake" and is torn apart at the hands of the Maenads (179c). (The musician Orpheus is a halfway point in the transformation of Dionysius into Apollo. Nietzsche observes that Socrates is an Orpheus dismembered by the public fury of the Athenian court.) An unwillingness to renounce one's lower self for the beloved and to obtain the benefits of *eros* at a discount leaves one torn and bereft of real fulfillment. Alcibiades in his speech will be torn between his higher and lower selves. Eros does not reward half-measures.

Achilles "learned from his mother [Athena] he would die if he killed Hector" and is praised by Phaedrus for sacrificing himself in revenge for the death of Patroclus. Achilles does this for a dead man and so could reap no reward (180a). Yet Phaedrus suppresses Achilles's mixed motives seen in Homer. As the son of a goddess, he knew he could trade a long life for an early death and lasting fame; he accepts. Achilles in Homer is also motivated by anger, not just by noble love. He sulks by the ships for losing his war-prize, costing his side dearly. He is no model, Plato implies. Phaedrus again filters the myths to fit his point. Love and its motives are more complicated than appearances suggest. He insists that Achilles was the beloved of the pair, thus contradicting his earlier observation that only lovers die for others. (The contradictory and self-undermining property of egoism is a common Socratic theme.) Diotima will later consider that the benefits of love for the self and others are not necessarily opposed.[5]

Phaedrus's speech is often passed over by commentators as surface introduction. On the contrary, however, it introduces some of the major questions and divisions of the dialogue. The self is divided into itself and its ego-ideal, according to which it strives to regard itself and to be regarded by others. Thus the public and private self are separate. There is the question of how love can benefit if the gods do not manifestly reward it. Do time and death have the last word over the lover, or are love and its fruits stronger than death; is redemption from time possible?

III. PAUSANIAS AND ERYXIMACHUS

Phaedrus views love under a single concept. Pausanias boldly divides *eros* into physical and spiritual types. Pausanias's division of love separates the body from the soul. Aristophanes and Socrates will try to resolve this tension. Eryximachus will maintain the split and emphasize the body as the center of love's fulfillment. Both speeches raise the problem of where the body and the sensate desires fit with respect to love's seeking fulfillment in something beyond the self.

Pausanias is a student of the Sophist Prodicus and is also the ardent and middle-aged lover of the beautiful young Agathon.[6] Pausanias observes that "considered in itself, no action is either good or bad, honorable or shameful" but its moral character "depends entirely on how it is performed" (181a). He is making more than the conventional point that acts apart from motives mean nothing; one can help an elderly lady across the street to rob or to aid her. Pausanias means that one's ends should be achieved with a certain outward decorum and should keep in mind the mutual benefit of the parties. Similarly, the character of love "depends on the behavior it gives rise to," or how one goes about it (183d). "Love," he notes, is not something in itself "noble and worthy of praise" but it is a matter of whether "the sentiments he produces in us are themselves noble" (181a). Pausanias is keen to note how variations in law or custom (*nomos*) shape people's views on taking a lover. A boy yielding to the older man's desires for material gain is a disgrace (185a). However, the boy can yield if "the young man is eager to be taught and improved by his lover" (184e). He leaves the nature of the improvement somewhat vague, and the lover's sentiments or the boy's s recompense leaves the same end in view. The idea seems to be that the older lover's gratification gains a noble face.[7]

As in Phaedrus's creation story, Pausanias initially locates the division between two kinds of love in Hesiod's *Theogony*. Cronus, the god of time, castrates Uranus, and the genitals floating upon the sea give rise to Heavenly Aphrodite. Pausanias, however, only alludes to this act of strife (*eris*) figuratively brought about by time. The spontaneous (and impossibly motherless) act of reproduction produces a love quite literally cut off from the body and thus from desire and temporality. (Agathon will castrate the older Pausanias and his stylized defense of pederasty in a speech scornful of old age and of the absence or loss of physical beauty.)

The Uranian Aphrodite is a lover of men and young boys, not of women, who are less worthy and intelligent. She is characterized by constancy, and she loves the soul rather than the body. Pausanias derides common Aphrodite as the lust "felt by the vulgar, who are attached to women no less than boys, and to the body no less than the soul ... all they care about is completing the sexual act" (181b). He who gives in to this acts "in a vile way" which is "truly disgraceful behavior" (183e). Vastly different is the lover who "loves the right sort of [virtuous] character, and who remains its lover for life" (183e). Heavenly Aphrodite signifies the male principle of reason over passion and is tied to the soul's search for wisdom (184e). It is significant, however, that it is a product of Sophist training and a person of uncertain motives who privileges males and male homosexuality. The female Diotima will be invoked to refute these claims. The ascent through the various stages of love in Socrates's, speech quickly moves beyond emphases on gender, orientation, and the body that occur in earlier speeches.[8]

Pausanias's sharp division of love separates the soul from the body and puts them at odds. Sexuality and procreative sex are cut off from higher love. In Pausanias, Plato caricatures the denigration of the bodily and physical realm, which in Western thought is a point of view he is often accused of holding. Plato will want to distinguish the self's alienation from the body from the integration of bodily *eros* into its rightful (if lower) place within the self. The Heavenly Aphrodite too must be procreative, and is not to be defined primarily in opposition to time and the body. As an aging lover of a younger man, Pausanias in his denigration of lower *eros* suggests his fear of the body's temporality and mortality. Paradoxically, his flight from his lower self leaves him attached to the body and the pleasures of youth, and this is rationalized by maintaining the appearance of virtue. Philosophy covers seduction. Pausanias is the sort of man whom Athenian fathers fear around their sons. His outward behavior is tragically indistinguishable to Athenians from that of the differently motivated Socrates.[9]

The body reinserts itself into the discussion when Aristophanes gets the hiccups and cannot take his turn. Pausanias's flight from corporeal *eros* is offset by the physician Eryximachus's emphasis on the primacy of the body and the material order. His technologically driven outlook and materialistic ontology present a formidable challenge to the Socratic philosophical approach. This challenge is easy to miss under his rambling and pedantic assessment. The physician goes well beyond his own expertise into areas as varied as varied as farming, music, and divination.

Eryximachus acknowledges the higher and lower kinds of love noted in Pausanias. Yet he expands the concept of love to encompass the proper or improper harmony of opposing elements in the psyche, body, and natural world (188a). Love becomes not only an attraction to beauty "in the human soul" but a force permeating the cosmos: "It certainly occurs within the animal kingdom and even in the world of plants ... it occurs everywhere in the universe" (186b). It is manifest "even [in] the seasons of the year," where opposing elements must balance to bring temperate climates and good harvests; the wrong sort of love brings "death and destruction" from nature (188b). His cosmology recalls forces of Love and Strife in Empedocles; in discussing love's origins, Eryximachus appeals to his own observations of nature and downplays the customary myths of its origins along with other gods.

Instead, love originates not so much in the realm of the gods as it controls the other gods: "Love is a deity of the greatest importance: he directs everything that occurs, not only in the human domain, but also in that of the gods" (186b). Furthermore, while love controls the gods, the aim of divination is the control of love. Its point is to "is to keep watch over these species of Love and to doctor them as necessary," and it is hoped that this will bring the proper relations between men and the gods (188d).

Not surprisingly, the self of the physician is primarily the bodily self. Eryximachus notes the honorable and shameful kinds of love that Pausanias sees are mirrored in the healthy and diseased constitutions of the body, and the task of the physician is to "effect a reconciliation and establish a mutual love" among bodily elements "opposed to one another, as hot is to cold, bitter to sweet, wet to dry, cases like those." The emphasis, then, is on love as a physiological phenomenon. Medicine's job is to mitigate the effects of overindulgence in bodily pleasures (187e). The trick to living well, then, involves the moderate enjoyment of sensual pleasures without ruining the body for further enjoyment. Plato here ties the fascination with technical artifice to a moderate hedonism and a lack of emphasis on higher aims.

Love in the technicism of Eryximachus, like the body under the physician's gaze, loses its distinctively human character and its ground in the psyche. Plato here links the striving for control over nature through artificial means to a vague confusion of psychic phenomena with biological and cosmological ones. The forces of the psyche are projected onto the latter two orders. Nature and the body ironically become things against which technical artifice must work.

The alienation of the soul from the body in Pausanias becomes in the scientifically and technologically oriented mindset of Eryximachus the irrelevance of the soul, its spiritual aims, and the spiritual realm. Both Pausanias and Eryximachus gravitate toward happiness and pleasure as the good. In a similar way, Descartes's radical dualism of the mind and the body will clear the path for scientific reductionism. The speeches of Pausanias and Eryximachus seem to be at odds with regard to the body. One disdains it; the other focuses on it. Yet Plato shows their underlying views to be linked, with one set of views easily leading to the other.

IV. ARISTOPHANES

The speeches of Aristophanes and Agathon also belong together. Aristophanes is a composer of comedies at the peak of his talents and fame. The young Agathon's literary star is rising for his recent victory with his tragedy. Of course, the literary qualities of each speech supersede the respective genres of the authors. Both argue for poetry as the superior vehicle of wisdom (over philosophy). Each directs *eros* to the self as its primary object.

The self of Aristophanes is haunted by an unrealizable vision of wholeness in this life. His speech attempts to heal the rift between higher and lower *eros* opened by Pausanias. His solution is to bring the psyche and its spiritual aims into a compromise with the body, which Socrates will be unable to accept. He lowers the transcendent aims in human nature to the worldly realm. This comes at the cost of a lesser happiness than Socrates envisions.

Aristophanes historically is interested in defending Athenian theology and mores. His elaborate satire of Socrates in *The Clouds* is frequently dismissed as caricature. Yet its argument received a hearing in Athens, as Plato has Socrates in the *Apology* allude to Aristophanes (18d) and *The Clouds* (19c) in connection with the "old" accusers turning the city against Socrates. *The*

Clouds alleges that scientific investigation of the cosmos leads to atheism and that the Socratic investigation of moral values leads to relativism. Both threaten the social and political orders.[10]

Plato responds here to Aristophanes's attack on Socrates by crafting the speech of Aristophanes as a comic masterpiece in the dialogue. The poet's *eris* toward his mentor is met with *eros*, in the form of a light-hearted and respectful forbearance. This does not mean that the poet's views escape substantive criticism. Diotima knocks down Aristophanes's dual thesis that the highest eros is romantic love and that love's goal is finding another self.[11] The Aristophanic desire to harmonize the *eros* of the body and the soul also anticipates Diotima's incorporation of them in her vision of hierarchical ascent.

Aristophanes describes humanity's bid for happiness in the myth of the circle-men. Humans were once double selves. They had two bodies with double sets of limbs, heads, and genitals. This made for three genders—male/male, female/female, and male/female. After storming heaven, Zeus splits each into two people, after which each person seeks his or her other half. Treating the gods "with due reverence" brings us a promised wholeness and completion in finding our lost selves, and "if we don't keep order before the gods, we'll be split in two again" (193a–b). Happiness lies in appropriating an other to oneself as another self. Aristophanes, however, clothes the idea in terms of finding a soul mate. Disaster awaits those who out of pride or ill fortune go it alone. This view of love would have been as well received by the Athenian in the street as it is nowadays is by modern readers of popular magazines.

The story brings to mind the Fall in Genesis. There is an original state of happiness occurring in a nonspecific time and place. The self's wholeness is expressed in physical terms. Adam and Eve were at one with nature, not subject to pain or mortality. The circle-men are formidable in their physical strength and ability to move. This power is also their source of pride. Their desire to replace the gods—the sin of their Biblical counterparts—suggests that they felt something was missing from themselves (190c). (Aristophanes uses the Olympian cohort instead of the older Uranian one.) The bid to replace the divine signifies a desire for a power and self-sufficiency that the self can never have. Society and the greater order cannot permit it. Attempts to achieve a superior isolation from others or from the constraints of society will end in painful reminders of who we are as limited individuals. (The myth has invited Freudian comparisons to a longed-for return to childhood.) Aristophanes has the perceived arrogance of philosophical reasoning in mind, which appropriates a knowledge and a freedom from convention reserved for a higher order. There can be only one Apollo (who cooperates with Zeus in fixing humanity in our present state).

Love, then, originates in a perceived lack within the self: "we used to be complete wholes in our original nature, and now 'Love' is the name for our pursuit of wholeness, for our desire to be complete" (192e). Romantic love is the closest we can come to happiness in this life. The longing for sexual union expresses a desire for a union of souls in the hope that love "will restore us to our original nature, and by healing us, will make us blessed and happy" (193d). Aristophanes is "speaking about everyone, men and women alike" of whatever orientation (192b, 193c). Thus, the doctrine of masculine superiority begins to fade with Aristophanes' speech.[12]

The whimsy of his speech distracts from its tragic significance. The division between higher and lower *eros*, and thus the body and soul, is somewhat mitigated by a common objective—the beloved. Yet, the promised completion and happiness remain limited to the body and the self. There is no goal transcending the self's satisfaction. The physical union can produce children, or at least temporary relief, but starts over after temporarily allowing people to go about their lives (191c). What the soul receives in the bargain is something Aristophanes has trouble articulating: "It's obvious that the soul of every lover longs for something else [apart from sex]; his soul cannot say what it is, but like an oracle it has a sense of what it wants, and like an oracle it hides behind a riddle" (192d). His poetry ultimately lacks the wisdom to make intelligible the point of *eros*, and by extension the self's destiny beyond its physical wants remains unclear.[13] There can be no literal union of the two selves. Spiritual longing cannot be fit into a physical union. The gods, moreover, remain on the periphery to punish or reward. They do not appear with assurances on how to live or on what the point of life is. Because romantic love is understood as the exemplar for *eros*, it is still a happiness ordered to the body and its temporality.

V. AGATHON

Agathon is well versed in the rhetorical techniques of the Sophists.[14] The previous speakers have only praised the salutary effects of love and have not described its character. As a young aesthete proud of his rhetorical gifts, Agathon characteristically confuses what is good with the beauty of appearance. Wisdom is identified with technical literary skill.

He opens with a challenge to Phaedrus. Love is not among the oldest of the gods but "is the youngest of the gods and stays young forever"; love "was born to hate old age and come nowhere near it" (195b–c). There is no love for the old or ugly. Pausanias's hopes are dashed. His elder couch-mate Socrates is meant to feel the cut as well. Even more than Phaedrus, Agathon suppresses love's connection with strife (and he takes greater liberties with Hesiod). The "violent deeds" of the gods in Hesiod and Parmenides—rebellions, maimings, imprisonments, and the like—"happened under Necessity, not love." Fate, not love, is to blame. Love would have permitted none of this.

Part of what marks him as a writer of tragedy is that he describes the features of the god.[15] He seeks to characterize the god's goodness, but ends up doing so in language used to describe the physical beauty of a boy—young, delicate, fluid and supple, of pleasing skin color (195d–196b). His descriptions of the god's virtues confuse virtue with power. This we find in Agathon's describing the god's excellence of character (*arête*) regarding the cardinal virtues of justice, moderation, courage, and wisdom (which Socrates treats in *Republic* II). Justice is only the absence of any violence, or whatever two people agree to do "when both are willing, that is right and just" (196c). It is not the unity of the other three virtues in the psyche, as Socrates holds in the *Republic*. Moderation is power in restraining unruly passions and desires, not what Plato and Aristotle hold to be the moderation (*sophrosune*) of a naturally even-tempered disposition needing no restraint. Instead of wisdom (*sofia*) being insight into reality and the wherewithal to act on it, Agathon treats wisdom primarily as the technical skill of an artisan or professional.

Initially he identifies love with poetic and rhetorical skill (196e) and notes "as for [all] artisans and professionals—don't we know that whoever has this god as a teacher ends up in the light of fame, while a man untouched by Love ends up in obscurity?" (197a). Eros becomes a desire for technical success in one's craft, which brings lasting fame:

Apollo, for one, invented archery, medicine, and prophecy when desire and love showed the way. Even he, therefore, would be a pupil of Love, and so would the Muses in music, Hephaestus in bronze work, Athena in weaving, and Zeus [quoting an unknown author] "in the governance of gods and men." (197a–b)

Here he identifies love with generic desire. The god of enlightenment and the goddess of wisdom would be ruled by artistry (techne).

His speech concludes in a crescendo of praise for love, imitating the rhetorical style of the Sophist, Gorgias, after which Socrates expresses fear and amazement that he has been thrown into a contest where eloquence and skill, that is, outward beauty and not truth, is the measure of goodness. Socrates first gets Agathon to return to the idea that love is desire. He has Agathon admit that a desire is either a desire for what one lacks or else it is a desire to continue to possess in the future something one has now. He then leads Agathon to the notion that love wants what is beautiful, so that therefore love lacks beauty. Socrates then presses the point that, if all goods things are also beautiful, love lacks goodness as well.[16] Agathon at this point shamefully admits that he must not have known what he was talking about when he made his speech. Agathon's speech is only beautiful in its appearance. Since it lacks truth, it is a beauty divorced from true goodness.

Agathon has projected onto love the outward beauty and technical competence he wants others to see in him. Agathon's hymn to love is really to an idealized self.[17] He hopes that outward beauty and creative rhetorical skill promise a quasi-divine self-sufficiency and freedom from Necessity. Pausanias, Eryximachus, and Aristophanes ground the self and its completion in the body. Agathon's self is the creative psyche of the poet. Imagination and literary artifice are used to try to free the body from its link to time and mortality. Happiness thus lies in ephemeral beauty made eternal in the imagination.

Socrates, in his love of authentic wisdom, brings Agathon to the hard truth about his own limits and the limits of his skills. Agathon and Alcibiades will tragically be supported in their illusions about themselves by Athens, at least for a time. Their common hope is that the appearance of goodness can substitute for the real thing.

VI. SOCRATES

Socrates's invocation of the mediator Diotima of Manitea offsets the exclusively masculine presence at the dinner and the glorification of the masculine in other speeches. She is credited with the most comprehensive and penetrating insights on love at a dinner at which only males are present.[18] The party unfolds in the cosmopolitan setting of Athens, which is watched over by its male-dominated Olympian pantheon. Manitea is in an archaic area where the earth goddess Demeter continued to be worshipped. The effete masculinity of Agathon is opposed by the masculine femininity of Diotima. She directs Socrates in philosophical dialectic, which Socrates normally carries on with interlocutors in other dialogues. She schools him in matters of love of which he feels ignorant. At times, she plays the role of a mystagogue initiating Socrates into mysteries beyond the point at which the careful reasoning of philosophizing will reach.[19] Socrates's speech corrects certain imbalances in previous speeches. He does this not by mere counter-emphasis, but by reintegrating previous emphases into a larger picture.

Diotima initially helps Socrates to understand what *eros* is by eliciting a series of transitions. (This shows that *eros* and its aims are somewhat intelligible to philosophical dialectic, which was not the case in Aristophanes's poetic reasoning.) The outcome is that *eros* desires beauty because it anticipates getting good things. We ultimately desire the perpetual possession of the good (206a), which will make us happy, and happiness has no higher end. Instead of *eros* being a beautiful god, Diotima locates it as a spiritual force (a *daimonion*) in the psyche. Love acts as a bridge, she says, spanning divisions between the human and divine realms, the physical and spiritual, and thus between temporality and eternity. It prevents the physical world from being split off from the spiritual world; it does this by preventing us from feeling too at home in one of these oppositions. Doing so divides and truncates the self. Love's home in the psyche connects us to the body and the passing of time; yet love reaches beyond the self.[20] Because *eros* is partly cognitive and not just inchoately physical, it can project beyond the present moment; similarly, it can attach to individuals and goals beyond the more immediate interests of the self.

Love has a dual character seen in its birth. Born of Poverty and Resource, Eros is self-aware desire able to be at home in its need and homelessness. It is never rich, but always resilient and never without resources. Love involves an awareness of a lack within ourselves, so it sends us beyond ourselves, but Aristophanes is also correct that we can never truly unite with what we want. Since wisdom is beautiful, then love is a lover of wisdom, without itself ever being fully wise. Love is still courageous and intense in seeking wisdom. Socrates thus portrays himself as the lover of wisdom, but without the falsely laudatory approach of Agathon. Also contrary to Agathon, Socrates places the love of wisdom at the core of the comprehensive sense accorded to "lover," while poets and craftsmen are lovers only in a more peripheral sense.[21] Finding the true good leading to happiness requires finding wisdom. Wisdom allows one to distinguish a higher from a lesser kind of good and true beauty from its surface appearance.

Perpetual possession of the good is impossible, and *eros* has a built-in consciousness of the self and its possessions as transient (207d). Instead, we seek vicarious immortality, or "immortal glory and remembrance" (209d, 208e), in physical or spiritual procreation. The next best thing to real immortality is "giving birth in beauty, whether in body or in soul" (206b).[22] Diotima thinks immortality is the motive for having children, as well as the propagation of one's blessed memory in heroic deeds, literary works, or the laws and customs given to states. (Lycurgus of Sparta is an example of the latter.) As various commentators point out, each part of the tripartite psyche has its corresponding type of immortality. The body achieves physical reproduction, the passions achieve lasting honor and fame, and the intellect gives birth to wisdom in law, poetry, philosophy, or education. The desire for happiness culminates in a kind of pre-conscious sacrifice of the self to larger things. Reproduction of beautiful and good things in the human domain constitutes the lesser mysteries of *eros*.[23]

She describes the route to the higher mysteries in the famous ladder of the ascending stages of our attraction to beauty. They are well known, but worth briefly noting. Love in its least mature stage is attracted to the beauty of a single person's body. One moves to an attraction to "all beautiful bodies" (210b). This move might also involve a shift from erotic attraction toward a distinctively more aesthetic appreciation of physical beauty. Desire to possess the other gives way to what Kant describes as a type of disinterested admiration that does not want to appropriate the object, but to let it be. Love at the third stage becomes a spiritual attraction to people's souls and characters, "so that if someone is decent in his soul... our lover must be content to love and care for him and to seek to give birth to such ideas as will make young men better" (210c). Such a lover will naturally have to be concerned with laws and customs. Then "after customs he will move on to [the beauty of] various kinds of knowledge." The beauty of knowledge in all its various branches presents a great "sea of beauty." In gazing upon this sea, the lover "gives birth to all manner of ideas and theories, in unstinting love of wisdom (*philosophia*)" (210d). The steps move from the material realm to the spiritual, and from a scope of consideration that is particular to an increasingly more universal one; knowledge and virtue become ends in themselves.

The accompaniment of effective philosophizing to the different strands of *eros* allows us to strive for things in due proportion to their relative worth. Opposed elements or aspects of something are brought into complementary roles. Both are brought into a comprehensive picture of the larger goals in aiming for the best way to live. The higher and lower *eros* of the body and soul work together. Neither is denigrated nor functioning in disharmony with the other. Plato is of course offering an ideal view of how the *eros* of the body can operate. This is not to ascribe to him a sunny view of the passions, which can easily lead to a wantonness dragging the whole personality down with it, as Socrates reflects in the *Phaedrus* (238b–c, 266a). The tyrannical personality in the *Republic* is ruled by a single degenerate passion identified as a kind of *eros*, which visits madness upon the entire soul (*Republic* IX, 572e–573e). The reverse side of this is that the lower passions are on a continuum with the attachments and satisfactions in the intellectual endeavors of art, literature, philosophy, and the sciences. Philosophy in the *Phaedo* prepares the soul for its separation from the body in death; in the *Symposium* it joins the two.[24] These are complementary, not contradictory, dynamic movements. *Eros* ideally harmonizes the respective desires of each in the common pursuit of virtue; the intellect is freed from distraction and is also bolstered by the passions in its higher pursuits.

The rise culminates (ideally) in the lover experiencing the universal essence of beauty. Plato places beauty at the terminus of both knowledge and desire, "all of a sudden he will catch sight of something wonderfully beautiful in its nature" (210e). Diotima refers to this in the following manner:

> if someone got to see the Beautiful itself, absolute, pure, unmixed, not polluted by human flesh or colors or any other great nonsense of mortality, but if [the lover] could see the divine Beauty itself in its one form? Do you think it would be a poor life for a human being to look there and to behold it by [the mind's eye], and to be with it? (211e–212a)

The appetitive and emotional life of the person (insofar as the emotions are desirous) aims at beauty, while the intellect has traversed the highest and most universal kinds of knowledge.[25] The ascent here parallels the ascent of cognition to the form of the good in the analogies of the divided line and the cave in the *Republic*. There the form of the good is the end and source of all intelligibility; beauty is also on the level of the forms. The separate accounts look more compatible if we consider that the *Republic* understands the ascent from the view of the intellect seeking wisdom. The *Symposium* approaches happiness and human ends from the view of human experience and the erotic side of human nature. Beauty in the *Symposium* shows up as the appetitive aspect or complement of the good, driving us toward fulfillment.

The psyche's embrace of absolute beauty allows the person

> to give birth not to images of virtue...but to true virtue (because he is in touch with the true Beauty). The love of the gods belongs to anyone who has given birth to true virtue and nourished it, and if any being can be immortal it would be he. (212a–b)

Contemplative eros, after reaching the height of its capacity, gives birth to genuine excellence in the self. Philosophy is a way of life and a mode of acting, not just an adherence to a collection of propositions. One aims to grasp and internalize the fundamental principles of order and valuation in order to internalize excellence in oneself, but also to bring it forth in others and in the world. Genuine happiness sees procreative *eros* bringing images of eternity into the temporal order. One becomes both a lover and also worthy of being beloved by uniting oneself to true beauty and bringing forth good things.[26] A lower self is exchanged for a higher self, meaning a higher stage of excellence. We are united to the divine order, made god-like, by seeking the true intelligible order of things and living in accord with excellence.[27] The lover leaves behind the lower forms of *eros* and beauty. However, this is not a withdrawal from the love of the beauty of bodies or of justice in individual souls or in the state. The enlightened self can better appreciate and bring forth good things that are patterned after the lover's grasp of universal knowledge. Such a lover stands to benefit both the self and others.[28] Plato became an example as an advisor to leaders, a founder of the Academy, and the author of his magnificent dialogues. He attempted to balance action with contemplation, and theory with practice (which is not to say that the accompanying tensions quite dissolve).

VII. ALCIBIADES

The importance of properly directed *eros* for the good life is underscored by the intrusion of Alcibiades as the final speaker. He, with Aristophanes, indirectly influenced the outcome of Socrates's trial. The prosecution could not mention Alcibiades but knew they could count on the jury to keep him in mind.

Alcibiades is self-tortured and a quintessentially unhappy man. Arriving drunk and wreathed in the image of an unruly Dionysius, Alcibiades embodies the destructive potential of *eros* when it is grievously channeled to the wrong ends. Xenophon characterizes Alcibiades as primarily driven by the lust to rule over other men.[29] He presents himself in front of Socrates as a lover scorned, although Socrates assures Alcibiades of his feelings for him (213c–d). The *Gorgias* sees Socrates compare his love for Alcibiades to his love for philosophy (481d) and later predicts that Callicles and Alcibiades will share a similar fate on account of their drive to rule their fellow Athenians (519a–b).[30]

Alcibiades asks Socrates to interject if what he says is not substantively true. Socrates never stops him. It is nevertheless unwise to consider Alcibiades's portrait of Socrates unreflectively. Alcibiades is a skilled dissembler. He is humiliated by Socrates' refusal to defer to his looks and charisma. He cannot distinguish true from superficial excellence, as his determination to crown Agathon the wisest and most beautiful shows. Yet Alcibiades's distortions about Socrates, depending on how they are read, still give Plato room for some sober assessment of both personalities.

Alcibiades's speech features images of himself and Socrates as divided selves. He compares Socrates to a statue of a Silenus and to the satyr Marsyas. The statue features an ugly exterior with a divine core, "[The statue] is split right down the middle, and inside it's full of tiny statues of the gods" (215b). Socrates's inner life imitates the divine and is of a perfection that is superhuman. Socrates has an inner but unerotic beauty. The image also hints at Socrates as in a way removed from ordinary human affairs. Socrates's discourse too, appears mundane and ridiculous, but is "truly worthy of a god" in its penetration and ability to entrance Alcibiades (222a).

The image of a satyr suggests a humanity separated from its animal nature. Marsyas was flayed alive after losing to Apollo in a flute-playing contest. Alcibiades is intimating that Socrates, like the circle-men, tries to usurp the place of the divine. Such hubris has a price. (Socrates's execution will happen near a time that the city is celebrating Apollo.) Alcibiades near the close of his speech says, "The best you can do is not compare him to anything human, but liken him, as I do, to Silenus and the satyrs" (221d).

Alcibiades relates that Socrates is oddly inured to seduction, drink, cold, sleep, and physical danger. Despite his awe-inspiring self-possession and moderation, Socrates experiences an intense attraction to beautiful young men, "To begin with, he's crazy about beautiful boys; he constantly follows them around in a perpetual daze." Presumably all youths, not just the beautiful ones, need educating. However, he regards people's wealth and looks "beneath contempt, and that's how he considers all of us as well" (216d–e). Socrates displays an awe-inspiring self-possession and moderation, but also seems separated from his instinctual life. He feels a powerful attraction to physical beauty, but also scorns it. Inside he is cold, like a statue of a god.

Alcibiades too is divided within himself. He feels a deep attraction to Socrates, and is profoundly ashamed in his presence. Alcibiades is deeply torn between his higher self and his worldly ambitions:

he makes me admit that my political career is a waste of time, while all that matters is just what I most neglect, my personal shortcomings, which cry out for the closest attention. So I refuse to listen to him ... yet, the moment I leave his side I go back to my old ways: I cave in to my desire to please the crowd (216a–b).

Socrates makes him aware that he chases only the appearance of excellence, but Alcibiades cannot tear himself away from it.

His sense of being torn partly originates in a deep pride in his own attractiveness and worldly skills. His attempted seduction of Socrates shows him to be drawn to an image of his own perfection, "Nothing is more important than being the best man I can be," and he hopes Socrates will aid him in pursuit of that goal (218d). He hopes the physical union will help him internalize something of Socrates's divine spirit. Unfortunately he hopes to "trade up" with Socrates without letting go of his worldly self. (Socrates sees this. Alcibiades also might think he can learn skills from Socrates that can further his political ends.) Alcibiades is an Orpheus who wants the perceived good of the philosophical life without actually giving himself up to it.

Socrates is committed to possession of the true good for himself and for Alcibiades. He must refuse the obvious complications sexuality would bring to the picture. After dismissing the relative worthlessness of Alcibiades's offer, Socrates proposes, "In the future let's consider things together. We'll always do what seems best to the two of us" (219b). Alcibiades accuses Socrates of hubris, though it is his own pride that Socrates turns back upon him. Their intertwining for the night is a kind of chaste Aristophanic union that their souls would never have.

Socrates in the end triumphs over the potentially disruptive entanglements of Dionysius and lower *eros*. However, tragically for Athens, Socrates does not get through to Alcibiades. Plato might be intimating that Socrates and Alcibiades each succumb to a certain pride in his own self-sufficiency that closes off the other. Socrates climbs to the heavenly sphere, but he is aloof from human and practical considerations that could have helped him to persuade the Athenians of his mission. Alcibiades can lead and be successful in the worldly sphere, but he is a self who lacks a higher vision beyond his own glorification.[31] If this is so, they are complementary halves of a whole. Socrates at the end of the party argues that an adept writer of tragedy should be skillful in writing comedy and vice versa. A truly great story holds together aspects of both genres.

VIII. CONCLUSION

The *Symposium* is Plato's mirror held up to our souls as well; it has us consider how it is we seek to complete ourselves and where we seek our own lost plenitude. Will we, like some of the symposiasts, seek our happiness in something that separates us from ourselves and from what is truly good? Being fully human in all our capacities is to be god-like. Yet being complete requires us to renounce our pride in holding onto an attenuated self in order to love what transcends the self. Plato intimates that it is paradoxically by both giving up and transcending ourselves that we can hope to possess the true measure of the good life.

Washington College, Maryland

NOTES

[1] Instead of "happiness," *eudaimonia* is better translated as "well-being" or "the good life." Happiness is associated with an elevated mood or frame of mind. The Greeks had in mind not so much a subjective state as one's overall situation in life. Plato ties *eudaimonia* to the excellent and harmonious condition of the psyche.

"*Eros*" can refer to desire in general and more particularly to an intense attachment characterized by sexual desire and passion. "*Philia*" usually has the sense of an affection or fondness indifferently applicable to friends, family, and lovers. It can also refer to an intense passion.

My interest in themes of opposition and integration in the *Symposium* originated in courses and discussions with the philosopher Karsten Harries at Yale several years ago. See his *The Broken Frame: Three Lectures* (Washington, DC: Catholic University of America Press, 1989), particularly pp. 11–18. Similar themes of opposition are emphasized by Seth Benardete, "On Plato's Symposium," in *Plato's Symposium*, transl. Seth Benardete, with commentaries by Allan Bloom and Seth Benardete (Chicago: University of Chicago Press, 1993), 179–199. Benardete notes on p.192 of his commentary: "And I would suggest what characterizes Platonic myths in general is precisely this: a principle is sundered in such a way that a two emerges from a one before it is reabsorbed into something that seems to be but no longer is one." Robert Wardly also examines dual opposites in the *Symposium*, mainly from the standpoint of the dialogue's literary structure, in "The Unity of the Self in Plato's Symposium," in *Oxford Studies in Ancient Philosophy: Volume XXIII*, ed. David Sedley (Oxford: Oxford University Press, 2002), 1–61. Wardly notes on p. 3: "The *Symposium* itself largely consists of combinations of opposites, so my Heraclitean proposal is that ... one or other apparent opposition is really a unity in dynamic tension." The basic idea is explored in Stanley Rosen's often speculative but highly stimulating commentary, *Plato's Symposium* (New Haven, CT: Yale University Press, 1968).

[2] All quotations are from the translation by Alexander Nehemas and Paul Woodruff. They cautiously estimate 406–400 BC as the setting; see Plato, *Symposium*, transl. Alexander Nehemas and Paul Woodruff, with an introduction by Alexander Nehemas (Indianapolis, IN: Hackett, 1989). Many commentators opt for around 400 or 401. R. G. Bury argues for around 400 BC in the introduction to his translation, *The Symposium of Plato* (Cambridge: W. Heffer and Sons, 1909), lxvi. Benardete agrees ("On Plato's Symposium," 180). Apollodorus upbraids Glaucon for "knowing very well" that Agathon (who left Athens in 408 or 407) has been gone "for many years," while Apollodorus had begun following Socrates just a few years earlier. Apollodorus's manner points to an appreciable gap between the two events (172b–173c). Glaucon is also unaware that the dinner celebrated Agathon's first victory for his tragedy and so happened, as Apollodorus says, "when we were still children." (Other translations are generally consistent with the above phrases.) Martha Nussbaum dates the setting shortly before Alcibiades's death in 404, mainly by arguing that Glaucon seems unaware of his death and would not have been unaware of it after 404. See her *Fragility of Goodness: Luck and Ethics in Greek Tragedy and Philosophy* (Cambridge: Cambridge University Press, 1986), 167–170. However, Glaucon's lines do not clearly indicate whether he thinks Alcibiades is alive or not. Alcibiades is simply mentioned once in passing as present at the dinner (172b). Nothing said in the setting is inconsistent with Alcibiades having been dead for some years.

[3] The similar-sounding first syllable of "Aristodemus" and "*eris*" was pointed out to me by Karsten Harries, who also explores the suppression of love's connection with strife in the speeches.

[4] Benardete, "On Plato's Symposium," 181.

[5] The *Symposium* shows that Plato is aware of what we consider the classic philosophical and psychological conundrum of altruism (as Greek culture was). Anders Nygren and others in the last century emphasized the contrast between Greek *eros* as egocentric and strictly possessive, while upholding the self-abnegation of *agape* in St. Paul as uniquely Christian; see Anders Nygren, *Agape and Eros*, transl. Philip Watson (Philadelphia: Westminster Press, 1953), 181. However, "*phila*" can mean seeking the good of another for his own sake, as we find, for instance, in Aristotle's *Nicomachean Ethics* (1166a) and *Rhetoric* (1380b35–1381a1).

[6] The *Protagoras* (315d–e) mentions Pausanias as Prodicus's student and refers to his love for Agathon.

[7] Robert Wardly notes, "Pausanias' speech is though ironically an elaborate rationalization for gratifying sexual desire"; see "The Unity of the Self in Plato's Symposium," 40. Rosen offers the same assessment in *Plato's Symposium*, 86–87.

[8] The *Symposium* is often understood as highly praising homosexual relations. Plato's views toward homosexual intercourse were complicated. The work's most sophisticated account of love (attributed to a female) quickly moves beyond considerations of gender, orientation, or the body. Socrates, when propositioned by one of the most sought-after men in Athens, makes light of it and goes to sleep. The *Phaedrus* sees intercourse between males characterized by Socrates as an "unnatural pleasure" (250e). The *Laws* regard it as "contrary to nature" (836b–c) and suggest that it is a man's duty to marry and raise children (721b). In 838e Plato prohibits "homosexual relations that deliberately wipe out the human race," while the natural end of sex is the generation of children. Diotima's speech will suggest that homoerotic love be sublimated to the pursuit of knowledge and excellence and their creative products. Athenian attitudes toward homosexual intercourse were a mix of permission and restraint, often depending on the parties involved, as K. J. Dover discusses in his classic *Greek Homosexuality* (New York: Random House, 1978); see particularly 104–107. See also his *Greek Popular Mythology in the Time of Plato and Aristotle* (Oxford: Basil Blackwell, 1974).

[9] Rosen, *Plato's Symposium*, 86–89.

[10] Stanley Rosen discusses this thesis in Aristophanes in *Plato's Symposium*, 122. See also K. J. Dover, "Aristophanes' Speech in Plato's Symposium," *Journal of Hellenic Studies* 86 (1966), 41.

[11] Diotima will note that ultimately we love something because it is good for us, not necessarily because it is another self. Love in its most noble manifestations involves us in attachments to larger things than persons (205d, 212c). Plato does not criticize a healthy self-regard spurring us to improve ourselves, but an excessive self-love keeping us from better things (*Laws* 731d–732b).

[12] Nehemas and Woodruff note that his speech considers all men and women, although at points he speaks to the homosexual proclivities of his audience, *Symposium*, 30 n.29. He also makes a mild quip at the expense of Agathon and Pausanias.

[13] Benardete notes, "Eros is an ever-to-be-thwarted longing for a second try in heaven"; "On Plato's Symposium," 186.

[14] Plato in the *Protagoras* has him listening to the Sophist Prodicus (315d–e). The introduction and conclusion of Agathon's speech in particular show the unmistakable influence of Gorgias, as Socrates notes afterward.

[15] Seth Benardete comments on the structure of Agathon's speech: "If anything makes Agathon a representative of tragedy it is in focusing on the being of a god. The being of a god is in his beauty. The causality of the good is in his virtue or goodness. The beautiful and the good are thus for the first time separated. The separation between the fourfold character of the beautiful and the fourfold character of the good which Agathon attributes to Eros...amounts to a distinction between the beloved and the lover. The beauty of Eros is manifest in the beloved, the goodness of Eros is conferred on the lover." "On Plato's Symposium," 188.

[16] Socrates' line of reasoning is not as cogent as it seems to Agathon. That all good things are beautiful does not guarantee all that is beautiful has to be good (in a relevant respect). Socrates's own mordant praise of Agathon's speech as beautiful but not good reveals this. Socrates as the philosopher must keep truth and sound reasoning in view. He is thus able to outwit the product of Sophist training, whose attention is drawn away from the implications of his own rhetoric by having to please a crowd. Agathon's pride in his own speech quickly turns to public shame and leaves him too flummoxed to respond to Socrates' challenge.

[17] See Rosen, *Plato's Symposium*, 177–178, 195–196.

[18] In *Republic* V, women are described as possessing a common, ideal human nature with men and enjoying the same rights and responsibilities. Women figured as property and as a liability in Greek law and custom. Aristotle, with tragic consequences for Western medieval thought, agrees that women have the same nature but he considers them immature in their biological development. Thus, they are said to lack the full range and intensity of human excellences. Aristophanes in his comedies portrays women as ideally affectionate and pretty, if often devious, but as fully human as the male characters. See Robert Brumbaugh's discussion of these matters in Chapter 17, "Four Definitions of Women in Classical Philosophy," of his *Platonic Studies of Greek Philosophy: Form, Arts, Gadgets, and Hemlock* (Albany: State University of New York Press, 1989).

[19] Robert Wardly suggests that Diotima's confidence and direction of Socrates reveals a masculine soul, in "The Unity of the Self in Plato's Symposium," in *Oxford Studies in Ancient Philosophy: Volume XXIII*, ed. David Sedley (Oxford: Oxford University Press, 2002), 1–61, 44–45. Diotima's statements directly refer back to Aristophanes (202e, 205d–e), suggesting that Socrates at least partly makes up her speech. She has neither been verified nor discounted as a historical figure.

[20] Karsten Harries in discussion has emphasized these contrasting aspects of reality being bridged by *eros*.

[21] Benardete, "On Plato's Symposium," 195.

[22] The phrase "birth in beauty" (*tokos en kaloi*) could mean "in" beauty or "in the presence of" beauty. The reference to children is not an afterthought to spiritual procreation. In *Laws* (721b) Plato writes: "A man must marry between the ages of thirty and thirty-five, reflecting that there is a sense in which nature has not only somehow endowed the human race with a degree of immortality, but also implanted in us a longing to achieve it, which we express in every way we can. One expression of that wish is the desire for fame and the wish not to lie nameless in the grave. Thus mankind is by nature a companion of eternity, and is linked to it, and will be linked to it forever. Mankind is immortal because it leaves later generations behind to preserve its unity and identity for all time: it gets its share of immortality by means of procreation." Transl. Trevor Saunders in *Plato: Complete Works*, edited, with an introduction and notes, by John M. Cooper (Indianapolis, IN: Hackett, 1997).

[23] Rosen observes, "Man is excellent to the degree he can transcend temporality," *Plato's Symposium*, 258.

[24] Benardete, "On Plato's Symposium," 191–192.

[25] As R. E. Allen notes in *Plato: The Symposium*, translated with commentary (New Haven, CT: Yale University Press, 1991), 85.

[26] After Lysias in the *Phaedrus* (230e–234c) grounds human relations in the lower forms of *eros*, the religious imagery surrounding the vision of the forms and the lover's return to the everyday world of beauty is emphasized in 251a: "A recent initiate, however, one who has seen much in heaven [in the vision of the forms]—when he sees a god-like face or bodily form that has captured Beauty well, first he shudders and a fear comes over him like those he felt at an earlier time; then he gazes at him with the reverence due a god, and if he weren't afraid people would think him completely mad, he'd even sacrifice to his boy as if he were the image of a god." Translated by Alexander Nehemas and Paul Woodruff in *Plato: Complete Works*, edited, with an introduction and notes, by John M. Cooper (Indianapolis, IN: Hackett, 1997). One's experience of the transcendent transforms and ennobles everyday experience, including human love, as R. E. Allen notes of the above passage in *The Symposium*, 91.

[27] On the theme of imitating the divine see *Phaedrus* 246d, 248a, 249c; *Timaeus* 47c; *Republic* 613a–b; *Theaetetus* 176a–c; *Phaedo* 78b–84b; and *Philebus* 28c–30e. Daniel Russell examines

this in "Virtue as 'Likeness to God' in Plato and Seneca," *Journal of the History of Philosophy* 42:3 (2004), 241–260.

[28] Gregory Vlastos writes that if love ultimately desires to possess the good, there would seem to be a twofold problem. Love ends up being about the interests of the self merely played out on the higher plane of enjoying philosophical contemplation. Second, Plato's ideal lover seems too aloof from interpersonal forms of love, while in fact the strongest ties are usually far more intense than the beloved's appearance or virtues warrant from a rational perspective, "What we are to love in persons is [only] the 'image' of the Idea (of beauty) in them"; see G. Vlastos, "The Individual as an Object of Love in Plato," in *Platonic Studies*, ed. G. Vlastos, 2nd edition (Princeton, NJ: Princeton University Press, 1981), 3–42, p. 31; see also pp. 30–32. Over the years, the critique has garnered a good deal of comment and response. (See, for example, Martin Warner, "Love, Self, and Plato's Symposium," *Philosophical Quarterly* 29:117 [October 1979], 329–339.) A similar observation that love is not often proportioned to the dignity or adequacy of a person was expressed earlier in the last century by John McTaggert, *The Nature of Existence*, Vol. II (Cambridge: Cambridge University Press, 1927), Book V, Chapter vli, Sections 465–468. Diotima might respond that the experience of true Beauty can enrich human thought and experience at the other levels of ascent, which it is not clear are completely left behind. R. E. Allen observes in this vein, "It is characteristic of the ladder that one leaves behind the lower rungs as one climbs. But one does not stop loving the beauty of bodies solely by reason of the fact that one has come to love the beauty of souls; or the beauty of souls because one has come to love the beauty of laws and institutions, ... or the beauty of the sciences ... solely because one has come to love Beauty itself. Plato here [in the *Symposium*], as in the analysis of society in *Republic* II, the account of the decline of the just state in *Republic* VIII and IX, and the origins of the world in the *Timaeus*, presents as a temporal sequence what is in fact a natural priority" (*The Symposium*, 82–83). It might also be argued that Diotima is not presenting an anthropological description of what usually happens with love. She is uncovering among our various attachments a reasoned and ideal set of priorities toward which we can strive, regardless of how we actually tend to feel.

[29] *Memorabilia* I.ii. 13–16.

[30] As noted by R. E. Allen, *The Symposium*, 104. The General Amnesty in Athens, declared in 401 BC after the fall of the Thirty Tyrants, prevented the explicit mention of Socrates's former associates at the trial in 399. For an interesting discussion of the figure of Alcibiades, see the introduction (pp. 1–28) of the study by David Gribbles, *Alcibiades and Athens: A Study in Literary Presentation* (Oxford: Clarendon Press, 1999).

[31] Karsten Harries pointed this out in discussion.

ANNIKA LJUNG-BARUTH

THE VIRTUE OF RESPONSIBILITY

Femininity, Temporality, and Space in Michael Cunningham's The Hours

Responsibility is a necessary part of subjectivity, as the ability to respond to the other is crucial to subjective self-constitution and self-awareness. By utilizing a methodological framework based on Luce Irigaray and Emmanuel Levinas, this essay will argue that responsibility in Michael Cunningham's *The Hours* is conditioned by temporality and by subjectivity's ability to phenomenologically "inhabit' the world."[1] I will elucidate how responsibility is canceled in this novel, and how this is due to an objectification of alterity, space, and time. At the end of the novel, we witness a turning point when subjectivity's ability to respond to the other is finally released with the liberation of time and transcendence.[2]

In *The Hours*, subjectivity is initially manifested as self-objectifying and as lacking the possibility of an infinite response to the other, that is, responsibility. This non-authentic nature of subjectivity is initially revealed as the characters' inability to "inhabit" (*TH*, 22, 35, 37) the world, or more specifically, the worlds that are supposedly theirs. True life, or real life, seems to them to reside "elsewhere" (*TH*, 42, 91), and the world that they do have seems "far from everything" real (*TH*, 111). It is a world in which they have "trouble believing in" themselves and in their surroundings (*TH*, 38). Their true selves seem to exist in a parallel dimension, as a "parallel purer self" (*TH*, 34), or in a "parallel world" (*TH*, 37) in which they could find their "true medium" (*TH*, 40). The protagonists predominantly experience reality as a realm resembling Levinas's concept of the *il y a*—anonymous and timeless being. Their destinies are caught up in sociopolitical situations that deprive them of their individuality (*Mrs. Richard Dalloway*, *Mrs. Woolf*, *Mrs. Brown*) and constrict their ability to confidently and creatively express themselves. For them, subjectivity itself is at stake because it has lost (or never found) its dwelling place, its point of departure. The characters fear a drifting into "unbeing" (*TH*, 188), into "detachment" (*TH*, 92). They experience a sense of "dislocation" (*TH*, 91) and "loss" (*TH*, 91), "the end of hope" (*TH*, 91). Theirs is a realm "worse than death" because in it the presence of death would signify "promise" and "release" (*TH*, 90). This sense of hopelessness can be characterized by the *il y a* as an atemporal "vigilance without possible recourse to sleep" (*TO*, 48–49), "the absence of all self, a without-self" in a world of sameness (*TO*, 49).

Luce Irigaray's philosophy of sexual difference serves well to elucidate the absence of self experienced by these women. For Irigaray, women have traditionally been deprived of the possibility of forming a subjective position, a selfsame identity. Instead, Irigaray claims (influenced by her predecessor de Beauvoir) that women are socialized to see themselves as "other," as non-subjective matter. Irigaray clarifies her point by defining the feminine as "the place" (*ES*, 10) that has traditionally been "separated from 'its' own place, deprived of its place" (*ES*, 10).[3] Instead, women have become the "available place" (*ES*, 84) for men, the *"thing"* (*ES*, 10) by which men can create their own site for dwelling and identity.[4] This objectification of selfhood as other-than-subjectivity positions women in a realm resembling Levinas's notion of the "il y a," a space in which subjectivity-as-identity and its dwelling are ruled out.[5] Furthermore, Levinas's idea that selfsame identity is necessary as a point of departure for the ethical relation (*TI*, 36) casts light on the inability of these women to form such a relationship.[6] They are unable to find an authentic dwelling place or form an identity. Instead, their experience of self-objectification results in an objectification of transcendence and temporality (the ethical relationship), and space (dwelling). Their spatial and temporal existence is subsumed under the objectifying power of the *il y a*.[7]

The Hours stages a timeless and anonymous zone in which responsibility is dislocated from sociality. Here, relationships to others are obscured and thwarted by a pervasive tendency to understand oneself and one's world primarily as "objects" (*TH*, 22). For Laura, responding to her son and husband is an "obligation" (*TH*, 38) only to be negotiated by fleeing into the world of literature. Clarissa wants to flee from the life she "pretends" to live with her partner Sally (*TH*, 92), and Virginia is desperate to escape from the life with her husband in Richmond that endlessly continues "in its decent, peaceful dream of itself" (*TH*, 34). Virginia, Laura, and Clarissa experience phenomenological reality as always being "elsewhere" (*TH*, 42, 91). This sense of dislocation is the result of an objectification of transcendence, that is, alterity. For them, subjectivity is locked into a prison-house of representation, excluding the possibility of authentic time, caring, sociality, or responsibility.

In objectified reality, we cannot meet each other "face to face" (*TI*, 52). This is because objectified reality does not allow for immediacy, that is, for "language" (*TI*, 52) or "saying" (*OB*, 5) in Levinas's terminology. Instead, objectified reality is "the said" (*OB*, 5): it is "already a thematization and a reference to a horizon (*TI*, 56). In *Otherwise than Being*, Levinas's distinction between the saying and the said helps us to understand the nature of language with and without immediacy.

> Saying... is the proximity of one to the other, the commitment of an approach, the one for the other, the very signifyingness of signification.... The original or pre-original saying, what is put forth in the foreword, weaves an intrigue of responsibility. It sets forth an order more grave than being and antecedent to being. By comparison, being appears like a game. Being is play... without responsibility, where everything possible is permitted.... Language permits us to utter... this *outside of being*, this *ex-ception* to being, as though being's other were an event of being. (*OB*, 5–6)

Before ontology (i.e., being) comes ethics. Ethics comes as saying, as language, as expression: the face that expresses itself necessarily undoing every attempt to thematize, to build an ontology of the said. Thematization is without limits because it cannot see beyond the realm of ipseity and selfsameness. Its freedom is not limited by the presence of the other. This is why its freedom also is a prison, blocking the possibility of an authentic relationship with the other. The relationship between the immediacy of saying and the thematization of the said casts light on the theme of motherhood in *The Hours*.

For Laura Brown, motherhood is a role, a performance, empty because of its disengagement from saying. Laura feels that she *should* be able to love her son Richie and that she *should* be able to fulfill the expectations placed on her by society. Laura has been caught in the thematization of domesticity imposed on her by society. Her life with her husband and son seems to her like a "performance" (*TH*, 43), as if she is taking part in "a play for which she is not appropriately dressed and for which she has not adequately rehearsed" (*TH*, 43). But because motherhood has become the said and Laura is deprived of her dwelling place, she is unable to have these feelings or live up to these expectations. In the words of Irigaray, she is not the point of departure for her own experience, she is not in her own "place" (*ES*, 10). She is the objectified other. Her unhappiness stems from an inability to understand or express, give voice to, her self. This is indeed being locked into a prison-house of representation, into an *other's* said, a space offering no access to one's own saying or a dialogue between the self and the other.

Laura Brown seeks to escape the representational reality of mid-twentieth-century idealized female domesticity when she leaves her son with a sitter and drives to the Normandy, the hotel in which she contemplates suicide but instead decides to leave her family. At this point, reality has for her become two dimensional and "flat" (*TH*, 141–142): "Everything she sees feels as if it's pinned to the day the way etherized butterflies are pinned to a board"

(*TH*, 141). The connection between time and domesticity in *The Hours* is illustrated by Laura's anonymous existence. At times, Laura can synchronize her existence with the time of the said as a futile attempt to find stability within a chronological, linear, synthesized, and thematized framework. At other times, she drops hopelessly into the anonymity of the "il y a," unable to contract an identity or to be a person. In both of these states of time, we witness an exclusion of alterity.

Levinas's concept of "diachrony," or the time of the other, is useful to deepen our analysis of Laura Brown's situation as well as the life of her son's future friend and lover, Clarissa Vaughan. The lack of alterity, or diachrony, in both of these women's lives has contributed to their inability to inhabit their worlds or to make them phenomenologically present.[8] Thus, Clarissa Vaughan, who lives with her long-time partner Sally, is also trapped in objectified reality. However, at times, Clarissa can remember her true self from an "elsewhere" (*TH*, 91) curiously connected to her childhood. This is the memory of the particular moment when she seems to have started to "inhabit" (*TH*, 22) the world. In her present life, Clarissa feels that she does not really "live" in an apartment with Sally, full of arbitrary objects, but rather in "a room where a tree gently taps against the glass as someone touches a needle on the phonograph record" (*TH*, 91):

> Clarissa would have been three or four in a house to which she would *never return*, about which she retains *no recollection* except this, utterly distinct, clearer than some things that happened yesterday: a branch tapping at a window as the sound of horns began: as if the tree, being unsettled by wind, had somehow caused the music. It seems that at that moment she began to *inhabit* the world" (*TH*, 22–23, emphasis added)

Clarissa's memory is an-archical, resisting a spatiotemporal framework. Like Levinas's "diachronous pre-original" past (*OB*, 10), it cannot be recuperated by a synchronizing historicizing gaze: "A linear regressive movement...would never be able to reach the absolutely diachronous pre-original which cannot be recuperated by...history" (*OB*, 10). In portraying alterity as the pathway through which Clarissa reconnects with her self, *The Hours* offers a reinterpretation of Levinas's thought that tends to identify the Absolute I with selfsame identity and an exclusion of alterity.[9] When Clarissa can feel her "essence" (*TH*, 92) and be "herself" (*TH*, 92) and stop "pretending to live in this apartment among these objects" (*TH*, 92), she is not selfsame identity but rather identity opened up to alterity. In *The Hours*, alterity, the time of the other (i.e., the time of the past that resists synchronization), coexists in fruition with the Absolute I.[10] Thus, in this novel, it is the lack of alterity that casts light on the lack of identity, essence, or "place" experienced by its female protagonists.

Cunningham's novel also shows that this new and other Absolute I is necessary for subjectivity's responsible relationship to the world. For Levinas, the "relationship with a past that is on the hither side of every present and every re-presentable... is included in the extraordinary and everyday event of my responsibility" (*OB*, 10). Likewise, in *The Hours*, Clarissa's memory serves as the starting point for a new connection with herself and with a responsible relation to the world around her. The importance of her memory is brought about by the sharp contrast it provides to the rest of her life, which largely consists in caring for her friend and former lover Richard, who is slowly dying of AIDS. Richard is about to receive a prize for his life's works of poetry, but has also recently published a novel in which Clarissa is a main character. Clarissa's caring for Richard is not authentic in Levinas's sense. Rather, it is based on a nostalgic thematization of the past produced by Clarissa herself and by her willingness to let herself be confined within Richard's interpretation of reality and semimocking reference to her as "Mrs. D" (*TH*, 55, 198). The inherent weakness of Clarissa's relationship with Richard and her feelings for his illness comes to light when she unexpectedly runs into her friend Walter Hardy, whose partner Evan is suffering from the same illness. Clarissa is filled with a desire to give a gift to Evan, to respond to his situation and his suffering, to respond to him as other, but she feels that a book or an "object" would not suffice. She fears that "art, even the greatest of it... belongs stubbornly to the world of objects" (*TH*, 22) and knows that "there is no comfort... in the world of objects" (*TH*, 22). Instead, remembering her moment of connection with herself and the distant unthematizable past, she realizes that she wants to give that *sense of self* to Evan: The "branch and the music matter more to her than do all the books in the store window. She wants for Evan and she wants for herself a book that can carry what that single memory carries" (*TH*, 22).

Just like Woolf's *Mrs. Dalloway*, Cunningham's *The Hours* reaches its climax when the poet commits suicide. Until Richard's death, Clarissa has largely been unable to experience the ethical relation, the pre-original commitment of responsibility. Her responsibility for Richard has been a quasi-responsibility enmeshed in her own overriding inability to face alterity and experience time. Her relationship to Richard has become an epos, already written, rather than true sociality based on a response to the other. Clarissa has been haunted by Woolf's (and Richard's) novel(s). She has searched in vain for herself and her life in Richard Brown's version of her as "Mrs. D" (*TH*, 55, 198). The sentimental and nostalgic nature of her attachment to Richard and his view of her as Mrs. D has set up an illusory reality in which she has looked for truth in the "said," in the thematized version of her life. Richard's novel and his view of her has woven a web of the past and synthesized it into sameness and comprehension. Ironically, in *The Hours*, the ethical relation is produced by the death of Richard Brown. Richard's suicide entails the sudden impossibility of thematizing the past. The past at once becomes unthematizable—it falls beyond the powers of representation and the said.

In *The Hours*, Richard Brown's death paradoxically entails a new birth—the birth of diachrony, the time of the other, the time that does not return. In and through diachrony, responsibility is liberated. For Clarissa, the change accomplished by Richard's death becomes immediately noticeable in the atmosphere. When Richard has jumped from an open window in his apartment, leaving her behind, the horror of the moment is strangely tinged by something vital to her own existence. As she runs down the stairs of the apartment building, she feels that the

> air itself seems to have changed, to have come *slightly apart*; as if the atmosphere were palpably made of *substance and its opposite*. She runs down ... and is aware (she will be ashamed of this later) of herself as a woman running down a set of stairs, uninjured, still alive.... In the lobby she suffers through a moment of confusion over how to get to the air shaft where Richard lies, and she feels, briefly, as if she's gone to hell. *Hell is a stale yellow box of a room, with no exit, shaded by an artificial tree, lined with scarred metal doors*... (*TH*, 200–201, emphasis added.)

With Richard's death, alterity becomes part of the atmosphere, and air is no longer saturated by selfsameness. Surprisingly for Clarissa, she herself is still alive, without the framework of representations provided by Richard. When she finds him, she suddenly seems to be liberated from the smothering "there is," the *il y a*. Significantly, hell here makes an appearance as the *il y a*, being without nothingness, without release or exit. Richard's body provides that exit, is in fact manifested as a break out of the *il y a* for Clarissa. Having found her way out to the shaft, Clarissa "knows ... that he is dead" (*TH*, 201). She "kneels beside him, puts a hand on his inert shoulder.... She tells herself she should go call the police" (*TH*, 202) but "puts [it] off, at least for another minute or two" (*TH*, 202): She remains with Richard, touching his shoulder. She feels (and is astonished at herself) slightly embarrassed by what has happened. She wonders why she doesn't weep. "*She is aware of the sound of her own breathing*" (*TH*, 202, emphasis added)

It is at the party originally intended to honor Richard that the ethical relation is released from its cancellation. This is brought about not only by the presence of Clarissa and Sally, but also by the return of the aging Laura Brown, Richard's condemned mother, who abandoned him when he was a child. Both Clarissa and Laura can now make their appearance outside the realm of the said. "It is time for this day to be over" (*TH*, 224), says Sally to Clarissa and it seems at that moment, that Richard begins truly to leave the world.... Soon... everyone who knew him will be asleep... and they'll wake up tomorrow morning to find that he's joined the realm of the dead.... Clarissa, *the figure in a novel* will vanish, as will Laura Brown, *the lost mother, the martyr and fiend.* Yes, Clarissa thinks, it's time for the day to be over (*TH*, 225, emphasis added).

Unexpectedly, with the lapse of time signaled by the ending of the day, we witness a re-establishing of the ethical relationship. It is only now that Richard's representations of Clarissa and Clarissa's life—its significance and non-significance—can truly drift into the past. It is only now that Laura for the first time enters the story with a voice, as herself, and not as an objectified other. Now she speaks to Clarissa about her own experiences, now there is dialogue. Now Clarissa and Laura are in the realm of saying and time. In contrast to the thematized past in Richard's novel, the past has now come to involve both representation and diachrony. The party that Clarissa has put together for Richard thus takes on a new meaning. It becomes a party for those who are still alive, those who can experience the ending (lapse) of one day and the dawning of another. The party has become "a party for the not-yet-dead; for the relatively undamaged; for those who for mysterious reasons have the fortune to be alive" (*TH*, 226). Clarissa is astounded to be "herself... not Mrs. Dalloway anymore; there is no one now to call her that. Here she is with *another hour before her*" (*TH*, 226, emphasis added). Thus the lapse of time brought about by diachrony makes its appearance in *The Hours* as something gained. For Clarissa and Laura, that which is gained is a dwelling place, a distinctive personal "envelope" in Irigaray's terms, big enough to contain their female identity and to enable its expression.[11] The loss of that which falls beyond thematization involves a release of time. Now, Clarissa and Laura have "an hour before" them (*TH*, 226). Theirs is now a past that "does not return—a diachrony refractory to all synchronization" (*OB*, 9).

University of Vermont

List of Abbreviations

ES: *An Ethics of Sexual Difference*

OB: *Otherwise than Being*

TH: *The Hours*

TI: *Totality and Infinity*

TO: *Time and the Other*

NOTES

[1] This essay is part of a larger research project that utilizes the phenomenology of Emmanuel Levinas, Edmund Husserl, and Luce Irigaray to examine the relation between female subjectivity and time in Virginia Woolf's *Mrs. Dalloway* (1925) and Michael Cunningham's *The Hours* (1998). Because of limited space, I have here chosen to focus mainly on *The Hours*.

[2] To my knowledge, no research on *The Hours* from a Levinasian perspective has hitherto been published. The issue of self-representation and identity in this novel has been studied, however. One of the most notable articles on this topic is Natalia Povalyaeva's "The Issue of Self-Identification in Woolf's *Mrs. Dalloway* and Cunningham's *The Hours*." Povalyaeva investigates Woolf's and Cunningham's strategies to address the question of self-identity.

[3] Irigaray furthers her analysis by claiming that "[i]f traditionally, and as a mother, woman represents place for man, such a limit means that she becomes *a thing*.... She finds herself delineated as a thing. Moreover, the maternal-feminine also serves as an *envelope*, a *container*, the starting point from which man limits his things. The *relationship between envelope and things* constitute one of the aporias, or the aporia, of Aristotelianism and of the philosophical systems derived from it (*ES*, 10).

[4] According to Irigaray, "woman would theoretically be the envelope (which she provides). But she would have no essence or existence, given that she is the potential for essence and existence: *the available place*" (*ES*, 84).

[5] Irigaray's and Levinas's ideas complement each other in this instance. Their ideas are at odds in terms of their understanding of maternity however. In my opinion, this does not necessarily have to impede the fruitfulness of looking at their ideas jointly. On the contrary, their differences are fruitful in creating a juncture of possibilities.

[6] In *Totality and Infinity*, Levinas explains that a "term can remain absolutely at the point of departure of relationship only as I" (36), and that "[a]lterity is possible only starting from me" (40).

[7] Levinas's "I" is thus culturally gendered. Irigaray supplements his thoughts by showing how women traditionally have been deprived of such an "I." In Western culture, Levinas's "I" designates a place traditionally reserved for men. As we shall see, *The Hours* offers a rewriting of this notion of identity by introducing the idea that the absolute point of departure of the self is founded in a relationship with alterity.

[8] Consequently, I differentiate between phenomenological presence and metaphysical presence. In contrast to selfsame presence, I point to another kind of presence, which requires alterity as a condition of possibility for its constitution. Levinas's notion of maternity casts light on this phenomenological presence. The relationship between subjectivity, the ethical relation, and maternity is vital to the constitution of subjectivity in *The Hours*. The ethical encounter takes place on an intrasubjective level as well as between individual subjects. For Levinas, subjectivity is the "breaking point where [selfsame] essence is exceeded by the infinite" (*OB*, 12). This resembles his ideas about maternity. Maternity for Levinas delineates a pre-original welcoming: "Rather than a nature, earlier than nature, immediacy is this vulnerability, this maternity, this pre-birth or pre-nature in which the sensibility belongs" (*OB*, 75–76). In *The Hours*, maternity has become distorted and the protagonists have been deprived of this immediacy and the creativity it engenders. Here, subjectivity is not a breaking point where infinity exceeds and breaks up selfsame essence. Instead subjectivity seeks to reestablish itself as essence in and through self-representation and self-objectification. In contrast, maternity provides a way out of the dichotomy between presence and absence. It deepens the relationship between the self and the other and the notion of subjectivity itself.

In "Like a Maternal Body: Levinas and the Motherhood of Moses," Lisa Guenther provides an insightful analysis of Levinas's thoughts: "While some feminist readers have criticized Levinas for romanticizing mothers' self-sacrifice without acknowledging the political conditions of this sacrifice, others have also found in his work the starting point for a feminist ethics of maternity" (119). By placing emphasis on the word "like" in "like a maternal body" (OB, 67; AE 109), Guenther wishes to "destabilize any strict correlation between women and mothers, or even between motherhood and responsibility" (119).

[9] From now on, I will call Levinas's idea of the point of departure for the ethical relation the "Absolute I."

[10] In noting this, I am inspired by Luce Irigaray's critique of Levinas and of other male Western philosophers, who demonstrate a pervasive tendency to interpret phenomenological existence as based on an either/or relationship rather than a both/and relationship.

[11] In *An Ethics of Sexual Difference*, Irigaray furthers her analysis of the envelope and what it can mean to the interplay between the sexes: "If man and woman are both body and thought, they provide each other with finiteness, limit, and the possibility of access to the divine through the development of envelopes" (86).

REFERENCES

Cunningham, Michael. *The Hours*. New York: Picador, 1998.

Guenther, Lisa. "Like a Maternal Body: Emmanuel Levinas and the Motherhood of Moses," *Hypatia* 21.1 (2006), pp. 119–136.

Irigaray, Luce. *An Ethics of Sexual Difference*. Ithaca, New York: Cornell University Press, 1993.

Levinas, Emmanuel. *Totality and Infinity: An Essay on Exteriority*. Pittsburgh: Duquesne University Press, 1969.

Levinas, Emmanuel. *Otherwise than Being or Beyond Essence*. The Hague: Martinus Nijhoff, 1981.

Levinas, Emmanuel. *Time and The Other*. Pittsburgh: Duquesne University Press, 1987.

Povalyaeva, Natalia. "The Issue of Self-Identification in Woolf's *Mrs. Dalloway* and Cunningham's *The Hours*," in *Woolf across Cultures*, pp. 269–276.

Woolf, Virginia. *Mrs. Dalloway*. New York: Harcourt, 1981.

SECTION IV

VICTOR GERALD RIVAS

ENLIGHTENMENT, HUMANIZATION, AND BEAUTY IN THE LIGHT OF SCHILLER'S "LETTERS ON THE AESTHETIC EDUCATION OF MAN"

> So the world [...] becomes a living and blessed thing.
>
> Plotinus

I

There are some figures who resist any endeavor to classify them, and Schiller is with no doubt one of them; he embodied the enlightened identity of creativity and lucidity whose natural realm is culture. Indeed, he reached the acme of his genius as a great playwright and as an exceptional poet insofar as he was able to understand the social and theoretical sense of art without mistaking logical explanation for imaginative expression or vice versa, a feature whereby it is seasonable to study him in a time like ours, when the figures of the poet and the thinker have again been so oddly—and, for me, so wrongly—identified. Still more, on studying Schiller's thought concerning what he called "aesthetic education," I shall shed light on the vital and poetical course of modernity, whose archetype of the thinker is neither the wise person nor the scientist but the "intellectual," who must be carefully distinguished from the two other figures: the wise person, whose paradigm was embodied in the ancient philosopher, and the scientist, whose prototype is the empirical investigator. Whereas the former revealed an all-embracing theory of reality and existence whose ground was transcendent and the latter solves problems defined within a certain field of knowledge that can change in accordance with the discovery of new phenomena,[1] the intellectual supplies logical frameworks for the interaction of individual and society: for him, thought is more than anything else the representation of the possibility of participation in the social dynamics, and is not worth attention when it does not aim at that, which, of course, does not mean either that it must immediately be related to its object, for it can set it from a universal outlook, which shows that, contrary to what the philosopher upholds in principle, the intellectual does not heed any idea for itself, that is, whether as the self-subsistent form of reality (Plato) or as the ground of any coherent mental process (Descartes): He just deals with a thought when it stands for a specific action, and it comes to the same thing if it is a universal principle or a particular rule, provided that it makes feasible socioindividual transformation, which corroborates that for the intellectual, at least for the kind that Schiller embodied, the question is not what thought as such is but how it frames someone's reach in a determined situation,[2] which, on the other hand, agrees with the subjective ground of modern thought, as one of the initial paragraphs of Schiller's Letters seems to remind us:

> The liberty of action you prescribe is rather a necessity for me than a constraint. Little exercised in formal rules, I shall scarcely incur the risk of sinning against good taste by any undue use of them; my ideas, drawn rather from within than from reading or from an intimate experience with the world, will not disown their origin; they would rather incur any reproach than that of a sectarian bias, and would prefer to succumb by their innate feebleness than sustain themselves by borrowed authority and foreign support (I, 2).[3]

According to the intellectual, then, everyone must participate in the social configuration of culture not mainly because of the objective meaning of his ideas (however worthwhile this could be by itself) but because they express the unity of his consciousness within the social relativity, wherewith the participation, instead of being the arbitrary imposition or the defense of a despicable slant, stands for the achievement of a possibility that furthers sociability and simultaneously furnishes the individual with an identity before others, in such way that the social dimension of existence hinges upon the capacity of focusing one's ideal as a standard that anyone can use for his benefit, through a process of identification and universalization that, as we shall see, also is the very gist of aesthetic education.[4] Thus, there is, at least in principle, a community of meaning between the action of the intellectual and the person who has received an aesthetic education: for both of them, the main aim is to universalize the social framework of individuality, which would not be possible if the two elements, society and individuality, were not transcendentally integrated, just as, on the plane of the individual, reason and feelings are. The unity of existence is thus doubly transcendental: objectively, it comprises social and individual elements; subjectively, it identifies all the manifestations of the person; the link on the first plane is provided by history; on the second, by aesthetic education; and the final unity is the work of art. Therefore, if it is absurd to speak of someone without taking into account the social framework wherein he evolves, it is even more absurd to speak of a personal feature passing over the unity of subjectivity. Beyond certain cases or beyond the particular interests that determine the social interaction, the philosophical comprehension of someone entails taking him as an original unity, not as a conglomerate of gifts, talents, and features, whereby the intellectual always must consider the individual as such, that is, as a conscious being that is able to change in accordance with his thought, for that is the condition sine qua non to understand everyone as a man, as a being able to determinate his existence consciously, as the transcendental or universal outlook whose philosophical ground Schiller borrowed from Kant requires, an outlook that compels everyone to act not only according to a categorical imperative but only by it, whose utmost enunciation is, "*So act that you use humanity, whether in your own person or in the person of any other, always at the same time as an end, never merely as a means.*"[5] It does not matter if concrete individuals agree with the ideality of man and, by extension, with sociability; what is determinant here is, first, that everyone stands for an absolute end by the mere fact of being human and, second, that it is possible for everyone to act only by the respect to humanity and not by aleatory factors. Instead of rising to the occasion, acting morally demands rising to the universality of law that is, as Schiller also emphasizes, the patrimony of everyone:

If stripped of their technical shape, [...the moral laws...] will appear as the verdict of reason pronounced from time immemorial by common consent, and as facts of the moral instinct which nature, in her wisdom, has given to man in order to serve as guide and teacher until his enlightened intelligence gives him maturity" (I, 4).

Indeed, although not everyone is up to the philosophical elucidation of the moral law, the fact is that everyone is up to the understanding thereof.

Thus, in stating that Schiller embodies the modern intellectual, I do not mean that his ideas had had an eminently political rise or scope (as it mostly happens with would-be intellectuals nowadays, who tend to be inspired by the figure of the journalist or the reporter); far from that, he followed the mode discovered by the eighteenth-century French thinkers, above all by Voltaire and Rousseau, who, from a different conception of their work as intellectuals, sought, however, an aim similar to Schiller's: enlighten society and make everyone conscious of his dignity as a rational being. This similarity of aims among so diverse conceptions of literature and thought was possible because both Voltaire, Rousseau, and Schiller shared the idea that is the hub of modernity, concretely of the Enlightenment: Reason always is endlessly and universally operative, which, instead of reducing the action thereof to the field of knowledge and science, demands to extend it to every aspect of human existence, which changes reason itself into the highest ideal and at the same time into the frame of the process, provided that it embraces the singularity of the individual consciousness. In this manner, reason furnishes everyone with a cultural framework to identify himself with others and, vice versa, with a symbolic dignity to express his being before society, and the identity of this double dimension is fixed thanks to the aesthetic education, which unfolds the organic unity of sociability, sensibility, and ideality. Someone that had been educated as Schiller proposes will per force recognize that society is not a hindrance to his freedom, since, on the contrary, he only can be free together with others in the bosom of a enlightened society, never in the isolation of the individual existence that is brutally crushed by unbounded wants; at the same time, he will perceive how all his potentialities and gifts converge in only one aim, the fulfilment of humanity. Consequently, the aesthetic education, instead of fostering the projection of the individual as such, that is, as the formless psychological aggregate of wants and views, fosters the harmonic accomplishment of humanity as a universal that everyone must freely and spontaneously vindicate, an ideal that Schiller also calls beauty:

> By your permission I lay before you, in a series of letters, the results of my researches upon beauty and art. I am keenly sensible of the importance as well as of the charm and dignity of this undertaking. I shall treat a subject which is closely connected with the better portion of our happiness and not far removed from the moral nobility of human nature. I shall plead this cause of the Beautiful before a heart by which her whole power is felt and exercised, and which will take upon itself the most difficult part of my task in an investigation where one is compelled to appeal as frequently to feelings as to principles (I, 1).

This ideal goes hand in hand with the two theses that I consider the most axial contribution of Schiller as intellectual: First, that there is a reciprocal link between the framework of a determined society and the framework of the individual sensibility. In other words, when a society is ruled by abstract ideas and unbounded desires, individuals will be carried away by them and will spoil the ideal unity of their being that is reflected by their sensibility; vice versa, when they lack the sensibility required to act rationally or freely, the society will be alien to the ideal unity of human being; on the contrary, when a society furthers the harmonic development of its members, they will enjoy an ideal restraint that will make them coexist rationally. Second, that modern society, insofar as it has liberated the individuals without having previously educated them in the aesthetic sense of the word, has brought about the most terrible upheaval on the plane of average existence. This is blatant both by the reduction of every human want to the mere satisfaction of desire and by the brutal expression thereof: It is not enough to be carried away by the monstrous avalanche of bodily and mental impulses, one has still to exhibit them in the most grotesque way so as to excite others, which creates the illusion of a universal liberation when the fact is that such an orgiastic blast is rather aimed to deprive everyone of his capacity of reasoning.

Now, although it is true that neither of these theses appears explicitly in the Letters, their sense shapes them throughout and supplies so the bedrock of the argumentation, which also precludes the "*Letters*" from being a simple gloss of the Kantian conception of morals, since, notwithstanding his overt philosophical debts to Kant, Schiller is after a goal very different from laying the transcendental foundations of moral experience: He wants instead to bring to light the critical framework wherewith the Kantian ideals can be reified both individually and socially, which shows again the difference between an intellectual and a philosopher while reinforcing their common appellation to the universality of reason. Thus, the exposition of Schiller's thought will not be only logical like Kant's and will require a historical background that will be helpful to confirm the enlightened conception of reason both as a universal ideal and as personal undertaking whose accomplishment hinges, however, upon everyone's will, a conception with which Schiller supports his idealization of art as the medium by antonomasia for recovering the unity of man with nature and through it with himself, a unity that the process of history has destroyed but that must be reconstituted and universalized, this time not by the lurid strength of nature but by the conscious action of man.

II

Inasmuch as Schiller aimed his activity as intellectual to make everyone conscious of his own humanity, no other literary genre was more adequate for him to set out his thought than the letter. As a matter of fact, the letter agrees with the subjective frame, the publicity, and the universal relativity of truth that modernity has upheld from the onset; moreover, and this is much more important, the letter establishes an intimacy and betokens a personal experience and a common concern that are more or less absent from the other two modern genres that also match the critical stance of the intellectual before society: the manifesto and the essay; the former stands for how a group upholds a certain idea or belief without entailing per force an individual consciousness thereof (which also is the view of the theatre, to which Schiller owed most of his fame), while the latter leaves aside the demand of a timely answer implicit instead in every letter, even when the addressee is humanity as a whole or, as in the famous "*Philosophic Letters*" by Voltaire, the community of enlightened persons beyond the borders of a national culture.[6] In brief, the letter evokes the dialogical condition of the intellectual, who speaks simultaneously on behalf of himself and on behalf of everyone, a feature that allows him to present his ideas not merely as his but as everyone's, whereby they become ideals that are for articulating the action of everyone, taking into account that an ideal, unlike an idea, is not so much a preexistent form (whether metaphysical or logical) as a possibility that compels everyone to carry it out, which endows again the ideal action with an almost sacramental value that reminds one of the famous passage of Goethe's *Faust* wherein the protagonist, after asking what term could be the most suitable translation of the Hellenic "Logos" wherewith Christ is named at the beginning of John's Gospel, discards the traditional "Word" and opts for "Act,"[7] confirming so the imperative of participating in the conformation of reality, in this case, of the sociohistorical world that is the rise of culture.

This transcendental primacy of action supplies the thread in Schiller's "Letters" and aims to what can be considered the specific problem of German Classical Idealism whether in its cultural phenomena or in its properly philosophical trend: the identification of reason and reality, an identification that Hegel called "Spirit" and Schiller, loyal heir of the enlightened tradition of the eighteenth-century, "humanization," a concept whose full comprehension implies, as in the case of the Hegelian Spirit, overcoming the would-be opposition that in accordance with the metaphysical tradition existed between nature and man or, to set the question in transcendental concepts, between necessity and freedom. Concerning this subject, let us recall that the only way that the tradition found to overcome the opposition at issue was setting out the existence either of a teleological rationality or of a supernatural providence, which, instead of solving the problem, just made it harder. Now, this was utterly useless since necessity and freedom can also be denominated "concrete universals" insomuch as (paraphrasing the definition of a transcendental element that Kant offers in the *Critique of Pure Reason*),[8] they do not mean self-subsistent frameworks or realities but the elements of universal experience that must agree throughout with the fulfilment of the own personality within the limits of the sociocultural approach wherewith we deal: None can enjoy a fully free life in a society that does not heed the harmonic formation of all and sundry and must suffer therefore somehow the tyranny of necessity, whether this is expressed by an internal unbalance or by a social upheaval. After all, the only way to reconcile freedom and necessity is to see them as the universal or concrete ideals that sustain the development of society through history, wherewith Schiller forestalls the possible criticism that it is absurd to devote oneself to laying the foundations of the aesthetic education when the main problem that humanity faces is the lack of justice and of individual freedom that goes hand in hand with the terrible violence in society. Although Schiller was very aware of the relevance of these problems, he thought that they would remain unsolved while they were set out in the field where they are perceptible and not where their common cause is located, which is, oddly enough, in the carelessness regarding the education of individuals: "to arrive at a solution even in the political problem, the road of aesthetics must be pursued, because it is through beauty that we arrive at freedom" (II, 5). In other words, injustice and violence are in essence an outcome, not a cause. Independently of factors that escape the individual consciousness, they can be considered a consequence of the lack of rationality that rules the education of individuals, sprawls over society, and vice versa: A society of unbalanced individuals is a horde, however much it seems to be cosmopolitan and refined.

Thus, although Schiller's approach to the issue could be branded idealistic in the deprecatory sense of the word, the author shows—paraphrasing or rather reinterpreting what Kant had settled concerning the transcendental frame of knowledge[9]—that idealism simply means that whatever sociohistorical phenomenon must be assessed in accordance with the kind of human existence that it presupposes and simultaneously reproduces, not with parameters whose would-be objectivity varies drastically together with the way of thinking of the evaluator: "advance of learning," "distribution of richness," or whatever else does not mean by itself a human fulfilment if it is not determined by the furtherance of conscious individuals that are able to face and overcome rationally that blind law of necessity that Schiller calls "the natural condition," wherein man is the same as any other living and is carried away by his immediate wants:

Now the term "natural condition" can be applied to every political body which owes its establishment originally to forces and not to laws, and such a state contradicts the moral nature of man, because lawfulness can alone have authority over this. At the same time this natural condition is quite sufficient for the physical man, who only gives himself laws in order to get rid of brute force. Moreover, the physical man is a reality, and the moral man problematical. Therefore when reason suppresses the natural condition, as she must if she wishes to substitute her own, she weighs the real physical man against the problematical moral man, she weighs the existence of society against a possible, though morally necessary, ideal of society (III, 3).

Now, this natural condition is neither a historical fiction like Rousseau's nor a symbol of human selfishness like Hobbes'; it is a critical concept that is for bringing to light the contradictions existing between the economical and political development of modern society vis-à-vis the harmony that should rule the individual formation, harmony that Schiller, unlike Rousseau, does not bind to a mythical nature but to the integral enlightenment that aesthetic education stands for, which from this outlook is superior to the moral law because this could not be universally fulfilled in the natural condition that is utterly alien to reason and only obeys physical power, so that the question is how to change a society that does not recognize the ideal condition of human life without threatening, on the other hand, the continuity thereof. For however sublime the idea of revolution can be and although no transformation will be useful unless it comprises the whole of the ideals that a society is supposed to respect, the case is that any harm against social order must be precluded. This outright refusal of any measure or action that endangers the stability of society, far from entailing a concession to the natural condition or an invitation to choose the lesser of two evils, agrees throughout with the hub of Schiller's proposal: that social development must be based on the freedom of each and every man and not vice versa. Due to the gruesome irrationality that any revolution sparks off and to the upheaval that even the fairest individuals experience whenever the social order crumbles, it would be preposterous to consider revolution as a remedy for injustice, an idea that Schiller, borrowed from Kant, who although supported the French Revolution as a symbol of a universal and spontaneous tendency to freedom, thought that it was preferable not to resort to such a measure and take care instead of the enlightenment of people and of the furtherance of the respect to the constitution that has to rule the State.[10] Thus, focusing the question from the perspective of the individual freedom and balance that both Kant and Schiller so eagerly upheld, the revolution, instead of solving social problems, tends to aggravate them because it blasts and is sustained at the cost of thousands of individuals that are brutally carried away by the tyranny of the majority or, what is a lot worse, indulge those untamable strengths that upset man, whereby Schiller remarks that

it would be necessary to qualify as unseasonable every attempt to effect a similar change in the state, and all hope as chimerical that would be based on such an attempt, until the division of the inner man ceases, and nature has been sufficiently developed to become herself the instrument of this great change and secure the reality of the political creation of reason (VII, 1).

Consequently, the improvement of a society cannot be assessed by the richness or the comfort wherewith it furnishes individuals, let alone by the would-be adaptability of intersubjective relationships, for these elements more often than not further a high degree of unconsciousness and brutality, facing which the moral law seems to be a chimera that is only useful to palliate the misery of existence or, which is almost the same, to deceive the foolish ones that are not up to it. Therefore, moral law will be meaningless unless the individual commands his inner complexity, which cannot be the outcome of a solitary or rather heroic decision that only some few can make as a last resort; on the contrary, this must be reachable for everyone, at least as a social determination:

This prop is not found in the natural character of man, who, being selfish and violent, directs his energies rather to the destruction than to the preservation of society. Nor is it found in his moral character, which has to be formed, which can never be worked upon or calculated on by the lawgiver, because it is free and never appears. It would seem therefore that another measure must be adopted. It would seem that the physical character of the arbitrary must be separated from moral freedom; that it is incumbent to make the former harmonize with the laws and the latter dependent on impressions; it would be expedient to remove the former still farther from matter and to bring the latter somewhat more near to it; in short to produce a third character related to both the others—the physical and the moral—paving the way to a transition from the sway of mere force to that of law, without preventing the proper development of the moral character, but serving rather as a pledge in the sensuous sphere of a morality in the unseen (III, 4).

III

We have so far seen that Schiller, unlike most of the critics of modern reason, whether contemporaries of his or not, instead of tilting at the systematic paradigm of knowledge, morals, and aesthetic experience (which comprises the entire development of Kant's critical work), praises it because it furnishes everyone with a full consciousness of his or her humanity. Still more, inasmuch as the first function of reason is precisely the determination of the limits and sense both of knowledge and of the moral law, a philosophical analysis of reason cannot leave aside the question of social coexistence and of the cultural function of knowledge, which was, as we have just recalled, vouched for by Kant, who dealt successively with the a priori framework of theoretical and practical knowledge and culminated in the *Critique of Judgement* with the question of the total unity that reason requires to provide a systematic experience beyond the division of the theoretical and the practical realms.[11] According to this, the merit of Kant lies in having realized before than anyone else that reason, focused as a whole process of determination of experience, goes beyond the objective knowledge or the subjective fulfilment of law and comprises the multiplicity of states of mind that rationalism, still under the command of the dualism inherent to the ancient metaphysics, had instead discarded as undeterminable manifestations of imagination linked to the world of appearances.[12] The multiplicity of subjective phenomena that had remained outside the realm of reason could thenceforth be ordered by the aesthetic judgment and (which was a lot more relevant for Schiller's goals) betokened a sui generis affinity between man and nature. Now, what is very remarkable is that Kant had also applied this way of thinking to lay the foundations of a critical conception of history that, as we have just seen, shows that the most brutal violence by no means gainsays the highest ideal and that is rather for supporting a kind of rational faith in man that Schiller for his part upholds and that is the background of the strong criticism that he aims not at reason (as done time and time again before and after him) but, on the contrary, at the irrationality of society that Enlightenment brought to light on claiming the boundless dignity of each man; before the injustice and the absurd prevailing in all the social processes and institutions, above all in the field of education, Schiller makes us become aware not of the abstract character of reason but of the reduction thereof to a mere tool to exploit nature and abuse others, which goes hand in hand with the terrible mistake of taking "freedom" for "liberation": whereas the former is a positive expression of reason, the latter is a negative answer to the social establishment.

Oddly enough, this double reduction of reason to instrumental determination and of freedom to liberation has mostly been passed over by intellectuals of all the tendencies, although it is overt that the two aspects always work as a whole, which shows that the miscomprehension of the integrative function of nature and culture through knowledge is the reverse of the oblivion of the regulative framework of individual freedom. Ignorant of the theoretic advances of enlightenment and alien to a rational vision of morals, the average individual of modern society degenerates very soon and ends up squeezed by selfishness as if he were an inhabitant of the natural condition whereof we have already spoken, and Schiller was doubtlessly one of the first to realize this problem and to offer a solution to it.[13]

Now, Schiller unfolds the process through which dehumanization and irrationality are finally one and the same by the elemental opposition of what he calls the savage and the barbarian:

Now man can be opposed to himself in a twofold manner: either as a savage, when his feelings rule over his principles; or as a barbarian, when his principles destroy his feelings. The savage despises art, and acknowledges nature as his despotic ruler; the barbarian laughs at nature, and dishonours it, but he often proceeds in a more contemptible way than the savage, to be the slave of his senses. The cultivated man makes of nature his friend, and honours its friendship, while only bridling its caprice (IIII, 6).

This opposition is insurmountable in principle in the natural condition because the continuity of objective violence and subjective imbalance distorts the very basis of coexistence, which is the universal recognition of the ideal humanity of each individual. Thus, any attempt to overcome the opposition will be useless since, although someone may possess an objective feature, the import thereof will be merely individual and will mar the capability of being level-headed, which everyone experiences not so much before some objective distress but before the very inner dynamics of vital strength: Far from relying on a general tendency to equanimity and self-assurance, the modern individual tends toward permanent imbalance and to a diffidence that is more often than not hidden by the furtherance of all and sundry inclinations and desires, which gives the impression that everyone is unboundedly free and that the ideal of a full life has been achieved, which is, however, utterly false:

> How different is the course followed by us moderns! We also displace and magnify individuals to form the image of the species, but we do this in a fragmentary way, not by altered combinations, so that it is necessary to gather up from different individuals the elements that form the species in its totality. It would almost appear as if the powers of mind express themselves with us in real life or empirically as separately as the psychologist distinguishes them in the representation. For we see not only individual subjects, but whole classes of men, uphold their capacities only in part, while the rest of their faculties scarcely show a germ of activity, as in the case of the stunted growth of plants (VI, 3).

Thus, instead of having been released from the burden of savagery and unsettling that is the token of the natural condition and that had always been disparaged both by the upper and the lower classes, modern society has preposterously vindicated it in all the fields of coexistence, so that the atrocities that were formerly reduced to war or to the collapse of the legal order are nowadays considered practically an unavoidable condition of existence or as the forceful concession that man must make to nature, an irrational tenet that finds its reflection on the plane of individuality, wherein desire is mistaken for an uncheckable instinct that demands to be satisfied in the coarsest ways; bereft of any ideality and reduced either to bodily wants or to mental outbursts, desire is metamorphosed into an abstract instinct that crushes alike identity and conscious preferences to the extent that it is almost the same to be barbarian or to be savage, for in any case both extremes contradict real humanity, which, nevertheless, makes more compelling the want of plunging into the dizziness of relations, procedures, and performances that characterizes modern life.

Concerning this, it is very remarkable the way Schiller figures out the aberrant unity of efficiency and unsettlement that is the very kernel of modern society, a unity that, as I emphasized, has provided the critics of modernity with their main argument to denounce the would-be tyranny of reason over existence; nevertheless, Schiller, as Kant had done before him, underlines time and time again that the only sound solution to the unbalance of modernity, at least from the individual outlook, lies in fostering the universalization of conscious responsibility and of sociopolitical ideality.[14] This aim is doubly important in a time when society has lost its traditional framework and is ruled or rather carried away by the shallowest understanding of the part that culture plays in the unfolding of life, a phenomenon that is perhaps unparalleled in history:

Man paints himself in his actions, and what is the form depicted in the drama of the present time? On the one hand, he is seen running wild, on the other in a state of lethargy; the two extremest stages of human degeneracy, and both seen in one and the same period. In the lower larger masses, coarse, lawless impulses come to view, breaking loose when the bonds of civil order are burst asunder, and hastening with unbridled fury to satisfy their savage instinct [...] On the other hand, the civilized classes give us the still more repulsive sight of lethargy, and of a depravity of character which is the more revolting because it roots in culture [...] The enlightenment of the understanding, on which the more refined classes pride themselves with some ground, shows on the whole so little of an ennobling influence on the mind that it seems rather to confirm corruption by its maxims. We deny nature in her legitimate field and feel her tyranny in the moral sphere, and while resisting her impressions, we receive our principles from her (V, 3–5).

For, independent of the particular valorization of tradition, there is no doubt that no time has questioned the value of culture as modernity has done, which also has brought about that the would-be depositaries of tradition, namely, the learned classes, have lost as a whole their cultural function and are incapable of setting an example to the rest of society, whereof Schiller makes the most to prop the want of the aesthetic or integral education of all and sundry individuals: Since no class embodies by itself the ideals of tradition, everyone must assume them for himself. Thus, Schiller sets out the so-called crisis or death of culture, which has caused a lot of talk for more than a century and a half, as a process of decadence that has, anyhow, played an axial part in the unfolding of freedom:

My subject has led me naturally to place in relief the distressing tendency of the character of our own times to show the sources of the evil, without its being my province to point out the compensations offered by nature. I will readily admit to you that, although this splitting up of their being was unfavourable for individuals, it was the only road open for the progress of the race [...] There was no other way to develop the manifold aptitudes of man than to bring them in opposition with one another. This antagonism of forces is the great instrument of culture, but it is only an instrument; for as long as this antagonism lasts, man is only on the road to culture (VI, 11).

Beyond the terrible effects that the decadence might have on the plane of individual existence, wherein the lack of a common ideality and of the corresponding establishment has more often than not sparked off an unheard-of distress, the same process has been for the consciousness of the originality and dignity of everyone, for if it is true that "transcendence" has become a meaningless term, it is also true that it has brought to light the philosophical complexity of sociocultural existence.

Thus, the crisis of tradition must be not mistaken for the sudden fall of a humanistic valorization of man's being; on the contrary, any conception of humanism that does not take into account the radical transformation of the function and meaning of reason after Kant is doubtlessly doomed to failure because it has to resort to a transcendence incompatible with the intellectual and cultural conditions of modernity, which by no means is tantamount to saying that there is no way of upholding a kind of transcendence, above all of a religious one, which will be perfectly feasible provided that such a transcendence agrees somehow with the critical bedrock of sociocultural life, as Kant shows, for instance, in *Religion Within the Limits of Reason Alone*, wherein all the ritual and ecclesiastical aspects of the question are in principle left aside and the very faith is changed into a ground of morals,[15] which is also what Schiller suggests on the final paragraph of the "*Letters*", when he sums up its content:

> In the aesthetic state the most slavish tool is a free citizen, having the same rights as the noblest; and the intellect which shapes the mass to its intent must consult it concerning its destination. Consequently in the realm of aesthetic appearance, the idea of equality is realized, which the political zealot would gladly see carried out socially. It has often been said that perfect politeness is only found near a throne. If thus restricted in the material, man has, as elsewhere appears, to find compensation in the ideal world. Does such a state of beauty in appearance exist, and where? It must be in every finely harmonized soul; but as a fact, only in select circles, like the pure ideal of the church and state—in circles where manners are not formed by the empty imitations of the foreign, but by the very beauty of nature; where man passes through all sorts of complications in all simplicity and innocence, neither forced to trench on another's freedom to preserve his own, nor to show grace at the cost of dignity (XXVII, 11–12).

In a word, if a critical or modern reason makes impossible to resort to any theological explanation of reality, it does not preclude philosophy or, in general, the humanities from dealing with the lack of a religious or theological ideal if it leads to deepen the understanding of man.

IV

I showed in the foregoing section that modernity (at least in its enlightened version, which is what Schiller vindicated), far from entailing an abstract idealization of man, has from the onset postulated that the double dimension of existence, objective or sociocultural and subjective or aesthetic-humanistic, possesses a rational framework thanks to which "State" and "person" are reciprocal terms,[16] which always must be taken into account so as to preclude the State from overpowering the person (as happens in the traditional or premodern society) or, contrariwise, to preclude the person from being alien to the State (as it happens more often than not in modernity). Together with this, we also have shown that the modern concept of reason that culminates in the Kantian Critiques rebuffs any theological or—to say it more properly— dogmatic transcendence, and asserts the unbounded moral dignity of every man, wherein the only philosophical import of culture lies, for Schiller—as for so many of his contemporaries—in disparaging alike the reduction of culture to the refinement of customs, to the canonization of a style or activity (whether it is artistic or not) and to the perfunctory handling of themes that ends up changing real comprehension into a bundle of truisms. This threefold import of the concept, which links respectively to politeness, to the academy, and to the false cultivation that becomes pedantry, leaves aside the question of the aesthetic identity of man and society, which is, nevertheless, the philosophical ground of culture. Now, what is really remarkable (considering the temporal proximity of Schiller with the romantic myth of folklore that above all in Germany was hand in hand with the metaphysical preponderance of the so-called Spirit of People)[17] is that our author never mentions in the *Letters* the relevance of folklore or of national tradition for aesthetic education and unfolds the question from the subjective plane. This, of course, more than implying that Schiller is blind to the national culture (which doubtlessly offers the bedrock of any individual formation), shows that what he is after is not the understanding of the individual as such but as a human being. In other words, although it is undeniable that a German or a Mexican will always be defined by the sense and reach of their respective folklore, a human being will pass over that and only will be determined by the transcendental framework of his being, not by his ties to a tradition, which shows that Schiller would surely have assented to the famous dictum of Voltaire: "I am French by incident and human being by nature."

The problem that Schiller and, in general, intellectuals like him must face is so how to identify empirically State and person. For although these two terms mean each other on a transcendental outlook (which is what Schiller adopted following Kant), its correspondence must also be evident on the empirical plane; otherwise, all the discourse concerning the fulfilment of humanity will be simply a heap of words, a display of rhetoric, perhaps brilliant, but nothing more. That is why Schiller introduces his theory of the elemental strengths of man, the instincts, which will have the universal scope that the transcendental outlook requires and the concrete sense that the empirical one imposes:

> Reason has done all that she could in finding the law and promulgating it; it is for the energy of the will and the ardor of feeling to carry it out. To issue victoriously from her contest with force, truth herself must first become a force, and turn one of the instincts of man into her champion in the empire of phaenomena. For instincts are the only motive forces in the material world. If hitherto truth has so little manifested her victorious power, this has not depended on the understanding, which could not have unveiled it, but on the heart which remained closed to it, and on instinct which did not act with it (VIII, 3).

Unlike Kant, who was devoted throughout to laying the foundations of the formal order of experience, Schiller is after the overcoming of any metaphysical approach to the formation or education of the individual consciousness, which is precisely his badge in the history of thought and why I have considered him the first embodiment—both chronologically and logically—of the modern intellectual. He could not pass over the problem of how to give a material content to the transcendental framework of experience, and his theory of instincts is for that without meaning, on the other hand, in resorting to it he is not somehow yielding either to the precritical metaphysics or to a coarse explanation of the organic functions of man. Far from that, he discovered in the concept of "instinct" the possibility of identifying the formal and the material elements of experience and—which was a lot more axial for him—of human being, wherewith, instead of appealing to the metaphysics whose theoretical barrenness Kant had once and for all proved, he resorted to the affinity of form and matter that is the very kernel of any idealistic conception of aesthetics and whose explanation is simultaneously the subject of the First Part of the *Critique of Judgement* by Kant and the rise of aesthetics as a philosophical field with proper limits. And it is in the exposition of the issue where one notes the great independence wherewith Schiller proceeds concerning his philosophical links whether to Kant or to other eighteenth-century thinkers,[18] for he puts the aesthetic determination of existence before any other, even before the moral one, not in hierarchy but in the part that it plays in providing man with the fulcrum required to identity self-consciousness and sociability. For more than "society," the concept that allows understanding the sense of Schiller's argumentation is "sociability," the penchant for coexisting and enjoying together with others, which, as I mentioned, contradicts throughout the penchant for isolating oneself that characterizes the modern individual. Now, sociability, unlike the universal determination of moral law, has to be furthered not against but through the resistance of the natural penchant to overpower others that man, as any other living being, experiences, which has been wrongly interpreted as an evil force by the metaphysical tradition of Platonic inclination, whereas the fact is that in the case of man (whose being must be fathomed with categories completely different to those of the other animals) it betokens the unmistakable recognition of the transcendent dignity of everyone. Furthermore, human brutality only works on a very narrow realm, namely, through the physical wants that by principle cannot prevail over freedom. In other words, Schiller dismisses the general orientation of the metaphysical tradition but makes the most of the transcendence by which it had focused individual freedom so as to reinforce the affinity of form and content or, to say it properly, of form and instinct, which after the critical work of Kant could no longer be set out as two metaphysically opposed elements but as the two aspects of the same process, as the author states in one of the most clarifying passages of the "Letters", which is worth quoting in extenso:

> This twofold labour or task, which consists in making the necessary pass into reality in us and in making out of us reality subject to the law of necessity, is urged upon us as a duty by two opposing forces, which are justly styled impulsions or instincts, because they impel us to realise their object. The first of these impulsions, which I shall call the sensuous instinct, issues from the physical existence of man, or from sensuous nature; and it is this instinct which tends to enclose him in the limits of time and to make of him a material being; I do not say to give him matter, for to dot that a certain free activity of the personality would be necessary, which, receiving matter, distinguishes it from the Ego, or what is permanent. By matter I only understand in this place the change or reality that fills time. Consequently the instinct requires that there should be change, and that time should contain something. This simply filled state of time is named sensation, and it is only in this state that physical existence manifests itself [...] The second impulsion, which may be named the formal instinct, issues from the absolute existence of man, or from his rational nature, and tends to set free, and bring harmony into the diversity of its manifestations, and to maintain personality notwithstanding all the changes of state. As this personality, being an absolute and indivisible unity, can never be in contradiction with itself, as we are ourselves for ever, this impulsion, which tends to maintain personality, can never exact in one time anything but what it exacts and requires for ever [...] It wishes the real to be necessary and eternal, and it wishes the eternal and the necessary to be real; in other terms, it tends to truth and justice (XII, 1–4).

As we see, Schiller's thought agrees point by point with the goal that any modern intellectual is after, which is making everyone become conscious of the inviolable right of self-determination that he possesses by the mere fact of being man, which, on the other hand, is tantamount to stating that the balanced development of one's own sensibility for dignity or freedom must be reflected by happiness: What would be the use of being free if one should pay for it with wretchedness? Fortunately, the affinity existing between nature and man reveals on the individual plane—barring pathological cases that are the exception that proves the rule—the one existing among the elemental instincts and the sundry possibilities wherein they are expressed.[19] Now, the precise form of manifestation cannot be anticipated because it stems from freedom, which is the only kind of absolute transcendence compatible with critical reason; however, once it has been manifested, everyone recognizes it because it stands for a transcendental feature and (taking advantage of the organic outlook that nurtures the theory of instincts) for the universality of vital strengths alike: No one can foresee how his personality is going finally to be since, beyond the concrete elements everyone uses to shape his character, there is a multiplicity of factors that is not reducible to a single rule, which explains why every individual, even the dullest or the shallowest one, is at the same time unique and common, unrepeatable and imitable, singular and universal.[20] Of course, these pairs of opposites, instead of referring to the dualism inherent in the precritical metaphysics, work simply as milestones in the process of fulfilment of one's own being: the formal instinct and the material one evolve together and neither of them is superior to the other; rather, their common manifestation endows each one with that diversity of states of mind and behavior that makes one's personality always seems to be modifiable however much it is almost impossible to change it when one proposes to do so. This odd harmony of immanency and transcendence wherein freedom is experienced, which is irreducible to any demonstration although its potency is undeniable, is what Schiller, sharing the term by which his contemporaries meant the everlasting unity of reality that is a lot more felt when everything is changing and disintegrating, styled "mind," whose action concerning the instincts lies in keeping the integrity of consciousness when they express their utmost difference:

> Moreover, this immanence of two fundamental impulses does not in any degree contradict the absolute unity of the mind, as soon as the mind itself,—its selfhood—is distinguished from these two motors. No doubt, these two impulses exist and act in it, but itself is neither matter nor form, nor the sensuous nor reason, and this is a point that does not seem always to have occurred to those who only look upon the mind as itself acting when its acts are in harmony with reason, and who declare it passive when its acts contradict reason (XIX, 9).

The mind, instead of gainsaying the natural and physical determinations of human existence, confirms the affinity of man and nature, whereas the metaphysical tradition had asserted the contrary because it had an abstract conception of the very being of man and defined it either as soul or as mere reason, leaving aside the comprehension of the universal framework of life both on the sociohistorical plane and on the aesthetic or individual one. With the unity of existence, Schiller seems to have at once overcome the dualism of the metaphysical tradition, but it is hardly understandable at any rate how according to him the mind acts upon the instincts, considering that it must be not only an a priori framework or a logical condition: In the field of knowledge or in the realm of morals it makes perfect sense to speak of a purely formal determination, but that is useless facing the passional complexity of life, where the aleatory potency of time and freedom always must be taken into account; Schiller, then, seems to have simply displaced the dualism more than overcome it, considering that his main purpose is to show how freedom can be fulfilled by everyone without betraying or contradicting its transcendental universality. Of course, the problem is more apparent than real, for the mind is not a metaphysical or rather a theological absolute but a determination of human existence that is much more perceptible through the aesthetic identification of any vital phenomenon, when its trace is recognizable in how a person becomes someone utterly new by the fleeting appearances and sudden outbursts that make up such a variegated vision of existence that should in principle gainsay the perfect unity of spirituality, when the fact is that the more something in life is unsettling, the more it can yield an unheard-of possibility of being to the person experiences it: For instance, death is spiritual when someone dies to save his loved ones, and the same happens when a stabbing passion strengthen the will that resists it. This shows doubtlessly that the aesthetic or vital action of the mind is misunderstood when it is conceived as the substantial unity of being and action that should be proper of God; man, for his part, experiences this unity only through his social interaction, whereby Schiller himself reminds us that

> Here we must remember that we have before us, not the infinite mind, but the finite. The finite mind is that which only becomes active through the passive, only arrives at the absolute through limitation, and only acts and fashions in as far as it receives matter. Accordingly, a mind of this nature must associate with the impulse towards form or the absolute, an impulse towards matter or limitation, conditions without which it could not have the former impulse nor satisfy it (XIX, 9).

The aim of the modern intellectual is not the comprehension of the divine being —whatever this expression means—but the elucidation of the socio-individual existence that is the very fulcrum of humanity insofar as it precludes everyone from selfishness; thereat, on explaining the spiritual condition of life one must be aware of the temporal, unpredictable condition thereof. In other words, the mind embraces or rather is in itself rise and becoming, import and sense, action and outcome, form, mater and instinct. Considering that Schiller aims at the subversion of the traditional explanation of the sense of culture on restating the spirituality of existence, it is not so surprising that he chooses as the paradigm of human activity one that would in principle be utterly alien to mind, at least to the metaphysical or abstract import thereof: Play is, indeed, a term that, due to its semantic richness,[21] is linked both with the highest dramatic works, with the act of performing them, and, oddly enough, with the humblest entertainments of everyday life, whereby it works as a matrix of the aesthetic identity of man with form and, by extension, of the fulfilment of his freedom, inasmuch as it encompasses the diversity of socio-historic existence, which explains why it also can be taken as a third elemental instinct:

> The sensuous instinct wishes to be determined, it wishes to receive an object; the formal instinct wishes to determine itself, it wishes to produce an object. Therefore the instinct of play will endeavour to receive as it would itself have produced, and to produce as it aspires to receive (XIV, 4).

Now, the main feature of this instinct of play is that it, unlike the formal and the material ones whereof we have already spoken, does not evolve through opposition or, on the contrary, by complementation, but through articulation or rather metamorphosis of its object, which supposes a completely different way of setting out existence; in sooth, whether "form" and "matter" are metaphysically, physically, or transcendentally defined, they stand for essences or frameworks that cannot be thought one without the other; still more, as the development of the modern philosophy shows, all the problems that metaphysics faced from its onset and until Kant stemmed from the untenable pretension of postulating a form that existed by itself and without content whatever, which is particularly blatant in the Platonic thought. This, on the other hand, had a decisive consequence on the plane of society and of sociability, for the tenet of the pure form widely used to support the idea that social order and the being of man (whether good or evil) were equally evitemal. Instead, Schiller, on subordinating the opposition or complementation of form and matter to the development of an activity such as play, overcomes the conception of an evitemal order in favor of a dynamic one and furnishes the comprehension of culture and society with a critical outlook that is particularly valuable to understand the interaction of all the planes of existence by the conscious participation of everyone, since play possesses a total sense whether it is successful or not, which is why it stirs up such an unquenchable passion in people of all ages and conditions.

Moreover, although Schiller dismisses a psychological approach to the subject,[22] it must be considered that, when someone plays, he actualizes a possibility that is worthwhile only by his will but whose sense does not hinge only upon it, considering that even when one plays alone, one must abide by the rules of the play at issue.[23] In other words, form and matter are indistinguishable in playing, and the same happens with sense and performance, which has three axial consequences for our subject: first, that one gets on playing a vivid consciousness of the identity of freedom and determination that no other activity supplies; second, that that consciousness always unfolds before a social background, which is a lot more evident when one plays alone; third, that playing begets a sui generis unity of form and matter through time, which Schiller calls beauty:

The object of the sensuous instinct, expressed in a universal conception, is named Life in the widest acceptation: a conception that expresses all material existence and all that is immediately present in the senses. The object of the formal instinct, expressed in a universal conception, is called shape or form, as well in an exact as in an inexact acceptation; a conception that embraces all formal qualities of things and all relations of the same to the thinking powers. The object of the play instinct, represented in a general statement, may therefore bear the name of living form; a term that serves to describe all aesthetic qualities of phaenomena, and what people style, in the widest sense, beauty (XV, 2).

With the intervention of this last term, the analysis of the question goes beyond the plane of aesthetic education and enters into the plane of the ideal that rules it.

V

Put briefly, Schiller's approach to beauty, although retakes the transcendental kernel of Kant's, develops it in a totally diverse way, for its goal, unlike the latter's, is not the final affinity of reason and nature (which is in fact the thread of the *Critique of Judgement*) but the final identity of man and freedom that springs from the conscious self-education of each one, an identity that from the plane of the individual is called dignity and, from the plane of ideals, beauty. In other words, if we have shown that State and person always go hand in hand because one's very individuality is only conceivable by reference to the social whole and vice versa (which, as I emphasized, leaves aside any conception of society that is only based either on custom or on mere convention), now I must unfold the complex part that freedom plays in the aesthetic projection of individual life, whose understanding demands that we take into account the peculiar double import, transcendental and psychological, that Schiller gives to all the concepts that he uses, to which I alluded on speaking of how he and his contemporaries understood the action of reason as an intellectual and social framework. When it is transcendentally defined, a concept provides the condition sine qua non for having a formally universal experience, whereas when it is used in a psychological sense, it is for articulating the diversity and the development of the individual consciousness, as happens with concepts such as "State," "person," or "beauty," which work as the logical ground and also as the psychological unity of any vital process, whose final outcome is a new socioindividual identity. Now, concerning beauty, this double approach means that Schiller had to show, first, how it prevails over the boundless differences of individual tastes and cultural paradigms and, second, that it is an ideal for each one that must be reified in a cultural world; in other words, Schiller had to show that beauty can simultaneously be objectively determined and subjectively enjoyed, which at first sight seemed to be practically impossible because experience has shown that beauty hinges upon who assesses it, and that although there are some objects, whether natural or cultural (such as some landscapes and masterworks), which have almost universally been considered beautiful, the fact is that no sound reason can be claimed to explicate why they are so and the question has to be set out again from the individual taste, which, however, is unsteady. Schiller could fortunately make the most of the philosophical investigations regarding beauty that from Descartes onward had mostly been aimed to elucidate the ontological and epistemological status of the so-called "world of appearances" that, in accordance with ancient metaphysics, contradicted the purely ideal essence of reality and that, from the subjective framework of modern thought, required a principle to be clearly and distinctly determined.[24] As a matter of fact, these investigations had made evident that a specific reflection on sensibility and beauty was axial to the full understanding of "human nature," which Hume, epitomizing a whole epoch, considered the new and incontrovertible bedrock of science and morals. Thus, the theoretical foundation of aesthetics went hand in hand with the enthroning of man as the hub of objective knowledge, as the paradigm of behavior, and, above all, as the idealization of a kind of freedom that, instead of demanding the existence of a postmortem realm so as to make up for the injustices of the earthly condition, had to be sociohistorically fulfilled.[25] Of course, this matched perfectly the active conception of social consciousness that rules the archetype of the intellectual whereof Schiller partook and with which he reinterpreted the fundamental contribution of Kant, which, briefly said, lies in the idea that beauty is not an objective feature (whether physical or metaphysical) but a subjective representation that pleases spontaneously without requiring to be conceptually determined because it betokens the universal affinity of subject and nature that everyone experiences as a total inner harmony.[26]

Now, although Schiller eagerly devoted himself to the philosophical explanation of the theme, the fruit of which was his work "Kallias or on Beauty,"[27] he was aware from the onset that more than working out a transcendental theory, he wanted to figure out the effect of beauty in individual life as well as in culture in order to show how the subjective harmony agrees with social affinity and the ideal creativity that make up as a whole the transcendental framework of human existence, by which Schiller intended to develop an all-embracing theory of life and culture without passing over the really metaphysical import of beauty, namely, the unfathomable originality of each human being:

But the genesis of beauty is by no means declared because we know how to point out the component parts, which in their combination produce beauty. For to this end it would be necessary to comprehend that combination itself, which continues to defy our exploration, as well as all mutual operation between the finite and the infinite [...] Accordingly, as soon as reason issues the mandate, "a humanity shall exist," it proclaims at the same time the law, "there shall be a beauty." Experience can answer us if there is a beauty, and we shall know it as soon as she has taught us if humanity can exist. But neither reason nor experience can tell us how beauty can be, and how humanity is possible (XV, 4).

Let us dwell on the triple plane wherein Schiller unfolds the vital function of beauty, the first of which is, so to speak, the logical one, which he sets out through the natural condition of the individual mind, which lies in the indetermination or rather the bewilderment before the plethora of stimuli with which reality pours itself upon man. This bewilderment is mostly mistaken for a great sensibility when the fact is that it conceals the inner fecklessness and the absentmindedness that always frame a hazy vision of reality, which has to be overcome not so much to get a theoretical precision, as the rationalist tradition claimed, as to get a full vital relationship with one oneself and with others, and the only way to do it is precisely to develop a sound thought, which is nevertheless impossible if man wants aesthetic education, since, as the opposition of the barbarian and the savage shows, no reason resists the charge of life when there is no personality that supports it; contrary to what some shallow epigones of Descartes might uphold, the logic order of thought is based on one's own sensibility, and the concatenation of ideas and instincts is feasible not because of an arbitrary overlapping of them but because of the transcendental affinity of understanding and sensibility that Schiller formerly called "mind" and now calls "beauty" because it stands for the unity of form and content that is simultaneously the token of any spiritual phenomenon and of the harmony that tradition identified with beauty:

> It follows from this, that when it is affirmed of beauty that it mediates for man, the transition from feeling to thought, this must not be understood to mean that beauty can fill up the gap that separates feeling from thought, the passive from the active. This gap is infinite; and, without the interposition of a new and independent faculty, it is impossible for the general to issue from the individual, the necessary from the contingent. Thought is the immediate act of this absolute power, which, I admit, can only be manifested in connection with sensuous impressions, but which in this manifestation depends so little on the sensuous that it reveals itself specially in an opposition to it. The spontaneity or autonomy with which it acts excludes every foreign influence; and it is not in as far as it helps thought—which comprehends a manifest contradiction—but only in as far as it procures for the intellectual faculties the freedom to manifest themselves in conformity with their proper laws (XIX, 6).

The first effect of beauty is the integration of thought and sensibility which is the very bedrock of the individual personality insofar as it endows everyone with the conscious of his own mental activity, which, unlike what is more often than not said, is or tends to be passed over, which is why even individuals that are up to the hardest technical tasks are nevertheless incapable of reasoning when they face some vital situation that would require their utmost lucidity. As the Greeks so deeply understood, "having knowledge" and "being sensible" are two completely different things.

Now, if beauty secures the harmony of the individual thought, with all the more reason it will help everyone to overcome the unsettlements that the organic constitution of human existence sparks off, which unfolds on the second plane of the import of the concept, the psychosomatic one. It is not enough to have an ordered thought to cope with life; it is necessary to unfold the complexity of one's being both in the mental and in the bodily dimension, whose common origin is the mind. Thus, the determination of one's own thought has to be enriched with the adequate assessment of the aesthetics possibilities that one's temperament supplies:

> For if the perfection of man consists in the harmonious energy of his sensuous and spiritual forces, he can only lack this perfection through the want of harmony and the want of energy [...] These opposite limits are, as we have now to prove, suppressed by the beautiful, which reestablishes harmony in man when excited, and energy in man when relaxed; and which, in this way, in conformity with the nature of the beautiful, restores the state of limitation to an absolute state, and makes of man a whole, complete in himself (XVII, 2).

Beauty is always one and the same from a transcendental outlook, but its effects upon the individual sensibility are not, whereby it should be better to consider that there are at least two kinds of beauty whose effects are completely diverse, for whereas the "energetic" beauty enlivens the individual, the "tender" one soothes him without sacrificing his temperament for the sake of normality, a point where the originality of Schiller is still more remarkable if one takes into account that, for lack either of a transcendent paradigm of character such as the one that ancient culture had close at hand or of a real understanding of the aesthetic education that Schiller proposes, the solution that modern society has found to the problematic diversity of individual temperaments has lain in imposing an abstract standard of behavior and sensibility whose effectiveness has largely been reinforced thanks to the mass culture whose historic roots coincide somehow with Schiller's epoch, so that, although this question cannot properly be set out now, it is anyhow the background of what is at stake here, for insofar as Schiller vindicated the boundless psychological originality of every human being, he needs to deal with the problem of how to integrate it socially, and his answer lies in appealing to the wholesome effects of beauty, which seems not to be so surprising since it has a decisive antecedent in the metaphysical tradition concerning the identity of good and beauty whose first upholder is Plato. However, Schiller's approach has nothing to do neither with the Platonic identification of good and beauty nor with the distinction made also by Plato between a celestial beauty and an earthly one that is the thread of Eriximacus' discourse in the *Symposium* (186a and ff.), since neither of the two kinds of beauty implies for our author the would-be supremacy of soul or mind over body. Beauty is, as it were, a tool to get organic balance and it is not for helping soul to get out of body, which possesses, furthermore, a decisive consequence on the moral plane, namely, that more than upholding an ascetic paradigm as metaphysics had done from Plato onward, the diversity of beauty unfolds all the possibilities that the singular sensibility offers, provided, of course, that none of them will contradict the absolute respect that everyone deserves by the very fact of being human, an idea that gets its fulfillment in the experience of the sundry feelings that a person can discover in the course of his life, which all of a sudden becomes a lot more interesting than what the metaphysical or specifically Platonic conception would allow us to suppose.

This opening to a sentimental projection of the individual life leads us to the third and last plane where beauty acts, the sociocultural one, which endows intersubjective relationships with an ideal of originality that more than artistic is aesthetic because it embraces imaginatively all the vital possibilities of each person, who is unique by definition. Thus, everyone, on becoming conscious that society stands for the natural condition of the human being, feels the lack of ideals that preclude the diversity of cultural interactions from degenerating into the hustle and bustle where none recognizes spontaneously others or, on the contrary, from being crushed by the constraints of the tradition. Of course, this would not be possible if the ideality of beauty were understood as the ancient metaphysical tradition set it out, that is, either as the mysterious harmony that came from a superior realm[28] or as an ineffable emanation of the very principle of reality,[29] which on the plane on which we are located now means that the individual life must be shaped by a preexistent archetype instead of creating a new one in accordance with the imagination and with the circumstances of each one. Now, since the ancient approach entailed a relative predetermination that is inconsistent with his outright apology for individual freedom, Schiller left it aside and considered that beauty is the ideal form of human existence that betokens the poetic nature that freedom possesses insofar as it is simultaneously a transcendental condition and also a voluntary accomplishment, by which although the former is not determinable as an objective feature, it possesses at any rate the universality required to be the bedrock of sociocultural life and not only an arbitrary connotation that passes over the moral import of any human relationship, which confirms the criticism against modern society that Schiller sets out at the onset of his Letters, when he compares the ancient Hellenes with the modern individual and shows that although the former had a life harder than the latter considering its material conditions, they were incomparably better considering their individuality as such because all of their culture was aimed at the development of a personality up to the immanent character of life, which is what Schiller calls the "aesthetic state"[30] :

The soul traverses a medium position, in which sensibility and reason are at the same time active, and thus they mutually destroy their determinant power, and by their antagonism produce a negation. This medium situation in which the soul is neither physically nor morally constrained, and yet is in both ways active, merits essentially the name of a free situation; and if we call the state of sensuous determination physical, and the state of rational determination logical or moral, that state of real and active determination should be called the aesthetic.

The transcendental identity of culture and personality goes throughout the triple plane of beauty, so that everyone gets an integral consciousness that allows him to partake in the cultural world without reducing his scope; on the contrary, he will really be able to trace goals that will also be inspiring for others, whether they are contemporaries or belong to future generations, creating in such a way a tradition that is not sustained in the transmission of past archetypes but of the only sound ideal, the universal man. *Vale*.

Meritorious University of Puebla, Mexico

NOTES

[1] This relativity of knowledge was canonized by Thomas Kuhn in his classic book *The Structure of Scientific Revolutions* (Chicago: University of Chicago Press, 1962), a work that was supposed to uphold for the first time an idea whose deepest import could be traced, however, to the Kantian concept of a Copernican Revolution (*Critique of Pure Reason*, B XVI), insofar as the determination of knowledge does not hinge upon any object whatever but upon the transcendental subject. Of course, this by no means entails that Kuhn was not the first thinker to lay out the foundations of a sociohistorical process, whereas Kant only heeded the logical conditions of the question.

[2] Without risking a theoretical link that could seem farfetched, this condition of the intellectual reminds me of the interesting remarks that Foucault and Deleuze made concerning the relation of theory and practice in the second half of the twentieth century and the part that intellectuals play in society. See "Un Dialogo sobre el Poder," in *Un Dialogo sobre el Poder*, ed. Miguel Morey, trans. Francisco Monge, *El libro de bolsillo 816* (Madrid: Alianza Editorial, 1981), pp. 7–19. Of course, Foucault's approach to the matter contradicts the apology for man that is the bedrock of Schiller and of the Enlightenment.

[3] Johann Christoph Friedrich Schiller, "Letters on the Aesthetic Education of Man," in *Literary and Philosophical Essays* (The Harvard Classics, 32) (Collier: New York, 1910). I quote the English text of the work as available at: Modern History Source Book (http://www.fordham.edu/halsall/mod/modsbook15.html). The Roman and Arabic numerals at the end of each quotation will correspond respectively to the letter and paragraph.

[4] Hume more successfully used the idea of standard to reconcile the apparent opposition of individual originality and social universality, as he did in his celebrated work *On the Standard of Taste*, which could have influenced Schiller through Kant. On this question, see my essay "Beauty, Taste, and Enlightenment in Hume's Aesthetic Thought" in this volume.

[5] Immanuel Kant, *Groundwork of the Metaphysics of Morals*, ed. and trans. Mary Gregor (Cambridge: Cambridge University Press, 1998), p. 38. The italics are Kant's.

⁶ If it is tempting to trace a certain parallel between Schiller's and Voltaire's respective Letters, it would only be for bringing to light the abyssal differences between the two extremes that define the function of the intellectual as we have understood it: the criticism of society and the idealization. Although I cannot deal with such a study here, I mention that whereas Schiller pursues a very uniform exposition throughout his work, Voltaire rather interpolates subjects as dissimilar as the smallpox, the condition of science in his epoch, and the advantages of certain forms of Christian creed regarding Catholicism. However, the intention of the author is very blatant from the onset: to show the benefits that an enlightened society like England's offers to the diffusion of culture. See Voltaire, *Lettres Philosophiques*, ed. Frédéric Deloffre, Folio Classique 1703 (Paris: Gallimard, 1986).

⁷ I offer an analysis of this passage and of the whole work in my essay "A Life beyond Go (od): a Criticism of Wisdom and the Foundation of a Poetic Conception of Life Based on Goethe's Faust," in *The Enigma of Good and Evil; the Moral Sentiment in Literature*, ed. Anna-Teresa Tymieniecka, Analecta Husserliana Vol. LXXXV (Dordrecht: Springer, 2005), pp. 749–785. The passage at issue is analyzed on pp. 771ff. On the other hand, it must be taken into account that if the definitive version of the First Part of *Faust* was published in 1808, three years after Schiller's premature death, the passionate friendship that he and Goethe had for more than ten years (they met in 1794) makes it very likely that he had exerted a great influence in the gestation and development of the work.

⁸ A12. Of course, Kant focuses the meaning of the concept in the passage at issue from an epistemological outlook, although the same can be widen to the delimitation of the historical experience, which agrees, on the other hand, with the general tendency of Kantian philosophy, as Schiller so clearly understood.

⁹ I mean concretely the explanatory note that Kant interpolates in the *Prolegomena to Any Future Metaphysics* (Ak IV, pp. 293–294), where he distinguishes between the critical or transcendental conception of idealism and the metaphysical or chimerical one: the former, which is Kant's, entails that whatever knowledge is determined by the subject's faculties and not by the would-be nature of the object; the latter, which Kant attributes to Berkeley, upholds the existence of transcendent or intellectual beings.

¹⁰ See "An Old Question Raised Again: Is the Human Race Constantly Progressing?" in *Emmanuel Kant, Filosofia de la Historia*, 2nd ed., ed. and Spanish trans. Eugenio Imaz, Coleccion Popular 147 (Mexico City: FCE, 1979), pp. 95–118.

¹¹ This axial aim of the third *Critique* has been widely emphasized by all of the most distinguished Kant scholars, who have shown that the reflection on the aesthetical judgment is a lot more decisive than what it seems to be at first sight. See, among others, Robert Rodriguez Aramayo and Gerard Vilar (eds.), *En la Cumbre del Criticismo. Simposio sobre la Critica del Juicio de Kant*, Filosofia 39 (Madrid: Anthropos/UAM, 1992), J. L. Villicañas et al., *Estudios sobre la "Critica del Juicio"*, La balsa de la Medusa 34 (Madrid: Visor, 1990), and Eva Schaper, *Studies in Kant's Aesthetics* (Edinburgh: Edinburgh University Press, 1979).

¹² I am aware that this approach to the question passes over the elemental fact that the philosophical interest in aesthetics stemmed originally from the rationalist tradition to which Baumgarten belonged; however, it is also true that rationalism could not have integrated aesthetics into the process of reason because of its metaphysical conception thereof. Concerning this, see the second chapter of the book by Marc Jimenez, *Qu'est-ce que l'Esthétique?* Essais 303 (Paris: Gallimard, 1997).

¹³ I know that this last remark changes Schiller's thought into an anachronistic vindication of reason against the so-called suspicion aroused by Nietzsche and Heidegger against the former; nevertheless, since my general approach to the author lies in the identification of him with the

modern figure of the intellectual, I think that such a vindication, which is properly mine, is perfectly compatible with his blatant defense of enlightenment (in the broad import of the term that he explains) as the only way to fulfill human freedom.

[14] Dilthey takes advantage of this feature to frame his interesting exegesis of Schiller's thought and artistic creations, and he explains how Schiller always rebuffed any romantic approach to the issue and upheld throughout the worth of consciousness. See "Schiller," in *Obras Completas*, ed. Eugenio Imaz and trans. Wenceslao Roces (Mexico City: FCE, 1945), Vol. IV, pp. 188–189, passim.

[15] See above all the foreword to the first edition of the work, which I quote from the Spanish edition: Immanuel Kant, *La Religion Dentro de los Limites de la Mera Razon*, 2nd ed., ed. and trans. Felipe Martinez Marzoa, Libro de bolsillo 163 (Madrid: Alianza, 1981), pp. 19–26, passim.

[16] Contrary to what has so often been said, this feature is by no means absent from the rationalist tradition: Descartes integrates the analysis of knowledge into a social framework in the *Discourse on Method*, above all when he reflects on the question of how to link the determination of behavior with the lack of coexistence in a society that more often than not is alien (Third Part) or, at the very end of the work, where he aims at a cosmopolitan society of learned people that interchange their respective knowledge so as to enhance mankind as a whole. For his part, Spinoza devotes to the question of the State two axial works, the *Theological-Political Treatise* and the *Political Treatise*, not to mention the deep questioning of coexistence that the philosopher undertakes in the two final parts of the *Ethics*.

[17] From this outlook, one can oppose Schiller's stance to the most ambitious and deep exposition of the preponderance of national heritage, which is contained in the "Lessons on the Philosophy of Universal History" by Hegel, where he says that Germany betokens through modernity the triumph of the Absolute Spirit over the abstract determinations of the Roman World, for the former solves thanks to the constitutional State but also to tradition the antagonism between the objective plane of history and the subjective one, which blatantly contradicts Schiller's idea that the State cannot overcome the crisis of modernity because it is subdued by the tyranny of the majority and, withal, because modernity is at bottom a conception of subject, not of an idealized tradition.

[18] With regard to this point, and in addition to the deep and clarifying essay by Dilthey mentioned in note 14, see the admirable biography *Schiller o la Invencion del Idealismo Aleman* by Rüdiger Safranski [*Schiller oder die Erfindung des Deutschen Idealismus*, Spanish trans. Raul Gabas, Tiempo de memoria 53 (Barcelona: Tusquets, 2006)].

[19] On the ripening of these ideas in the thought of the young Schiller, see the book mentioned in the previous note, Chapter 5.

[20] See my article "An Enquiry Concerning the Dialectic of Personality and its Practical Consequences," in *Logos of Phenomenology and Phenomenology of the Logos*, Book Two, ed. Anna-Teresa Tymieniecka, Analecta Husserliana, Vol. LXXXIX (Dordrecht: Springer, 2006), pp. 61–89.

[21] Present in German and in English alike, whereof Gadamer and hermeneutics make the most. See the exhaustive Gadamerian analysis of playing in *Truth and Method*, 4th ed., Spanish trans. Ana Agud Aparicio and Rafael de Agapito, Hermeneia 7 (Salamanca: Sigueme, 1991), pp. 143–181.

[22] It is worth recalling that the deepest study of the state of mind proper to playing is contained in Dostoevsky's *The Gambler*, where one sees how someone who never before had played roulette loses his whole fortune to the consternation of the narrator. Of course, this instance, although contradicts the positive exegesis of playing and the function thereof in Schiller's thought, emphasizes the terrible consequences that faces someone who lacks an aesthetic education and has obeyed a rigorous moral code without having put it at stake before the real instinct of life.

[23] It is very meaningful that Schiller's interest in playing had subsisted until our time, when its treatment by Gadamer and his followers has shown new aspects of the subject, as mentioned in note 21. In addition to *Truth and Method*, see *La Actualidad de lo Bello* [Die Aktualität des Schäonen], Spanish trans. Antonio Gomez Ramos, Pensamiento Contemporaneo 15 (Barcelona: Piados/ICE–UAB, 1991), pp. 66–83. Another book on the theme is the masterful work *Homo Ludens* by Johan Huizinga, ed. Juan D. Castillo, Spanish trans. Eugenio Imaz, Grandes Obras de Historia 29 (Barcelona: Altaya, 1997).

[24] Of the several works that I have devoted to the axial part that the investigation of this subject played on the development of modern thought, I only emphasize my article "'With Foolish Shadows, With Hollow Signs': A Reflection on Subjective Perception and Personal Identity in Hispano–American Golden Age Intrigue Comedies," in *The Enigma of Good and Evil; The Moral Sentiment in Literature*, ed. Anna-Teresa Tymieniecka (Dordrecht: Springer, 2005), pp. 491–516.

[25] Concerning this issue, see above all the introduction of *Eighteenth-Century British Aesthetics*, ed. Dabney Townsend (Amityville, NY: Baywood, 1999), as well as Luc Ferry, H*omo Aestheticus. L'Invention du Gout à l'Age Classique* (Paris: Bernard Grasset, 1990).

[26] *Critique of Judgement*, A35, paragraph 11.

[27] It is included together with the "Letters on the Aesthetic Education of Man" and other works in *Escritos sobre Estetica*, ed. Juan Manuel Navarro Cordon and trans. Manuel Garcia Morente et al., Clasicos del pensamiento 84 (Madrid: Tecnos, 1990), pp. 3–64. The work is made up of the letters that Schiller sent to his friend Körner, although it is very interesting because it shows the deep interest that Schiller felt regarding the subject as well as his early intellectual independence concerning Kant. See also Rüdiger Safranski, op. cit., pp. 349ff.

[28] See Plato's masterly exposition of the metaphysical transcendence of beauty in the *Phaedrus* (250a and ff.)

[29] See Plotinus' treatise On the Intellectual Beauty, *Enneads*, V, VIII, in *Philosophies of Art and Beauty. Selected Readings in Aesthetics from Plato to Heidegger*, ed. Albert Hofstadter and Richard Kuhns, trans. Stephen Mackenna (Chicago: University of Chicago Press, 1976), pp. 151–164.

[30] The general approach of my exegesis prevents me from dealing with another fundamental import of beauty that Schiller explicates in Letter XXII—the artistic one. Briefly, he upholds that any specific art must provide the spectator or the reader with an aesthetic fullness independent of its concrete materials, subject, or ways of expression.

LAWRENCE F. RHU

BEYOND ADAPTATION
Stoicism, Transcendence, and Moviegoing in Walker Percy and Stanley Cavell

When Walker Percy was invited to deliver the Phi Beta Kappa Address at Harvard in 1987, he declined. The year and the event would have inevitably commemorated Emerson's famous address on the same occasion one hundred and fifty years earlier, "The American Scholar," delivered in August of 1837. Percy felt profound dismay about the cultural legacy of Emerson's career, as described by his friend Lewis Simpson, and he also considered himself ill educated in the actual writings of Emerson, as he acknowledged in a letter to his friend Robert Coles at Harvard. To become the sesquicentennial voice of such an inheritance obviously made him uneasy. It would put him in a false position.[1]

Yet Percy shares basic affinities with that intellectual tradition, especially as it has recently been elaborated by Stanley Cavell. Once they are noted and explored, the ties that link these two writers illuminate their accomplishments both as individual writers and as participants in cultural conversations of major significance in the last half century. Each is preoccupied with the ordinary or everyday and its vulnerability to the mood of its reception. Each discovers in film provocations to thought and ways of finding words for his responses, not only to movies, but to life as we are likely to live or imagine it on screen and off. Each uses continental philosophy, and especially the existentialist tradition from Kierkegaard and Nietzsche to Camus and Sartre, as a means of moving beyond American orthodoxies that potentially confine him—for Percy, Southerness and medical science; for Cavell, analytical philosophy and pragmatism.

By focusing on stoicism, transcendence, and moviegoing, this essay demonstrates these basic affinities between Percy and Cavell both in the terms just mentioned—the ordinary, film, continental philosophy—and also through the idea of the American scholar as Emerson famously characterizes this figure, however unlikely such an affiliation may have struck Percy in the mid-1980s. Perhaps one must read Percy against the American (or, rather, the Southern) grain to show his kinship with transcendentalism Concord-style. Though Cavell's reading of Emerson is controversial, it offers us a philosopher

199

A-T. Tymieniecka (ed.), Analecta Husserliana XCVI, 199–209.
© 2008 *Springer.*

and a writer whose resonant representations of consciousness anticipate the preoccupations of phenomenology and the literary turn that its inheritors, like Walker Percy, will ultimately take to say most effectively what is on their minds: "man thinking," as Emerson represents the American scholar. For all three of these writers, one might say, paraphrasing Emerson, that the virtue most in demand is clear-headedness or presence of mind. It is a condition preliminary to moral action and decision-making, whence such conduct can spring once the spell of routine and received opinion is broken.

This essay aims to clarify the spiritual kinship among these apparently different writers—Percy, Cavell, and Emerson—and to demonstrate the worth of attending to it. To my knowledge, no one has yet made the connections among these writers explicitly and in depth.[2] They all mean to inhabit, as fully as possible, their place in time without falling prey to needless provincialism and fixated categories of critical fashion. Such efforts make them secret sharers of an American tradition whose present viability becomes fully apparent once we recognize its persistence in their writings and those of their inheritors, as well as its resonance with continental philosophy as it has evolved in the last two centuries, from Königsberg to Concord and from Covington to Cambridge.[3]

Among film scholars, the relative neglect of Cavell's remarkable writings has not gone unnoticed. William Rothman and Marian Keane have recently made a commendable effort to remedy this situation in their careful study of the first of Cavell's four books about film, *Reading Cavell's The World Viewed: A Philosophical Perspective on Film*. In introducing their monograph, these authors observe the almost total divergence from mainstream thinking that distinguishes Cavell's film criticism. Then they add their hopeful anticipation of productive challenges that may arise from the expanded awareness of alternative approaches made possible by an acquaintance with Cavell's thought. "Almost invariably," Rothman and Keane aver,

Cavell's intuitions run counter to views generally accepted.... In providing a meaningful alternative to views that are so often accepted without question within the field of film study, *The World Viewed* is capable of challenging the field to question the unquestionable, to check its theories against the test of experience, thereby opening for exploration regions that have remained closed.[4]

This claim justly characterizes the value of Cavell's other books on film as well, although suspicious readers, viewing his work through the lenses of feminist and Marxist approaches, have characterized Cavell's responses to Hollywood movies as naïve and mystifying.[5] Given Cavell's insistence upon art's fundamental value in helping to realize the wish for selfhood, perhaps such suspicions are unavoidable.[6] The process of reading requires belief before it can confer understanding, as Cavell sees it, and we are thus vulnerable to mistaken identification.[7] But standing coolly apart has its hazards as well. Though fools rush in where angels fear to tread, we do not have wings, so we may need to make the most of our folly. Taking instruction from our mistakes can turn our errors into a truer direction, but we must first take the steps necessary to test our intuitions. No theory, however grand, can protect us from fallibility.

There is a prostitute in Flannery O'Connor's *Wise Blood* who receives this memorable characterization: "[S]he was so well adjusted that she didn't have to think any more."[8] At this juncture, O'Connor's sharp satire takes its cue from the secular religion of mental health that widely prevailed when her novel first appeared in 1952. Celebration of the ability to adjust, regardless of circumstances, often seemed prized above any other accomplishment. No matter what question of value was at stake, emotionalism betokened trouble. Though lack of affect could occasion concern, the passions appeared bleached of all color in the clinical discourse of popular psychology at mid century. This discourse set standards for the assessment of character by social scientists, and society at large widely accepted their authority. Professional jargon of this sort thus became the frequent target of mordant satire such as O'Connor's.

The reasonable sort of accommodation commended by detached analysis became even easier to dismiss when cries of injustice were heard in the series of political struggles that soon emerged over civil rights, Vietnam, and the status of women during the early decades of Cavell's academic career, the 1960s and 1970s. Dispassionate reason in the interest of human advancement, the Enlightenment project if you will, lost credibility in strife over matters of race, gender, class, and empire. Detached analysis of one's own psychological condition and that of others became similarly liable to characterization as an empty gesture. Likewise, an even older model of such equanimity, the stoic ideal of the will's masterful transcendence of the passions, had long ago fallen into disfavor. Yet its hierarchical partitioning of the self into reason and passion and its affirmation of the will's capacity to rise above storms of emotion retained a surprising allure. This claim of individual sovereignty despite the most adverse of circumstances remained a compelling alternative even in the triumphant Christian culture that supposedly put such rival pagan philosophies into decisive eclipse.[9]

In his explorations of the film genre that he labels the Hollywood melodrama of the unknown woman, Stanley Cavell discusses his protagonists' capacity to judge the world at certain junctures where one could mistakenly claim that they simply rise above it, mystically taking their leave of the human realm altogether.[10] For example, Charlotte Vale (Bette Davis) decisively transcends the understanding of her circumstances expressed by Jerry Durrance (Paul Henreid) at the end of *Now, Voyager*. Yet she remains very much a worldling, a resident of this Earth who consciously selects a course of life that Jerry fails to comprehend. Indeed, he construes her situation in such conventional and sanctimonious terms that Charlotte directly chastens him for what finally seems his dim-witted misprision of her self-understanding in the film's closing moment.

But Charlotte's painful unknownness to Jerry does not make her completely unintelligible, for the film does not confine us to Jerry's perspective. Likewise, according to Cavell, Stella Dallas (Barbara Stanwyck) makes recognizable choices that determine her fortunes at the end of the 1936 film named after her. She is not merely a victim of others' class prejudice or her own envy of their privileges. She makes choices that indicate her distaste for their world, which she once aspired to join but now decisively rejects. Stella Dallas exercises her capacity to judge *their* world and, finding it wanting, she walks ecstatically away from a life she no longer desires. But such ecstasy is not simply "blissing out." As Thoreau puts it, "With thinking we may be beside ourselves in a sane sense."[11]

Almost three decades earlier, Cavell makes a kindred point about Shakespeare's *King Lear*. Cavell confronts the unbearability of this tragedy, registered most notoriously by Dr. Johnson's reaction to the death of Cordelia,[12] and he directly counters the despair that such a moment can awaken. "There is hope in this play," Cavell opines; and he pointedly adds "it is not in heaven." This obvious echo of a resonant biblical claim from Deuteronomy 30.12 directly counters the presumption that such hope is escapism in the same way that the transcendence Cavell attributes to Stella Dallas and Charlotte Vale, in their unknownness, need not be at all otherworldly or despairing. Where then does Cavell find this hope in *King Lear*? He answers this question in the following manner:

> In the realm of the spirit, Kierkegaard says, there is absolute justice. Fortunately, because if all we had to go on were the way the world goes, we would lose the concept of justice altogether, and then human life would become unbearable. Kant banked the immortality of the soul on the fact that in *this* world goodness and happiness are unaligned—a condition which, if never righted, is incompatible with moral sanity, and hence the existence of God. But immortality is not necessary for the soul's satisfaction. What is necessary is its own coherence, its ability to judge a world in which evil is successful and the good are doomed; and in particular its knowledge that while injustice may flourish, it cannot rest content.[13]

The argument that Cavell advances in *Contesting Tears* defines melodrama as a genre that purposefully trades in emotional excess. Its hyperbolic gestures aim to open hearts otherwise inclined to lose touch with currents of feeling whose expression convention constrains. By "figuring our hidden screams, and then understanding us despite ourselves, despite our inexpressiveness," melodrama represents the realm of the spirit in such a way that passion can inform reason and animate judgment.[14]

Passion, of course, is conventionally assigned a gender, and that is female. Cavell challenges this customary attribution most memorably when he describes Adam Bonner, Spencer Tracy's character in *Adam's Rib*, as "something of an unknown woman himself."[15] Of course, Adam just pretends to cry in the scene that earns him this characterization, and he subsequently calls this performance a "little trick." But the very theatricality of his gesture indicates that neither sex holds exclusive title to certain regions of feeling. Rather, behavioral styles and the conformity that they tend to enforce arbitrarily link maleness to stoical impassivity and femaleness to emotional expressiveness. Granted that Adam's timely improvisation of tears may express genuine feeling despite his avowal that it was merely a ploy, still the surprise it produces in Adam's wife, Amanda (Katharine Hepburn), also indicates the arbitrariness of certain social roles, what we commonly call their constructedness.

One of the most memorable representations of stoic resignation in modern fiction appears in *The Moviegoer* by Walker Percy. It is Emily Cutrer, the formidable great-aunt of that novel's alert narrator and questing protagonist, Binx Bolling. This generally uneventful novel tells the story of a week in the life of a New Orleans stockbroker who quietly makes some changes in his way of life and suffers a few others as well. Besides attending to financial matters, Binx habitually goes to the movies and tries to enjoy the company of attractive young women whenever occasion allows. Movies fascinate him precisely because of their seductive allure and their power to enthrall our imaginations. Though Binx usually stands securely aloof from this power, he revealingly succumbs to it and becomes their thrall at a decisive turn in the novel, its deceptively undramatic climax. Mediated exclusively through Binx's perspective, the novel's main subject is human attachment, or what you might call love, if you qualify that claim with a healthy dose of irony about romance in reduced circumstances.

The stoic Aunt Emily herself amounts to something of an unknown man inasmuch as William Alexander Percy, the novelist's second cousin and beloved "Uncle Will," served as the model for this figure.[16] She quotes Marcus Aurelius and keeps the stiff upper lip required of such types when they face what they deem the deterioration of cherished values and modes of conduct.[17] As the old order passes and is replaced by questionable upstarts who neither esteem nor embody the noble codes that allegedly guided their precursors, a studied detachment offers such stoics refuge. Aunt Emily bears unmistakable marks of this view of the world, which Percy no longer considered an option for his generation of Southerners despite his high regard for William Alexander Percy.[18] Aunt Emily even compounds her recourse to detachment by identifying herself as "spiritually a Buddhist."[19] The anodyne of indifference commended in that Eastern tradition bears a recognizable affinity with the equanimity achieved via stoic detachment.

The ultimate legacy of stoic high-mindedness that haunted Walker Percy was the suicide of his father. He would reckon more directly with this traumatic inheritance in his second novel, *The Last Gentleman*, but Binx Bolling's fiancée, Kate Cutrer, confronts him with a comparable challenge in *The Moviegoer*. Her self-destructive behavior, however, manifests itself in mood swings that represent precisely the opposite of stoic impassivity. Indeed, her instability and the desperation that goes with her consequent inability to find peace ironically enable her to take Binx's measure with disarming candor. This philosophical charmer can get very cozy with the reader, who is mainly confined to his perspective as narrator except for occasions of dialogue. But then Kate can take on a life of her own, prodding Binx, even "figuring [his] hidden screams," to borrow Cavell's phrases about melodrama, "and then understanding [him] despite [himself]."[20] Or, at the very least, Kate can make Binx confront his own coldness and detachment in their frank conversations.

Ironically, film of no kind has this effect on Binx. His moviegoing habit entails, almost as a fundamental principle, a pervasive, even absolute, distrust of the stories he sees on screen, despite the fascination they stir in him. Their characters and, in a way, the actors who play them do not impress Binx at all as real people. Cavell's alleged gullibility seems the last kind of weakness Binx would display. He views movies with dogmatically skeptical detachment.

> The movies are onto the search, but they screw it up. The search always ends in despair. They like to show a fellow coming to himself in a strange place—but what does he do? He takes up with the local librarian, sets about proving to the local children what a nice fellow he is, and settles down with a vengeance. In two weeks time he is so sunk in everydayness that he might just as well be dead.[21]

Binx's own story takes the form of an avowed search, which, ultimately, has no specific object and remains conspicuously inconclusive at the novel's close. Still, if it were not for Binx's resolute anti-romanticism, the title of one of Cavell's books, *In Quest of the Ordinary*, would capture a good bit of Binx's search. For Binx, however, the ordinary remains elusive, when it is not simply dispiriting. There are, in Wallace Stevens's wonderful phrase, no "tootings at the weddings of the soul" for Binx.[22] Yet the philosophy of

Kierkegaard that resonates most deeply with the ambitions of Binx's search and permeates Percy's fiction appears in the description of the knight of faith in *Fear and Trembling*, and Cavell explicitly notes its congruence with the Emersonian quest to recover the ordinary that he invokes as a prime provocation for his study of Hollywood comedies of remarriage.[23]

Cavell's responsiveness to Hollywood at its best differs significantly from the forgone conclusion at which Binx has arrived: "The search *always* ends in despair" (emphasis added). Binx's knowing anticipation of hackneyed routines reveals an understandable impatience with formulaic products of the studio system, whose happy endings arrive on schedule like a timely fix. However, it also preempts other possibilities. As Cavell argues, the excesses of melodrama aim to open these options up precisely because of the everydayness into which we too readily sink without recourse to such extreme measures. These emotional extravaganzas mean to break the trances into which ordinary routines all too often lull us. They aim to awaken our hearts and thus make us think with more passion than usual and with greater consequences.

The Moviegoer is also a story about what Cavell calls thinking, as he discerns it in Emerson, for whom passion, or what Kant calls inclination, requires no apology. It is told from a point of view whose changes of mood are at least as important as the events of the plot, if it is even possible to distinguish between these two elements in this text. Percy would have balked at such a distinction, as his response to suggested revisions from his editor, Stanley Kaufmann, reveals. Kaufmann urged Percy to tighten the plot of *The Moviegoer*, and he replied,

Your calling attention to dropped characters and interrupted story strands is certainly valid novelistic criticism, but it does not seem applicable here—at least it does not strike a chord with me. *Passage to India* is a much better constructed novel than [Jean-Paul Sartre's] *Nausea*, but *Nausea* would be wrecked by a revision along these lines. I suppose I am trying to say that the fragmented alienated consciousness that is Mr. Binx Bolling, cannot be done up in a *novel* in the usual sense of the word [emphasis Percy's].[24]

At the beginning of *The Moviegoer*, Binx becomes, you might say, an American scholar: he wakes up and starts thinking about the predicament in which he discovers himself. He thus becomes not merely a thinker, but man thinking, as Emerson defines the scholar, a man who brings active reflection to bear upon the world as he finds it. He ceases to haunt his life and begins to live it because of no more than a change of mood, a funny feeling he has one morning as he contemplates his "personal effects"—the wallet and keys, change and cards strewn on top of his dresser. Somehow he sees them differently after he wakes up and gets ready to go out for the day. It dawns upon him that his personal effects could easily turn into his "last remains."

Thus, he becomes a philosopher in one of the oldest senses of that term, which claims that to philosophize is to learn how to die. At an odd moment, Binx is graced with an awareness of his mortality. That awareness sticks, and it starts to change his everyday approach to his passage through life. As Emerson remarks,

> We must be very suspicious of the deceptions of the element of time. It takes a good deal of time to eat or to sleep, or to earn a hundred dollars, and a very little time to entertain a hope and an insight which becomes the light of our life.[25]

Walker Percy's favorite philosopher, Søren Kierkegaard, distinguishes between being and existence in a way that enables us to appreciate the change that Binx begins to undergo: "A human being can forget to exist," the Danish philosopher declares.[26] Binx's casually glimpsed insight into his own finitude helps to save him from becoming a casualty of his own obliviousness. What happens to Binx is that he starts to remember to exist and thus ceases to be a mere thinker; or, in Percy's way of making this process clear, Binx abandons mere spectatorship and idle moviegoing, and he becomes more responsive and engaged in his life as it passes. The epigraph of *The Moviegoer* offers another version of this same perception from Søren Kierkegaard: "The specific character of despair is precisely this: it is unaware of being despair." Binx becomes conscious of the despair in which he has been living. That consciousness dawns upon Binx in the way that Emerson characterizes as intuition. One day it just happens to happen that Binx sees himself in a new light, and that fresh perspective makes him wonder enough to pay much steadier attention than usual to life as it passes thereafter.

Furthermore, Binx is responding in an Emersonian fashion to his unforeseen insight inasmuch as "Self-Reliance" insists that every intuition requires a tuition, a follow-up that seeks to discover where such intuitions will lead. Binx calls his response, with merciful restraint, a search; ultimately, it leads him nowhere, if you are expecting revelations of the sort that the idea of a quest can melodramatically make us anticipate. He gets married, becomes a medical student, and sees his beloved through a painful loss—no more, nor less, than these ordinary events sum up where he is bound when we leave him at the novel's end. But if we listen to his words and his voice, and if we trust our own intuition, we may know what Emerson says we can know instantly—whose words are loaded with life and whose are not.[27] Those of Walker Percy undeniably abound in their capacity to make that impression upon us.

The hazards of moviegoing in Percy's novel coincide with those of reading in "The American Scholar." In distinguishing between a mere thinker and man thinking, Emerson wants to give books no more than their due and to warn the scholar away from the dangers of becoming a bookworm. "Books are for the scholar's idle times," he writes; and he expresses his wariness of their over-influence when he declares, "I had better never see a book than to be warped clean out of my own orbit and made a satellite instead of a system."[28] Star-gazing and the fixations of cultish celebrity are versions of this hazard that Walker Percy investigates in his novel, and it stands in a long and distinguished line of literary works that explore this kind of idolatry and its manifold complexities.

Forgetting that figures in fiction are creatures of the imagination is the sort of mental lapse that creators of fiction have often taken as their central theme. In *The Moviegoer*, Walker Percy offers us an account of exactly what this sort of obliviousness might look like at the movies. As such a story, this novel deserves an estimable place in the tradition of exploring the fortunes of gullible readers like Don Quixote and Emma Bovary in the works named after them—and like Stanley Cavell, according to Marxist and feminist critics who characterize him as a credulous, if not simply gullible, moviegoer.[29] Like Binx, those devotees of the fashionable narratives of their times were too emotionally responsive to discern the difference between, on one hand, their own lives' options and circumstances and, on the other, the fictional realm inhabited by the figures of whom they read in romances and novels. They became, for better or worse, unwitting victims of the imaginary lives to which they unguardedly opened their hearts.

Binx Bolling, however, seems nothing if not guarded about his susceptibilities to film narratives. As we have seen, his knowingness leads him to the dogmatic dismissal of their routines when he speaks of how they "screw up" the search that preoccupies him. Binx's ironic detachment about movies will not go unpunished, if that is the right word. During a crisis at the novel's climax, a helpless relapse into despair will expose Binx's own vulnerability to these film narratives that he deems so predictable and feels he can view with such impenetrable skepticism about their power. Still, despite the dogmatism of this particular view, Binx's capacity for rational supervision of his own conduct and that of others also becomes a resource for stability in both his professional and private lives rather than merely a temptation to absent himself from felt connection with others. In the novel's epilogue, he helps his new wife, Kate Cutrer, face the death of his stepbrother Lonnie, one of the novel's two other characters who is explicitly labeled a moviegoer.[30] We may take the occasion of that moviegoer's death as a hopeful sign, inasmuch as it also becomes a moment when the other moviegoer, Binx, seems to have decisively returned to a world not merely viewed but inhabited.

NOTES

[1] Jay Tolson, *Pilgrim in the Ruins: A Life of Walker Percy* (New York: Simon & Schuster, 1992), 466. For the essay in question, see Lewis P. Simpson, "Home by Way of California: The Southerner as the Last European," in *Heritage and Promise: Southern Literature in Transition*, eds. Philip Castille and William Osborne (Memphis, TN: Memphis State University Press, 1983), 55–70. Coincidentally, in a briefer form, this essay ("Beyond Adaptation") was first read as a paper on Emerson's birthday, May 25, at the Phenomenology and Literature Conference at the Harvard Divinity School in 2005.

[2] I try to do so in *Stanley Cavell's American Dream: Shakespeare, Philosophy, and Hollywood Movies* (New York: Fordham University Press, 2006). Stephen Mulhall is on the right track in "Reading, Writing, Re-Membering: What Cavell and Heidegger Call Thinking," in *Ordinary Language Criticism: Literary Thinking after Cavell after Wittgenstein*, eds. Kenneth Dauber and Walter Jost (Evanston, IL: Northwestern University Press, 2003), 115–133. However, either Mulhall cannot hear, or chooses not to respond to, Emersonian echoes quite audible both in arguments made and in passages cited on pp. 121–122 and 127–130 of his own essay. Though Mulhall is very much in sympathy with Cavell's explicitly Emersonian project, he seems to demur at what he calls "the case for Emerson as a serious philosopher" in his review of Cavell's 2003 book, *Emerson's Transcendental Etudes* (*Times Literary Supplement*, 21 May 2004). At least, he initially remarks that it is "hard to say" whether Cavell's claim to this effect "will seem more obviously ludicrous in the United States or in Europe."

[3] Among Percy's inheritors, Richard Ford's three Frank Bascombe novels—*The Sportswriter* (1986), *Independence Day* (1995), and *The Lay of the Land* (2006)—especially warrant note. In *The Southern Writer and the Postmodern World* (Athens: University of Georgia Press, 1991), 41–58, Fred Hobson has persuasively demonstrated how the first of these, *The Sportswriter*, owes much to Percy's fiction. The second, *Independence Day*, repeatedly engages Emerson's "Self-Reliance" because Frank has given his son a copy of that essay in the hope that its edifying potential may prove beneficial. Ford called *The Moviegoer* his "favorite novel" during his turn in a series under that rubric on the NPR show "On Point" in 2005. Interestingly enough, he said that *The Moviegoer*, embedded though it is in the suggestive specificity of Percy's beloved New Orleans, made him feel he "could write about anywhere." In *Independence Day*, Haddam, New Jersey, where Frank lives, contains a run of streets named after the nine muses, like the sequence of streets that crosses St. Charles Avenue "uptown" in New Orleans.

[4] William Rothman and Marian Keane, *Reading Cavell's* The World Viewed: *A Philosophical Perspective on Film* (Detroit: Wayne State University Press, 2000), 26. In *Disclosure of the Everyday: Undramatic Achievement in Narrative Film* (Trowbridge, Wiltshire, England: Flick Books, 2000), 5 n. 2, Andrew Klevan acknowledges the pervasive presence in his book of Cavell's work on film by making a kindred observation about its lack of recognition by film scholars in Britain.

[5] E. Ann Kaplan, review of *Contesting Tears*, by Stanley Cavell, *Film Quarterly* 52.1 (fall 1998), 77–81, p. 80. Maria DiBattista, *Fast-Talking Dames* (New Haven, CT: Yale University Press, 2001). David R. Shumway, "Mystifying Marriage," in *Modern Love: Romance, Intimacy, and the Marriage Crisis* (New York: New York University Press, 2003), 89–100.

[6] See Stanley Cavell, *The World Viewed: Reflections on the Ontology of Cinema*, enl. ed. (Cambridge, MA: Harvard University Press, 1979), 22: "Apart from the wish for selfhood (hence the simultaneous granting of otherness as well), I do not understand the value of art."

[7] See Lawrence F. Rhu, "An American Philosopher at the Movies," *DoubleTake* 7.2 (spring 2001), 115–119, p. 116, where Cavell says, "The problem here is of requiring belief before

achieving understanding—a dangerous demand from philosophy, a necessary demand (if dangerous still) from religion. But I think commitment of this sort is required of what we used to think of as the humanities. Commitment gets formed long before one has arrived at an understanding sufficient to justify the commitment."

[8] Flannery O'Connor, *Wise Blood*, in *Collected Works* (New York: Library of America, 1988), 34.

[9] Paul Tillich, *The Courage to Be* (New Haven, CT: Yale University Press, 1952), 9–17. In his recent exposition of what he calls Stanley Cavell's "embrace of the human," Ronald Hall takes particular care to distinguish between Cavell's overcoming of skepticism and stoic resignation. See Hall, *The Human Embrace: The Love of Philosophy and the Philosophy of Love: Kierkegaard, Cavell, Nussbaum* (University Park: University of Pennsylvania Press, 2000), 107.

[10] Cavell, *Contesting Tears: The Hollywood Melodrama of the Unknown Woman* (Chicago: University of Chicago Press, 1996), 16–17.

[11] Henry David Thoreau, *Walden and Resistance to Civil Government*, 2d ed. (New York: Norton, 1992), 91.

[12] Samuel Johnson, *Selections from Johnson on Shakespeare*, ed. Bertrand H. Bronson (New Haven, CT: Yale University Press, 1986), 240.

[13] Cavell, *Disowning Knowledge in Seven Plays of Shakespeare*, updated ed. (Cambridge: Cambridge University Press, 2003), 80-81.

[14] Cavell, *Contesting Tears*, 40.

[15] Ibid., 190.

[16] Jay Tolson, *Pilgrim in the Ruins: A Life of Walker Percy*, 277, 315–316.

[17] Walker Percy, *The Moviegoer* (New York: Knopf, 1961), 78.

[18] Walker Percy, "Stoicism in the South," in *Signposts in a Strange Land* (New York: Farrar, Straus, and Giroux, 1991), 83–88, pp. 85–86.

[19] Percy, *The Moviegoer*, 23.

[20] Cavell, *Contesting Tears*, 40.

[21] Percy, *The Moviegoer* (New York: Knopf, 1961), 13.

[22] Wallace Stevens, "The Sense of the Sleight-of-Hand Man," in *The Collected Poems of Wallace Stevens* (New York: Alfred A. Knopf, 1965), 222.

[23] Stanley Cavell, *Pursuits of Happiness: The Hollywood Comedy of Remarriage* (Cambridge, MA: Harvard University Press), 14–15. The relevant phrase in Kierkegaard occurs during his discussion of the knight of faith's ability "absolutely to express the sublime in the pedestrian." See Søren Kierkegaard, *Fear and Trembling* in *Kierkegaard's Writings*, Vol. 6, trans. Howard V. Hong and Edna H. Hong (Princeton, NJ: Princeton University Press, 1983), 41.

[24] Walker Percy, Letter to Stanley Kauffmann, 2/11/60, quoted in Tolson's *Pilgrim in the Ruins*, 286.

[25] Emerson, "Experience," in *Emerson: Essays and Poems*, ed. Joel Porte, college ed. (New York: Library of America, 1996), 471–492, p. 492.

[26] Cited in James Conant, "Cavell and the Concept of America," *Contending with Stanley Cavell*, 55–81, p. 59. See Johannes Climacus, *Concluding Unscientific Postscript*, ed. S. Kierkegaard, trans. Walter Lowrie (Princeton, NJ: Princeton University Press, 1968), 49. "[T]hat we humans must decide to be human" is the central theme of Ronald Hall's *The Human Embrace*. See Hall, *The Human Embrace*, 1.

[27] Emerson, "The American Scholar," in *Essays and Poems*, 53–71, p. 60.

[28] Ibid., 57–58.

[29] See note 5.

[30] Percy, *The Moviegoer*, 238–241. See p. 216 for the other.

JOHN BALDACCINO

BETWEEN THE IRONIC AND THE IRENIC

Happiness, Contingency, and the Poetics of Recurrence

I

This essay starts by discussing a number of assumptions about happiness. These are partly prompted by the language and philosophy of a fragmentary history and the ensuing notion of 'historical contingency.'[1] I want to do this with respect to a discussion of happiness as I see it move between the irenic and the ironic in various artistic forms and their diverse manifestations. This suggestion emerges from an interest to seek a definition of happiness between the following two views:

1. An ironic engagement with the world. This is done as a way of understanding the world from a point of view that is critical, by being at best humorous and at worst sardonic. Furthermore, this engagement could be seen as part of a larger 'formative' intentionality.
2. The irenic ideals of human consciousness. By such ideals we anticipate and wish for the realization of our teleological projects—projects that are intended to transcend the contingent nature of the human condition.

While irony seems quite accessible through the various arts (popular, high, on the fringe, or in the mainstream), the irenic may appear as rather problematic when the very notion of teleology—especially what Lukàcs calls our "teleological projects"—is fundamentally challenged by historical contingency.

Although the argument of this essay is philosophically informed, its main intent is to revisit happiness through questions that arise around aesthetics and more particularly as an argument for the contemporary arts. This is a solid argument for the arts even when currently it could be argued that our aesthetic experience has entered a kind of 'lull,' a 'pause,' or even a 'drop' in what is universally expected as a horizon of artistic activity. The irony—here implicit in the argument of art (not to mention the content that comes from art)—is also evident in a condition of stasis. What I mean by "a condition of stasis" is that although many artists are still producing what is presumed to be a continuous engagement with various forms of artistic creation, this often comes to us as a suspended activity, almost an activity that is willfully self-alienated from what the arts—even through Modernism—have always been expected to 'be' or 'do.' I would never argue that contemporary artists

are producing 'rubbish' (as some critics may say). However, I would say that the contemporary arts are caught between the following:
1. The contingency that fragments any argument for a universal narrative.
2. The need to reclaim art as a universal narrative that allows us to live and survive our historical contingency.

In this way, art's expression of content comes out as a negotiation between a desired irenic state and an existing ironic reaction to the fact that that state is not at hand, although it remains a desirable and important human objective. While the arts cannot afford to be cynical—even when they appear to be so, especially in their contemporary forms—artists need to make use of the implements of irony to engage, learn, and indeed do art by ways that often appear to be erroneous, partial, and vulgar, if not downright nonsense.

In this context I see Richard Rorty's well-known definition of the 'ironist' as very apt – even though I would still debate the liberal assumption by which he invests irony, although to many extents I am not inimical to such an argument.[2] As Rorty puts it,

> 'ironist' (…) name[s] the sort of person who faces up to the contingency of his or her most central beliefs and desires—someone sufficiently historicist and nominalist to have abandoned the idea that those central beliefs and desires refer back to something beyond the reach of time and chance. Liberal ironists are people who include among these ungroundable desires their own hope that suffering will be diminished, that the humiliation of human beings by other human beings may cease.[3]

As I have said elsewhere, the recognition of a state of groundlessness gives us a hope beyond the contingency that conditions many of our objectives.[4] I think that this hope could be articulated by those who converge on the notion of irony from their different philosophical, political, and artistic traditions. Why this is possible is precisely because ironists are by definition attendant to the contingent nature of traditions. I happen to see the arts as main facilitators of the ironic recognition of groundlessness, and this is because, more than any other human activity, the arts are adept at irony. Likewise, I regard the arts as preserving the irenic in potentiality.

It is this to-ing and fro-ing between the ironic and the irenic that I want to discuss in this essay. It is also in this particular context that I want to make an argument for happiness. This is what animates most of the thinking behind this essay. I say this while bearing in mind that both the ironic and the irenic aspects of the contemporary arts attest to an understanding of the dynamics of happiness in the forms of hope, empathy, love, friendship, community, philanthropy, and so on, even when—or perhaps more so when—the comforts of totality are deemed to be a fallacy. A further caveat to this discussion is that while happiness as a human quality remains a must in our desire to fulfill and make sense of our lives, the contemporary arts also warn us off any hope to achieve happiness through identitarian routes—specially when throughout history such qualities have been deformed and manipulated by oligarchs and hegemonies of all persuasions.

Agnes Heller prefaces her book *A Philosophy of History in Fragments* as follows:

> This book is not a book on history. It is a philosophy of history after the demise of the grand narratives. The leftover of the past is historical consciousness itself; post-moderns understand themselves as dwellers in the prison house of our contemporary/history/historicity. This is why we cannot get rid of the awareness of historicity and history, although one can give it a try. I have attempted this a few times, but, on the whole, this book manifests rather the entanglement of modern men and women caught within this prison house.[5]

She goes on to argue

> Post-moderns inherited historical consciousness, but not the self-complacency of the grand narratives. The confidence in an increasing transparency of the world is gone. This is not a good time for writing systems. On the other hand, it is quite a good time for writing fragments.

The notion that philosophically the idea of history is more akin to that of a multiplicity of fragments is confirmed by the very fact that it is inconceivable for philosophy, morality, or aesthetics to univocally sustain a totality. Those who know their history of philosophy, and indeed that of the arts, know well that this argument is not simply an assumption limited to the whims of a post-modern condition. This preoccupation with the unfeasibility of totality is argued out of the essential anxiety by which men and women engage with their other permanent condition: that of sustaining human reason in the face of the human catastrophes that emerged from total views and practices.

History as a multiplicity of fragments is not a rhetorical argument. In modern times it comes to a sharp edge in Kant, whose *Critique of Judgement* confirms the implicit gap between the grammars of the understanding and those of reason; of the conformity to law and the final purpose; of nature and freedom. This apparent separation, or alienation, emerges from the fact that in his rational construction of these grammars, Kant could not avoid the imperatives of an equally rational structure by whose implements these grammars preserve themselves as philosophically legitimate and thereby distinct from each other. Such dilemmas simply leave us (with Kant) with an aesthetic that is alienated from reason and ethics where the traditional triangle of the true, the good, and the beautiful is no more.

Recently, Slavoy Zizek has invited us to read such dilemmas by the way of a so-called parallax view, where what we have, is, in this case (at least as I read it) two perspectives (the rational and moral) that are positioned with an interstitial space 'between' them.[6] Indeed this interstitial space is not simply a fictive or logical construction of philosophy, discourse, or sheer rational perception. It pertains to the fragmentary condition with which the moderns of today—the so-called 'post-moderns'—still have to grapple, not only in philosophy, but also in their reflection on every aspect of their lives.

Whether (as Kant suggests in his third critique) judgment, purposiveness, and art could respectively bridge this gap remains a major philosophical question, which to many extents has also redefined and set the foundations for the aesthetics of modernity and what is deemed to 'follow' it. Surely beyond this alienation of the beautiful from the true and the good, Kant's third critique offers the conceivability of notions that otherwise would have been considered as either illogical or simply nonsense. Here I refer to Kant's concept of purposiveness without purpose in matters of beauty; of disinterestedness in matters of taste; and of his re-articulation of the Sublime (beyond that of Longinus and Burke) as a 'short-circuited' system (as Lyotard calls it) that comes in full effect with the matter of judgement.[7]

One could react to such reiterations by raising one's arms in despair with the expected sigh of "Here we go again!" However, on the other side of the argument there is an optimistic interpretation (if that is allowable, philosophically) that would regard this state of affairs as necessary for the opening of those possibilities by which we could, as Heller suggests, "write fragments."

Indeed "writing fragments" is an opening of the possible. This opening allows us to proceed by dint of our historical consciousness (albeit deprived of the comforts of grand narratives) to re-assume our responsibilities toward history. This is possible even when, philosophically, history emerges in fragmentary forms. This also means that the question of happiness—which, to my mind, is an integral part of any historical consciousness (in whichever way it is defined)—retains relevance within the wider moral and aesthetic corollaries of our lives.

The need to write fragments, rather than 'mend "middles"'[8] is the only option we have. We do not need the post-moderns to confirm this. We need only recall the work of Kierkegaard and Nietzsche, who, still experiencing the Hegelian ghost in the philosophical corridors of academia, came to conclusions that are not dissimilar from ours, which is why we find in their work a way of surviving the dilemmas of modernity.

Those attempts to 'emancipate' Kant's 'deferrals'[9] into a dialectically embedded history have ended in disaster. They failed not because of Hegel's system, but because modern history is the history of Capital. By the pragmatic and positivistic assumptions with which the power of Capital has reigned supreme everywhere, Hegelianism has been relegated to totalitarianism. The latter found its fulfilment in the ideological reification of human reason—done (and justified) by the hopes with which the Enlightenment gave way to the positivist assumptions of Capital. In practice, these assumptions emerged in Capital's individualist and collectivist immediacies in the form of market and command economies, respectively.[10]

Adorno articulates this state of affairs as follows:

> History is the unity of continuity and discontinuity. Society stays alive, not despite its antagonism, but by means of it; the profit interest and thus the class relationship make up the objective motor of the production process which the life of all men hangs by, and the primacy of which has its vanishing point in the death of all. This also implies the reconciling side of the irreconcilable; since nothing else permits men to live, not even a changed life would be possible without it. What historically made this possibility may as well destroy it.[11]

To 'write' fragmented histories is not to declare an end or failure of humanity. It is another way of saying that our philosophical, artistic, ethical, and political articulations of history could only be deemed as fragments and not totalities. This is because the conceptual building blocks by which we as human beings have constructed our philosophical horizons remain insufficient, or at best remain willfully suspended in philosophical discourse—as one finds in Kierkegaard, Nietzsche, and Husserl. This is because philosophy is unable to fully convey the very immanence by which women and men can declare themselves to be 'historical beings' without descending into the mire of sophistic tautologies by which fascism has, under many guises, caused human thought to degenerate. This is also a realization that a history that comes to us in fragments is a reversal—indeed a categorical refutation—of the identitarian aspirations by which history itself is often forced on us. I concur with Adorno when he argues that the identity principle—as imbued in the notion of a 'world spirit'—is the real source of catastrophe:

> The World spirit, a worthy object of definition, would have to be defined as permanent catastrophe. Under the all-subjugating identity principle, whatever does not enter into identity, whatever eludes rational planning in the realm of means, turns into frightening retribution for the calamity which identity brought on the nonidentical. There is hardly another way to interpret history philosophically without enchanting it into an idea.[12]

II

In his second thesis on the philosophy of history, Walter Benjamin writes that "[r]eflection shows us that our image of happiness is thoroughly coloured by the time to which the course of existence has assigned us."[13] In *The Gay Science* (§276), Nietzsche wants "to learn more and more to see what is necessary in things as the beautiful in them—thus I shall become one of those who makes things beautiful." Benjamin qualifies the happiness that "could arouse envy in us" as existing "only in the air we have breathed, among people we could have talked to." In this way, he sees our image of happiness as "indissolubly bound up with the image of redemption." But what is this redemption, one could ask, if it were to be framed in a history that is essentially fragmentary?

In the sixth thesis on the philosophy of history, Benjamin argues that "to articulate the past historically does not mean to recognize it 'the way it really was' [...]. It means to seize hold of a memory as it flashes up at a moment of danger." In this, one can hear echoes of Nietzsche:

> Amor fati! May that be my love from now on! I want to wage no war against the ugly. I do not want to accuse, I do not want even to accuse the accusers. May looking away be my only form of negation! And, all in all: I want to be at all times hereafter only an affirmer! (*The Gay Science* §230)

Nietzsche's moment is not unlike Benjamin's. The moment begets a history that is taken on not by simply recounting backward to other moments, but by recognizing its 'redemption' from the teleological prescriptions of a causal chain. If the past is, as Benjamin remarks (in the fifth thesis), "seized only as an image which flashes up at the instant when it can be recognized and is never seen again,"[14] this also means that far from being simply bereft of history, this moment—which may well be deemed fragmentary—is beheld by the present. In this present, we beheld the past as a moment that is not unlike happiness as "an image of redemption." Benjamin says that "[t]he past carries with it a temporal index by which it is referred to redemption. This is a secret agreement between past generations and the present one."[15] One would read in this a redemptive possibility that survives without having to be quashed under the identitarian imperatives of an ethical system (and with it a definition of happiness) that is held hostage to its own grammatical rigors.

The redemptive qualities that Benjamin attributes to happiness and the past might sit well with Zarathustra's "Of the Vision of the Riddle," where he tells of a gateway with "two aspects":

> Two paths come together here: no one has ever reached their end.
> This long lane behind us: it goes on for eternity. And that long lane ahead of us—that is another eternity.
> They are in opposition to one another, these paths; they abut on one another and it is here at this gateway that they come together. The name of the gateway is written above it: "Moment."[16]

We know that the gate, the "Moment," recurs eternally. It is in this context that Nietzsche reminds us how "all things that can run have already run along this lane." The same goes for "all things that can happen have already happened, been done, run past."[17] What is emphasized is the possibility of the running of things and the very recurrence of the possibility of what happens. In this way, the happiness that is made possible by the recurrence is one that is not beheld by one identity but by the recurrence of several identities that pass through the moment. The moment—one could even say the moment of happiness—is single, but it is a singularity that is in itself plural and nonidentical even when recurrent.

So if we talk of happiness as a moment, we need not hang happiness on a causal line that is premeditated—or indeed pre-mediated—by strictly identified origins and ends. This also distances happiness from a process by which happiness is anticipated, or worse still, conditioned by ethical assumptions that are tied to a legislative frame that ends up proscribing the very irenic assumptions that it makes. Traditionally, we have assumed that the irenic is a state of mind that would need to be gained, and thereby framed by the preconditions that would regale us with a state of happiness that would in turn take on a transcendental distancing from the contingencies of life. This is found in many religious assumptions of happiness, where it is almost invariably linked to a negotiation with states of suffering. Here one would recognize a stoic characterization of the attainment of happiness, which proscribes immediate happiness through gratification. Happiness as gratification seems too hedonistic to the minds of those who still misconstrue hedonism as a kind of unscrupulous search for constant pleasure. While it is not the intent of this essay to revisit the division between hedonism and stoicism, it is worth noting that often the assumptions of an irenic state are distanced from hedonism because the latter is misconstrued as temporary, whereas a more stoic-like route to happiness remains worthier in the eyes of those who closely tie happiness to a view of ethical happiness, where the latter is gained almost in a prolonged process of self-amelioration.

However, this difficulty—and one could add, this classical dichotomy between immediate gratification and gained irenic states—would be avoided if happiness was to be seen not as an overcoming of a contingent state, but as a realization that contingency is a reality of the human condition. In the latter case, one could then take the concept of the irenic beyond that which is limited to a teleological and narrowly conceived view. Indeed the nobility of self-sacrifice in stoicism could still hold value in a perspective of the irenic that emerges from a concept of happiness that is open to the possibilities that would emerge from our writing—and indeed doing and living—of fragments.

This is where the irenic by itself is not sufficient to the definition of happiness. This is also where the irenic needs to travel to (and from) the ironic and 'back'—whereby the interstices of the fragments that we 'write,' 'see,' and 'do' emerge in their recurrent states. For this to become clearer—at least in my mind—I would need to resort to the philosophical narratives that are regaled to us by the arts.

III

In Pier Paolo Pasolini's drama *Affabulazione*, which is characterized by the relationship between a father and his son (taking off from where Sophocles leaves in his Oedipus), we come across a re-articulation of the *Pater Noster*, the Lord's Prayer, that starts like this:

> Padre nostro che sei nei Cieli,
> io non sono mai stato ridicolo in tutta la vita.
> Ho sempre avuto negli occhi un velo d'ironia.
> Padre nostro che sei nei Cieli:
> ecco un tuo figlio che, in terra, è padre...
> (Our Father who art in Heaven,
> I have never been ridiculous in all my life.
> I have always had a veil of irony over my eyes.
> Our Father who art in Heaven:
> here is a son of yours who, on earth, is [a] father...)

In the 'earthly' father's invocation of the heavenly Father's attention, Pasolini draws our attention to a filial–paternal recurrence that is re-projected by the same force with which Sophocles traps his audience in his tragic cycles. Ultimately the father is trapped in the same state of ridicule that he continuously sought to avoid through his ironic outlook. This is a tautology bent on itself, an 'oedipal' recurrence that even goes to suggest—almost by way of blasphemy—that the Father–Son recurrence starts with the heavenly Father, who is the only One who could put a stop to this incestuous cycle. In this way, the heavenly aspect to which the earthly father resorts, will realize the eternal aspect of the recurrent route. This larger, eternal, recurrence could be deemed less Freudian and more Nietszchean in that it presents us with the transient nature by which the gate of the Moment moves from one eternal route to another.

As a moment of the Moment, the mortal father's prayer to the immortal heavenly Father also suggests that the fragments by which one writes life could only be seen (and understood) through the veil of irony but never that of ridicule. Irony is there to use but also to ultimately avoid and rid us from ridicule. This distinction between irony and ridicule is very important because it also frames irony in a light that has nothing to do with the immediate and (sometimes cruel) guises that it may take. From under the veil of irony, we could write, do, and live fragments in a way that will not simply lead to nothing but further irony. Unlike ridicule, irony enables the seizure of the image of redemption that Benjamin casts in the realms of happiness. In this case, happiness is not temporary—as an elated moment that becomes excessive and thereby short-lived. Rather, this time, irony aspires to a longer form of happiness by which an understanding leads to the possibility of the irenic—perhaps to be understood as that understanding of the world in its limitations and possibilities.

The recurrence between the ironic and the irenic is made more manifest in Pasolini's film *Uccellacci e Uccellini* (1966), where one is presented with two confluent stories, positioned in different time frames but conjoined by a recurrence that is reflected forward and backward, between a father and son, and an old Franciscan and a young novice. The father and son, Innocenti Totò and Innocenti Ninetto, meet a talking raven on their erratic and hopeless journey. The raven declares that he comes from a distant land called Ideologia and his parents were Mr. Doubt and Mrs. Conscience. The raven tells them of the story of Frate Cicillo and Frate Ninetto, an old monk and a young novice, who are ordered by Saint Francis to evangelize the birds. Frate Cicillo and Frate Ninetto spend a long time seeking to learn how the birds speak, and after a long pilgrimage, they finally reach their objective, realizing that the small birds (the *uccellini*) can be spoken to by chirping, while the big birds (the *uccellacci*) communicate between each other using strange leaps and dances.

At the end of their pilgrimage, the two monks realize that although they have been evangelized, the big birds remain adept at killing and devouring the smaller birds. This is catastrophic to the monks, who in their journey have had to come to terms with the tragedy of the relativism by which love itself remains in fragments. The bigger and stronger birds love each other per se—as *uccellacci*, as a stronger species; while meek, small, and weak birds do the same, loving each other as a smaller and weaker species per se. But when it comes to the larger, plural, and diverse species of birds (*uccelli*) comprising large and small, *uccellacci* and *uccellini*, together, it is a different story.

In this film, the relationship between Frate Cicillo and Frate Ninetto is characterized by episodes of buffoonery, affection, and a boundless love toward the world as God's creation. This love remains uninterrupted even when the Franciscans' irenic passage to understanding is marred by the irony of its fragmentary ways. The overall state of irony becomes more acute when we are taken back to the errant and erratic journey of Totò and Ninetto, who, though mentored by the wise words of the raven about every aspect of human life—sexuality, morality, birth control, politics, religion, and economics—end up making a supper of the raven. Being hungry and lost in a world that they could not really cope with and fully understand, they eat the raven and move on!

Apart from having as its main protagonist the most loved comedian in Italy, Antonio de Curtis (better known as Totò), Pasolini's *Uccellacci e Uccellini* is celebrated in terms of how this work of comedy delivers the most sensitive account of empathy and compassion. This relationship between irony and the extent of human tragedy recalls another film, whose protagonist is yet another prominent Italian comedian and director, Roberto Benigni. Benigni's film *La Vita è Bella* (1997) represents a most incisive commentary on the tragedy of the Holocaust by depicting human tragedy through the implements of irony, which in its comedic (but never ridiculous) parameters, carries the audience to a deeper understanding of one of the worst tragedies in human history.

In Benigni's *La Vita è Bella*, the irenic is internalized in the boundless love between Dora, Guido, and their son Giosué. This love prevails beyond the horrific tragedy of the Holocaust in which Guido (played by Benigni) is caught and executed by an SS guard while Guido, dressed as a woman, is attempting to enter the female wing of the camp to meet his wife.[18] *La Vita è Bella* brings together the powers of tragedy and comedy where the ironic moves in tandem with moments of the irenic—moments of happiness that prevail over the anguish and deadly sadness caused by the horrors of fascism. *La Vita è Bella* deals with fascism first with the sharp tools of irony, by which tyranny is ridiculed and brought into absolute disrepute. Then the same comedic implements become cathartic in moments when Guido decides to fight fatalism while hiding the horrible truth from his young son Giosué, telling the young boy that the labor camp is actually a theme park and that they are entering a competition of "hide and seek," with the winners taking the prize of a much-coveted armored tank. This rather controversial mechanism in no way denigrates the dignity and remembrance of the victims of the Holocaust. Guido makes the ultimate sacrifice and dies for the happiness and salvation of his son and wife. The outcome is heartbreaking. This film fulfils the classic expectations of an art form that intends to redeem its audience by doing 'good' in the face of the horrendously irrational. The ironic never moves to the grotesque, and Benigni scrupulously protects the victims of history. Instead, he reserves the grotesque for the perpetrators of the horrors of the labor camp and their allies. By means of a comedic irony, Benigni not only obliterates fascism's cynicism and arrogance, but he also restores the hope of happiness by turning the moment of the past into the irenic moments of possibility.

IV

The recurrent moves between the irenic and the ironic could probably be captured in works of fine art—more specifically visual works—where the condition of contingency comes to immediate focus in ways that are shockingly clear, as well as intimately personal. By the latter I mean that ironically (!) we come to realize that contingency becomes a universal condition with which we all identify at a personal level even when we do not know any of the individual details by which we share it.

One example is Peter Breugel the Elder's work, best known in English as *The Land of Milk and Honey* (*The Land of Cockaigne*, 1567). Breugel's depiction of an impossible utopia is sufficiently punchy to suggest that it is ironic to think of an irenic state, especially when the attainment of such an ironic statement appears to be one marked by a laidback and lazy dreaming. In this respect, the ethical critique of this hope for the irenic is chastised by an array of symbolic cues that are in themselves an admonition against the easy way.

What is of specific interest in Breugel is the observer's ability to bypass the need to acquire the art historian's tool and instead make use of what Baxandall calls the consumer's "picture-troc." The consumer's troc—her ability to barter—seems to be a consumer prerogative in this respect where "the consumer can respond or not to classes of things that have been made" by the artist, even when there is no sufficient knowledge of the work except for one's own observations.[19] Although Baxandall is discussing Picasso and what could have been his 'Brief' when he painted his *Portrait of Daniel Henry Kahnweiler*, in my relationship with Breugel's work, as Breugel's 'consumer,' I can barter his perusal of irony. I can recognize Breugel's irony through the universal character of human contingency that he captures. Even by a cursory, immediate, and very uninformed appreciation of Breugel, I partake of his strongly ironic social commentary by which he captures everyone's imagination beyond the historical, cultural, or even epistemological limitations by which we approach his art.

Could we then argue that the ironic facilitates the bartering of meaning, by which we are invited to consider happiness and to some extents weigh the value of the irenic?

Another set of works, this time contemporary (though not immediately considered as such if one is not attentive) are John Currin's, in which the ironic is facilitated not simply by the caricatured social and cultural deformities of his subjects, but also his take on a figurative style that is so often attributed to an influence from classical Flemish art. The latter attribution is mainly given to his nudes—works like *Pink Tree* (1999) and *The Go See* (1999).

Yet this attribution may or may not be more important than the intention that emerges from Currin's work as an act of social commentary in the form of irony. Indeed the ironic gestures and stylized positioning of the nudes are already suggestive of something odd going on with figures that retain a certain twentieth- and twenty-first-century look even when unclothed and strangely figured and staged as if they were posing for a Memling or a Cranach in the fifteenth or sixteenth century. This is an irony that remains intrinsic to the form, which is best illustrated in other works by Currin in which his Memling-like figures are garbed in contemporary clothing, suggesting another narrative that may well be interpreted—in terms of how we come to barter our meanings and intentions with the artist and the picture—as a commentary on the ideal (read: *irenic*) attributes that we give to a certain puritan slant that is often read in sixteenth- and seventeenth-century Flemish and German art. This puritan (and I would say, Protestant) streak tends to suggest a recapitulation of the desired irenic stages of purity by which we would expect art itself to reconfigure the world—or is it?[20]

In Currin's *Stamford After Brunch* (2000) and *Thanksgiving* (2003), we are left with a taste of an ironicized reinterpretation of an irenic desire that somehow goes wrong by the fact that contingency creeps in and leaves no space for the assumed 'perfection' and presumed 'innocence' by which Cranach's *Three Graces* (1535) or Memling's *Vanity* (1485) are meant to come across—at least in the eyes of a twenty-first-century audience, and more so, as read alongside Currin's nudes.

V

Richard Rorty sets three conditions for the definition of an "ironist":

(1) She has radical and continuing doubts about the final vocabulary she currently uses, because she has been impressed by other vocabularies, vocabularies taken as final by people or books she has encountered; (2) she realizes that argument phrased in her present vocabulary can neither underwrite nor dissolve these doubts; (3) insofar as she philosophizes about her situation, she does not think that her vocabulary is closer to reality than others, that it is in touch with power not herself.[21]

He also adds that the terms by which ironists describe themselves are always subject to change—a change that they are always aware of. Ironists are "always aware of the contingency and fragility of their final vocabularies; and thus of their selves."[22] This is evidenced by the works that I have discussed. In the case of the arts, the vocabularies themselves are always challenged and we see this not only in the very case by which one could engage—perhaps endlessly and uselessly—over Currin's "Flemish" style, but more so in the works of Benigni and Pasolini, where it is not just the story line that attests to the awareness of contingency, but more palpably the art work itself. These ironic works often emerge as fluid in their own rigor to challenge the art form by which the narrative is conveyed.

When I try to understand how irony and the irenic somehow come together in each other's defiance in a work of art, two images come to mind—Beuys's and Catellan's *La Rivoluzione siamo noi! (We are the revolution!)* (1972 and 2000). This is compounded by the title, which itself is a commentary on those irenic utopias that we always assume as catalysts of historical change. In this case it is not a Land of Milk and Honey, but the overtriumphant and equally utopian notion of historic change embodied and catalyzed by the Revolution.

Joseph Beuys's *La Rivoluzione siamo noi!* and Maurizio Catellan's later version of it are superb examples of how irony, the irenic, and the awaited happiness by which we confront the contingency of the human condition can take different aspects in the minds of those who have to barter meaning with hope in a world in which we could still do good—and, like little Giosué, live to see a future beyond the spoils of human tragedy.

Teachers College, Columbia University

NOTES

[1] Heller, A. *A Philosophy of History in Fragments* (Oxford: Blackwell, 1993).
[2] I remain skeptical of the liberal argument because, although it challenges the grounds of conservatism, liberalism as a philosophy and a political argument—in its various strands in liberal and social democracies—does not offer an alternative to what ultimately is the failed critique of conservatism. In view of what I argue later, I think that in opting for the primacy of capital, liberalism does not take us out of the morass that traps us between command and free market economies, that is, between the communist and capitalist frames of mind. Likewise, liberalism has not managed to offer a nonidentitarian stand that could eliminate the traps of the sociology of knowledge. Rather, liberalism acquiesces to ideologies even when, as here, Rorty rightly advocates the opposite. This is a dilemma between agreeing and hailing Rorty's argument for irony and solidarity and ultimately remaining doubtful about its ultimate ideological fallbacks.
[3] Rorty, R. *Contingency, Irony and Solidarity* (Cambridge: Cambridge University Press 1990), p. xv
[4] Baldacchino, J. "Hope in groundlessness: Art's denial as pedagogy", *Journal of Maltese Educational Research* (University of Malta), Vol. 3, Issue 1, June 2005 (available online at http://www.educ.um.edu.mt/jmer/).
[5] Heller, *A Philosophy of History in Fragments*, p. viii
[6] Zizek, S. *The Parallax View* (Cambridge, MA: MIT Press. 2006).
[7] Lyotard, J. F. *Lessons on the Analytic of the Sublime* (Stanford, CA: Stanford University Press, 1994).
[8] To which Gillian Rose strongly objects; see Rose, G. *The Broken Middle* (Oxford: Blackwell, 1992).

[9] Hegel's Introduction to his Lectures on Fine Art. See Hegel, G. W. F. *Hegel's Aesthetics. Lectures on Fine Art* (Oxford: Oxford University Press, 1998).
[10] Meszaros, I. *Beyond Capital* (London: Merlin Press, 1995).
[11] Adorno, T. *Negative Dialectics* (London: Routledge, 1990), p. 320.
[12] Adorno, ibid.
[13] Benjamin, W. "Theses on the Philosophy of History", in *Illuminations* (Glasgow: Fontana/Collins, 1973), p. 244.
[14] Benjamin, op cit., p. 247.
[15] Benjamin, op cit., pp. 245–246.
[16] Nietzsche, F. *Thus Spoke Zarathustra* (Harmondsworth, UK: Penguin, 1980), p. 178.
[17] Nietzsche, ibid.
[18] This state of affairs is made more poignant by how Dora 'volunteers' herself to the camp. Although she was not listed as Jewish—and therefore was of no interest to the Nazi butchers—Dora insisted on following Guido and little Giosué.
[19] Baxandall, M. *Patterns of Intention: On the Historical Explanation of Pictures* (New Haven, CT: Yale University Press, 1985), p. 48.
[20] I am here thinking of the Protestant ethic and its historical and iconic effects on visual art. In Currin's case, I am not sure it becomes an issue, but his work reminds me of a certain Protestant New England streak which he comes to use, perhaps in a critical way, via the implements of irony. The predominance of white middle-class subjects does appear as an ironic statement. Likewise, his visual commentary on streaky bodies and plasticized add-ons (such as enormous breasts) are invariably critical commentaries of certain identifiable forms of social and economic conventions.
[21] Rorty, *Contingency, Irony and Solidarity*, p. 73.
[22] Rorty, ibid., p. 74.

RAJIV KAUSHIK

PHENOMENOLOGICAL TEMPORALITY AND PROUSTIAN NOSTALGIA

INTRODUCTION

In Vol. XXIII of the Husserliana, entitled *Phantasie, Bildbewusstsein, Erinnerung*,[1] Husserl joins Freud in the attempt to show how a present consciousness can be comported toward itself in its non-present and particularly foreign forms. For both thinkers, the problem is how through phantasy, image-consciousness, and memory there is a 'loss of self' (*Selbsteverlust*), how there could be an appearing for the self that is not merely a matter of presence, but also of withdrawing. For Freud in particular, however, it is the desires of such phantasy and image-consciousness that are complicit with what they also exclude. We desire what is forbidden, and if that is true, it amounts to a fundamental diagnosis about selfhood: To be a self is to always be asking and wishing for something, specifically where that something is never fully present. The subject could never do otherwise than desire, which is to say, s/he desires and desires without ever the possibility of satiating all desire. Thus desire marks an impossibility. In fact, Freud goes so far as to claim that, because of this, to be a self is to be an-other to oneself, to be alien to oneself. It is because of this that we have the ability to absent ourselves from ourselves, for example, in the figurative, symbolic formations of phantasy-consciousness that are different than perception proper.

At times, Husserl agrees with Freud's analyses of consciousness as alien to itself. In § 70 of the *Ideen*, for example, he proposes that phantasies acquire a position of primacy over perception, and that thinking and speaking occur on their basis.[2] As John Sallis writes, here it seems that Husserl admits a distinction between,

on the one side, sensation, which is such as to resist being taken as a mere image of something, which itself the very hallmark of reality, which is primary actual presence (*primäre, aktuelle Gegenwart*); and, on the other side, phantasm, the sensible content of phantasy, which is given as non-present (*gibt sich als nichtgegenwärtig*), which is such as to resist being taken as present, which bears the character of irreality.[3]

Because in phantasies we encounter something that is not perception, something that knows itself as other than perception because it is strictly innerly performed, this primacy of phantasy consciousness apparently initiates a unique problem for phenomenology, that of an 'exteriority.' It initiates the problem of a "fracturing," a "hovering," a "spacing imagination" that is *created* in phantasies and seems to "question the fundamental securities of phenomenology."[4] In other words, if there is introduced into phenomenology a phantasy consciousness that takes precedence over intellection in the sense that the inner performativity of phantasy enables the performativity of intellection, then it seems that phantasies are beyond the possibility of phenomenologizing about. Instead, they seem to be of an imagining exteriority that is 'spaced' away from or above phenomenological consciousness.

What I want to show in this essay is that the problem of an 'otherness' within oneself need not arise in phenomenology, not even in connection with discussions of phantasies, image-consciousness, and memories. Especially in the light of Husserl's genetic-phenomenology, we can emphasize a sort of remembrance, namely, nostalgia, which does indeed reveal a 'loss' or 'not-ness' of self but not a radical one that collapses into exteriority. Where phantasy and imagining, considered narrowly and in themselves, might lead to something fractured above phenomenology, the phantasies of nostalgic remembrances by no means denote a spacing of consciousness from itself. But why does nostalgia specifically give us an instance of phantasy that does not initiate an otherness of the self? And, in this connection, why should we insist on using the word over and above desiring, hoping or wishing, etc. for what is lost, forbidden, or esoteric from consciousness? It is the claim of this essay that the word nostalgia in particular highlights a very specific brand of consciousness' esotericism. Even if nostalgia is called a "yearning for the beyond of memories,"[5] this nostalgia does not put phenomenology to the test. In fact, Proustian nostalgia is a particularly helpful determination of that which phenomenology dis-covers.

It is often said that Proust was influenced by the philosophy of Henri Bergson, and that he also helped to create a certain climate for French Existentialist thought.[6] But here I argue that, although there is no question of a direct influence, in fact Proust manages to highlight a material temporality within nostalgia that phenomenology also moves toward and, moreover, that his reflections on such temporality should have significance for phenomenology, especially should it want to avoid the thesis of a 'spacing imagination.' In particular, it is a consideration of Proust's descriptions of the sudden emergence of nostalgia in the *mémoire involontaire* that are helpful to phenomenology. Upon tasting a *petite madeleine* dipped in tea, for instance,

Proust writes of how the protagonist comes to re-collect a past joyful memory of his childhood home:

And soon, mechanically, weary after a dull day with the prospect of a depressing morrow, I raised to my lips a spoonful of the tea in which I had soaked a morsel of the cake. No sooner had the warm liquid, and the crumbs with it, touched my palate than a shudder ran through my whole body, and I stopped, intent upon the extraordinary changes that were taking place. An exquisite pleasure had invaded my senses, but individual, detached, with no suggestion of its origin.[7]

Here the present taste sensation stimulates the recollection of the past taste sensation and hence the past occasion itself.[8] It is not a question of a mere 'external' association between two distinct and discriminate sensations and events, since in this case the two moments are not experienced as merely 'similar' but 'identical.' The past and present have been made to intrude on one another,[9] and thus the ordinary experience of time as a series of separated 'nows' is transformed into a perpetual recapturing and recalling of the past. The past is in this sense preserved rather than nihilated.[10] For here the *petite madeleine* evokes a sense of temporality that is not subject to the vicissitudes of ordinary temporal mutability but goes beyond the limits of such a time.[11] The traversal of time in the *mémoire involontaire* rests upon the fact that the mind itself has no role in recalling the past because it happens when the past has been completely forgotten, literally 'lost.' Proust thus introduces us to a lost self that is different than the Freudian past self; it is thought not so much in terms of childhood traumas or forbidden desires, for example, but rather as a forgotten or fugitive place that is the cradle for a renewable world. In this connection, there is for Proust a material world to which our pre-consciousness belongs that is understood and re-arrived at in terms of a symbolic-imagination, which preserves the simultaneity of all temporal moments, past, present, and future, at once.

Proust's treatment of nostalgia, which is seen in the *mémoire involontaire*, therefore helps us to bring into scope a unique picture of the temporal being of consciousness as something pre-objective. We see in Proust's writings something that phenomenological-temporality merely suggests, namely, that it is an episodic time in which the movement of the real is expressed. In this case, Proust also helps us to see that it is myths, narratives, poems, and so on that alleviates[12] nostalgia, and therefore we might say that nostalgia is more fundamental to phantasy-consciousness because without it there would no phantasies. It is argued that insofar as Proust thrusts the wishes and desires of phantasies back into the context of a nostalgic-temporality, it is the nostalgic phenomenon that brings us away from the thesis of an exteriority, say, in the spacing imagination.

An analysis of the nostalgia of phenomenology is methodologically beneficial because it helps us see that consciousness can be located within this temporal and physical possibility. It allows us to undermine the notion of a radical alienation within phenomenological-temporality, since here what is most fundamental to consciousness is a nostalgia in which there occurs a 'loss of self' but only (e.g., in the *mémoire involontaire*) in the context of a temporal being of the things past, which does not radicalize this loss and make it wholly alien. To frame genetic-phenomenology in terms of a nostalgia thus forces us to reel phenomenology in, back toward its original impulse as a philosophy that seeks to discover nothing beyond the experience of this world, nothing other to the phenomena, no thing in itself, no other world to the sensible one. For instance, a phrase like the one we find in Husserl's *On the Phenomenology of the Consciousness of Internal Time*, which characterizes temporality as an incessant modification or a "continuity of reverberation,"[13] is meant to dispel any so-called 'metaphysical grammar' (to use Nietzsche's phrase) that consists in doubling the event of becoming with a second world beyond it.

Admittedly, this essay does not seek to perform a phenomenology of nostalgia per se, but rather to say that the characterization of phenomenological temporality as nostalgic, which then allows for the possibility of phantasies, pre-empts the thesis of exteriority. To come to see this nostalgia in phenomenology there are first two important stages that we must work through in our treatment of phenomenology as such: (1) We will need to see that in Husserl's analysis of a bodily-consciousness the phenomenologist shows that the withdrawing of the self is in fact present; but also therefore (2) Husserl's analysis of a withdrawing carnality is not another route toward a philosophy of exteriority but rather that the withdrawal of carnality, also having presence, is for Husserl an *Abgrund* in genesis in which there is nothing that is not presencing. What we have to see in other words is that in Husserl's dis-covery of a bodily-consciousness there is an intentionality that lacks objectivity, and even subjectivity, and that this lack must be seen to belong to an upheaval and time of the things past. Proustian nostalgia adds something after this point, namely, a sort of case study of how in fact we can place a phantasy consciousness within the context of this withdrawing carnality so that it does not refer to a fracturing over and above phenomenology. It is not merely that Proust makes clear that nostalgia is a temporal matter—phenomenology can show that on its own accord—but that he is able to make vivid, and with particular reference to nostalgia, the fullest sense of a dissatisfied consciousness in such a way that phenomenology has hitherto only theoretically indicated.

BODILY-CONSCIOUSNESS: AN INTENTIONALITY WITHOUT SUBJECT AND OBJECT

The manuscripts of 1929–1930, compiled by Landgrebe under the title *Erfahrung und Urteil*, are perhaps the first to speak of the world as a "field of passive doxa," as the "horizon of all possible judgment substrates."[14] This level of primal constitution (*Urkonstitution*) is by no means the transparency of an absolute to itself. It requires a passivity of a primal impression (*Urimpression*) that is understood against the backdrop of an obscurity of the *hyte*, in order to overcome the Cartesian thesis of an 'indubitable given.' What phenomenology aims at is to bring to the light of day a unity between consciousness and nature that is hidden by theoretical consciousness. In doing so, it wants to found the idea of the real and the categorical on the sensible and to expose the false thought of a being that does not affect us. That is, phenomenology hopes to witness the origins of the correlation of consciousness with its object and thus to expose the myth of a spontaneous understanding that is completely detached from the receptivity of the sensible. In still other words, phenomenology shows that consciousness is first and irrevocably "an interested party," that it exists in the world as a "collaborator."[15] The phrase that Eugen Fink uses to describe consciousness is applicable here as well: According to phenomenology, he says, there is a "temporality of the analytic situation" of consciousness that stands in a "discordant unity" with the world.[16]

The field of passive doxa allows us to think of an originary experience of the world in its pre-given, pre-logical sense that contains protological structures out of which a structure of the higher-order logic arises through the process of idealization. In this case, this passive doxa forces us to see that the distinctions 'known' and 'unknown,' 'determinable and 'determinate,' for example, occur against the background of a horizon of typical familiarity. Husserl is forced to broaden the notion of 'presentation' to show that it involves a subjacent intentionality that includes the temporal considerations of an object as "having-been-itself there," a "recapitulating" of the "sequence of subjective 'exhibitions of' having been in my earlier ontic validities."[17] He sometimes employs the term 'perspectivization' rather than 'perspective' in order to refer to something that is potentially a fact and to consider perceiving beyond its now-phase, as a primary-remembering and awakening and as forward directing. Here Husserl understands conscious life on the basis of a 'unity of becoming,' a unity of waking and hidden life that acts as a concrete background to later abstraction.[18]

Which is to say: The presented thing, qua thing, is only there by virtue of a retention that is constitutive of the act of perception and allows us to see the datum in the unity of a consciousness that encompasses intentionally "what is present and what is past."[19] Husserl's example of tonality in his *Phenomenology of Internal Time-Consciousness* shows that the tone does not unravel linearly but is rather a matter of constitution that obeys a twofold movement of protention and retention, where it is perpetually merged into a melody.[20] A reflection on our experience of this movement shows that consciousness has to be within a continuum. One's expectations of what is to come in the music may or may not be correct, but what is significant is that underneath this expectation is a 'pointing into' its horizon. I therefore cannot say that a sound begins, continues, or stops without bringing into question the issue of duration and succession. In the movement from one tone to another, for example, I implicitly ascertain the internal, primordial character of succession underlying two distinct phenomena in which already there is a promise of repetition. "The consciousness of succession," as Husserl writes, "is consciousness that gives its object originally; it is 'perception' of this succession."[21] The key is that any 'now-phase' of my perceptions must occur not merely as a point but through a 'zone' or 'span' that brings an object into actualization for consciousness.[22] In this sense, natural experience is for Husserl a complex of both full (which is to say present) and empty (which is to say absent) intentions.

This demonstrates a shift, a de-centering of the subject into the continuum that must somehow itself be meaningful, albeit latently. The latency of meaning happens in the moments of absence: The tension created by a crescendo, for example, happens not in the now but from the past of the now, and even in the future of the crescendo, with the anticipation that the tension previously created must somehow be resolved. In the production of meaning, phenomenology therefore posits a more latent, nascent logos that is neither totally absent nor distinct from predication but is a non-presence inherent to the thing that must be somehow meaningful in the now-phase of perception. If the absence of a thing's appearance is inextricably linked to its predication, intentionality now also includes an 'objectivism' that forces the phenomenologist to posit a streaming-consciousness into that absence. The constituting subject is an 'enworlding' (*Verweltigung*) one; as a human existing in the world, it is literally in the midst of it.[23] The question is how Husserl should understand this collaboration in the world, that is, literally the corporeal subject that feels itself as 'flesh' (*Leib*), conjointly with the way in which he conceives the originary perceptions of the spatial things around that body. What does natural experience have to do with absence? If the things are not themselves indissoluble unities, they are instead for Husserl ever-changing. Insofar as this once again implicates the issue of a primordial succession in the context of enworldment, it is a topology that contains a promise of the non-absent to come. Thus, as Rudolf Bernet writes, being "does not arise without its withdrawal and concealment for the benefit of the massive and visible presence of the things of the world."[24] And it follows that there is a bodily "intentionality without an object in Husserl" that is not an "impressional selfmanifestation which could scarcely be said to belong to a life of subject-ivity."[25] More needs to be said as to how this pre-subjective intentionality without an object does not create the problem of a total lack that has nothing to do with the visibility of things. If indeed Husserl can envisage the withdrawal of carnality as presence, here is the connection we will make with nostalgia in order to overcome any absolutistic reading of the absent of consciousness and its impossibility.

THE TEMPORALITY OF WHAT IS LOST IN CONSCIOUSNESS

To accomplish this, we now have to see the withdrawn in the context of timeliness, and, to do this, we first had to stress that the withdrawing must be understood in light of an interweaving between 'what is present and what is past.' The aim of this is simply to expose that in the field of passive doxa whatever is 'true' is true because of what has proceeded it and urged it on to become so. Husserl's analysis of this so-called 'living present' (*Lebendige Gegenwort*) of consciousness shows us that the true is only so afterward, on the basis of what has already been; it needs to be made true in the sense that it must await verification. When he notes in *On the Phenomenology of the Consciousness of Internal Time* that the "now apprehension is, as it were, the head attached to the comet's tail of retentions relating to the earlier now points of the motion,"[26] he means to highlight the retroactive quality of the true, and therefore to tell us that whatever is true is originally in constant movement. Or, as he puts it elsewhere, that there is a "single continuum that is continuously modified."[27] It is also significant that when Husserl remarks on this modifying continuum he notes that it lacks a name and can only indirectly, that is, metaphorically, be designated as 'flow.'[28]

Husserl is keen here to show the reader that he does not think that his discovery of the living-present of consciousness should reveal a new problem in which a continuum forces the ontical decision of whether or not after death, for example, still another kind of life is possible or whether there is an after-life to consciousness. It does not follow, however, that a subjacent intentionality is wholly contingent. For then it seems that a universal intentional consciousness would lead nowhere and come to a halt within temporally constituted being. The request to think of a temporality of consciousness as a 'flow' not in any metaphysical sense but rather as something metaphorical implies that he hopes to catch a glimpse of this temporality before we have done anything to it in scientific language. In that case, the remark reminds us of Heidegger's comment that "any true phenomenological chronology has nothing to do with the order or success and the science of established dates"[29] because it should not force us to question its absolute beginnings or absolute endings. Fundamentally, it never attempts to answer the question of its own ultimacy.

In fact, Husserl is at pains to criticize any in-itself that would invoke such a logic, as is evidenced, for instance, in the explicitly anti-Copernican attitude of a manuscript note from 1934 bearing the title "Reversal of the Copernican Doctrine." The note opens:

Distinction: the world in the openness of the surrounding world—posited conceptually as infinite. The sense of this infinity "world existing in the ideality of infinity." What is the sense of this existence, the existing infinite world? The openness as horizonality that is not completely conceived, represented, but that is already implicitly formed.[30]

This distinction is a typically phenomenological move, namely, an interest not in the principled foundation of the infinite per se but in the articulation of the sense of the infinite. The attempt here is to re-temporalize this notion of the infinite by seeing it not through the eyes of an 'evasive transcendentalism' that wrongly tries to reconstruct a beginning from the point of view of its results but always without appeal to some external logic. Thus, whereas the infinite as ideality is "expressed in judgments by ontology"[31] in which "the form of the world is taken into consideration along with its ontic possibilities,"[32] phenomenology "penetrates the horizon... and grasps actually, intuitively, as confirmed being, a fragment of the mundane field that is being offered."[33] In that way, the form of the world emerges from within "an open range of possibilities"[34] and is thus founded from within a "deformation and continual inner motion"[35] or "within the open and indeterminate horizon of earthly space."[36]

This move can be understood to adhere to the notion of the *Fundierung*, the reciprocal founding-founded relation first presented in the *Logical Investigations*,[37] which refuses the Kantian 'Copernican Revolution' that instigates an absolute idealism, for example, the world as a transcendental postulate of reason. Otherwise, a temporality of the analytical situation would always remain impossible because, as a stasis, this continuity would only be a situation to which the analytic position would be juxtaposed and in mere discord. Thus, any continuity must exist more exactly as an ongoing multiformity in order for it to be the theoretical intermediate stage in the final elucidation of any philosophical logic. In this case, it is the earth itself that is a series of possibilities that allows for the conceptuality of a world as infinite. Gérard Granel helpfully notes that insofar as Husserl's aim is to problematize any theme of a "perfect given of the thing," the given no longer appears in phenomenology as an external limit but as an "internal telos"[38] in which we discover its more original "furtiveness, its withdrawal, its modesty, its *Gelichtetheit*."[39] Here phenomenology "succeeds in representing even the silence of being."[40]

In this way Husserl's dis-covery of the temporality of consciousness shares a significant theme with Proust's novels: The search for a lost time also ends in phenomenology with a time retrieved, but only (as I attempted to clarify in the last section) where phenomenological remembering is not concerned merely with a past from a perspective of the present but also with the future from the perspective of the past.[41] This is especially evident in Husserl's famous paper "On the Origins of Geometry," in which he seamlessly relates a "chain of historical back-references" that are also "enigmatically given in the present"[42] to an "entelechy" in which "psychic humanity has never been and never will be."[43] Entelechy—Coming back to Granel's characterization, what this telos of an inner-chain entails is that the seed of the past is perpetually planted anew in the present. Husserl understands the historicity of consciousness against the backdrop of an unlimited fecundity, forever re-appearing. Exposing a present remembrance of a previous world, which at the same time belongs to this world, can only be done if remembering and the previous world are both called from this same present. This in turn requires a consistent abandonment of a 'metaphysics of presence,' which is in fact the lesson learned from Proust as well. Merleau-Ponty for one also makes a link to the author on behalf of phenomenology at the very end of his last, incomplete work: "No one has gone further than Proust," he writes, "in fixing the relations between the visible and the invisible, in describing an idea that is not the contrary of the sensible, that is its lining and its depth." And later: "The difference is simply that [in Proust] this invisible, these ideas, unlike those of science cannot be detached from the sensible appearances and erected into second positivity."[44] If no one has gone further than Proust in avoiding what Merleau-Ponty calls here a 'second positivity' of a world beyond this one, it is because he fulfills a suggestion made by phenomenology, namely, to show how an absence that bears temporality and physicality brings to the light of day all of consciousness' disaffectedness without referring to an absolute impossibility of consciousness. In particular, Proust is engaged in a task that should be read into phenomenology, that of reading the nostalgic desires of remembrance toward a worldview that leads nowhere other than to this same world.

THE TEMPORALITY OF WHAT IS LOST IN PROUSTIAN NOSTALGIA

Let us consider, Proust's reflection on the *mémoire involontaire* that is provoked, for instance, by a paving stone:

> I felt the flutter of a past that I did not recognize; it was just as I set foot on a certain paving-stone that this feeling of perplexity came over me. I felt an invading happiness, I knew that I was going to be enriched by that purely personal thing, a past impression, a fragment of life in unsullied preservation (something we can only know in preservation, for while we live in it, it is not the present in the memory, since other sensations accompany and smother it) which asked only that it should be set free, that it should come and augment my wealth of life and poetry.[45]

This *mémoire involontaire* is different than an intellectual memory. The latter is the normal sense of memory because here the past is irretrievably past—it is a 'dead past' insofar as there is no genuine preservation of the past in a living way.[46] The intellectual memory is thus at our disposal, and in this sense is voluntary.[47] The *mémoire involontaire*, on the other hand, insofar as it is invoked by a chance encounter with some significant object, reveals to us that in fact the past can be given back in some other, livelier manner. Here the stone releases a memory of something more than just itself, an 'aura' of the thing that coincides with the cognition of a desirable set of relations from a time recalled. The *mémoire involontaire* in fact reveals that there is no absolute past in Proust, and that the things past are not absolutely absent in remembrances.[48] In other words, it reveals that the past does not rest as absent, like a solitary atom that is itself incapable of evoking its own sense.[49] Instead, there is a past that reenacts itself as a rejuvenating force that is not itself temporalizable, which is to say, is not itself a singular moment from a time far gone and, strictly speaking, no longer.

This is not to suggest that in the *mémoire involontaire* we find an 'actual'— which is to say, factual—constitution of the past but, as James Hart writes in an article entitled "Towards a Phenomenology of Nostalgia," a "memory world" that is "founded in the actual present horizon" and in this sense is a particular sort of "imaginative reconstitution of the past."[50] This nostalgic-phenomenon is thus rooted in a phantasy-world that does not purely coincided with the actual present of the imagining-I because the latter has its own time orientation rooted in the phantasy world and not in the actual present. It seems therefore that nostalgia highlights a fundamental non-identity between a self and the self who the former attempts to recapture by recapturing a past time. This non-identity is what Julia Kristeva's treatment of the 'little phrases' of the violinist that Swann hears one evening at a dinner part seems to suggest. She points out that these little phrases, which to Swann is a "liquid rippling of sound, multiform," "pleasing", "enrapturing," and "exquisite,"[51] are from the beginning endowed with a power of recollection that is expressed in a series of metaphors.[52] For example, she says, when Swann returns home, he experiences the little phrase "as a woman he has seen for a moment passing by" so that a woman can become for Swann the metamorphosis of falling in love with a piece of music.[53] It seems to Kristeva, therefore, that in Proust there is a constant succession of "overprintings," an "imaginary journeying from metaphor to metaphor" in Swann that "both irradiate and contaminate each other" that "chain the meaning of one another."[54]

We should not be tempted to reduce Proustian remembrances to a mere psychical meaning that becomes evident only through a chain of metaphors. If we treat the little phrases in the context of what we discover from the *mémoire involontaire*, Hart's remark that nostalgia denotes an imaginative reconstitution of a memory world leads us to another conclusion, since here this memory world is primarily founded in the actual present horizon. We come across what we might call a 'corporeal memory,' a memory of 'having been there' and inhabiting this memory world because of some chance encounter with an actually presented object.[55] Here remembrances operate as a "past-present,"[56] that is, there is a consciousness of what has been perceived as having been perceived and thus as having its own horizons of the past and future. In this case, time does not 'come to an end' but is overcome because "there is a coincidence of a manifold of horizons,"[57] or an overlapping of successive times in which the present includes the past and the past includes the present.

In fact, the very way in which Proust writes about the *petite madeleine* makes this vivid to the reader:

And as soon as I had recognized the taste of the piece of Madeleine dipped in lime-blossom tea that my aunt used to give me (though I did not yet know and had to put off to much later discovery why this memory made me so happy), immediately the old gray house on the street, where her bedroom was, came like a stage set to attach itself to the little wing opening onto the garden that had been built for my parents behind it (that truncated section which was all I had seen before then); and with the house the town, from morning to night and in all weathers, the Square, where they sent me before lunch, the streets where I went on errands, the paths we took if the weather was fine.[58]

The parentheses, for instance, provide a tool here for the author to interject a vital detail of the past and in this way link it to the childhood home of Combray that is presently being recalled. His use of commas too is a way for him to relate these two events seamlessly, like a stream rather than separated events. Proust's way of writing is in this sense more earnest. It bespeaks of the way in which, even in conversation, we need to make life into a life story because, insofar as we are temporal, we need to constantly interpret and reinterpret our selves by referring in remembrances to our past, to some primal experience as well as to a new world of possibility that is opened up by this primacy. What this implies is that because it is replete with a potentiality for all other times, this past is not ended so much as it is a 'beginning.' The time of which Proust speaks, in other words, refers not to pre-established dates, which are chrono-logical, but to eras, aeons, epochs, episodes, and so on.[59] What Kristeva says is true, that this time is 'metaphorical,' and that inherent in this twofold movement of recollection and projection is the possibility of a hiddenness of desires. But for Proust the meaning that is absent to consciousness does not belong to a simple 'psychical' life: There is meaning here precisely because it belongs to an absence of the things past that is in the present.

The Proustian "reciprocal metaphor"[60] is made possible in this case by a thing past whose meaning is not static but forever in movement and thus with the ability to forever replant itself in the present. On this view, the 'liquid rippling of sound' of the violinist's little phrases are from the beginning endowed with metaphor because of its own nature as something that is not per se a 'thing' that is past but as an absencing, vanishing, changing, dying, and so on, a past that is always in retreat.[61] Even when Proust refers to the little phrases as "pure music," he does not mean to say that this past has been, *nunc flumens*, somehow stilled,[62] but rather to say that it belongs to an inchoate succession of time before it has become 'historical.' That is after all how it can be revived time and again through Swann's lover, Odette; the past itself creates space for Odette to stand in the place of the little phrases. It is even argued that Proustian metaphor thus operates only insofar as it is first supported by metonymy and that it is in fact metonymy that opens up metaphorical possibilities for Proust.[63] In this case, the succession of metaphors is made possible by the underlying juxtapositions and associations that are always already inherent within the little phrases prior to the intellectual establishment of musical notation.

This inherent succession of time forces the present *stricto senso* to be subtended in the direction of the past and toward the future. As Merleau-Ponty writes in a section called "Temporality" in *Phenomenology of Perception* that relates this Proustian time to a Husserlian 'operative intentionality,' "My present outruns itself in the direction of an immediate future and an immediate past and impinges upon them where the actually are, namely, in the past and in the future themselves."[64] There is actually a reopening of time on the basis of something implicated in the present, and this is possible only when this lost time does not become something non-temporal (as a chrono-logy would have it), but, as temporalizable, possibly enveloped by the present (as an episodic time would have it). One can therefore literally re-collect the past in nostalgia, since such an experience is not itself retained in the field of presence. The last achievement of nostalgia is thus that it issues unto us a certain completeness inasmuch as it overflows the now-moment. What first seems to be an irrevocable past that has absolutely nothing to do with the present becomes in nostalgia a past in the present that even provides the possibility of some desired future. We might say that this past is a sort of burdensome loss such that in our own present hopes we are compelled to return to it. In speaking of an epochal time, nostalgia therefore evokes an eschatology of some 'proposed world' that is furthermore based on some concrete remembrance.

What Proust teaches us is thus that nostalgia itself belongs to an unreflective dimension of memory that coexists with the things of the past in their very forgottenness. It is not merely that the interwovenness of the temporal moments in nostalgia preempts absence from becoming exteriorized because it has to be seen in connection with its having presence. More precisely, it is also that this preemption happens at a corporeal dimension of remembrances. As Proust shows us, after all, it is really a furtive, epochal time of the things past of which the nostalgic phenomenon and its resultant phantasies bespeak and thus not of an-other world to this one. Reading phenomenology in the light of nostalgia helps to bring the former back toward its original attitude, which does not posit the thesis of exteriority. Although Proustian nostalgia does of course allow for an absence of self, it also suggests that this absence is made possible not by an exteriority per se but by a withdrawing carnality. The importance of characterizing phenomenology as revealing a secret nostalgia, it therefore turns out, is that it highlights a means by which we should treat the foreignness of consciousness: The topos that is, precisely because of its prosaic quality, absent to the self is exactly the place that we can understand from whence come the insatiability of desires without referencing an exterior phantasy consciousness. At no point therefore does a nostalgia of phenomenology offer any turn away from phenomenology; for what is nonphenomenological and absent in nostalgia is in fact necessary for the possibility of phenomenology itself. Perhaps also in keeping with the Freudian theme of an 'unhappy love' in which the heart bears an endless capacity to break over and again, here the very painfulness in the nostalgia of phenomenology is a 'melancholic pleasure,' a dissatisfactory-satisfaction of temporality: It offers a glimpse of an absence that is presencing, and therefore, paradoxically, without ever the remedy of a complete and absolute absence.

CONCLUSION

The difficulty in Freud is how the unconscious relates, if at all, to the concrete world. Indeed, in his 1908 essay "Writers and Day-Dreaming," Freud says that the "motive force of phantasies [is] unsatisfied wishes, and every single phantasy is the fulfillment of a wish, a correction of unsatisfying reality" so that "past present and future are strung together, as it were, on the thread of a wish that runs through them."[65] But once we place this thread on a wish in the context of Proustian nostalgia, we gain a picture of what exactly it means to speak of an 'unsatisfying reality' of which all of our wishes and desires speak. Here the real is literally unsatisfying insofar as it is nowise fully present or even absent, except, in the so-called 'art of memory,' in the essential prosaic and epochal character of a bodily-consciousness.

We also see in Husserl's analyses of passive synthesis a latent criticism of the Freudian unconscious as belonging to a body, the unconscious is not per se the negation of conscious but a return to a pre-personal and unthought living situation.[66] In that case, instead of a phantasy consciousness trumping the securities of phenomenology, when the former is seen against the backdrop of the living situation that is itself withdrawing, it can in fact trump the spacings of the imagination. One wonders how this is possible if phantasies have precedence over any, say, linguistic or intellectual significations. It is true, however, especially if such spacings are thought along the lines of a phenomenological-temporality, where an original absence is actually the very key for the possibility of thought and so does not, strictly speaking, defy thought. At this point, what we glean from Proustian nostalgia is that consciousness is not an efficient telos, and that there is indeed an unreflectivity that strangely belongs to a fecund temporality. Here Proust adds something to the phenomenological understanding of the temporal being of consciousness, and by showing how in this unreflectivity we can understand its own hidden meaning of wishes, he in fact furthers the phenomenological quest to describe a withdrawn of consciousness without breaking consciousness toward a second world, a world beyond.

Brock University, Canada

NOTES

[1] This work has now been translated into English. Husserl, Edmund, *Phantasy, Image Consciousness and Memory*, translated John B. Brough (Berlin: Springer, 2005).

[2] Husserl, Edmund, *Ideas Pertaining to a Pure Phenomenology and to a Phenomenological Philosophy — First Book: General Introduction to a Pure Phenomenology*, translated by F. Kersten (The Hague: Nijhoff, 1982).

[3] Sallis, John, "Spacing Imagination," in *Eros and Eris: Contributions to a Hermeneutical Phenomenology Liber Amicorum for Adrian Peperzak*, edited by Paul Van Tongeron, Paul Sars, Chris Bremmers, and Koen Boey (Dordrecht: Kluwer Academic, 1992), p. 211.
[4] Ibid.
[5] "De nostalgie is dus het verlangen naar het 'au-delá' van herinneringen, zoals het geëvoceerd wordt door souvenirs." Breeur, Roland, "Souvenirs, Dood en Nostalgie," *Tijdschrift voor Filosofie*, Vol. 55, June 1993.
[6] Morrison, James, and Stack, George J, "Proust and Phenomenology," *Man and World: An International Philosophical Review*, Vol. 1, November 1968, p. 604.
[7] Proust, Marcel, *Remembrance of Things Past: Book I. Swann's Way*, translated by Terence Kilmartin and C. K. Scott Moncrieff (New York: Penguin Classics, 1998), p. 36.
[8] Morrison and Stack, "Proust and Phenomenology," p. 605.
[9] Ibid., p. 606.
[10] Ibid.
[11] Ibid.
[12] I use the word 'alleviates' here in reference to the origin of the word 'nostalgia.' The term, a neologism of medical student Johannes Hofer in 1678, refers to the 'illness' of homesickness. In fact, the Greek words *nostos* (returning home) and *algos* (pain) that form the word nostalgia highlights a less psychical painfulness from the lost, since here the pain of *algos*, for example, describes the pain of childbirth or labor pains. The German word *Heimweh*, which is translated into English both as homesickness and nostalgia, also highlights this interconnection between the physical loss and nostalgia. See Hart, James G, "Toward a Phenomenology of Nostalgia," *Man and World: An International Philosophical Review*, Vol. 6, November 1973, pp. 397–420.
[13] Husserl, Edmund, *On the Phenomenology of the Consciousness of Internal Time*, translated by John Carnett Brough (Dordrecht: Kluwer Academic, 1991), p. 44.
[14] Husserl, Edmund, *Erfahrung und Urteil*, edited by Ludwig Landgrebe (Hamburg: F. Meiner, 1999), Section 9.
[15] Husserl, Edmund, *Crisis of the European Sciences and Transcendental Phenomenology: An Introduction to Phenomenological Philosophy*, translated by David Carr (Evanston, IL: Northwestern University Press, 1970), p. 136.
[16] Fink, Eugen, *Sixth Cartesian Meditation: The Idea of a Transcendental Theory of Method* (Indianapolis: Indiana University Press, 1995), p. 53.
[17] Husserl, Edmund, *Experience and Judgment* (Evanston, IL: Northwestern University Press, 1975), pp. 105–106.
[18] Steinbock, Anthony J., *Homeworld / Alienworld: A Generative Phenomenology* (Ann Arbor, MI: UMI Dissertation Services, 1997), p. 120.
[19] Husserl, *The Phenomenology of the Consciousness of Internal Time*, p. 16.
[20] Ibid., p. 33.
[21] Ibid., p. 44.
[22] For a helpful article on this matter, see Rodemeyer, Lanei, "Developments in the Theory of Time Consciousness," in *The New Husserl* (Bloomington: Indiana University Press, 2003), p. 132.
[23] Here, I borrow the terminology found in Fink's *Sixth Cartesian Meditation*.
[24] Bernet, Rudolf, "An Intentionality Without Subject or Object?," *Man and World: An International Philosophical Review*, Vol. 27, 1994, p. 249.
[25] Ibid., pp. 250–251.
[26] Husserl, *On the Phenomenology of the Consciousness of Internal Time*, p. 32.
[27] Ibid., p. 78.

[28] Ibid., p. 75.
[29] Heidegger, Martin, *Gesamtausgabe 21* (Frankfurt am Main: Klostermann, 1978).
[30] Merleau-Ponty, Maurice, *Husserl at the Limits of Phenomenology*, with a note by Husserl entitled "Foundational Investigations of the Phenomenological Origin of the Spatiality of Nature: The Originary Ark, the Earth, Does Not Move" (Evanston, IL: Northwestern University Press, 2003), p. 117.
[31] Ibid., p. 120.
[32] Ibid.
[33] Ibid.
[34] Ibid,
[35] Ibid., pp. 122–123.
[36] Ibid., p. 127.
[37] This is Dastur's point in reference to the same manuscript notes. See Dastur, Françoise, *Telling Time: Sketch of a Phenomenological Chrono-logy*, translated by Edward Bullard (London: Athlone Press, 2000), p. 115.
[38] Granel, Gérard, *Le Sens du temps et de la perception chez E. Husserl* (Paris: Gallimard, 1968), p. 82.
[39] Ibid. p. 120.
[40] Ibid.
[41] Bernet, Rudolf, "My Time and the Time of the Other," in *Self-awareness, Temporality and Alterity*, edited by Dan Zahavi (Dordrecht: Kluwer Academic, 1998), p. 140. The comparison to Proust here is not mine, but Bernet's.
[42] Husserl, *Crisis*, p. 273.
[43] Ibid., p. 275.
[44] Merleau-Ponty, Maurice, *The Visible and the Invisible*, translated by Alphonso Lingis (Evanston, IL: Northwestern University Press, 2000), p. 149.
[45] Proust, Marcel, *Proust on Art and Literature 1896–1919*, translated by Sylvia Townsend Warner (New York: Carroll & Graf, 1997), p. 21.
[46] Hart, "Towards a Phenomenology of Nostalgia," p. 401.
[47] Ibid.
[48] Breeur, Roland, *Singularité et sujet. Une lecture phénoménologique de Proust* (Paris: Jérôme Millon, 2000), pp. 154, 157.
[49] Ibid., p. 157.
[50] Hart, "Towards a Phenomenology of Nostalgia," p. 402.
[51] Proust, *Remembrance of Things Past*, pp. 294–296.
[52] Kristeva, Julia, *Proust and the Sense of Time*, translated by Stephen Bann (London: Faber and Faber, 1993), p. 60.
[53] Ibid.
[54] Ibid.
[55] Ricoeur, Paul, *Memory, History, Forgetting*, translated by Kathleen Blamey and David Pellauer (Chicago: University of Chicago Press, 2004), pp. 40–41.
[56] Hart, "Toward a Phenomenology of Nostalgia," p. 404.
[57] Ibid.
[58] Proust, *Remembrance of Things Past: Book I. Swann's Way*, pp. 47–48.
[59] Ibid.
[60] Kristeva, *Proust and the Sense of Time*, p. 61.
[61] Breeur, R. *Singularité et sujet*, p. 155.
[62] Morrison and Stack, "Proust and Phenomenology," p. 607.

[63] See, for example, Genette, Gérard, "Métonymie chez Proust," *Figures*, Vol. 3, 1972.

[64] Merleau-Ponty, Maurice, *Phenomenology of Perception*, translated by Colin Smith (London: Routledge, 1992), p. 418.

[65] Freud, Sigmund, "Writers and Day-Dreaming," in *The Standard Edition of the Complete Psychological Works of Sigmund Freud*, Vol. 14, translated under the general editorship of James Strachey (London: Hogarth Press, 1964), pp. 134, 135.

[66] Merleau-Ponty's readings of phenomenology are especially helpful here. For him in particular, the Freudian unconsciousness can be submitted to a criticism by way of passive synthesis. In one of his earlier lectures, for example, he argues that "the cleavage between the real and the imaginary" can be rendered suspect through an analysis of a passive bodily-intentionality in which we "return to a prepersonal relation to the world." After all, if in phenomenology the unconsciousness of the body is not the negation of the consciousness, this means that its absence to consciousness is somehow also a presencing; "our waking relationships with objects," Merleau-Ponty writes, "have an oneiric character as a matter of principle...in the way dreams are, the way myths are" (Merleau-Ponty, Maurice, *Themes from Lectures at the Collège de France 1952–1960*, translated by John O'Neill (Evanston, IL: Northwestern Press, 1970), p. 48. Hence Merleau-Ponty equates what is lacking in perception with the qualities of a pre-consciousness. In this connection, his essay "Cézanne's Doubt" directly contrasts his treatment of Leonardo with that of Freud's in "Leonardo da Vinci and a Memory of his Childhood," attempting to show that what is faded into memories and perpetually recalled in the art-working of the artist has everything to do with the first moments in which the flesh come into contact with the world.

SECTION V

JAIMIE JANDOVITZ

ART AND AWARENESS

INSIGHT FROM A MONASTIC AESTHETE

An adequate account of the nature of art—specifically, the nature of aesthetic objects—should fit coherently within a like account of the nature of the aesthetic in general. Not only do we encounter paintings and operas in the realm of the aesthetic, but we are similarly confronted with aesthetic sunsets, aesthetic moments, and even aesthetic people. While the latter certainly are not objects on display in a museum, I believe that they have a part to play in our understanding of the nature of art. The following passage is from the late Thomas Merton, who beautifully describes his surroundings as experienced from the monastery in Kentucky:

> Today, Father, this blue sky lauds you. The delicate green and orange flowers of the tulip poplar trees praise you. The distant blue hills praise you, together with the sweet-smelling air that is full of brilliant light. The bickering flycatchers praise you with the lowing cattle and the quails that whistle over there. I too, Father, praise you, with all these my brothers, and they give voice to my own heart and to my own silence. We are all one silence, and a diversity of voices.
>
> You have made us together, you have made us one and many, you have placed me here in the midst as witness, as awareness, and as joy. Here I am. In me the world is present, and you are present. I am a link in the chain of light and of presence. You have made me a kind of center, but a center that is nowhere. And yet also I am 'here,' let us say I am 'here' under these trees, not others. (Merton, 1968, 177)

I think this prayer of Merton's offers insight for a sound conception of the aesthetic. In this essay, I will analyze art in terms of "witness, awareness, and joy," focusing on awareness as the defining outcome of the aesthetic. I will argue that art is a means of awareness, which is central to its nature. In order to accomplish this, I will draw on Nelson Goodman's account of the role of cognition in art and on Martin Heidegger's ideas concerning art opening a world.

WITNESS

In the passage from Merton, he responds to the landscape in part by declaring that he is "witness." A witness testifies to something other than—or outside of—himself; aesthetic objects, occurrences, and people may testify, for example. Even in the case of deeply personal subjective experiences, such as emotions, the artist assumes that the work produced will convey these experiences—will testify to them in some way. Symbols function as witnesses, since they exist in relation to something outside themselves that came first. Goodman states "Symbols are indispensable to communication," while allowing that communication does not constitute the whole picture (Goodman, 1994, "Languages of Art," 248). For now, it is crucial to note two things: (1) Art objects and aesthetes almost exclusively witness to something beyond themselves; and (2) art assumes a rational audience as recipient of a message. I assume here that Goodman has successfully argued against the existence of "pure art": art objects that contain only intrinsic references. I agree with him that "even the purist's purest painting symbolizes" (Goodman, 1994, "When Is Art," 243).

Concerning point 2, it is important for the purposes of this essay to ask: Could art exist without a rational audience? I conclude that this possibility appears unlikely. A bird does not create nests for any purpose other than nesting, let alone for aesthetic purposes! "A stone is worldless. Plant and animal likewise have no world; but they belong to the covert throng of a surrounding into which they are linked. The peasant woman, on the other hand, has a world" (Heidegger, 1994, 265). It appears that the condition of having or experiencing a world—what I will later argue is crucial to awareness— is only possible for rational beings. Nellie the elephant's paintings are sold for fifty dollars on http://animalschoolnet.com, but her elephant friends—and she—don't seem very interested in contemplating them. They are for her only a "daily enrichment activity," according to the phrasing on the website.

JOY

Merton delights in the landscape. He perceives it as beautiful, and it moves him to pray to its Creator. Yet the essence of art is neither an aesthetic emotion nor aesthetic beauty, whether interested or disinterested. Goodman points out that "the best pictures are often obviously not pretty. But again, many of them are in the most obvious sense ugly. If the beautiful excludes the ugly, beauty is no measure of aesthetic merit" (Goodman, 1994, "Languages of Art," 247). Merton could have had an aesthetic experience as a result of a gloomy, rainy day in winter—a day that he may have perceived as ugly. "Satisfaction cannot be identified with pleasure, and positing a special aesthetic feeling begs the question" (Goodman, 1994, "Languages of Art," 247).

I think feelings are certainly an important aspect of art, but the nature of art does not hinge on a special "aesthetic emotion," as Clive Bell has urged.

Nevertheless, satisfaction is a recurring element of aesthetic experience. This satisfaction occurs even when the object is not satisfying, and often this satisfaction is such that it leaves a lasting impression on us, even crescendos to elation or joy. Later I will suggest that this satisfaction attends revelation.

AWARENESS

"In me the world is present, and you are present," Merton proclaims. He is demonstrating awareness with this statement. Cognizant of entities outside himself—namely, here, the landscape and God—Merton becomes alert to their realities in relation to his own subjective experience. By meditating on or contemplating the scene, he is exercising awareness. He perceives relations between creation and Creator, between himself and creation, and between himself and God. His inner world becomes attuned to that what he contemplates.

I mean 'awareness' in a different sense than 'consciousness.' It is possible to be conscious of the colors in the landscape without being aware of them; I assume awareness to signify an additional element of recognizing relationships. During consciousness, I exist and the colors exist. With awareness, however, there is a connection made between me and the colors and between the colors themselves. Rational agents are needed to perceive not merely what exists, but to perceive the relations between entities that exist and those entities and the perceiver.

Contemplation manifests not only in abstract thought, such as abstract contemplation, but also more frequently through concrete means. Repetitive activities may become meditative. Slave songs in the U.S. South were born of workers' repetitive activity in the fields: The slaves were aware of both their hope of freedom (to which the songs testified) and their rhythmic activity. Contemplation in art, religion, or life often entwines with a specific object, occurrence, or even emotion. This concrete entity (for example, a rosary), apprehended by perception, is interacted with repetitively. Much has been said about art as imitation, especially from Plato and Aristotle. But what is imitation other than a repetitive invocation of awareness? In trying to copy something, we try to really see it; we try to preserve its import glimpsed during that window of awareness.

ART AS THE OBJECT OF AWARENESS

Of course, imitation is not required in order to bring the aesthetic into existence. Nellie the elephant's randomized paintings may justly be admired by enthusiasts of abstraction. And "the holedigging and filling functions as a work insofar as our attention is directed to it as an exemplifying symbol" (Goodman, 1994, "When Is Art?," 244). Objects that came into existence apart from an artist's experience of awareness may still be considered aesthetic, may still be art. And their status as art is malleable: "A thing may function as a work of art at some times and not at others. In crucial cases, the real question is not 'What objects are (permanently) works of art?' but 'When is an object a work of art?'" (244). Goodman concludes that an object becomes art "by virtue of functioning as a symbol in a certain way"—that is, when the object "exemplifies certain of its properties—e.g., properties of shape, color, texture" (244).

I am in full agreement with Goodman, although I want to push his argument further. Why do we care about symbols or their properties, such as color and texture? How does merely being a symbol—as opposed to being a road sign—give an object its aesthetic significance? Goodman gives us a clue in his example of "the hole digging and filling": Our attention must be directed toward it. In order for an object to function as art, it must foster awareness. This awareness consists both of something beyond the image and of relations within the image: The abstract and the concrete are wedded. In the case of a symbol, we are aware of the outside relation of something to which the symbol refers. More directly, however, we are aware of the relation of the elements of the art object to one another: the interplay of colors, forms, textures, and so on. In fact, Gestalt theory applied to art claims that the whole is greater than the sum of the parts.

In sum, a central part of art's nature is that art is an object cultivating awareness. It is something perceivable by the senses that exhibits relations between and beyond this input. These relations may be apprehended—analytically, or subconsciously, or any number of ways—by rational perceivers, in whom awareness is cultivated. Good art is attended by satisfaction stemming from a holistic cognitive balance occurring during awareness that, for the purposes of this essay, I will label revelation.

GOODMAN: THE AIM IS ENLIGHTENMENT

What all three [explanations of "what constitutes effective symbolization"] miss is that the drive is curiosity and the aim enlightenment. Use of symbols beyond immediate need is for the sake of understanding, not practice; what compels is the urge to know, what delights is discovery, and communication is secondary to the apprehension and formulation of what is to be communicated. The primary purpose is cognition in and for itself; the practicality, pleasure, compulsion, and communicative utility all depend upon this. (Goodman, 1994, "Languages of Art," 248)

In declaring that the primary purpose of art is cognition, Goodman's theory of art is on par with a theory of art reliant on awareness. Cognition, again, requires rational perceivers. It is important to note here that cognition is not entirely intellectual:

> The cognitive... does not exclude the sensory or the emotive, that what we know through art is felt in our bones and nerves and muscles as well as grasped by our minds, that all the sensitivity and responsiveness of the organism participates in the invention and interpretation of symbols. (Goodman, 1994, "Languages of Art," 249)

Two important aspects of cognition in art that are imperative to awareness are imagination and discovery. Imagination is a well-traversed subject in theories of aesthetics. "The aesthetic experience is an imaginative experience.... The only power which can generate it is the power of the experient's consciousness. But it is not generated out of nothing. Being an imaginative experience, it presupposes a corresponding sensuous experience" (Collingwood, 1994, 200). (Collingwood seems to be using the word 'consciousness' here in the same manner that I have been using 'awareness.') Dewey declares, "Esthetic experience is imaginative.... All conscious experience has of necessity some degree of imaginative quality" (Dewey, 1994, 218). Dewey explains that the imaginative operation of the work of art "is to concentrate and enlarge an immediate experience" (219). This is a beautiful description of a window of awareness occurring in a rational perceiver.

The second aspect of cognition examined here—discovery—indicates awareness' function as mentioned by Goodman: enlightenment. Exploration is as much a part of the artistic journey as attainment. Goodman speaks of a "constructive search" that comes about through "theme and variation" (Goodman, 1994, "Languages of Art," 250). Art is not mere diversion; it is a teacher. One of its cognitive functions is "conforming to and reforming our knowledge and our world" (251).

REVELATION

Goodman continues, "We focus upon frontiers; the peak of interest in a symbol tends to occur at the time of revelation, somewhere midway in the passage from the obscure to the obvious" (Goodman, 1994, "Languages of Art," 249). That "somewhere midway" is the timeframe where awareness arises.

Heidegger gives an account of art opening a world (Heidegger, 1994, 264). I will briefly compare his view of art with the view discussed in this essay. To begin, Heidegger observes that all art objects have a "thingly element" that is "irremovably present in the art work" (255). This corresponds closely to the concrete sensual object of contemplation; the "thingly element" contains internal characteristics such as texture and color. It is composed of materials from our everyday environment that may not be employed in contemplation unless imaginatively transformed into an art object.

Heidegger states, "The art work is something else over and above the thingly element. This something else in the work constitutes its artistic nature" (Heidegger, 1994, 256). I aim to challenge this point, suggesting instead that thingly relations are one of the two modes of awareness harnessed by art; they are the internal relations that must harmonize with the symbolic (or abstract) witness to something outside the work. The thingly is half the weight of the work of art—not something to be shed. Heidegger designates the concrete aspect of a work as the Earth element, which "is present as the sheltering agent" (263), yet he refuses to acknowledge it as "work-material" after it has been transformed into the work (266). This sheltering agent strives against the world, which is defined as "the self-disclosing openness of the broad paths of the simple and essential decisions in the destiny of an historical people" (267). World and earth "are never separated" (267). This idea is compatible with the view I have been elaborating. 'World' corresponds with the world that is opened to cognition via symbols; it is a network of relations outside of the artwork. When a world opens to a person, that person experiences awareness.

Awareness occurs in the Open, during intermittent periods of unconcealedness, at the point of revelation. "To the Open there belong a world and the earth" (Heidegger, 1994, 271). Heidegger explains this concept in terms of Van Gogh's painting of the peasant woman's shoes: "The revelation of the equipmental being of the shoes, that which is as a whole—world and earth in their counterplay—attains to unconcealedness" (272). A balance is achieved between the concrete and abstract aspects of the painting of the peasant shoes. The degree to which the artwork is successful depends upon the congruence of the concrete and abstract elements: that which calls for contemplation, and that which is contemplated—the concrete materials and the ideas they indicate.

As many subjects (and more) as have been presented to us as objects of awareness await our relating to them through understanding. Both we and the objects seem transformed as we become aware. "At bottom, the ordinary is not ordinary; it is extra-ordinary, uncanny" (Heidegger, 1994, 271).

CONCLUSION

To summarize, I have thought of art in terms of "witness, awareness, and joy," discussing how aesthetic objects testify (through symbolism) to something outside themselves, forming relations between these entities and the perceiver, who must be a rational being. What this rational perceiver seeks and receives from art (that he or she experiences as art) is awareness. Revelation accompanies awareness and is the source of the satisfaction that one finds in art. Finally, I have examined Goodman's account of the role of cognition in art and compared features of Heidegger's theory to the theme of this essay.

Emmanuel College, Boston

REFERENCES

Animalschoolnet, "Elephant Paintings," Hollywood Animals: Exotic Animal Training School and Animal Adventures.

R. G. Collingwood, "Principles of Art," in Stephen David Ross, ed., *Art and Its Significance: An Anthology of Aesthetic Theory*, 3rd ed. (Albany, NY: SUNY Press, 1994), pp. 192–201.

John Dewey, "Art as Experience," in Stephen David Ross, ed., *Art and Its Significance: An Anthology of Aesthetic Theory*, 3rd ed. (Albany, NY: SUNY Press, 1994), pp. 204–220.

Nelson Goodman, "Languages of Art," in Stephen David Ross, ed., *Art and Its Significance: An Anthology of Aesthetic Theory*, 3rd ed. (Albany, NY: SUNY Press), 1994, pp. 247–252.

Nelson Goodman, "When Is Art?," in Stephen David Ross, ed., *Art and Its Significance: An Anthology of Aesthetic Theory*, 3rd ed. (Albany, NY: SUNY Press, 1994), pp. 238–246.

Martin Heidegger, "The Origin of the Work of Art," in Stephen David Ross, ed., *Art and Its Significance: An Anthology of Aesthetic Theory*, 3rd ed. (Albany, NY: SUNY Press, 1994), pp. 254–280.

Thomas Merton, *Conjectures of a Guilty Bystander* (New York: Image Books, 1968).

Stephen David Ross, *Art and Its Significance: An Anthology of Aesthetic Theory*, 3rd ed. (Albany: SUNY Press, 1994).

ENRICO ESCHER

THE IMAGE IN THE HISTORY OF THOUGHT

The concept of the image has both a media and a philosophical value; it is one of the most important issues regarding understanding in the field of human action, not least in information technology, forever caught between research into its theoretical basis and its relative empirical realizations.

The concept of the image is not a simple one because it falls between imitation, tracing, and convention. It is impossible to provide an unequivocal definition of it. Indeed, writes M. Joly, at a first glance what do a child's drawing, a mural, an impressionist painting, graffiti, posters, a mental operation—individual or collective—a dream, a vision, a visual hallucination, a perceptive scheme, the image of a trademark, a media image, and so on have in common? All this not to mention the image in the scientific field, from astronomy to optics, from medicine, to physics, to information technology, to biology, to mechanics, to nuclear science. Or the image in the virtual field. The image, also used as a synonym for "metaphor," brings two terms together, stimulating the discovery "of unsuspected points in common"; it is along these lines that the surrealist image in literature, in painting, and in cinema works.

And yet, despite the fact that the term has such varied meanings, we are able—each time we come to it and in different contexts—to understand it in its double situation of visualization and similarity. We understand that it indicates something that, although it does not refer to the visible, can draw some elements from the visible; in any case, we interpret it as something that depends on the production of a subject: "imaginary or concrete, the image passes through someone, who produces it or recognizes it."[1]

Plato, in the *Republic*, wrote, "And by images I mean, in the first place, shadows, and in the second place, reflections in water and in solid, smooth and polished bodies and the like." The image, therefore, recalls the mirror; it is a secondary object with respect to another; it carries with itself an aura of ambiguity.

Aristotle wrote in *De anima* (III, 8, 432a9) that images are sensitive like things themselves, except that they have no matter. In this sense, the image is both the product of the imagination and the sensation or perception itself as seen by the person who receives it. This distinction was taken up again by the Stoics and was even used for theological purposes during the Middle Ages.

In modern philosophy the theme crops up again in Hobbes, for whom the image is the act of feeling and differs not from sensation except for its differing from the fact (*De corpore*, 25, §3); it also appears again in Descartes, Wolff, Bergson, and so on, although its meaning changes according to whether the accent is placed on the sensitive or the conceptual origin of the ideas of the representation available to the person.

This brief consideration serves to demonstrate how the concept of "image" runs throughout the history of thought and how, despite its differences, it carries with it the being of a trace or sign of the things, which can remain distinct from the things themselves.

In any case, it comes from far away: "everywhere in the world man has left on the rocks traces of his imaginative faculties in the form of drawings, from the most ancient times of the stone age to the modern day."[2] These drawings were destined to communicate messages or were limited to a schematic description of people or objects from the real world. Sometimes they corresponded to precise magic or religious procedures.

In any case, the image runs through the entire history of art, but, as we have already seen, through the history of philosophy as well, beginning with Plato and Aristotle. Quite rightly, Scarafile, writing on the spectator–flaneur, suggests that the image has always generated a certain embarrassment for Western philosophy and its eminently scientific vocation. Be it a copy of a copy of the real, as Plato had it, or a phenomenological representation of a separate reality, as in Kant's position, the image has always been the object of widespread suspicion, relegated as it was to being on the side of a distortion of reality and not to being a vehicle for its improvement. But if it continues to worry us, there is nevertheless no doubt that today we are in the presence of a recovery of its "other reality" in terms of scientific methodology and its conventional procedures, realizing above all else in the metaphor and the narrative redescription of reality its subversive suggestion of recall (it would be enough to think of Gadamer and Ricoeur).[3]

Traditionally, images have been imprisoned in their statute of reflection, constrained to be a copy of that which exists, shadows projected by real objects, "At best a substitute, at worst deceptions, but always illusions" (R. Debray).

Today, the meaning of the image has undergone a shift, acquiring connotations as a language, a visual message made up of different types of signs; in other terms, as an instrument of expression and communication.

Time changes continuously the aspect of things and in the end it cancels them definitively; images, instead, remain and give substance to appearances, removing them from their ephemeral nature. They are a sign of reaction to death, to its manifestation as a dissolving of individuality.

The image, therefore, is not only the place where the echo of the world is repeated: It is also the means that allows us to feel the world more easily as ours.

Both expressive and communicative, the image always constitutes a "message for others," even when the "others" are "us." It is for this reason that in order to understand a visual message it is necessary to identify the recipient for whom it has been produced. In order to do this we need at least two criteria of reference: (1) to place the different types of image in the scheme of communication; and (2) to compare the uses of the visual message to those of the main human productions created with the purpose of establishing a relationship between man and the world.

Indeed, the image organizes this relationship, it identifies the visible. It can tell us many things: It communicates information, it inspires feelings, it tells us a story, and so on. We must not, however, forget two factors: (1) the physical elements that transmit this information and (2) the fact that these elements are preceded by an investment of sense.

It follows that in the disassembly of the image, we have to keep in mind the interaction between the expressive elements and the operations of meaning carried out by the subject. The reconstruction of that particular functioning of the image that is the narration also displays a constant interaction between the various expressive instruments of the image, but among these there is also the activity of the receiver. Not only does this activity in the mare magnum of personal and social memory preserve memories and control the past; it has a function of evocation, archiving, recording, and memory. But it is above all a sign.

But the image is also historical and is of its time, subjected as it is to the transformation of the mechanisms and the conditions of possibility of communication of which it forms a part. This transformation becomes tangible, for example, in the passage from television to the virtual. Indeed television passes from a phase characterized by the mutation of the thing into an image to a phase characterized by the mutation of the image into a "thing": The world, "fragmented by the dissolving force of video," slowly recomposes itself "around empty ectoplasms, that are our companions today."[4] In other words, while through television the medium becomes the world, with virtual reality it is the world that becomes the medium. And this comes about not through an operation of dissolving and impoverishment, but through a "thingification," a thingification, however, that involves an inverse route with regard to the route effected by a simulacrization: It is rather that the simulacra, put into action by the virtual, cannibalizes the real, replacing its status; it is no longer the image that triumphs over the thing, remaining an image, but it is the image that devours the thing, becoming a thing in itself: Realism is substituted by a new ontology. In this sense we can reread McLuhan's famous statement that "the medium is the message".

Along these lines, Fausto Colombo, who underlines the limits of the "simulacral" reading of "Baudrillardism," maintains that the new technologies of the image do transform our conception of the real, but in a sense that is the opposite of that indicated by Baudrillard. The icons and the simulacra of communication become inserted into daily life, becoming and integral and insuppressible part of it. The electronic image is so pervasive that not only does it penetrate the world and tend to double it, but it also often goes so far as to modify the perceptive habits of our eye.

But if the image is everywhere around us and within us, we can no longer think of any experience totally free from its representation: Our project of knowledge ultimately is nothing less than the hope of an iconic or iconographic reconstruction. Thus, with regard to the so-called "ingenuous conceptions" of the image society, for which the problem consists of the interposition of icons between man and reality, Colombo's hypothesis, which I share completely, is that the status of "thing" passes from reality to the image.

To ask oneself therefore what the expression "image society" means has an explicative utility only if by this we mean an aspect of that society "in which the technical image plays an essential role in both processes of mass information and in the constitution of a new imaginary."[5]

For Colombo, the nature of electronic pseudo-reality, or neo-reality, is that of a "real" experience, that is, in synthesis with the experience, the new reality does not superimpose or interpose on or between the subject and a presumed "other" reality, but rather enters to form part of the environment and the lived experience of the subject. It "gives life to a part of reality [...] thanks to its apparently purely communicative contribution": "Behind the shadows, world, we think. And we seem not to realize that those shadows are our world, that their laws, their forms, their vague materiality are our reality, a dimension of ours."[6]

Indeed, the media modify our concept of reality, or rather the conscious operations with which we control the existence of something, generating a new virtual space, that does not possess the characteristics of the space that we experience in our daily lives, but which, in its way, is equally real. The "liquid architecture" becomes the spatial structure of virtual reality[7]—a space in which it is possible to move, communicate, interact with others, without leaving one's own room. It is enough to put on a pair of special glasses and a glove equipped with sensors, and it possible to (perceptively) fly, walk under water, enter into a molecule. And then there is the varied entertainment market, from the journey myth of American culture in the 1960s, out of which in some way virtual reality was born, to safe sex, to individual and group games (Penge). Furthermore, it should not be forgotten that bits, too, have their reality, given that, to produce effects, they have to materialize in electrical signals (electrons in movement), and to be memorized, they have to written on physical media. Even the full immersion that virtual reality machines allow is completely physical: "Visual or sound information (perhaps even olfactory information) reach our sensorial receptors. And these are not in any way 'deceived,' but simply transmit input to the cerebral cortex, so that it can process them as it knows how."[8] Thus, rather than denying that the virtual image has no corresponding physical reality, we can perhaps state that with it we enter, with incalculable consequences, "into a completely other visual order" that subordinates "the optical sphere to that of modelling and calculus."[9]

This is a prelude to the future ways of life of the von Neumann Galaxy.[10] "Therefore allow your thoughts to leave this world for a while so that they come to see another, new world that I will bring to life in its image in imaginary spaces." Thus wrote Descartes.

But Descartes could never have thought that his dream would have another context above and beyond narrative expedient. Today, instead, the "imaginary spaces" have the same minute exactness as reality.

Indeed, it has become a commonplace to state that the image has overtaken reality, with a progressive emptying of its function as witness.

In these movements towards disenchantment, the real world, as Nietzsche announced, seems to have become a "tale"; and the appearance, the dream, sang Calderon de La Barca, seems to have sucked the real world into it.

If ours has been called a "neo-Baroque epoch," it is indeed because reality, as in the Baroque period, has become rarefied in its transitory and ineffable representation. Indeed, what metaphysics defined as "substance" would be progressively declined in form, or better, as Gilles Deleuze writes, in the different repetitions (copies) or an original metaphysical substance (model) the traces of which are now lost.

And since relations among men, work, and intelligence depend in effect on the incessant metamorphosis of informational devices of all kinds, with the arrival of the virtual, new ways of both thinking and of being have been worked out.

I can visual and manipulate things that are completely beyond me in real reality, and this can change my sense of reality. The virtual—indeed, above all else the virtual—brings with it, in its shadow, the problem of "reality," or rather of the legitimacy of continuing today to use—and in which sense—this term. Thus we return to the same question: what do we mean by "reality"? It is here that physics—especially in the version provided by the Copenhagen school—philosophy, and media meet.

In any case, there is no doubt that the advent of the virtual is changing the relationship between man and his world, between reality and fiction, between hypothesis and factual verification. Thus, "Even the mind builds its own cathedrals and its own museums: capacity for imaginative thought and capacity for its realization are almost equal for the first time in history" (F. Scianò). A new language is born, a new mode of communicating, new actors of communication, a new concept of the image.

But if the process toward a contraction of the universe of material objects, objects that will be substituted by processes and services that are increasingly immaterial, is undeniable, does this authorize us to speak of dematerialization? That is to say, as Maldonado wonders, is it reasonable to think that in this century, "We will only deal with intangible realities, with illusory, evanescent images, with something approaching a world populated by spectres, hallucinations, by ectoplasms?"[11]

Although this question, from an "operative" and pragmatic point of view, has its raison d'être, it does not have an equally strong one from the scientific point of view. To believe the concept of "real" to be highly problematic does not mean in itself to identify it with the concept of "spectre." Rather, it means identifying it with "subjective" in the meaning that Heisenberg gives to this term.[12]

In the case of nuclear physics, writes Heisenberg, if we formulate its laws completely, we cannot ignore the fact that our body and the instruments with which we carry out our observations are in themselves subject to the laws of nuclear physics: "Here our knowledge of a state of things takes the place of a physical fact." To an even greater degree this will be true, for example, in psychology.

Therefore, when Heisenberg speaks of an order that ascends from the objective to the subjective, he intends to say that the process of knowing that gives us information on reality "represents in itself an integral part of the connections that constitute the context in question." We could object that this route leads not to an ordering of reality, but only to an ordering of our knowledge of reality. But already the concept of ordering, replies Heisenberg, has as a presupposition not only the thing to be ordered, but ourselves as well, and therefore there is no wonder "that in an ordering we cannot decide if it manifests itself as an ordering of reality or of our understanding of reality." In any case, we have to bear in mind always that the reality of which we can speak is never reality "in itself" but is a reality filtered by our consciousness or even, in many cases, made by us. For us "there is" indeed only the world in which the expression "there is" makes sense.[13]

The conclusions of Heisenberg and the Copenhagen school are controversial and are not shared by the entire scientific world; we cannot ignore them, however, to take refuge in the undoubtedly more reassuring, but not necessarily more reliable, world of common sense.

What interests me above all, however, is the type of communication that the virtual image carries and, above all else, its "nature as object," which brings with it worrying questions (What type of experience does it involve? Of what use is it to our literacy and background?) and its ethical and political consequences.

The distance of the world from the image, a critical as well as physical distance, is abolished with the virtual: "If Neotelevision is a window on the world of wonders, Virtual Reality allows us to go beyond the mirror. It is beyond the glass, in medias res" (M. W. Bruno).

But the problem is also technological. Recent developments in information technology and telematics have opened the world of communication to a new dimension, in which it is possible to realize incredible links between sound, images, and signs, processing information in almost real time and allowing access from remote terminals, connected online to the central processing unit: "This dimension is profoundly different from the silent and immobile word." In addition, it also involves the sensorial apparatus in new and different ways compared to the past, bringing about an "integration among the senses" through a plastic organization that changes in relation to the context in which it is used:

The multimedia society has combined traditional instruments of communication with electronic technologies, and in this sense it has allowed for the preservation and the transmission of information in a multiplicity of forms, which being to the traditional written text the dynamics of image and the musicality of sound. This flexibility in the modes of representing knowledge determines by reflex a greater plasticity in the sensorial organization involved in the processes of perception and learning. Space proves to be almost cancelled; terrestrial distances are shortened and almost lose their meaning. Even time acquires a new sense, that implies immediacy and simultaneousness. Space and time are abstracted completely by the rhythmic–corporeal dimension to which man, given his biological nature, is inevitably tied.[14]

The use of the concept of the image in the virtual therefore has strong repercussions in the philosophical, media, and technological fields.

In recent years it has become ever more difficult to carry out a rigorous separation of the fields of influence of virtual reality—entertainment, scientific research, technology—from what Maldonado calls, using a word coined in the imaginative spirit of the Italian writer Gadda, *viurtuovaglie* (virtual victuals); certainly complicit in this process are technological acceleration, the vast spread of the media of the immaterial, such as the Internet, cell phones, credit cards, and everything that functions without concreteness.[15] To sum up, the final frontiers of virtual reality have come to revolutionize the traditional dichotomy between natural and artificial.

For this reason ours has been defined as the civilization of images.[16]

For Maldonado, we can accept this definition if we add that ours is an epoch in which a particular type of image, the trompe-l'oeil image, reach, thanks to the contribution of new technologies, "a prodigious yield in realistic terms." This had appeared to be clear with the invention of photography and, in a more evident way, with the invention of cinematography and television. But the most incisive confirmation comes today from the advent of computerized graphics, especially if we think of its latest developments aimed at the production of virtual realities.[17]

But not everyone believes that the route traced out by these developments is an easy one to go down and even less so that over a short time span we can reach the amazing results publicized by the mass media as having already been achieved. The most reliable exponents of research into virtual realities have indeed considerable doubts in this regard and seek to dampen enthusiasm. Indeed, they express concern about how the nonspecialist press presents the theme.[18]

Now, although this caution from a scientific point of view is more than pertinent, there is no doubt that the versions provided by the media can in any case be useful in that they allow us, even given the different approaches, to deal with the problem. Indeed, while for some critics the spread of virtual reality can contribute to modeling a computerized world, "a lighter world from which one could expect [...] not only a more efficient social and economic organization, but even a more democratic one," for others, instead, these technologies represent "the long-awaited chance to 'come out of the world'."

In Maldonado's view, nevertheless, this drastic bipolarization—"on the one hand, unsophisticated proclaimers of Panglossian possible worlds; on the other careful predictors of a transcendental coming out of the world"—does not describe all the varied panorama of the makers of virtual reality intended as an alternative, substitutive, or parallel reality to "real reality," and above all else it does not allow us to understand the repercussions of the various incursions into possible worlds, into identities of the self and the sense of self, into the relationships that the self has with the world outside, and so on. Indeed, it does not allow us to understand whether there is a place for the private and a place for the public.

But Franco Carlini too invites us to regard the rough bipolarity between natural and virtual with diffidence, between a "natural" that an enthusiastic journalist might look upon nostalgically and a "virtual" that this journalist might attribute principally negative and above all "fictional," "dematerialized," and "artificial" values.[19]

What we cannot ignore in any case is that the procedures have moved progressively, with a clear break with regard to the "first." Carlini writes that both for individuals and for social organizations (government, businesses, associations) "this virtual so real" becomes an element of salutary crisis, even if accompanied by worries and fears as far as the traditional spheres of public opinion and the polis are concerned. Therefore, if we can be serene and in believing that there will be no disappearance of media and forms, nevertheless it is completely understandable that many are worried about the new dynamics and the redefinitions of themselves that they are called to perform:

The basic reason for many conservative reactions towards the virtual and the net lies just here. Not because of pornography or computer crime, which are pure accidents that are very similar too and much less serious than what happens in the real world [...], but because of the potential shock (in the true sense and to the very letter: virtual) that is destabilizing roles and powers.[20]

One thing is nevertheless certain, and that is that—alongside the traditional one that lives in the daily grind—a new map of the human is being drawn, a new generation, that allocates the image in a hyper-real world, in a hyper-real culture, where everything is paradox, skepticism, irony. This generation is formed by men grown in "common-interest developments," in a world of "just-in-time" occupation, men "more therapeutic than ideological," "more emotive than analytic," who think more in images than in words.[21]

All things told, we have the development of the "proteoform" generation (R. J. Lifton) of the cyberman, who lives and nurtures himself with the image. The objective is to know how to resolve the contrast—if this is a contrast—between the two cultures, without living in the nostalgia of the past, but also without falling into the enthusiasm of the multimedialists, of the prophets of the digital world and cybernavigation, in the telematic technopolis, that is, without blindly taking vows to the concept of "virtual miracles." Perhaps good sense can point a middle way between technological utopianism and mystical frenzy.

Obviously, this gives new challenges to ethics: What are the consequences of these innovations? What are the rules that emerge from this electronic economy? These are questions to which must be added questions regarding the appearance of images on the contemporary cultural scene, regarding the consequences of there being there and their ever-widening influence. Is it possible to have a new consciousness of the responsibility of communication through images? Indeed, are the same ethics possible?

These are questions behind that the problems of the impact of the image with reality manifest themselves together with those, more complex, of a refounding of the role of users immersed in an ever-spreading neo-reality.[22]

For Colombo, the genuine future of the image is played out beyond the space in which it is constituted technologically; it is played out rather within a choice made above this, perhaps even behind it. Here, perhaps, is the only possible reasonable commitment: The gnoseological crisis comes out of extra-theoretical reasons, recognizable in ethical and political parameters, even if behind such parameters there continues to persist the problem of realism and its plausibility, albeit as a problem to be placed within parentheses because it is "unspeakable" and "irresolvable."

This does not e mean an abandoning the "heaviness" of meanings in favor of their "lightness." This means rather formulating a new paradigm of "ethical realism," beginning with the analysis of a spectacle that today is central in the television industry: so-called reality television, a statement of its becoming the world, an expression of the its vocation for annulling the differences between the world both that side and this side of the screen, to present itself ever-increasingly as a pure mirror of the spectator.

To sum up, the problem, irresolvable from the ontological point of view, or rather denied by that point of view, becomes ethical, deontological, striking man in his very being, which, for him, is his only reality.

University of Catania

NOTES

[1] M. Joly, *Introduzione all'analisi dell'immagine* (1994), translation by D. Buzzolan, Turin, 1999, p. 17.

[2] I.-J. Gelb, *Pour une histoire de l'écriture*, Paris, 1973.

[3] By this, nevertheless, I do not wish to emphasize a sort of aristocratic supremacy of art over science. Indeed, I utterly disagree with Gadamer, who, with regard to the epistemological problem, is certainly not an avant-garde scholar. His thesis of an understanding in opposition to knowing and explaining reveals a conception of knowledge that is of the objectivistic, reflecting, type, that has no position contemporary epistemology beginning from 1912. To give an example, the publication, at a few years distance from *Truth and Method*, of Thomas Kuhn's *The Structure of Scientific Revolutions* provides evidence of the falsity of the conviction, which is indeed very widespread, that epistemology is still founded on an objective model of knowledge and is subject to a homogeneous process of development. On this topic, see R. Egidi, *La svolta relativistica*

nell'epistemologia contemporanea, Milan, 1992, p. 11, and the observations of A. Escher Di Stefano, *Historismus e Ermeneutica*, Presentazione by F. Tessitore, Premessa by G. Cantillo, Naples, 1997, p. 811.

[4] F. Colombo, *Ombre sintetiche. Saggio di teoria dell'immagine elettronica*, Milan, 1999, p. 115.

[5] Ibid., p. 24.

[6] Ibid., p. 60.

[7] On the importance of the concept of space within virtual reality, see N. Benedikt, *Cyberspace*, Padua, 1993.

[8] G. Bettetini, Internet, in *La realtà virtuale*, edited by J. Jacobelli, Rome, 1998, p. 36.

[9] A. Renaud, Pensare l'immagine oggi, in *Videoculture di fine secolo*, edited by A. Piromalo and A. Abruzzese, Naples, 1989, p. 20.

[10] It was J. von Neumann, at the end of the 1940s, who made the first design of an electronic computer that without too many changes continues to be used today.

[11] T. Maldonado, *Reale e virtuale* (1992), Milan 2005, p. 12.

[12] W. Heisenberg, *Indeterminazione e realtà* (1927), edited by G. Gembillo, Naples, 1991, p. 97.

[13] Ibid., p. 99.

[14] M. Groppo and A. Bartolomeo, Il potere dell'informatica e il suo viraggio culturale, *Rivista dell'istruzione*, 1998, 6, p. 779. But see M. Groppo and M. C. Locatelli, *Mente e cultura*, Milan, 1996.

[15] L. Lipperini, Se Platone è il padre del digitale, *La Repubblica*, 2 November 2003, p. 33. Or seems to do without concreteness.

[16] On closer inspection, nevertheless, all civilizations have been image civilizations.

[17] T. Maldonado, *Disegno industriale, Un riesame*, Milan, 2005, VII ed. p. 48.

[18] T. Maldonado, *Reale e virtuale*, op. cit., pp. 50–51.

[19] F. Carlini, *Un plus di realtà*, Milan, 1995, pp. 38–39.

[20] Ibid., p. 39.

[21] J. Rifkin, *L'era dell'accesso* La rivoluzione della New Economy, translated by P. Cantoni, Milan, 2000, p. 250.

[22] G. Bettetini, Preface to F. Colombo, *Ombre sintetiche. Saggio di teoria dell'immagine elettronica*, Naples, 1995, p. 8.

MARTIN HOLT

THE NARRATIVE MODEL

I want to develop and defend a new theory of narrative representation based on the traditional causal view that narratives are primarily about human events and their causes and effects, and that represented chains of events are crucial to the form of any story. In a forthcoming paper I will defend this idea in the light of recent work In philosophy; I will look at the possible forms these chains can have, and argue that these forms reflect the structure of causal chains in reality, and that the events depicted in narratives reflect real events, and that the real events depicted, when psychological or social, do not reduce to physical events. But even if this realism is wrong, I will argue in this paper that conventional human events of all sorts, from coronations to christenings, can still be accurately represented in narratives. If I am right, narratives can represent human life accurately, even if human life is composed of conventions and nothing more.

This leaves open the crucial question of how something can be accurately represented in a narrative, which is the subject of this paper. I think there are two main methods: reference and modelling. Reference, whether it works by description, ostension, causation, or some complex mixture of these, is not exactly a clear notion, but it is a generally accepted part of modern philosophy of language; I think it is clear enough, at least in central cases, when reference occurs, but not how it works, and I will rely on the former and leave the latter in its current obscurity. The only point I want to make about reference as it is directly used in fiction, is that often fictional narrative works refer to real things, even if these real things - such as Napoleon, or the Napoleonic wars in *War and Peace* -are sometimes referred to via conventional categories. But as we shall see, reference plays a crucial if oblique role in the issue I want to investigate, the more controversial notion of modelling. I will attempt to provide a theory of what modelling is, how it works, and how it, along with reference, can be used to explain how narratives can sometimes accurately but often usefully represent the world.

After discussing the nature of modelling, I will look briefly at a vital element of narratives, that of character and the notion of logic of character.[1] Finally, I will illustrate the theory of narratives as models using parts of two film narratives.

What is a model? I think a useful signpost at the outset for the direction I'm travelling in is to say that a model is a tool, a tool that we use to think about or act toward part of the world. (The part of the world a model represents, I shall from now on call the original of the model). Before I go into more detail, I would like to explain my motivation for using this notion to explain how narratives work, rather than sticking with the notion of representation.

One might argue defining modelling in terms of representation runs the risk of being a circular. Doesn't a representation model, as much as a model represents?[2] Actually, I think not; I think that modelling is a kind of representation; for example, I think that a representation can also be a copy, or an index. Sound recordings, I count as copies as well as indices of what they record, and x-ray plates as indices but not copies of what has been x-rayed; I am happy to count both as representations, although I do not think they are models.[3] And I am happy to count what Nelson Goodman would call a model as what I would call a diagrammatic model.[4]

Diagrammatic models are not confined to diagrams, but rather diagrams illustrate their nature; they are representations where the fine grain of the form does not matter for the purposes of the representation, so that small changes in form need not be accompanied by a change in the representation, or indeed, in what is represented. Diagrammatic models are not, to use Goodman's terminology, syntactically dense.[5] Examples of such models include circuit diagrams and medical illustrations, which one can contrast with landscape paintings or portraits in which small changes in contour or colour, say, can transform a hill into a mountain or a happy smile into a sardonic one. Even if the same things are represented in a painting or portrait after the changes, these changes could radically alter the character of the content.

Since I want my theory of modelling to include scale models, and paintings, and since these things are often 'syntactically dense,' I am not content to keep to Goodman's notion of model. I also include as models, amongst other things, maps, architectural plans and models, models of anatomy, the hydraulic model of the British economy at the London School of Economics, orreries and other automata, and computer simulations.

I do not include mathematical models in this list, but I do include dynamic causal models, such things as wind tunnels, animals used to model the human body in experiments, and scale models of rivers to check flooding risks and consequences. All these things fit my rough guide of being tools for thinking about and acting towards the world. But both mathematical and causal models stand out from the others in the list in one crucial respect. Dynamic causal models work by re-creating the same kinds of causal relations between the same kinds of causes and effects as in the original. Mathematical models work by making explicit real mathematical relationships between the elements modelled, or at least objectively testable approximations to these.[6] I can see no convincing conventionalist account of why these models should work, though, of course, a hard bitten skeptic might argue that they are conventional; I think they directly reflect the way the world is, the real mathematical relationships and the real cause-and-effect relationships between kinds. But narratives and most other models are evidently highly conventional in significant ways and don't work by causal re-creation or mathematical modelling; they are not directly testable in the same way, but they can still be very useful.

My primary motivation for using the notion of model to explain fictional representation, and for not giving a special explanation for fiction, is that it fits the facts, and fits with my pragmatist leanings; "model" is a notion with a much wider application than fictional representation, and it is uncontroversial that models are useful. Models are practical tools in everyday use by engineers, designers, scientists, and the general public. My plan is to ally fictional representations—fraught as they are, from a realist point of view, with the problems of fiction and convention—to this down-to-earth notion. Defending this idea is not an easy task in itself, but the other and perhaps harder task I will take on is to give a good account of how models work. This is what I will tackle first.

The most popular way of looking at models is that they capture the structure of what they model; the obvious way of explaining what structure is and how models capture it is in terms of similarity. In one commonly accepted version of similarity, (1) x can be said to be similar to y to the extent that it has properties in common with y, which I will expand upon to allow (2) that x can be similar to y if some of its parts are of the same type as the parts of y or share properties with parts of y or if some of the same or similar parts of x are related to each other in the same way as the parts of y. Using (2) we can get an idea of structure, based on the internal relations between parts, and similar structure based on comparisons between things with similar parts or parts of the same type that have the same internal relations. x is similar in structure to y if x has the some of the same relations between some of its parts as in y.

Similarity is often thought of in objective terms, but these kinds of similarity need not be objective, since they depend on the categorization of objects and parts, which one can allow is sometimes done objectively, but not always. Another immediate problem is that similarity is a rather promiscuous notion: anything is similar to anything else, in some way or other, since anything shares some properties with anything else. But surely comparatively few things qualify as models, so how similar does something have to be to something else to qualify as a model of it? Also similarity is at best necessary for modelling, but not sufficient, since similarity is symmetric, but modelling is not – the Eiffel Tower is not a model of the tourist's paperweight.

In the face of these problems, another way to account for modelling sometimes advocated is to use isomorphism, a technical device derived from mathematics.[7] In effect, isomorphism guarantees that if your model has a relation in it, then the original has what we might loosely call a matching relation—it might be the same relation, but it could be a different one—relating exactly the same number of elements.[8] There is a one-to-one correspondence between model and original, if the one is isomorphic with the other.

A little more formally, we can say that If there is a function such that there is a one-to-one mapping of all the elements in set A related in an R way to all the elements in set B related in an S way, then there is an isomorphism between A and B. Isomorphism holds between ordered sets, and so doesn't directly apply between originals and their models, but we can construct ordered sets out of each and then test these for isomorphism. So the relative widths of blocks of wood, expressed by the relations 'is as wide as' and 'is wider than' might be used—via ordered sets—to map indirectly all the blocks of wood onto all the stones in Stone Henge using the relative heights of the stone and the relations 'is as tall as' and 'is taller than.' These blocks of wood would then have a partial isomorphism with Stone Henge, and on that basis, would serve as a model of it.

I call this isormorphism 'partial' because usually isomorphism is taken to map all the relations of one set, which in our case derives from the model, onto another set, which in our case derives from the original. But since I am talking about the isomorphism of ordered sets constructed from empirical systems, we can be as blinkered as we like when considering which sets to construct, or for that matter, the relations to map from one set to another. We may, for example, ignore relations such as 'is heavier than' and 'is taller than' or 'deeper than' between the blocks of wood, and, as I've suggested, use the relation 'is wider than' of the blocks to represent 'is taller than' between the stones. This partial isomorphism, where we can ignore relations in the model that are not useful and relations in the original we are not interested in, allows us the necessary latitude for modelling, whereas complete isomorphism is much too demanding a condition. It requires that for each relation between elements in the model, there needs to be a one-to-one mapping to the elements in the original, and indeed a kind of correspondence between model and original, since isomorphism guarantees that for all the mappings from model to original there is a reverse mapping from original to model. But very few, if any, of the models I enumerated earlier would have a complete isomorphism with their originals.

If for some relations in the set constructed from original X there is a partial isomorphism from elements with relations in the set constructed from model Y, then we may say X shares some of its structure with Y. If we allow that one sense of structure is captured in this way by isomorphism, then it comes down to a precise if abstract notion of how elements in the original are related to one another and to elements in its model. With a complete isomorphism, we may say that in this sense X and Y have the same structure, even though in another sense they may be entirely different.

To illustrate this, let us alter our example a bit, so that most of the relational properties are capable of being matched between the blocks of wood and Stone Henge because they are the same. So elements in the model related by 'is as heavy as' are mapped onto elements related by 'is as heavy as' in the original, and so on. But now let us suppose that the relational properties 'is taller than' and 'is wider than' can only be mapped onto the original by swapping them in the model. One gets a complete isomorphism, but with respect to the relations 'is wider than' and 'is taller than', the blocks in the models and originals are not similar. With partial isomorphism, where we have no practical restraints of using all the relations in our model to map its elements onto the elements in its original, we can easily have relations such as 'is happier than' being used to map elements in the model onto elements related by 'is taller than,' in the original, but there is no theoretical reason why we couldn't get a complete isomorphism between a model and original that weren't at all similar.

These examples of the possible mappings between models and originals of elements related by 'is taller than,' 'is wider than,' and 'is happier than' are rather suggestive. Let me digress for a moment to make an important point to which I will return later in my account of modelling. All of these relations are dependent on monadic properties: respectively, height, width, and happiness.[9] If we fix the monadic properties, we fix these relations, and so we can say that in this case the relations supervene on the monadic properties. Also, all these monadic properties are similar in having similar relations that they fix; so height fixes 'is taller than,' which is asymmetric and transitive, and this is similar to 'is wider than' and 'is a happier than' fixed by width and happiness. And height fixes 'is as tall as,' which is symmetric and transitive, which is similar to 'is as wide as' and 'is as happy as' fixed by width and happiness.[10] We can find these similarities between all the relations that height fixes and those fixed by happiness and width.[11]

Isomorphism guarantees that the relation used to do the mapping between sets must have the same properties as the relation between elements mapped onto; so, for example if the relation in the model is symmetric, the relation in the original must also be symmetric. But there is nothing in isomorphism that requires that the relations that are fixed by a monadic property in the set doing the mapping are fixed by a matching monadic property in the set mapped onto. Thus, elements related by 'is as wide as' in the model may be mapped onto elements related by 'as tall as', in the original, but at the same time elements related by 'is wider than' in the model may be mapped onto elements related by 'is heavier than' in the original. Indirectly, this raises one problem with using isomorphism as an account of modelling, namely, how do we know how to read the model? But if we knew width in a model stood for height in the original so that all relational properties fixed by width were matched in this way by all relational properties fixed by height, we could instantly read all the supervening matched relations, and this is an idea I'll make use of later, but it isn't part of isomorphism.

Despite its precision, in an important way isomorphism is very permissive, which is, I think, an attraction of the theory: elements in the model and original can be anything we allow, constrained either by set theory, logic, or metaphysics, so one can allow sets, numbers, parts, and properties, as well as objects, to be used to construct ordered sets. This permissiveness immediately undermines the apparent objectivity of the scheme; whether something is isomorphic depends on how generally permissive we are about elements and their relations, and also on how we categorize things and properties in a particular case, which may even be on a purely conventional basis. Sometimes we may use parts, and sometimes only whole objects or events in our model and original, and what we count as any of these things may depend on our culture. Virtually any kind of thing can share structure with any other kind of thing, and mapping can take place between very disparate things. The structure of a texture gradient might be shared by a colour gradient, an ordered series of weights, and even a group of happy people.

This illustrates how different isomorphism is from our traditional notion of similarity. A model may have a partial isomorphism with its original, or even have many partial isomorphisms or a complete isormorphism with it, and yet only a very weak similarity to it; it may not even be counted by us as at all similar to its original, not even similar in structure – that is according to some non-isomorphic notion of structure, such as similarity (2).

I doubt many of us would count the London underground map as similar to the real underground system. How could a diagrammatic design, or even the tokens of it printed on pieces of paper, be at all similar to real train lines and stations? The printed lines are at best similar in the weakest second-order and perspectival way to train lines, perhaps vaguely tracing the same forms from an overhead point of view. The simplified milk-bottle outline of the central portion of the map – drawn to a much larger scale than the outer portion, with straight lines, and uniform curves at the corners - has little to do with the form of the real train tracks, which would be better described by spaghetti-like entangled coils. And yet there is a partial isomorphism between the labelled 'interchanges' at the line crossings of the coloured lines on the map and the real interchanges of train lines on the underground.

If partial isomorphism seems a better account of modelling than similarity with diagrammatic models, what about scale models? A scale model needn't share any partial isomorphisms with the original, for example, because of simplification; here similarity seems a better explanation of what is happening. This raises what I think it the biggest problem with the isomorphism view of modelling, namely that isomorphism is too precise. Usually models and originals only share part of a structure and for only some relations. Models are imperfect man-made tools, which can nonetheless be very useful. Another problem for isomorphism as a full account of modelling is that it isn't clear why something that is isomorphic should be readable, and to make it so we need to add extra conditions. Similarity, at least of a close enough sort, has readability built in.

Perhaps similarity and isomorphism are jointly necessary for modelling? Actually, I think that both similarity and isomorphism are, in their different ways, too strict as jointly necessary conditions for modelling, and that models may make use of isomorphism or similarity, which are both, in their different ways suggestive, but they need not use either. Instead I think elements in models are props for thinking about the original and acting towards it, stand-ins, with stand-in relations between the elements only having to approximate the relations in the original.

An orrery doesn't tell you exactly what the solar system is like, but it enables you to think about the solar system in more detail, more precisely, and with more understanding than otherwise. An orrery can hardly be said to be similar to the solar system, except in the weakest kind of way. You understand how the planets are related to one another and the Sun and what happens when there is an eclipse via the prop Earth, Moon, and Sun. In a way this understanding is rough as the model is highly simplified because many real relationships between the planets - such as relative mass - are not modelled, and nor are many smaller but still large scale heavenly bodies in the system. But in another way the understanding is precise, since you can derive many true sentences about the solar system using the model: that Mercury is nearer to the Sun than is Earth, and that the Moon comes between the Sun and Earth during a solar eclipse and is of such a size and distance so as to almost perfectly occlude the one from the point of view of the other, and so on. You are also able to have a visual understanding of complex relations, such as those involved in an eclipse. Of course, you have to be able to distinguish between model and mechanism, or other irrelevant elements—you have to know what bits are stand-ins. And to reliably derive truth from the model, you have to understand what is approximate.

A model depends on an original, and indeed is guided in its construction and use by it, and my theory accounts for this, since props can only be understood by reference to the kind of thing they are props for. Another advantage of my theory is that you can, without paradox, or even difficulty, have props for things that don't exist: architectural models of buildings that are never built and models of floods that never happen contain props of this type. The paradox of fiction doesn't even arise with these models, because it is clear that we are not thinking about nothings that somehow half subsist in a fictional world, but thinking about models, which we can only understand in relation to the actual world. Sometimes models are of things that are, in a sense, currently impossible, as in architectural plans of skyscrapers that demand stronger material than we currently have. Are fairies so different from the strangest of the architectural follies in plans or scale models? Fairies and follies are based on something, though—the plans for follies are an exaggeration of normal architecture, and fairies are roughly humanoid, and beyond that rely on the descriptions of a pre-existing folklore. But new and fantastic things, without any references to kinds, are extremely hard to understand in a model, and at best can only be given a kind of half-life.

The totally new, and one might even say, the totally fictional, is opaque in a model. The only life it has consists in the internal relations it makes to props for things we know. If it doesn't even do this, it is totally redundant as an element. How can we know what to make of it, or what to do with it? (Here lies the problem of futurology in architecture and in science fiction, and the problem of the fantasy and horror genres in fiction—how to represent something startlingly new and imaginative without being too new and ultimately representing little or nothing.)

I want to flesh out my idea of model elements as stand-ins or props using another approach to the problem of modelling, which I am adapting from Arthur Danto's work. Danto does not intend this work as a account of modelling, or even of artistic representation, but rather of what one might call the content in all art, even the most abstract, but I think we can use some of what he says in an account of modelling:

"There is an is that figures prominently in statements concerning artworks which is not the is of either identity or predication; nor is the is of existence, or identification it is in common usage, and readily mastered by children. It is the sense of is in accordance with which a child, shown a circle and a triangle and asked which is him and which his sister, will point to the triangle saying "That is me"; or, in response to my question, the person next to me points to the man in purple and says "That one is Lear"; or in the gallery I point for my companion's benefit, to a spot in the painting before us and say "That white dab is Icarus."[12]

Danto goes on to say that he calls this is the is of artistic identification, and that what in a work of art can be identified with something else is a part or property of the work. He elaborates his idea with an illustration involving two indiscernible paintings, by artists A and B, oblong rectangles drawn with black lines on a white ground, bisected half way up by a black line. Each oblong stands perpendicular on one of its shortest sides. A's painting is called *Newton's first law*, B's is called *Newton's third law* :

"B explains his work as follows: a mass pressing downward is met by a mass pressing upward: the lower mass reacts equally and oppositely to the upper one. A explains his work as follows: the line through the space is the path of an isolated particle. The path goes from edge to edge, to give the sense of going beyond.[13]"

A bit later he adds that what initial artistic identifications are made makes a big change in how the picture can be interpreted. "To regard the middle line as an edge (mass meeting mass) imposes the need to identify the top and bottom half of the picture as rectangles, and as two distinct parts (not necessarily as two masses, for the line could be the edge of one mass jutting up)."[14]

But the scheme is initially very flexible, and we can regard the flat surface of the oblong as an area seen from below and the line as a jet in *Jet-Flight* or a line seen from above as in *Submarine*: "We could indeed, enter a quiet poetic world by identifying the upper area with a clear and cloudless sky, reflected in the still surface of the water below, whiteness kept from whiteness by the unreal boundary of the horizon."[15]

Once we make these initial choices, some other identifications will be forced on us and others will be precluded. And some identifications, Danto claims, are senseless, "No one could, I think, sensibly read the middle horizontal as Love's Labour's Lost or The Ascendancy of St Erasmus."

Artistic identifications seem, initially, to be a matter of stipulation, so in order to know what the picture is, we need quite a number of crucial initial stipulations from the artist to know what he or she is doing. I have a problem with this, rather analogous to the problem many people feel about the programme notes in programmatic music; it seems much too mechanical and arbitrary. However, if after these initial identifications, a complex of identifications were forced on the viewer and the content of the work naturally followed, then I would be less worried.

I think there is a tension in Danto's thought at this point, between identification by stipulation on the one hand, and identification by cultural context and artistic theory on the other. No doubt this is because he is addressing himself to the problem of the literal invisibility of modern art that has a strongly 'conceptual' element–where the message is not in the medium, and a large part of it resides in the story told by the artist about work. Anyway in his example of the two paintings, all we have initially is stipulation, and it is far from clear to me that other artistic identifications are so clearly ruled out given the initial identifications, or even that some initial identifications are so clearly ruled out as senseless, unless we have a cultural milieu or artistic theory as a background. But even then the pictures he has chosen seem to me to be too minimal to rule out multiple interpretations.

I suspect that no theory or piece of cultural context can tell us how to read pictures such as A's or B's, unless it provides a key, or in effect stipulates what the parts or properties of the pictures stand for. But meaning by stipulation has a long history; for example, we get it in classical iconography, telling us that the dove is the Holy Ghost, and the still-life stands for the vanitas theme, and so on. These stipulations, though, based on stories, ideas, and images rich with cultural associations, are ripe with meaning, and have become so deeply embedded in our culture that in their context they take on a natural feel quite different in kind from the arbitrary stipulations of an artist. But suppose oblongs on a white ground are identified by our iconography as an overhead view of the heavenly choir – all lined up, shoulder to shoulder, in a neat rectangle, Busby Berkley style. Then it may not be such a big leap to identifying the middle line as Saint Erasmus, a lengthways view—although, no doubt, we still have to be told this—and given the title, it may be a short step, if not an irresistible one, for us to understand the picture as showing him ascending to heaven. But floating up lengthways? Well why not? Perhaps he is floating to heaven lying on his back.

I am sure that Danto means artistic identification to be guided by artistic theory and the cultural context, as well the artist's intentions and stipulations, although this is not clear in his example, but, anyway, I shall take this to be a constraint on what we can correctly identify in paintings. I see a strong parallel here to how models work: maps, for example, usually have a key, which in effect identifies some elements by stipulation, but also we are very used to reading maps, and there are theories and methods of making maps and methods of using maps, and all our understanding of this transfers when we come to a new map. In art, maps are more analogous to renaissance paintings than to one of Danto's oblongs, or, for that matter, than to conceptual art.

I should also note that renaissance painting - and many other painting styles before and since - make use of something else, illusion, or a weaker condition, such as recognition, something which automatically sustains what I call a cognitive transfer: that is, the transfer of various perceptual or other cognitive skills or propositional knowledge from the world to a representation. So, for example, arguably, we 'see' perspective in these paintings naturally, using some of the same cognitive processes we use when seeing real perspective, and we can even say that 'seeing' the perspective in paintings depends on our ability to see the perspective in reality; without being able to see real perspective, we wouldn't be able to see perspective in a painting. We can still agree with Goodman, that classical perspective in paintings does not represent perspective in the world by means of similarity – after all, the representation is flat, the original isn't, and it also involves conventional distortions – for example parallel vertical lines are not drawn as converging - ruling out even partial isomorphism between original and representation. Sometimes, then, perhaps we immediately recognise elements in a model without making use of isomorphism, objective similarity, stipulation, or convention, but using something else, which I will refer to from now on as 'recognition'.[16]

Danto's scheme, if transferred to modelling, is, in a way, much more liberal than isomorphism since we don't have the constraint of precise mapping of elements. As with isomorphism, anything can stand for anything. But for a prop to function as such and to get us to think about it as an instance of a kind, I will add the extra constraints that the cultural context, illusion or recognition, stipulation, isomorphism, or similarity sustain converse denotation from the prop to the kind for which it is a stand-in.

Instead of 'artistic identifications' we can talk of 'modelling identifications.' Since models need to be readable, and clarity is generally aimed for, we can expect that the modelling identifications are made by illusion, recognition, or some such condition enabling immediate cognitive transfer, or when these identifications are conventionally made, that they are often made according to a commonly accepted code, or cultural practice, rather than according to simple stipulation.

However, stipulation need not always be so simple. In drawing, there is the phenomenon known as transfer—not to be confused with my notion of cognitive transfer—whereby, it is argued, if you can recognise a dog from a drawing of it, you will be able to recognise a cat from a drawing, though you have not seen a cat before. So even if drawing is in a way conventional, it doesn't work entirely by simple stipulation. Part of the explanation for this might well be an illusionistic one, but leaving that to one side, for the sake of argument, let us say that once we understand, by stipulation that a line stands-in for a contour, we can understand an indefinite number of drawings. From one stipulation, much follows, and with each new picture we don't need the artist stipulating what it is a picture of. I will call such a stipulation seminal, in contrast to simple stipulation in which an element in a model is stipulated as standing for a particular in the original of the model. When a prop stands for an instance of a kind, in such a way that we can recognise similar props as standing for instances of the same kind, the prop is also seminal. If you know a stick is a stand-in for a sword, then you don't have to keep being told this about other sticks. Props are usually seminal in this sense.

Earlier I noted something similar and even more powerful with some monadic properties; if it's stipulated that width in a model stands for height in its original, then in the right context you can quickly, perhaps even automatically, gain the idea that all the relational properties such as 'is wider than' and 'is as wide as' will stand for matching relations, in the original such as 'is taller than' and 'is as tall as.' Some props may have a monadic property that fix relational properties between them, and that matches its original in this way, or the monadic property may be matched across all props for a more general matching with its original. I will call monadic properties of props seminal if they function in this way. Partial isomorphism matching different kinds of relations between model and original is also seminal, though in a more limited way. Another example of seminal modelling is if a prop has an abstract property in common with its original. In Orson Welles' theatrical production of Moby Dick, horizontal ropes were agitated to create prop waves; the 'waves' in the ropes had a certain amplitude, and the audience didn't need to be told which agitations stood for calm seas and which for stormy ones.

If the model is ultimately clearer and more useful in a new form than using old ones, then relatively more stipulation may initially be needed. Before Harry Beck's map of the London underground, the maps of underground systems were made according to the principles of geographic map making, and not only were the interchanges between stations and train lines represented, but also the real spatial relations between stations and their real distances from one another. Beck created a much simpler diagrammatic map, realizing that the most important information to passengers wanting to get from one station to another was where the interchanges were, and what the different lines were. The real distances between stations and their spatial locations relative to one another and the real paths of the train lines were at best only very roughly represented. Passengers, unused to the new style of map, were initially confused, but quickly caught on. Other underground maps copied the diagrammatic style, and now these maps are a firm part of international culture, and if we come across a new underground map from another country, it's easy to read.

The map of the underground works, so how can it be completely conventional? Yes, it's a complex cultural product, modelling another complex cultural product, but it's a tool with a function— dispositional causal powers that are realized when people use the map and follow a route. Our culture has created something that does something, like a corkscrew or a car, and it does that independent of whether we believe it or not, and even of whether we share the culture. What we have to learn is how to use the map.

But notice how important it is that the model user knows what is being modelled, and above all what kind of thing. If you don't know what a station interchange is, or a stile or river, then having a symbol for it on a map is not very useful; a description in the model key helps, and complex modelled interrelations with things in the model we do know helps even more, but best of all is personal experience. Compare this with the child's problems in understanding Chekhov, even if he or she understands all the words. What is lacking is experience, and this experience transfers to the model. A model is a tool with a function, but it can only fulfil its function with the right kinds of knowledge and cognitive skills from the user—without which there is no cognitive transfer. A model, like any other tool, has to be used in the right way or it is inert.

Danto's scheme modified to account for modelling also allows that not all or even most of the structure of the original being modelled is captured. What is captured depends on the function of the model and on what is useful for that function, and what is captured is inflected by model making theories and culture and from a point of view—captured, one might say, in intension or under a description.

When a part or property, event, or object of a model is identified as a part or property, event, or object of an original, I shall call the thing identified a stand-in for what it is identified as.[17] A stand-in is a kind of substitute, a prop. Unlike a name, which refers to an object, a stand-in for an object is to be used or thought about as if it were something different, as if it were the object. The prop dagger that Macbeth uses to kill Duncan is to be thought about by the audience as a real dagger, and even to be used by actors to an extent as a real dagger would be in the original of the situation; in this case it might be looked at with expressions of horror and fascination.

Since the episode is fictional, it does not refer to a real dagger, yet we know what kind of thing it is a prop for. With a stand-in, we have converse denotation from a thing to a label, although in the case of models the label usually doesn't apply literally to the thing, but rather has a non-literal and transferred application to the thing.[18]

"Token x of type z is a stand-in for a token of type y" means that x is interpreted or understood or read as a token of type y, and one way to explain how this can come about is that to start with "x refers to type y," and then type y can be used, in a non-literal, or transferred sense, to refer to x.

It's important to introduce another degree of flexibility into our scheme: props may be composed of other props. We may have prop objects or prop events composed of parts made by other props – for example the characters who take part in a modelled event. This in turn reflects the fact that real objects and events have parts. If the prop event arises from its prop parts in a typical and repeatable way which is exploited in the rest of the narrative, we can regard the parts and their interrelations as seminal.

A crucial aspect of modelling is that it is testable against the world. Props may have monadic properties matching properties in the original, or they may have the same monadic properties as in the original; and props may be related to other props, with relations that are stand-ins for relations between elements in the original, or are the same relations. We then have two dimensions of good modelling: 1) the extent to which the props behave like the originals in terms of their monadic properties and 2) the extent to which the props behave like their originals in terms of their relations to each other. However, more indirectly, we can also ask, using similarity or partial isomorphism as our metric, do model and original share some of the same structure? The result of this test might be quantified by us, but it may, instead be relied on, as we use the model to understand the original and guide us; just as we rely on maps, without usually knowing in precise numerical terms, how accurate they are. (And the question of accuracy hardly seems appropriate for the hastily scribbled - and no doubt diagrammatic - map of a friend giving directions, though the map may still prove very useful.) If the map is no good, we will find out sooner or later.

Standing-in relies on reference, both referring to a label for a kind and then having that label refer to it, but it is not defined simply in terms of this two-way reference. Goodman says that this two-way reference happens with what he calls exemplification, which can be both literal and metaphorical. A tailor's swatch might literally exemplify a paisley pattern, a picture might metaphorically exemplify sadness; the swatch refers to the label 'paisley', the picture to the label 'sadness'. In both cases they serve as samples of what they exemplify, and as we look at them we are meant to think of the property they exemplify—the converse denotation is a constant feature of them, when they are functioning as samples.[19] But props, unlike samples, do not have to refer constantly to the kinds that label what they are props for in order to function as props; the converse reference explains the initial modelling identification and then its job is usually done. But where it persists, the model becomes a sort of sample, and rather than just modelling an instance, even where this instance is typical in some way, the instance goes beyond this to talk about the kinds involved— following Goodman, we can say this sort of model exemplifies what it models. It serves as a sample, a mode of modelling quite popular in fictional narratives, and even more popular in biological and chemical models.

Although we can talk about this modelling process from a realist perspective, as though the elements of the model and the relations between them are real, I want to stress that this account of modelling need not be restricted to realism. Perhaps, instead, models reflect human and conventional categories; perhaps kinds, properties and relations don't really exist, or, less paradoxically, reduce to sets of objects taken in extension - categories produced by human conventions. If this were true, then my account still tells us how novels, plays, and films can accurately represent human events, people, and their interrelations, but only given our culture and conventions. A model will still be valid and useful in the culture, since these conventional categories can still be more or less accurately modelled - a good model of them would be an invaluable tool for a visiting anthropologist. Our realist narratives of human life, like a child's letter to Father Christmas, are unwitting testimony to the culturally inflected lives we lead. And postmodern narratives, presumably, may actually be witting testimony. However, I'm not sure how something wholly conventional can allow someone to find his or her way, as maps do. I am a pragmatist, not a realist, but realism, or at least reality, lurks in the background.

If narratives are maps, what then are the elements of the terrain, and how do we use these maps? Well, events and characters are supreme as the elements modelled in narratives, and the two are closely linked. Characters cause, are affected by, or are components of most events in narratives. In a forthcoming paper I will look at the notion of 'event' in greater detail. Here I want to take this notion for granted and spend a little time explicating the notion of 'character'. There is an unfortunate ambiguity in the word 'character' as used in the context of narrative; sometimes by 'character' we mean 'character type,' sometimes 'represented person'; I mean character in the latter sense when I talk generally about character and its role in narrative, but character type is very important too.

Many would claim that character types have no place in real life, and are empty stereotypes or fictions. But I think that human beings can be classified according to virtues—courageous or wise, for example—or according to other relatively stable dispositions, either to behave in certain ways or to have certain psychological reactions or states. Some people are melancholy types, others are fussy, and so on. And I don't think we have been mesmerized by Dickens if we call someone a real Uriah Heep. We mean that he is entirely untrustworthy, has a disposition to dissimulate and to be falsely humble as a manipulation device, and perhaps leaves a slick of sweat and oil on your hands after a falsely hearty handshake. Such people, I think, really exist. And it is this idea that narratives exploit when they use a logic of character.

But a character type is only part of a person, and a small part at that, to add to the general psychology, memories, and motivations of an individual. Human nature, and the individual operation of desires and beliefs, may entirely cut across character type, as the coward acts courageously, the talker falls silent, and the sage is foolish. But just as a sense of order is lent to a narrative whose events are linked in strong causal chains, so a sense of order is lent a narrative if character types are used as the key for understanding the important actions of the characters; this often happens in tragedies and the like, to add to the sense of fatality. And here the course of events is fatally altered or even initiated by the actions of the tragic hero or heroine, and these actions often spring from a flaw in his or her character -the classic hamartia.

But the strong use of character types can also provide some unity to the anti-narrative composed of a chaotic series of depicted events, as in the film *The Big Lebowski*. In this film, the central character - strongly characterized by his ability to drift with style - has little control over the course of events, and the events themselves are often atypically linked. It's very hard to know what will happen next. (This technique of imposing an order of character type on a loose or chaotic narrative is quite a popular one with a long tradition, which we can trace through such key works as *Don Quixote*, *Tristram Shandy*, and *Waiting for Godot*.)

Before I look in some detail at a couple of illustrations of how characters and events are modelled in film narratives I should at least give a rough sketch of what the props and parts in a film actually are. I will count shots of a film as parts of the film. Shots can be stand-ins by themselves, but often they serve as stand-ins in groups, and often the shots decompose into smaller parts. So a shot may stand in for an event, but usually a sequence of shots depicts an event, which, in any case, we are often only shown part of; and a shot or part of a shot may stand in for a physical object, but often a group of shots does; and a shot may stand in for a character, but usually a shot stands in for a character together with other shots of the character. The event, the physical object, the character as modelled, are composed of all the parts with stand-ins that by resemblance to one another, illusion or recognition, stipulation, or convention are of the same event, object, or character. So, to take the case of character, we don't notice the double instead of the actor in the action sequence because of resemblance, or we realize by the flashback convention that this is the character as a young boy, though obviously played by a different actor, or we understand that Dracula has changed off screen from a bat into a man, by stipulation, before a convention is formed. When a modelled event part, object part, or character part appears in a shot in such a way that we can think of the part as the event, or the object, or person then this shot is a stand-in for the original by itself.[20]

Shots may be made into stand-ins for an event by linking them by cuts between some or all of the ingredients of the event: for example cuts between characters that are part of an event acting or reacting in certain ways. These parts have temporal and spatial relationships, indicated often by recognition, but sometimes by convention. Cuts also often signify, at least partly by convention, a cause-and-effect relation between shots. The relation may be proximal or one of a distant antecedent cause to an effect. Events may also be shown to be analogous by cuts, an effect often heightened by a visual match. Cuts between events can also be related by contrast, comparison, and similarity. All of these relations between cuts can be used to describe the props in greater detail.

The film model can be divided into two broad types of description: the description of physical events in physical terms; and the description of human events and characters. These distinctions are rather fuzzy edged, but easy enough to make at the extremes, since a film needs the first type of description but can exist without the second, and a narrative needs the second type of description but can exist without the first.

How can editing model human events? Continuity editing allows us mentally to reconstruct the scene of physical events; we see humans and other objects interacting at a basic physical level, and we locate them in time and space; this can be enough to reconstruct the human events, since the physical events modelled in the shots and editing include human behaviour. We actively reconstruct the physical scene using recognition, convention, inference, and some of the same cognitive processes we would undertake in real life, reaching the same sorts of conclusions: she's on his left, eating, as he bumps into her and her wine glass falls over and so on. In action films and slapstick such physical events are often crucial to the gags; the exposition is frequently very careful so that we understand what is going on, since the joke or action can depend on it.[21]

Cuts also work as human descriptions, by modelling persons and their interrelations and the events in which they take part. Any kind of shot can be used in such a cut, which, like a physical continuity cut, is picked out by function as much as form. I argue in a forthcoming paper that there is a reality of human events out there: falling in love, grieving, washing the dishes, and so on. Some events only happen in some cultures, others seem to cross cultures, but none may be essential to human life—there may be no essential human nature—just as there isn't any economics if there are no people exchanging goods. Money may not have existed, but once it does, it fulfils a certain function; the same is as true, I think, of events like falling in love, or dishwashing. Narratives model these human events and the sequences they can form, and so provide a kind of map of life.

Most, if not all cuts, either by convention, or perhaps sometimes because of the nature of human perceptual mechanisms, suggest some sort of connection between the shots they join; in physical continuity editing this connection is one of space and time, place, physical structure, cause and effect, or some mixture of these. One frequent sort of human description cut occurs in the transition from one scene to another. Death is followed by a funeral—not a convention of narrative but a matter of our culture—but even this obvious causal transition can, with a little alteration, make an important narrative point in an original way.

In *Longtime Companion*, a film about the gay community in California at the start of the AIDS epidemic, one of the main characters cares for his partner until the partner's death at home. The cut from his partner's death takes us to a funeral, but that of the carer, not his partner, though it takes a while for this to dawn on us—he wasn't even ill before the cut—which adds to the cut's impact. It simplifies a complex chain of cause and effect, by cutting a lot of it out. We understand the point that if you were in a long-term relationships with someone with AIDS before the disease was properly recognised, then you were likely to catch the disease yourself. But the cut's effect is more complicated than that.

The man, not his partner, is one of the main characters, and we identify with him to an extent, preparing ourselves for the death of his partner, which would not be so upsetting, and even seems like a blessed relief for his partner from pain, indignity, and failing mental faculties. So the cut to the man's funeral comes as a double shock: it is not only unexpected, since he is apparently healthy in the previous scene, but also we are more attached to this character.

And the situation isn't even symmetric between the two; the man's death will have been worse, since he knew what to expect, and had no one so close and devoted to look after him at home when the end came. With one cut the structure and significance of a whole sequence of events is suggested to us, but only because we can use our understanding of human events to grasp it, and onto this structure we can then project our emotions and concerns.

Because the cut exploits our knowledge and understanding in this way, it is not simply conventional, although it certainly is a causal cut, and one could argue that we expect cuts to stand in for causal relations by convention. But the causal links represented are not, I think, conventional, although in this case, highly culturally inflected, and very much 'of the time'. This cut also exploits our expectations of a cut being followed by a closer relevant effect than this, which, again, one could argue is an expectation generated by film convention; in this case we also expect the representation of a person's death to be often followed by his or her funeral. So as it dawns that it is the 'wrong' funeral, we are surprised and thrown off balance. But much more important, the cut exploits what we now know about the high mortality and transmissibility of AIDS; without this knowledge the cut risks being too confusing; Our realization that the apparently healthy partner has died crucially relies on this knowledge to work.

Causal cuts connect events and parts of events as modelled in shots as causes and effects. Human description cuts that are causal often show us human actions and reactions, and often suggest to us the thoughts and motivations of the characters involved in them. Alfred Hitchcock was a master at representing the inner life of his characters in this way, and one of his more subtle trademarks is the large number of scenes that he includes in his films where these cuts are crucial.

Let us take the scene in Notorious in which Ingrid Bergman's character first realizes that she is being poisoned by her husband and mother-in-law as she takes coffee with them. Obviously, the substance of that scene is not in the dialogue, which is, on the surface at least, strictly conventional, but in what these three people are thinking about. Also present is the hapless but kindly Nazi doctor who knows nothing and is the cause of the other characters' circumspection; he is a necessary character, since without this circumspection the scene would lose much of its interest. The interest lies in having human thought, emotions, and understanding mapped out for us to observe and infer, using many of the cognitive skills that we would use in real life.

Notice how clear we are about the mise en scéne and the relative positions of the characters to one another, which is necessary to understand where the characters are looking, or to use film terminology, to understand the eyelines.

Notice also how this scene links up to previous scenes: We learn of the plot to poison her in an earlier scene, and suspect that she is sick because they are carrying it out, though we haven't been shown this directly.

Although this knowledge of previous events is essential to the meaning of the scene, it is still true to say that we find out in detail what the characters are thinking by watching. The classic Hitchcock style exposes everything to view. Although some of this exposition is conventional, such as the outsize image of Bergman's coffee cup used in one angle, this still allows for the substance of the scene to be modelled, even if by conventional means—in this case the well-worn convention that large image equals significant image.[22]

Much of Hitchcock's exposition of the undercurrents in this scene is not conventional - or so I want to argue. In a film we usually make the assumption that the character is reacting in a way closely connected to what he or she is looking at, or sometimes looking away from —that this gives us a clue as to the thoughts or emotions of the character—and I think we often make the same assumptions about people in reality.[23] Anyway, this is certainly easy enough to test against personal experience, or even experimentally, should we feel the need. One strong piece of evidence for this view comes from the heights to which Hitchcock manages to take this technique, communicating highly complex information to a wide audience about the interior of his characters. His technique is so readily understood by us, which is a bit of a puzzle if it is entirely conventional.

When Ingrid Bergman's character Alicia struggles to her feet in such a dramatic way, after the Doctor accidentally goes to drink from her coffee cup, we immediately know she is not paranoid or hysterical or simply sick; we know this because of events before this scene, but also because of events within the scene. Sebastian, her husband, and his mother - the two poisoners - overreact when the Doctor mistakenly picks up Alicia's cup. This overreaction is rather subtle - although magnified by the way it's shot and edited - but we can see Alicia notices it and has a strong reaction which swiftly intensifies, and from this we see that she has realized she's being poisoned. Meanwhile, we can see throughout the scene that the kindly Doctor is oblivious to these undercurrents, but concerned at Alicia's evident sickness. This is exactly the sort of observation and inference we make from people's behaviours in real life, although, thankfully, what we discover is usually not as dramatic.

How can the scene do all this? The style we have just described is largely brought about by shots of characters looking cut together with shots of what they are looking at. This sits on top of our general scheme for film models, so within the scene we have props for parts of events and events, such as coffee drinking, pouring, talking, poisoning, and realizing you are being poisoned. These props are composed of shots, or parts of shots, and we have cuts standing in as causal connections linking these prop events together as sequences or parts of sequences – for example, pouring coffee followed by drinking it; and we have props for characters - shots of them in long shots or close ups - and props made from shots for other objects, such as coffee cups. And then we have a number of non-causal relations modelled between all these props, often by cuts, on the basis of relations between the props matching (often different) relations in the original, for example the spatial relations between the characters and objects modelled by the shot/reverse angle shot - three dimensions modelled in two. All of these things sustain the cognitive transfer, so we can understand what the characters are doing, and even what they are secretly thinking and feeling.

I have argued that models are successful either because they model the way things are in the original, or because they model the way we conventionally classify things in the original, but of course, I'm not neutral on this issue. I think a film can sustain a profound transfer from the observation of human behaviour and the understanding of human events and persons to their modelled counterparts, a transfer that can to lead to a profound insight; in a way, human life is captured. One can return to the model at any time to see some part of life again in a detail that eludes us during the original experience of it and would be impossible to derive from a memory. One can return to see the casual patterns and complex interrelations of the parts of life and to think about them as one would think about their originals.

If films are like maps—as I have argued all narratives are, in a way—then despite conventions of various sorts, they are tools with which to think about the world and act towards it. A map is a tool not only for planning and finding a route, but also for reliving a journey and seeing the lay of the land; narratives can be guides to living and places of re-experience, and even, at times, places to gain an overview of life.

There is an important sense in which maps go beyond their creators. Beck cannot have known all the possible routes people would take using his tube map, or indeed, how someone might point to the Northern Line between London Bridge and Bank and say, "This is where I was stuck for an hour." In a more dramatic way, the orrery takes on a new meaning for the modern physicist steeped in Einstein, relativity theory, and space-time than it originally had for the eighteenth-century physicist steeped in Newton and absolute space. It still works as a model, but the framework in which it is understood has dramatically changed.[24] In the same way, novels, films, and plays can go beyond their creators; we can have insights and make discoveries that go well beyond the scope of the author's intentions as we bring our own experience to bear on the story and make our own value judgements about events and characters. And the Freudian critic who turns to Shakespeare will see Hamlet in an entirely different psychological framework, which casts a new light on it in a way analogous to the orrery case.[25]

Sometimes maps are almost purely composed of conventional meanings and are largely decorative objects; medieval maps, for example, may tell us something about the conventions of the time, the folklore, and social hierarchies, but they surely tell us little about the lay of the land. Some narratives are of the same ilk, more concerned with form and conventional meanings than function, but if we want to engage with the stories of Dickens, Tolstoy, or Chekhov, of Shakespeare, Ingmar Bergman, or Hitchcock, then we have to go beyond such idle decorations.

We can normally judge the good maps from the bad on the basis of what we can recognise and on how easy they are to use to find a route or on how perplexing they are and on how much we fumble around with them and become lost; in short, we judge maps according to how well they help us fit the world. In a narrative, we recognize human behaviour and the events of life. And in a way we can find a route or become lost by seeing a good or poor modelling in a story of these typical human events or characters or chains of events, events we want to understand or at least think about more.

Perhaps there are postmodern map experts who are only concerned with maps as conventional artefacts and how they are made; while this is an essential part of judging their design, without seeing the useful maps as tools, our map experts have no means of judging how good these maps are or how well they are designed. Postmodernist inspired narrative theorists have a parallel problem when judging many narratives.

King's College, London

NOTES

[1] Eventually, I want to put my theory to use to see if any of a whole family of related realist notions, rather undermined by recent narrative theory, can be defended as more than simple convention. These notions include authenticity, plausibility, and realism itself. However this task is beyond the scope of this essay.

[2] For a more radical separation of models from representations, see Nelson Goodman, Languages of Art (Brighton: Harvester Press, second edition, 1981) pp 170–173.

[3] But this is a purely definitional matter; the reader may find that my concept of 'representation' is too broad when I include both x-ray plates and sound recordings. If the concept of representation is much narrower than I take it to be, and is in fact synonymous with the concept of model, then in what follows, and in blissful ignorance of the fact, I will have provided an

account of both. But I will still have grounded myself in the pragmatic and modelling aspect of the notion, with all the benefits of that that I describe in this essay.

[4] I also think a diagrammatic model can be a vital part of an artistic representation, contra Goodman. See Nelson Goodman, Languages of Art (Brighton: Harvester Press, second edition, 1981) pp 170–173 for his discussion of models and his arguments for the narrower definition.

[5] Ibid, pp. 103–142, for Goodman's general discussion of syntactic requirements and p. 136 for his characterisation of syntactic density.

[6] Why I exclude mathematical models in my account is tangential to this essay, and so I won't return to it in the body of the paper, but if the reader wants to know why, I suggest reading through the essay and returning to the rest of this note.

Briefly, my main reason for excluding mathematical models is that although they give us real relations (mathematical ones) or approximations to these between elements modelled—and this fits in with my account of models—the elements in mathematical models are symbolised by names or variables for kinds, or objects falling under kinds, not stand-ins, so they don't work as props, and there is no modelling identification. Using the mathematical model, we think about the objects or kinds directly, if abstractly, and this way of thinking is relatively novel, guided by the discovery of the mathematical relationships, and not transferred from our previous well established ways of thinking about or knowing the world. Also, what we get directly from a model are equations. I think equations are too far removed from the structure that we normally grasp of the original to fit in with my condition of cognitive transfer for modelling, and that mathematical models are unable to sustain all but the most abstract thought about the original. Computer models—those, for example, used in meteorology—can have graphic representations that are stand-ins and also there are relations between these, and when computer models do this, I will count them as models, although they will be built with a mathematical model programmed in, driving the graphics.

Note that in mathematical models and computer models, we can often rigorously test the models, and a useful model of either sort can fail some tests. The mathematical relationships that are discovered and used in these tools are often approximate, even when these things work well, and not like laws of nature.

[7] An early example of isomorphism used in an account of modelling, perhaps the first, is in Max Black, Models and Metaphors (Cornell University Press, 1962), p. 222. Black did not intend isomorphism to be a complete account of modelling but only a necessary condition of it, and he was primarily focused on giving an account of models used in science to mediate between the abstract equations of scientific theory and the world; these models, he argued, are necessary if the theory is to be applied to the world. I do not look at scientific models in this essay. But Black's idea that models function like metaphors and his account of metaphors involving transfer were not only very influential on Nelson Goodman and his account of metaphor, it has also heavily influenced my account of cognitive transfer.

[8] I provide this broad brushstroke version of isomorphism in case the reader is not interested in technicalities and wants to skip the next section, where I go into more technical detail, although the reader might find still find it useful to read the illustrative examples I use in this section and scan over the rest. However, I have tried to explain all key technical terms in this next section in footnotes, so it may make some sense even if the reader is not familiar with logic or set theory.

[9] A monadic property of a thing, such as 'is red' or 'is tall,' is a property that is non-relational; it is had by the thing alone, and not in relation to other things. A relational property, such as 'is taller than' or 'is redder than,' relates two or more things.

[10] A symmetric relation is such that it works both ways, as in 'is equal to' or 'is similar to'; if x*R*y, then y*R*x. A transitive relation is such that if one thing bears the relation to another, which bears the relation to a third, and so on, the first bears the relation to the third, and so on; if x*R*y and y*R*z, then x*R*z. 'Is taller than', 'is wider than' are both transitive.

[11] The idea that some relational properties supervene on some monadic properties is, of course, very different from saying that all relational properties do. This latter idea echoes the classic idea defended most vigorously by Leibniz that only monadic properties are 'intrinsic' and relations are somehow unreal.

[12] Arthur C. Danto, "The Artworld," in The Philosophy of Art, Readings Ancient and Modern, ed. Alex Neil and Aaron Ridley (McGraw-Hill, 1995). p. 206.

[13] Ibid, p. 207.

[14] Ibid, p. 207.

[15] Ibid, p. 208.

[16] For the classic defence of illusion theory, see Ernst Gombrich, Art and Illusion: a Study in the Psychology of Pictorial Representation (Phaidon Press, 1983) for the original statement of his view, and also "Visual Discovery in Art," in The Image and the Eye (Phaidon Press, 1982); here he replaces the condition of illusion with the weaker condition of recognition. For a recent and important variant in this tradition, see Flint Schier, Deeper Into Pictures (Cambridge University Press, 1980). I talk about all kinds of psychological transfer including cognitive and emotional transfer, at greater length in "Virtual Decadence," in Analecta Husserliana, ed. Anna-TeresaTymieniecka (Springer 2006), Vol. XC, pp. 373–399.

[17] I use the term 'stand in' rather than 'stand for' because often the later is used synonymously with 'reference' by philosophers, although in everyday language I think they often come down to the same thing.

[18] For a parallel scheme used in his account of samples, see Nelson Goodman, Languages of Art, pp. 52–57.

[19] Ibid., pp. 52–57.

[20] Parts can be of events or objects or systems, and sub-parts may themselves be objects or events or systems or sections of these. I am using the following scheme when talking about parts: parts have boundaries; parts may be concrete, in that only one part can be in the same time and place with the same boundary, but parts may be abstract – for example two events, one mental, the other physical, may be in the same time and place; we can allow that a part can be part of another part and parts can be overlapping; and a thing is divisible into its parts with no remainder.

[21] Nowadays, however, lots of action in action films is depicted in a highly fragmented 'impressionistic' style, so that the viewer only has a vague idea of what is happening.

[22] Even in the case of the outsize cup image, she is in the background, and the spatial relationship of her to her cup is represented non-conventionally as is the cup itself. For conventional and technical reasons, this outsize image was achieved by using a giant coffee cup, but the shot is still naturalistic, in that is looks like the camera is very close to an ordinary cup.

[23] A related point was made by Lev Kuleshov's famous 'experiment' in which the same neutral shot of the same actor looking was intercut with three shots depicting very different things—a child playing, a funeral, and a bowl of soup. People were said to interpret the actor as happy, sad, and hungry, respectively. This result is questionable—a wooden actor looks wooden!—but it contains a kernel of truth: expressions are always ambiguous. A sad expression cannot normally be mistaken for a happy expression, but the object of the emotion is not etched in the face, and if it can be determined at all, it will be determined using the context. Is he sad because of the funeral, or sad because he can't afford soup? Hitchcock's Rear Window contains hundreds of

shots/reaction shots that work in this way and can be seen as an exercise in exploiting this effect to the limit. Kuleshov's little experiment is also further evidence for my view that this 'shot reaction shot' technique has a natural - as opposed to conventional - interpretation

[24] As I write, astronomers have agreed that Pluto should no longer be counted as a planet, and that it should be regarded as one of three "dwarf planets." In Newton's day only six planets had been discovered. Using an eighteenth-century orrery today is a bit like using Beck's original underground map today, where some things are missing from the map, but the map is still useful.

[25] See Ernst Jones, Hamlet and Oedipus (Victor Gollancz, 1949).

WILLIAM ROBERTS

POLITICAL SYMBOLISM IN THE SAINT ANTOINE GATE, 1585–1672

Sur les autres Cités cette ville l'emporte Autant que du cyprès les superbes rameaux S'élèvent au-dessus des faibles arbrisseaux

> Virgil, Eglogue 1

Since the time of King Philip Augustus, the principal entrance to Paris from the east opened into rue St. Antoine. Like rue St. Honoré, it marked the principal Roman east-west cross-street (a *decumanus*). In 1369 Charles V ordered an upgrade to the earlier defensive gate. At the same time he added the six towers of the nearby Bastille fortress.

Various seventeenth- and eighteenth-century historians, including its last architect, believed that the next gate was built in 1549 for a royal entry of Henri II. However a modern scholar, Louis Hautecoeur (514, n. 3), determined that this king traditionally passed through the St. Denis gate instead. In 1573, when Henri III, King of Poland, returned to Paris after the death of his brother Charles IX, he entered through a Tuscan arch that was completed in 1585, a date generally accepted. Brice and Lerouge state that it was intended to serve as a triumphal arch in memory of Henri II.

In the earlier part of the seventeenth century this district, the Marais, was the most prestigious in the city. When on August 26, 1660, Louis XIV brought his new queen home following their marriage at l'Ile des Faisans, the royal party did not pass through the traditional but crumbling Porte St. Denis. Instead they entered by the sixteenth-century Porte St. Antoine, next to the Bastille. For the occasion, additional wooden and plaster ornaments were reportedly applied to the gate. On the wide rue St. Antoine, spectators filled the balconies of the numerous *hôtels* lining this principal artery. Then in 1670, for the upcoming tenth anniversary of Louis' assuming the kingship, François Blondel, that *"habile architecte"* of the time, was commissioned to update this portal but not replace it.[1] The project particularly celebrated the results of Louis' very advantageous marriage. The gate was demolished in 1778, and so in order to visualize the details of its originality one needs to compare contemporary accounts with extant prints and with modern research.

Standing next to the Bastille, this eastern gate was the official one for foreign ambassadors entering the city, and hence the external side needed to be, and was, all the more impressive.

Jean Marot engraved what is purported to be a faithful elevation of the original 1585 "*Arc de pierre sur le pont dormant*" as seen from the east and said to have been built by Thibault Métezeau, member of a dynasty of French architects (Fig. 1).[2] Marot's view of the exterior confirms many assertions that its original style was Doric, with stones of the pilasters and arch cut in strong horizontal and oblique lines (*corps de refends*). The central section contained the vehicle entry, covered by a pediment ("*frontonarrazé*"). Through this open

Figure 1.

archway in Marot's *première état* engraving, one sees three statues decorating the Charles V gate, across the second bridge.

On a small console extending from the keystone is a royal bust by the Flemish sculptor Gerard Van Opstal. It was painted in bronze so as to stand out against the white stone: Historians agree that it represented young Louis XIV, *"fait d'après naturel."*

Above it, on the inclines of the pediment (*les rempants*), the two reclining figures in low relief have sometimes been interpreted as representing Ceres and Apollo. But these elongated sixteenth-century century figures have also been seen as Maître Ponce's, Germain Pilon's, or Jean Goujon's "very fine" river gods: la Seine et la Marne, *"figures d'un ouvrage exquis"* (Blondel 605).[3] They support a large panel dated MDC.LX (1660) and inscribed in Latin abbreviations. This text credits the victory of peace—the Treaty of the Pyrenees—to the military might of Louis, the advice of his mother Anne of Austria, his august marriage, and the assiduity of Cardinal Mazarin.[4] This panel can be clearly read, and is depicted as standing much taller in Marot's than in prints by later artists. Yet on either side of the panel a pair of large letters "H" indicates an originally intended tribute to the Valois Kings Henri II and/or Henri III. These motifs disappear in the Perelle and Poilly versions.

Between two small pediments on the pilasters, a wide broken pediment (*fronton brisé*) contains a large double escutcheon. Set between military trophies and under a closed crown, the two shields joined together contain the arms of France and Navarre inside chains of the honorary French Orders Saint Michel and Saint Esprit. Atop this second pediment are placed two additional reclining female figures, larger and fully clothed. Wearing headdresses shaped like castellated towers and joining hands, they represent a newly strengthened alliance. Significantly, in her lap France has a crown bearing fleurs-de-lys, while Spain holds a shield and some darts. Above them on a small pedestal stands the handsome adolescent Roman god Hymen, son of Apollo. Watching over the King's marriage, he holds a flaming torch and a bridal veil—not a mouchoir, as one eighteenth-century historian would have it. Brice and Hurtaut credit these statues to Van Opstal, who died in 1668. Cynthia Lawrence concludes that "His best known sculptural decoration in Paris was for the Porte St. Antoine (c. 1660)."

Above the pedestrian entries, François Anguier's allegorical statues of Hope and Public Safety—*"figures d'un assez bon travail"* (Blondel)—stand in niches over their identifying overdoor panels. Climbing an anchor at the feet of Hope is a barely discernible dolphin (read Louis XIV's son, le Grand Dauphin, who will in fact be born on November 1, 1661, during the gate's refurbishing). Safety ("*le Salut Public*"), with reassuring demeanor, leans on a column—just at the time when the King was ordering the city fortifications to be dismantled.[5] Such thematic allusions clearly pertain to the circumstances of the 1660s and not the period of the Henris. Contradicting Lerouge, Hautecoeur (II, 515) attributes these statues to Michel Anguier; by 1669 his brother François (*l'aîné*) had died.

In Marot's title print (*deuxième état*) the large left console seems to be torn, or at least very hastily drawn in.[6] All of the foregoing facts suggest that Marot's engraving represents some mid-seventeenth-century hybrid state of the east facade—some compromise or last-minute documentary effort, perhaps made shortly before Blondel carried out his major changes.

Over the niches, two high reliefs of galleons in full sail—traditional allegories for the arms of Paris—function as square metopes between four triglyphs. Over the small end pediments stands a pair of slender obelisks or pyramids, which bear golden fleurs-de-lys on top of golden globes. The gate's overall linearity (the horizontal piled-up lines and the consoles joining the sides to the pillars, which then climb up to the obelisks) contributes to a clearly vertical impression. The much lower side sections are joined to the center by other consoles. At the ends of these are smaller flat pillars, surmounted by pairs of winged "*marmousets*" who hold up Roman military trophies. No internal staircase is visible. In a time-honored, traditional gesture, an artist (Lepautre) seems to be portraying himself, sitting at his easel in the near left corner. A nobleman by the oval window might be seen as a "peeping Tom" of the period.

Nicolas de Poilly's and Adam Perelle's late–seventeenth-century engraved "perspectives" and the latter's drawing of this same east facade of the gate all apparently represent François Blondel's embellishments of 1671–1672 and are very similar to each other (Figs. 2 and 3). Poilly exaggerates proportions and depicts much more of the Bastille and of the taller buildings in the Marais (Mansart's Visitation Church, St. Paul's remaining Gothic belfry, and the dome of the famed Saint-Louis des Jesuites Church). Perelle omits the Visitation dome, barely suggests the Bastille, and centers on the gate and its foreground.[7] A later engraver, Jacques Rigaud, draws from an angle and includes the entire east front of the Bastille. All the prints more or less concur with Sauval's judgment (I, 105) that Blondel's gate was decorated with the finest taste that Architecture could offer ("*ornée de ce que l'Architecture a de plus achevé*").

Blondel, in lectures preserved in his Cours d'Architecture a few years after the construction, summarizes his commission, established by the city officials ("Praefectus et Aediles"). It is not the opportunity for great new invention, but rather an upgrading (as he calls it, a "*rabillage*") of the Métezeau gate, which had so many sentimental associations for the City. He recalls his major

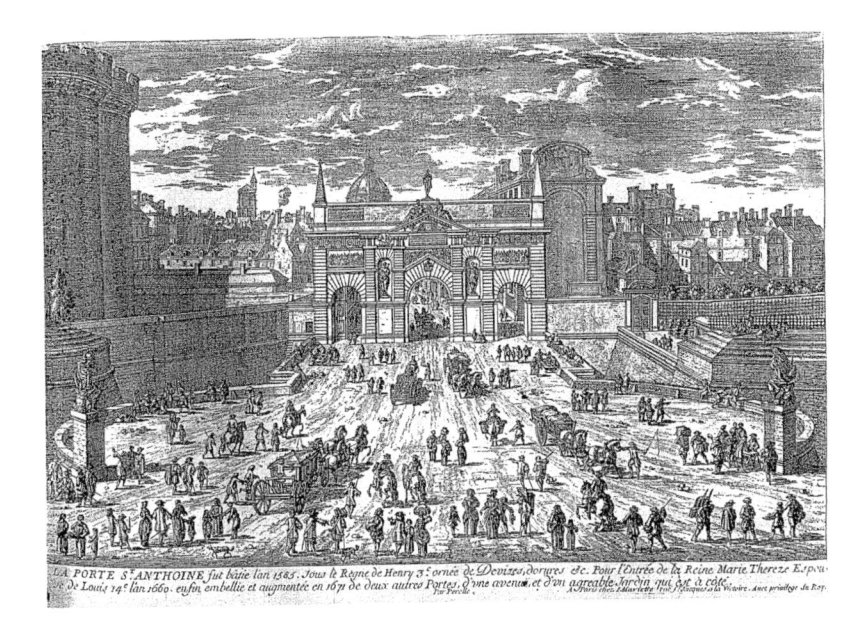

Figure 2.

Figure 3.

problems: first, how to free up the traffic jams and subsequent quarrels at this choke point leading into the very wide rue St. Antoine. To alleviate the situation he added two tall wings to the centerpiece (which he was obliged to maintain), with side openings ("*portes collatérales*") in the gate.[8] This involved reinforcing the foundations at the head of the *pont dormant* (fixed bridge) because of the Bastille and Bastion moats; he then had to widen the parapets. Both Perelle and Poilly illustrate how Blondel created a very nonclassical indented section of the walls (back to original size, and probably because of the drainage ditch), just before they fan out into the semicircular esplanade and the three major streets outside.

The second serious problem was stylistic: how to blend his preferred "*Dorique correcte*" with what he disdainfully calls the "*Dorique Gotique*" of the earlier construction—"*en quoi*," writes Brice (238), "*on peut dire qu' il a réussi très - heureusement.*" However, according to Blomfield (II, 94), "To his mind Gothic architecture was not architecture at all." In order to permit the side openings, he blocked up what he calls two "*fausses portes*" below the niche statues in the "*entrecolonnes*" and installed high stone sills under them, both solid and lined, as the later engravers indicate. But Marot shows that these original pedestrian doorways had earlier opened at ground level, and that well-dressed people were indeed passing through. Over these Blondel took off the small panels identifying the niche statues—probably since Hope and external Public Safety were no longer problematic in 1671.

Over the side doors, in his "*seconde ordonnance*" he inserted wide bas relief panels representing apparent enemy surrenders (doubtless to Louis), and continued the two-pilaster format. He removed the pair of quaint mini-pediments that crowned the outside pilasters, "*parce qu'ils étoient trop vilains*" (606). In Perelle and Poilly's works, the "H" letters, references to previous monarchs, clearly seem to have been suppressed—even though, in the planning stage, Blondel's own "*Elévation*" shows the "H's" still in place. The keystones of all three arches seem to be somewhat flattened. Mutules on the existing triglyphs are augmented from three to five, but the galleons appear to be unchanged. Extending from either side in the frieze, a row of mutules and five new metopes have been added, with rosettes in their centers.

Atop Blondel's new full attic, which unites the three archways, the obelisks have been moved to the far ends and are crowned by fleurs-de-lys, but without their golden balls. A wide panel reportedly of black marble separates new lettered panels at either side.[9] The double shield in the broken tympanum is now changed to a single one bearing the three fleurs-de-lys, but not the arms of Navarre, nor is it inside the honorary chains. It is under a complete row of mutules. The central statue of Hymen has been moved to the highest level and onto a smaller pedestal. He is portrayed somewhat differently in each later print, with and without a torch. The contemporary historian Brice mistakenly thought that this top statue represented Louis XIV himself; Blondel (607) calls him simply *"une figure debout dans le milieu."*

The split stone style now gives a general impression of Doric horizontality. The blank end wall of the five-story building on the right suggests a deliberate harmonization with the style of Marot's gate. It holds a sundial in its rounded tympanum between its large consoles and matching pilasters. Lerouge in 1716 appeared to identify this as the house of the King's architect, Jules Hardouin Mansart.[10]

In their foreground, various engravers portray a large half-moon esplanade opening from the exterior faubourg onto the bridge and the gate itself. The area is filled with a very diverse traffic and activity. At its extremities two stone statues, larger than life and *"estimées"* by Lerouge (141), sit among military trophies and flags, atop rustic pediments. This decor, credited to the *"sculpteur habile"* Thomas Renaudin, had been reportedly created for the royal entry of 1660. On the engravers' right is Hercules in his legendary posture: He wears the pelt of the Lion of Nemea as a cloak, with the animal's head forming a hood. This costume recalls the hero's first labor: the freeing of the region from that fearsome beast. He leans on his club (*la massue*), which he had cut from a tree nearby. The statue has been seen as representing Louis XIV, returned from his early military exploits, to rest a bit in the capital of his burgeoning empire. (This interpretation, typically flattering to the King, may well have been a prime factor in angering him at the famous Fête de Vaux-le-Vicomte: From the Hercules door panel and remarkable "Apotheosis of Hercules" ceiling, to the focal statue high up in the Vaux gardens, it would have been clear to all the guests that a rich commoner had stunningly preceded his monarch in this symbolism).[11]

Opposite Hercules is a female figure: This is Pallas-Minerva wearing a plumed helmet, metal armor, and a skirt. She has been seen as a reference to Anne of Austria, mother of Louis, whose advice had contributed to the military triumphs of her son, just as Minerva had done for Hercules. Perelle and Poilly chose these two statues as fixed points on which to anchor their visual perspectives.

The form of the city-side (west) facade has been preserved for posterity through an engraving by François Nicolas Martinet (Fig. 4).[12] Published in 1779, the year after the gate's demolition, it illustrates the basic decorative scheme (the split stone pattern) that Blondel had retained also on the city facade. Partially duplicating the faubourg side, round-arched openings with keystones cover each side passage, with a pediment over the middle opening.

Figure 4.

Notable inside these, spherical triangles or double pendentives ("*arrière voussures/arceaux en cul de four*") are set on oversize double consoles ("*modillons*"). These are placed atop flat plain pilasters or piers that frame the gateways. In fact, Blondel himself stipulated (604) that a main reason for saving Métezau's gate was that it contained this special vaulting over its city entrance ("*la Voûte de la même Porte du côté de la ville, dont le trait est si beau*"). Despite his strongly professed classicism, François Blondel's willingness to preserve this feature would seem to hint that he retained a certain mannerist spirit.

The tympanum over the west center arch restores the double-shield motif of the arms of France and Navarre—and what seems to be a small "H." Over the new side doors are large bas relief copies of the medal struck in 1671 by the city in the King's honor (Fig. 4).[13] The left arch offers a handsome profile view of young Louis, with long, flowing hair and wearing a metal breastplate. It bears the momentous legend LUDOVICUS MAGNUS. FRAN. ET NAV. REX P.P. [Pater Patriae]. In the right arch, a reproduction of the medal's reverse side presents a seated allegory of "Vertu" (courage, valor). She holds a cornucopia, symbol of prosperity, and leans on a shield bearing the arms of Paris—once again the allegorical galleon of the Nautae—surrounded by the legends FELICITAS PUBLICA [sic] and LUTETIA. The pediment over the middle arch points up to the center of the entablature and the continuous attic. There, a world globe between two armored breastplates and flags is lit by a sunburst, already chosen by the king as his royal emblem (we are to understand by this that Louis with his armies enlightens the world). Under the obelisks are two square panels bearing pairs of scripted "L's," as one can still see at Versailles. For the foreground of his western facade Martinet chose to portray, not the usual street activity, but instead a crowd of costumed revelers and musicians dancing in front of the gate. Thus he evokes the spirit of Carnival, whose rites were held from time immemorial on this rue Saint Antoine.

Brice, along with most commentators, judges of the gate that *"La plus belle face regarde le faubourg."* Lerouge concurs that indeed this side of the gate is *"plus belle que celle du côté de la ville."* Yet despite the city side's not having the same ornamentation as the exterior, Blondel argues that it *"ne laisse pas d'avoir ses beautez."* Sauval writes (I, 105) that the east/faubourg side was the more attractive, and was "decorated with Architecture's most perfect features." In his opinion all the figures were "trophies to the King's glory or hieroglyphs of the anticipated peace, and to the commercial and cultural advantages to be derived from this august Alliance." Altogether it was an optimistic allegorical tableau of recent and hoped-for history, including the references to Anne, the latest regent of France, and to Cardinal Mazarin.

After 1788 the two highly considered bas reliefs of reclining rivers (supposedly by "Gougeon") and *"qu'il auroit esté cruel de détruire"* (Blondel) were salvaged when the gate was taken down. They then decorated a large facade arch at the home of the playwright Beaumarchais, author of "The Barber of Seville." After 1818 when the house was taken down they supposedly went to the Cluny Museum, then to the Louvre. The niche statues were sent to the Carnavalet Museum.[14]

A well-known seventeenth-century print was meant to illustrate the "Day of the Barricades" (August 27, 1648), the event that launched the Fronde uprising. Its combat scene is situated on the bridge in front of Métezeau's gate, under the cannon fire of the Bastille. Erroneously, this view features Blondel's 1671 construction as the authentic backdrop for an incident that had actually taken place a quarter century before. Such historical and artistic rewriting has only added to the confusion about la Porte St. Antoine.

In September 1683, after the death of Colbert, it seemed appropriate for the next Almanach for the year 1684 to celebrate the accomplishments of the new minister Louvois. Its right-hand column recalls the embellishments of Paris under Louis XIV, among which are featured the gate and the rampart of St. Antoine.

This gate, called *"admirable ouvrage"* and *"magnifique édifice,"* survived for over two centuries. Blondel, speaking as an architect, noted that, since the forming of Métezeau's (and his own) city-side arch vaults, they have been considered so beautiful that all similar constructions have taken the name "Voûte ou Arrière-Voussure saint-Antoine."

In 1765 Piganiol (V, 51), repeated in Hurtaut (IV, 117), granted that the gate contained "some remarkable parts, especially the admirable sculptures, but the taste of the overall composition was small and stingy [*mesquin*]." Moreover,

This monument has neither the grandeur nor the magnificence suitable for the exit from this superb suburb [St. Antoine], and which is intended to announce the immensity and beauty of a city such as Paris, which in spite of all its defects, is still today the most famous and most admirable of the universe.

Especially at such an important site, some believed that the gate should have been made twice as large and imposing. Hurtaut elsewhere regrets its being sacrificed to the convenience of passage [the 1788 solution], and the more so since it was intended to support the peace and was an appropriate decor for ambassadors entering the city

The symbolism of la Porte Saint Antoine marks an important point of evolution for the French monarchy. The original homage by the letter "H" to a Valois king could have referred to Henri II, son of the well-known François I, and who was fatally wounded in a joust exactly on the rue St. Antoine, just a few yards from the site of this gate. On the other hand, it has been credited as honoring Henri III after the latter's return from serving as King of Poland, and who in 1585 would have authorized its reconstruction. His own assassination four years later provoked a crisis in the monarchy. This was resolved by the religious conversion of Henri IV, the Protestant King of Navarre, who introduced the Bourbon dynasty. Excepting for the original "H's" and the small later one, the only reference to this popular grandfather of Louis XIV appears to be the coat of arms of Navarre, then part of the French identity. Yet it is surrounded by the chain of a royal order, le Saint Esprit, inaugurated in 1588 by the Valois King Henri III. Other than the scripted "L's," there seems to be no reference on this gate to Louis XIV's father, Louis XIII, who had done much to fortify the western walls of the city, but who died when the present king was only five.

Fortunately the engravers preserved its image at different stages. Its original theme was praise for the Treaty of the Pyrenees (1659), which allowed reconciliation in the long Franco-Hispanic rivalry. The Spanish Habsburg Infanta, Maria Teresa, was brought in to be queen of France, with all the rights of succession that this treaty could imply. Mazarin's vision in these negotiations was far-seeing: Besides the rich dowry and territorial acquisitions, its provisions led eventually to the Wars of Devolution and of the Spanish Succession (1701–1714), fought to maintain Louis' grandson, Philip V, as king of Spain.

Hence the importance of the decoration of this eastern facade: the bronzed bust of the new virile king, the allegorical statues of France and Spain announcing a new politics, the blessing of this marriage and its future progeny. The combination of Hope, the dolphin, and Hymen combined to predict dynastic success for the Bourbons.

In the engravings of this gate we note a trifold symbolism: first, that Paris is twice allegorized by windswept galleons. These have been part of its arms since medieval times and refer back to the early boatmen, the Nautae. The representative nymphs, Seine and Marne, are a Renaissance topos referring to the rivers that merge just before flowing into the city. The Nation itself is traditionally figured by fleurs-de-lys, by the arms of France and Navarre, and by the chains of knighthood. The early pair of "H's" stand for one or all of the last three Kings Henri. The Nation is also directly personified by the reclining statues on top of the pediment: While "France" wears a royal crown, Spain holds a defensive shield and darts. They do clasp hands, in sign of close friendship—not exactly a normal image, considering the history of their relationship over recent decades.

Here the symbolism narrows, on account of the Treaty that brought about this sudden closeness. Hymen presides over its major stipulation, that the French King would travel to Spain and marry its most eligible daughter, thus eliminating the long-term rivalry of the two countries. SPES (Hope) further confirms the optimistic scenario.

In a magnanimous gesture for the time, the earliest marble panel expresses an uncommon sense of acknowledgement of the young king's indebtedness. As I noted, it credits the new peace of 1659–1660 to (1) the young king's military successes in the north, (2) the counsel of his mother, who had been a Spanish Infanta and also the latest regent of France, preserving the throne for her son and stepping down at his majority, (3) his politically favorable marriage, and (4) the persistence of Cardinal Mazarin, who had arranged the strategic negotiations for the Treaty and also been a close adviser to Louis until his own death in March 1661.

These successes relate to the other statue of "Public Safety," for they had helped to guarantee the frontiers of the country from any Spanish aggression. The esplanade statues make further allusions to Louis and to his very supportive mother.

For the tenth anniversary of the famous royal entry, the city fathers had commissioned Blondel to provide an upgrade for this gate. In the planning stage, the architect's elevation drawing maintained the "H" allusions to earlier kings, but in all the later views of this facade, the "H's" seem to have been chiseled off. The now-single shield no longer shows the arms of Navarre, except on the other facade in 1672. Two new panels present scenes of apparent recent enemy surrenders.

The west (city-side) facade compounds the symbolism. Dating from 1672, it repeats the motif of the shield fleur-de-lys, inside the honorary chains. Military allusions, with flags and armor, recall the Dutch war currently being waged. Then the decor becomes more personal, with scripted "L's," the large profile bust on the medal, and the King's new sunburst emblem over all—implying that his powerful yet magnanimous influence now benefits the world. The year before, the city had commissioned that laudatory medal designating their monarch as "Louis the Great," a theme then recreated by the architect. For his next official project, la Porte St. Denis, Blondel will go further. In its frieze he will announce its dedication in very large gold letters that blaze in the early morning and afternoon sun—"LUDOVICO MAGNO."

ACKNOWLEDGMENTS

I thank the staffs of Special Collections at Northwestern University, the Houghton and Loeb Libraries at Harvard University, and the Ryerson Library at the Art Institute of Chicago for their assistance with this project.

Northwestern University, Evanston, Illinois.

NOTES

[1] It may have been a coincidence, but the city fathers must have noticed that Le Vau had just completed the Trianon de Porcelaine at Versailles.

[2] Marot's print occurs in two states: one is complete, the other has the main entry cut out as a title page. See 1014 in Préaud's *Inventaire*, where Lepautre is credited with drawing the figures. Métézeau's role is confirmed in Turner, Jane, ed. *The Dictionary of Art*, 21:345.

[3] F. Blondel, *Cours d'Architecture*, II, 604–608; cited in Blomfield as 12:604. Bénézit (VI, 325) reports that they are now considered to be from the School of Goujon, "but are in any case characteristic of his style." There are reasons for this confusion among earlier historians. On the

Pont Notre-Dame, for the "solemn entry" of Henri II (1649), Pilon is credited with sculpting the nymphs of the Seine and the Marne. Later, for the entry of Charles IX, a contract document from 1571 stipulates that Pilon provide figures of the Seine and the Marne for the décor of the Pont Notre-Dame. In 1573, for the entry of Henri III through the Porte St. Antoine, the poet Ronsard was in charge of a different "ballet of the nymphs" (J. Babelon, 21–41).

[4] Brice (239) and Hurtaut (IV, 116) transcribe the abbreviated Latin text.

[5] Vauban had provided much security in the north, and was eventually named Commissionnaire des fortifications (1678).

[6] But not in his *"première état,"* pictured in Lepautre;1014, p. 354. See note 2.

[7] Dethan (73) reproduces and annotates Perelle's original drawing of this gate.

[8] The new size is cited as being 9 toises wide × 7 toises high.

[9] Their text was composed by the architect himself; he admits (607) to having borrowed from Cicero's praise of Pompey.

[10] *"Voyez dans cette rue [St. Antoine] la Maison d'Hardouin Mansart, habile Architecte...elle donne sur le rampart, & le batiment en est tout agréable"* (Lerouge, II, 140).

[11] Lerouge (II, 265–271) describes Le Brun's ceiling: *"Hercule sur son char...Dans une partie du ciel éclairé paroît Jupiter avec les autres dieux qui s'empressent d'admettre ce héros au sein de la gloire."*

[12] Taken from Martinet's incomplete series of engravings "Descriptions Historiques de Paris" (1779), which is preserved in Béguillet, I, 70ff. Signature variant is "Martinete."

[13] Dethan (73) prints both sides of a similar medal struck by the City in 1671, dated here 1672).

[14] Hautecoeur 515 (n. 1); Hoffbauer, II, 41, "Bastille" section.

BIBLIOGRAPHY

Babelon, Jean. *Germain Pilon*. Paris, Beaux-Arts, 1927.

Béguillet, Edmé. *Description historique de Paris et de ses plus beaux monumens*. Paris, Chez les Auteurs, 1779–1781, 3 vols.

Bénézit, Emmanuel, ed. *Dictionnaire des peintres, sculpteurs, dessinateurs et graveurs*. Paris, Gründ, 1999, 14 vols.

Blomfield, Sir Reginald T. *History of French Architecture from the Death of Mazarin till the Death of Louis XV, 1661–1774*. London, Bell, 1921, 2 vols.

Blondel, François. *Cours d'architecture enseigné dans l'Acadèmie royale d'architecture*. Paris, L. Roulland, 1675–1683. Reprinted 1904–1915, 4 vols.

Blondel, Jacques-Francois. *Cours d'Architecture*. Paris, Desaint, 1771–1777, 6 vols. Reprinted in 4 vols., Paris, 1904–1905.

Bluche, François. *Dictionnaire du Grand Siècle*. Paris, Fayard, 1990.

Brice, Germain. *Description de la ville de Paris et de tout ce qu'elle contient de plus Remarquable*, 9th edition. Reprinted Geneva, Droz, 1971.

Dézallier d'Argenville, Antoine Nicolas. *Voyage pittoresque de Paris*, 4th ed. Paris, De Bure, 1765.

Dethan, Georges. *Paris au temps de Louis XIV*. Paris, Hachette, 1990.

Dulaure, J.-A. *Nouvelle Description de Paris*, 2nd enl. ed. Paris, Lejay, 1787, Vol. 2.

Hautecoeur, Louis. *Histoire de l'architecture classique en France*. Paris, A. Picard, 1943–1957, Vol. 2 (1).

Hoffbauer, M. F. *Paris à travers les àges (1875–82)*, Vol. 2, Pl. I, II, V.

Hurtaut, P. T. N. *Dictionnaire de la ville de Paris*. Paris, Moutard, 1779–, Vol. 4 (P–Z). Reprinted, 1973.

Lawrence, Cynthia. In Turner, Jane, ed. *The Dictionary of Art*. New York, Grove, 1996, 23:460.

Lerouge, G. L. *Curiositez de Paris*. Paris, Saugrin, 1716, 1733, 2 vols.

Piganiol de la Force, J. A. *Description historique de la ville de Paris et des environs*. Paris, Libraires associés, 1765, 10 vols.

Préaud, Maxime. *Les effets du soleil, Almanachs du règne de Louis XIV*. Paris, Louvre, 1995, p. 79, & num. 23.

Préaud, Maxime. *Inventaire du fonds français: Graveurs du XVIIe siècle (Lepautre)*. Paris, Bibliothèque Nationale, XI, 354; 1014 (première état).

Sauval, Henri. *Histoire et recherches des antiquités de la ville de Paris*. Paris, éditions du Palais Royal, 1974, 3 vols. (reprint of 1724 ed., publ. C. Moette).

Tadgell, Christophe. "N. F. Blondel," in Turner, Jane, ed. *The Dictionary of Art*. New York, Grove, 1996, 4:165–166.

Turner, Jane, ed. *The Dictionary of Art*. New York, Grove, 1996, 34 vols.

MÜNIR BEKEN

MUSIC THEORY AND PHENOMENOLOGY OF MUSICAL PERFORMANCE

A Case Study: Five Notes in Joël-François Durand's un feu distinct

INTRODUCTION

This essay attempts to reveal certain experiential nuances between music performers and audiences. To illustrate these differences I analyze a passage from Joël Durand's musical composition *un feu distinct*. I then compare it with the concept of enharmonic spelling in traditional music theory to show that Durand's composition is an extension of Western classical music that is conscious of these experiential differences and occasionally articulates them.

The French-American composer Joël-François Durand's evolving style embraces a complex set of compositional practices and develops new ones. "At first influenced by postwar European serialism, as in the early *String Trio* (1980–81), Durand quickly sought to distance himself from the system by developing an interaction between pre-determined compositional processes and more spontaneously derived musical elements."[1] In other words, he seeks a dialogue and balance between theoretical and, even though they may be justified theoretically, nontheoretical decision-making processes. This is especially true for *un feu distinct*. In the composer's words, from his guide for performers, "In... *un feu distinct*, there is no... opposition between the constraints of... large scale organizations [and] a number of elements [that] are often decided freely during the actual writing, as the two tendencies complement each other."

UN FEU DISTINCT

Un feu distinct was commissioned by the Ensemble Contrechamps, which premiered it in Geneva on March 27, 1992, under the direction of Farhad Mechkat. The instrumentation includes alto flute, piccolo, clarinet, bass clarinet, violin, cello, and piano played by only five players. In this composition Durand avoids experimentalist extended-unconventional techniques on individual instruments. While especially his piano writing is intentionally conservative, his rhythmic vocabulary and "irrational meters" are rich and inventive. The use of quarter-tones as well is not just for a coloristic effect, but has structural significance. The melodic materials are substantially generated by the use of the software "MAX" created at the I.R.C.A.M. (Institut de Recherche et Coordination Acoustique/Musique) by Miller Puckette. Above all, in this composition Durand emphasizes the melodic domain in a progressively polyphonic context in which individual parts become distinct and less connected.

Unity, balance, and individuality are very important to Durand's work. He achieves unity by a source melodic idea the derivations of which "progressively unfold" until he reveals the original material at the very end. He sees these derivations as "perceptible analogies" to the original melodic idea in a "pseudo-thematic" formal system.

He pays special attention to musicians' experience in a carefully controlled physical and social space. as evidenced by the special instructions he provides for the performance of the composition and program notes. For example, according to the Program Notes,

> The position of the piano on the stage, separated from the other four instruments, reinforces this double attitude of participation/isolation, which constitutes its musical reality. In this sense, the piece is a kind of mini-concerto in which the soloist is constantly alienated from the other performers, even when they all play together. This situation is maintained until the end of the work, where piano is included in the global texture at the moment when the other four instruments reach the maximum point of their polyphonic individuality. In this sense there is no social integration, at the most a superimposition of the individual differences.

He regulates the "participation" and "isolation" through especially precise control of dynamics and a set of instructions for specific performers. For example, in addition to the specifics of the composition, he states in his guide for performers that "during the measures, 2 to 23, the cello is in its own inner dreamy world, completely separated from the other three; later it mixes more with them." He also points out certain relationships between individual instruments. For example, for a certain passage "it is...important [to him] to work carefully at the dialogs between piccolo/clarinet and violin." Only when there is a technical necessity is "a certain amount of freedom... left to the performer in their interpretation."

The most extreme case of "isolation" appears later in the composition in the flute part.

THE FIVE NOTES

During the measures 164 and 165 of *un feu distinct* Durand asks the flutist to be silent for five particular notes written in parentheses. Since in both cases the performer is asked to be silent, the tendency to compare the passage with John

Cage's 4' 33" is unavoidable. However, upon a closer look, there are some fundamental differences in the initial motivation and philosophy of the two works.

In 4' 33" the impossibility of a silent environment is the basic assumption, and therefore the surrounding soundscape[2] is appropriated into the musical composition. While the pianist indicates the formal structure of the composition by opening and closing the lid of the instrument, the audience listens to the random sounds that happen to be present for four minutes and thirty seconds. Like a typical experimentalist work, in this composition the process is more important than the sonic result.

Durand's composition, on the other hand, provides a written musical passage in which "the notes in parentheses are not ... played. The keys [on the flute] corresponding to the written notes are depressed silently, as if the notes were going to sound, but no sound is emitted." Furthermore, the performer is asked to "take special care of 'thinking' the whole phrase as if it was played normally." What is interesting is that a sounding single note "A" in measure 165, surrounded by pseudo silence, is integrated into the middle of the passage. From the performer's perspective, this strengthens further the continuity of the passage as a whole.

ENHARMONIC SPELLING

In the Western classical tradition, enharmonic spelling, chromaticism, modulation, and polyrhythm are some of the theoretical concepts that could be compared conceptually with the silent notes in Durand's composition. I focus on the topic of enharmonic spelling.

Enharmonic spelling is a notation in which a particular sound with regular vibrations is named and written differently. For example: physically, D sharp and E flat are the same. In other words, they are both played by pressing the same key on the piano.

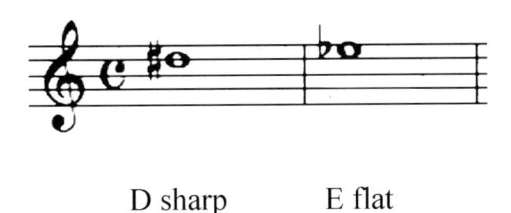

D sharp   E flat

However, for a musician who is also a theoretician, the implications of these two notes are quite different. In most pre–twentieth-century European compositions, when an unstable meaning is assigned to this pitch, E flat moves down to D or D flat and D sharp moves up to E:

      E flat   D   E flat   D flat   D sharp   E

Or with harmony:

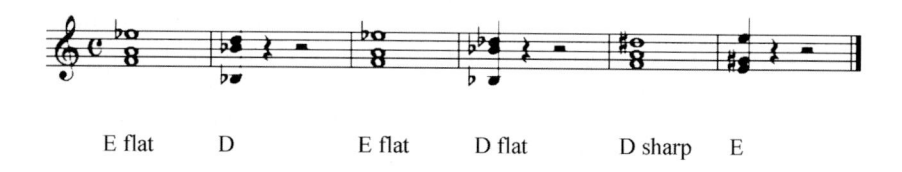

      E flat   D   E flat   D flat   D sharp   E

This practice becomes very complicated when a composition modulates to remote keys and uses double flats and double sharps, making the score very difficult to read for performers. In such instances, books on harmony, orchestration, and other aspects of music theory advise the composer to use practical alternatives. For example, when a composition calls for an E double flat, the enharmonic equivalent D is recommended instead. Some instruments, such as violin, viola, cello, double bass, and trombone, can play slightly different pitches to show the difference between enharmonic spellings. The following suggestion about violin writing in Cecil Forsyth's book on orchestration is exceptionally insightful:

> When the chromatic notes have time to sound and are of actual harmonic importance the player distinguishes between the enharmonics, both in the fingering and in the resultant pitch. The correct notes should therefore be written, especially in the case of the larger stringed-instruments such as Violas and Cellos, where the stopping is wider and the enharmonic differences more easily realized. Quick chromatic passing notes which have no harmonic value are generally best written in the simplest form possible. The inclusion of many double-flats in flat-keys and of double-sharps in sharp-keys serves no good purpose. (Forsyth, 1982, 312)

HOW DOES THE THEORY ALTER THE EXPERIENCE?

Although Forsyth thinks that keeping double flats and double sharps (in fast passages for violin, as well as writing for piano) "serves no good purpose," by simplifying the notation and getting rid of complicated accidentals, the composer would also sacrifice his or her communication with performers about any implied tonal meaning in that particular passage. In fact, some Romantic composers, like Chopin, insisted on employing double flats and double sharps in their compositions, even though it was more difficult for performers to read. I recall from my composition lessons how Cemal Resit Rey, a student of Gabriel Faure, would recommend that I read certain Chopin compositions like a harmonic narrative. Without the double flats and double sharps, some of these dimensions would have been obscured or lost. Even the twentieth-century American composer Morton Feldman, while exploring "sound as sound" and discovering "its own individual life in its own individual sound world," insisted on double flats and double sharps (Nyman, 1999, 71).

Therefore, my experience of the following identical sounding chords may be different than that of a person with no theoretical background:

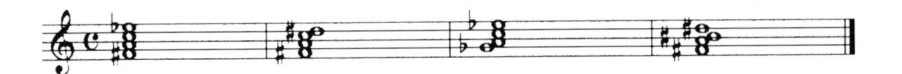

CONCLUSION

In conclusion, Joël-François Durand's composition is not a pretentious anomaly intended to create a niche for itself for its shock value, nor does it come from the American experimentalist tradition; instead, it belongs to the well-established Western classical tradition in which certain experiential differences between performers and audiences exist. Both Durand's *un feu distinct* and compositions in which enharmonic alternatives are not preferred contain special instructions intended only for the performers who know theory. A Chopin waltz, for example, would require a special learned ability to sense these nuances and, in the end, these instructions do not necessarily change the outcome or the experience of the audience who does not see the score. However, through these instructions in the scores, composers reveal certain additional sensory dimensions to be perceived by performers who live musical moments quite differently than listeners. The five notes in Durand's *un feu distinct* do just that.

I suspect that further studies in other facets of music theory, some non-Western musical cultures, and other artistic mediums might reveal similar phenomena.

ACKNOWLEDGMENT

I am grateful to Sally Hawkridge for her assistance in the writing of this work.

University of California, Los Angeles.

NOTES

[1] From Durand's official website, http://www.music.joelfdurand.com/Biography.html.
[2] From Durand's guide for performers.
[3] Ibid.
[4] Notice that I use the term soundscape in a different way than does Kay Kaufman Shelemay, who does not focus on noise and random sounds.

BIBLIOGRAPHY

Beken, Münir. 2004. *Teaching Tonality as Mode.* Paper presented at the Hawaii International Conference on Arts and Humanities, Hawaii University-West Oahu.

Bernard, Jonathan W., ed. 2005. *Joel Durand in the Mirror Land.* Seattle: University of Washington Press.

Forsyth, Cecil. 1982. Orchestration. New York: Dover Publications.

Griffiths, Paul. 2002. *Modern Music and After: Directions Since 1945.* Oxford: Oxford University Press.

Nyman, Michael. 1999. *Experimental Music: Cage and Beyond.* Cambridge: Cambridge University Press.

INDEX

Ba Jin, 10
Ban Zhao, 9
Beken, Münir, 305–310
Bergonzi, Bernard, 38, 44, 46
Blomfield, Sir Reginald T., 296, 302
Blondel, Jacques-Francois, 291, 293–294, 296–300, 302
Brice, Germain, 291, 293, 296–297, 299, 303
Burns, Norman T., 44, 46

Cao Xue-qin, 9
Carpentier, Alejo, 115, 117, 118, 119, 120, 121
Christopher J. Reagan, 44, 46
Collingwood, R. G., 249
Coward-McCann, 44
Cunningham, Michael, 159, 163, 166

Derrida, Jacques, 121
Dethan, Georges, 303
Dong Zhong-shu, 7
Dreyfus, Hubert, 123–126, 129
Du Qiy-niang, 5

Evanston, 43, 208, 239–241

Farnell, Lewis Richard, 19, 44
Forsyth, Cecil, 308
Frye, Northrop, 23, 28–29, 44–45
Fussell, Paul, 21, 32, 37–39, 44–46

Gadamer, Hans-Georg, 16–17, 27–29, 35–36, 43–45, 197–198, 254, 262
Goethe, Johann von, 94, 123, 126–131, 133–134, 176, 196
Golding, William, 124
Guenther, Lisa, 167

Hautecoeur, Louis, 291, 294, 303
Hurtaut, P. T. N., 293, 300, 303
Husserl, Edmund, 45, 118–119, 166, 215, 225, 228–233, 238–240
Hutcheon, Linda, 39, 46

Ibsen, Henrik, 123–125, 131, 133–134
Ingarden, Roman, 15–16, 21, 44–45
Irigaray, Luce, 159–161, 165–167
Iser, Wolfgang, 15, 21, 24, 29, 33–34, 39, 40, 43–46

John Dewey, 249
Jones, Gwyn, 27, 41, 45–46

Kant, Immanuel, 53, 55, 65, 74, 76, 77, 78, 81, 121, 123, 128, 130, 132, 150, 173, 175, 176, 177, 178, 179, 181–185, 189, 190–191, 195–198, 202, 205, 213–214, 232, 254
Kenneth R. Olson, 43

Lawrence, Cynthia, 293
Legge, James, 6
Lerouge, G. L., 291, 294, 297, 299, 303
Levinas, Emmanuel, 105, 159–163, 166–167
Li Ba, 7
Lu Xun, 10
Luo Guan-zhong, 11

Mailloux, Steven, 34, 45
Mann, Klaus, 130
Martin Heidegger, 240, 246, 249–250
Merleau-Ponty, Maurice, 233, 236, 240–241
Meyer, Michael, 131

Nelson Goodman, 245–246, 248–249, 251, 266, 275, 278–279, 286–288
Nyman, Michael, 309

Piganiol de la Force, J. A., 300
Pinter, Harold, 116, 118, 119
Povalyaeva, Natalia, 166
Préaud, Maxime, 302
Pu Sun-Lin, 11
Purkis, John, 31, 45

Raglan, 23, 25, 28, 44–45
Raymond Canon, 131
Reed, Walter L., 41, 46
Rutherford, Andrew, 22–23, 26, 33, 44–45

Sauval, Henri, 294, 299
She Nei-an, 12
Stallworthy, Jon, 40, 44–46

Thomas Merton, 94, 245
Turner, Jane, 302
Twain, Mark, 125

Wang Shih-fu, 9
Woolf, Virginia, 159, 163, 166
Wu Cheng-en, 8
Wu Jing-zi, 10

Analecta Husserliana

The Yearbook of Phenomenological Research

Editor-in-Chief

Anna-Teresa Tymieniecka

*The World Institute for Advanced Phenomenological Research and Learning,
Belmont, Massachusetts, U.S.A.*

1. Tymieniecka, A-T. (ed.), *Volume 1 of Analecta Husserliana*. 1971
   ISBN 90-277-0171-7
2. Tymieniecka, A-T. (ed.), *The Later Husserl and the Idea of Phenomenology*. Idealism – Realism, Historicity and Nature. 1972   ISBN 90-277-0223-3
3. Tymieniecka, A-T. (ed.), *The Phenomenological Realism of the Possible Worlds*. The "A Priori", Activity and Passivity of Consciousness, Phenomenology and Nature. 1974   ISBN 90-277-0426-0
4. Tymieniecka, A-T. (ed.), *Ingardeniana*. A Spectrum of Specialised Studies Establishing the Field of Research. 1976   ISBN 90-277-0628-X
5. Tymieniecka, A-T. (ed.), *The Crisis of Culture*. Steps to Reopen the Phenomenological Investigation of Man. 1976   ISBN 90-277-0632-8
6. Tymieniecka, A-T. (ed.), *The Self and the Other*. The Irreducible Element in Man, Part I. 1977   ISBN 90-277-0759-6
7. Tymieniecka, A-T. (ed.), *The Human Being in Action*. The Irreducible Element in Man, Part II. 1978   ISBN 90-277-0884-3
8. Nitta, Y. and Hirotaka Tatematsu (eds.), *Japanese Phenomenology*. Phenomenology as the Trans-cultural Philosophical Approach. 1979   ISBN 90-277-0924-6
9. Tymieniecka, A-T. (ed.), *The Teleologies in Husserlian Phenomenology*. The Irreducible Element in Man, Part III. 1979   ISBN 90-277-0981-5
10. Wojtyła, K., *The Acting Person*. Translated from Polish by A. Potocki. 1979
    ISBN Hb 90-277-0969-6; Pb 90-277-0985-8
11. Ales Bello, A. (ed.), *The Great Chain of Being* and *Italian Phenomenology*. 1981
    ISBN 90-277-1071-6
12. Tymieniecka, A-T. (ed.), *The Philosophical Reflection of Man in Literature*. Selected Papers from Several Conferences held by the International Society for Phenomenology and Literature in Cambridge, Massachusetts. Includes the essay by A-T. Tymieniecka, *Poetica Nova*. 1982   ISBN 90-277-1312-X
13. Kaelin, E. F., *The Unhappy Consciousness*. The Poetic Plight of Samuel Beckett. An Inquiry at the Intersection of Phenomenology and literature. 1981
    ISBN 90-277-1313-8
14. Tymieniecka, A-T. (ed.), *The Phenomenology of Man and of the Human Condition*. Individualisation of Nature and the Human Being. (Part I:) Plotting the Territory for Interdisciplinary Communication. 1983 *Part II* see below under Volume 21.
    ISBN 90-277-1447-9

Analecta Husserliana

15. Tymieniecka, A-T. and Calvin O. Schrag (eds.), *Foundations of Morality, Human Rights, and the Human Sciences*. Phenomenology in a Foundational Dialogue with Human Sciences. 1983 ISBN 90-277-1453-3
16. Tymieniecka, A-T. (ed.), *Soul and Body in Husserlian Phenomenology*. Man and Nature. 1983 ISBN 90-277-1518-1
17. Tymieniecka, A-T. (ed.), *Phenomenology of Life in a Dialogue Between Chinese and Occidental Philosophy*. 1984 ISBN 90-277-1620-X
18. Tymieniecka, A-T. (ed.), *The Existential Coordinates of the Human Condition: Poetic – Epic – Tragic*. The Literary Genre. 1984 ISBN 90-277-1702-8
19. Tymieniecka, A-T. (ed.), *Poetics of the Elements in the Human Condition*. (Part 1:) The Sea. From Elemental Stirrings to Symbolic Inspiration, Language, and Life-Significance in Literary Interpretation and Theory. 1985
For Part 2 and 3 *see below* under Volumes 23 and 28. ISBN 90-277-1906-3
20. Tymieniecka, A-T. (ed.), *The Moral Sense in the Communal Significance of Life*. Investigations in Phenomenological Praxeology: Psychiatric Therapeutics, Medical Ethics and Social Praxis within the Life- and Communal World. 1986
ISBN 90-277-2085-1
21. Tymieniecka, A-T. (ed.), *The Phenomenology of Man and of the Human Condition*. Part II: The Meeting Point Between Occidental and Oriental Philosophies. 1986
ISBN 90-277-2185-8
22. Tymieniecka, A-T. (ed.), *Morality within the Life- and Social World*. Interdisciplinary Phenomenology of the Authentic Life in the "Moral Sense". 1987
Sequel to Volumes 15 and 20. ISBN 90-277-2411-3
23. Tymieniecka, A-T. (ed.), *Poetics of the Elements in the Human Condition*. Part 2: The Airy Elements in Poetic Imagination. Breath, Breeze, Wind, Tempest, Thunder, Snow, Flame, Fire, Volcano... 1988 ISBN 90-277-2569-1
24. Tymieniecka, A-T., *Logos and Life*. Book I: Creative Experience and the Critique of Reason. 1988 ISBN Hb 90-277-2539-X; Pb 90-277-2540-3
25. Tymieniecka, A-T., *Logos and Life*. Book II: The Three Movements of the Soul. 1988 ISBN Hb 90-277-2556-X; Pb 90-277-2557-8
26. Kaelin, E. F. and Calvin O. Schrag (eds.), *American Phenomenology*. Origins and Developments. 1989 ISBN 90-277-2690-6
27. Tymieniecka, A-T. (ed.), *Man within his Life-World*. Contributions to Phenomenology by Scholars from East-Central Europe. 1989 ISBN 90-277-2767-8
28. Tymieniecka, A-T. (ed.), *The Elemental Passions of the Soul*. Poetics of the Elements in the Human Condition, Part 3. 1990 ISBN 0-7923-0180-3
29. Tymieniecka, A-T. (ed.), *Man's Self-Interpretation-in-Existence*. Phenomenology and Philosophy of Life. – Introducing the Spanish Perspective. 1990
ISBN 0-7923-0324-5
30. Rudnick, H. H. (ed.), *Ingardeniana II*. New Studies in the Philosophy of Roman Ingarden. With a New International Ingarden Bibliography. 1990
ISBN 0-7923-0627-9

Analecta Husserliana

31. Tymieniecka, A-T. (ed.), *The Moral Sense and Its Foundational Significance: Self, Person, Historicity, Community*. Phenomenological Praxeology and Psychiatry. 1990   ISBN 0-7923-0678-3
32. Kronegger, M. (ed.), *Phenomenology and Aesthetics*. Approaches to Comparative Literature and Other Arts. Homages to A-T. Tymieniecka. 1991   ISBN 0-7923-0738-0
33. Tymieniecka, A-T. (ed.), *Ingardeniana III*. Roman Ingarden's Aesthetics in a New Key and the Independent Approaches of Others: The Performing Arts, the Fine Arts, and Literature. 1991
    Sequel to Volumes 4 and 30   ISBN 0-7923-1014-4
34. Tymieniecka, A-T. (ed.), *The Turning Points of the New Phenomenological Era*. Husserl Research – Drawing upon the Full Extent of His Development. 1991   ISBN 0-7923-1134-5
35. Tymieniecka, A-T. (ed.), *Husserlian Phenomenology in a New Key*. Intersubjectivity, Ethos, the Societal Sphere, Human Encounter, Pathos. 1991   ISBN 0-7923-1146-9
36. Tymieniecka, A-T. (ed.), *Husserl's Legacy in Phenomenological Philosophies.* New Approaches to Reason, Language, Hermeneutics, the Human Condition. 1991   ISBN 0-7923-1178-7
37. Tymieniecka, A-T. (ed.), *New Queries in Aesthetics and Metaphysics*. Time, Historicity, Art, Culture, Metaphysics, the Transnatural. 1991   ISBN 0-7923-1195-7
38. Tymieniecka, A-T. (ed.), *The Elemental Dialectic of Light and Darkness*. The Passions of the Soul in the Onto-Poiesis of Life. 1992   ISBN 0-7923-1601-0
39. Tymieniecka, A-T. (ed.), *Reason, Life, Culture, Part I*. Phenomenology in the Baltics. 1993   ISBN 0-7923-1902-8
40. Tymieniecka, A-T. (ed.), *Manifestations of Reason: Life, Historicity, Culture*. Reason, Life, Culture, Part II. Phenomenology in the Adriatic Countries. 1993   ISBN 0-7923-2215-0
41. Tymieniecka, A-T. (ed.), *Allegory Revisited*. Ideals of Mankind. 1994   ISBN 0-7923-2312-2
42. Kronegger, M. and Tymieniecka, A-T. (eds.), *Allegory Old and New*. In Literature, the Fine Arts, Music and Theatre, and Its Continuity in Culture. 1994   ISBN 0-7923-2348-3
43. Tymieniecka, A-T. (ed.): *From the Sacred to the Divine*. A New Phenomenological Approach. 1994   ISBN 0-7923-2690-3
44. Tymieniecka, A-T. (ed.): *The Elemental Passion for Place in the Ontopoiesis of Life*. Passions of the Soul in the *Imaginatio Creatrix*. 1995   ISBN 0-7923-2749-7
45. Zhai, Z.: *The Radical Choice and Moral Theory*. Through Communicative Argumentation to Phenomenological Subjectivity. 1994   ISBN 0-7923-2891-4
46. Tymieniecka, A-T. (ed.): *The Logic of the Living Present*. Experience, Ordering, Onto-Poiesis of Culture. 1995   ISBN 0-7923-2930-9

Analecta Husserliana

47. Tymieniecka, A-T. (ed.): *Heaven, Earth, and In-Between in the Harmony of Life*. Phenomenology in the Continuing Oriental/Occidental Dialogue. 1995
 ISBN 0-7923-3373-X

48. Tymieniecka, A-T. (ed.): *Life. In the Glory of its Radiating Manifestations*. 25th Anniversary Publication. Book I. 1996 ISBN 0-7923-3825-1

49. Kronegger, M. and Tymieniecka, A-T. (eds.): *Life. The Human Quest for an Ideal*. 25th Anniversary Publication. Book II. 1996 ISBN 0-7923-3826-X

50. Tymieniecka, A-T. (ed.): *Life. Phenomenology of Life as the Starting Point of Philosophy*. 25th Anniversary Publication. Book III. 1997 ISBN 0-7923-4126-0

51. Tymieniecka, A-T. (ed.): *Passion for Place. Part II*. Between the Vital Spacing and the Creative Horizons of Fulfilment. 1997 ISBN 0-7923-4146-5

52. Tymieniecka, A-T. (ed.): *Phenomenology of Life and the Human Creative Condition*. Laying Down the Cornerstones of the Field. Book I. 1997
 ISBN 0-7923-4445-6

53. Tymieniecka, A-T. (ed.): *The Reincarnating Mind, or the Ontopoietic Outburst in Creative Virtualities*. Harmonisations and Attunement in Cognition, the Fine Arts, Literature. Phenomenology of Life and the Human Creative Condition. Book II. 1997 ISBN 0-7923-4461-8

54. Tymieniecka, A-T. (ed.): *Ontopoietic Expansion in Human Self-Interpretation-in-Existence*. The I and the Other in their Creative Spacing of the Societal Circuits of Life. Phenomenology of Life and the Creative Condition. Book III. 1997
 ISBN 0-7923-4462-6

55. Tymieniecka, A-T. (ed.): *Creative Virtualities in Human Self-Interpretation-in-Culture*. Phenomenology of Life and the Human Creative Condition. Book IV. 1997 ISBN 0-7923-4545-2

56. Tymieniecka, A-T. (ed.): *Enjoyment*. From Laughter to Delight in Philosophy, Literature, the Fine Arts and Aesthetics. 1998 ISBN 0-7923-4677-7

57. Kronegger, M. and Tymieniecka, A-T. (eds.): *Life. Differentiation and Harmony ...Vegetal, Animal, Human*. 1998 ISBN 0-7923-4887-7

58. Tymieniecka, A-T. and Matsuba, S. (eds.): *Immersing in the Concrete*. Maurice Merleau-Ponty in the Japanese Perspective. 1998 ISBN 0-7923-5093-6

59. Tymieniecka, A-T. (ed.): *Life – Scientific Philosophy/Phenomenology of Life and the Sciences of Life*. Ontopoiesis of Life and the Human Creative Condition. 1998 ISBN 0-7923-5141-X

60. Tymieniecka, A-T. (eds.): *Life – The Outburst of Life in the Human Sphere*. Scientific Philosophy/Phenomenology of Life and the Sciences of Life. Book II. 1998 ISBN 0-7923-5142-8

61. Tymieniecka, A-T. (ed.): *The Aesthetic Discourse of the Arts*. Breaking the Barriers. 2000 ISBN 0-7923-6006-0

Analecta Husserliana

62. Tymieniecka, A-T. (ed.): *Creative Mimesis of Emotion*. From Sorrow to Elation; Elegiac Virtuosity in Literature. 2000   ISBN 0-7923-6007-9

63. Kronegger, M. (ed).: *The Orchestration of The Arts – A Creative Symbiosis of Existential Powers*. The Vibrating Interplay of Sound, Color, Image, Gesture, Movement, Rhythm, Fragrance, Word, Touch. 2000   ISBN 0-7923-6008-7

64. Tymieniecka, A-T. and Z. Zalewski (eds.): *Life – The Human Being Between Life and Death*. A Dialogue Between Medicine and Philosophy, Recurrent Issues and New Approaches. 2000   ISBN 0-7923-5962-3

65. Kronegger, M. and Tymieniecka, A-T. (eds.): *The Aesthetics of Enchantment in the Fine Arts*. 2000   ISBN 0-7923-6183-0

66. Tymieniecka, A-T. (ed.): *The Origins of Life, Volume I: The Primogenital Matrix of Life and Its Context*. 2000   ISBN 0-7923-6246-2; Set ISBN 0-7923-6446-5

67. Tymieniecka, A-T. (ed.): *The Origins of Life, Volume II: The Origins of the Existential Sharing-in-Life*. 2000 ISBN 0-7923-6276-4; Set ISBN 0-7923-6446-5

68. Tymieniecka, A-T. (ed.): *PAIDEIA*. Philosophy/Phenomenology of Life Inspiring Education of our Times. 2000   ISBN 0-7923-6319-1

69. Tymieniecka, A-T. (ed.): *The Poetry of Life in Literature*. 2000
    ISBN 0-7923-6408-2

70. Tymieniecka, A-T. (ed.): *Impetus and Equipoise in the Life-Strategies of Reason*. Logos and Life, volume 4. 2000   ISBN 0-7923-6731-6; HB 0-7923-6730-8

71. Tymieniecka, A-T. (ed.): *Passions of the Earth in Human Existence, Creativity, and Literature*. 2001   ISBN 0-7923-6675-1

72. Tymieniecka, A-T. and E. Agazzi (eds.): *Life – Interpretation and the Sense of Illness within the Human Condition*. Medicine and Philosophy in a Dialogue. 2001   ISBN Hb 0-7923-6983-1; Pb 0-7923-6984-X

73. Tymieniecka, A-T. (ed.): *Life – The Play of Life on the Stage of the World in Fine Arts, Stage-Play, and Literature*. 2001   ISBN 0-7923-7032-5

74. Tymieniecka, A-T. (ed.): *Life-Energies, Forces and the Shaping of Life: Vital, Existential*. Book I. 2002   ISBN 1-4020-0627-6

75. Tymieniecka, A-T. (ed.): *The Visible and the Invisible in the Interplay between Philosophy, Literature and Reality*. 2002   ISBN 1-4020-0070-7

76. Tymieniecka, A-T. (ed.): *Life – Truth in its Various Perspectives*. Cognition, Self-Knowledge, Creativity, Scientific Research, Sharing-in-Life, Economics ......
    2002   ISBN 1-4020-0071-5

77. Tymieniecka, A-T. (ed.): *The Creative Matrix of the Origins*. Dynamisms, Forces and the Shaping of Life. 2003   ISBN 1-4020-0789-2

Analecta Husserliana

78. Tymieniecka, A-T. (ed.): *Gardens and the Passion for the Infinite.* 2003
    ISBN 1-4020-0858-9
79. Tymieniecka, A-T. (ed.): *Does the World exist?* Plurisignificant Ciphering of Reality. 2003
    ISBN 1-4020-1517-8
80. Tymieniecka, A-T. (ed.): *Phenomenology World-Wide.* Foundations – Expanding Dynamics – Life-engagements. A Guide for Research and Study. 2002
    ISBN 1-4020-0066-9
81. Tymieniecka, A-T. (ed.): *Metamorphosis.* Creative Imagination in Fine Arts, Life-Projects and Human Aesthetic Aspirations. 2004   ISBN 1-4020-1709-X
82. Tymieniecka, A-T. (ed.): *Mystery in its Passions.* Literary Explorations. 2004
    ISBN 1-4020-1705-7
83. Tymieniecka, A-T. (ed.): *Imaginatio Creatrix.* The Pivotal Force of the Genesis/Ontopoiesis of Human Life and Reality. 2004.   ISBN 1-4020-2244-1
84. Tymieniecka, A-T. (ed.): *Phenomenology of Life. Meeting the Challenges of the Present-Day World.* 2005.   ISBN 1-4020-2463-0
85. Tymieniecka, A-T. (ed.): *The Enigma of Good and Evil: The Moral Sentiment in Literature.* 2005.   ISBN 1-4020-3575-6
86. Tymieniecka, A-T. (ed.): *Temporality in Life as Seen Through Literature. Contributions to Phenomenology of Life.* 2006. HB.   ISBN 1-4020-5330-4
87. Tymieniecka, A-T. (ed.): *Human Creation Between Reality and Illusion.* 2005.
    ISBN 1-4020-3577-2
88. Tymieniecka, A-T. (ed.): *Logos of Phenomenology and Phenomenology of the Logos. Book One: Phenomenology as the Critique of Reason in Contemporary Criticism and Interpretation.* 2005.   ISBN 1-4020-3678-7
89. Tymieniecka, A-T. (ed.): *Logos of Phenomenology and Phenomenology of the Logos. Book Two: The Human Condition in-the-unity-of-everything-there-is-alive. Individuation, Self, Person, Self-determination, Freedom, Necessity.* 2005.
    ISBN 1-4020-3706-6
90. Tymieniecka, A-T. (ed.): *Logos of Phenomenology and Phenomenology of the Logos. Book Three: Logos of History - Logos of Life. Historicity, Time, Nature, Communication, Consciousness, Alterity, Culture.* 2005.   ISBN 1-4020-3717-1
91. Tymieniecka, A-T. (ed.): *Logos of Phenomenology and Phenomenology of the Logos. Book Four: The Logos of Scientific Interrogation. Participating in Nature – Life – Sharing in Life.* 2005.   ISBN 1-4020-3736-8
92. Tymieniecka, A-T. (ed.): *Logos of Phenomenology and Phenomenology of the Logos. Book Five: The Creative Logos. Aesthetic Ciphering in Fine Arts, Literature and Aesthetics.* 2005.   ISBN 1-4020-3743-0
93. Tymieniecka, A-T. (ed.): *Phenomenology of Life - From the Animal Soul to the Human Mind. Book One: In Search of Experience.* 2007.   ISBN 978-1-4020-5191-3

Analecta Husserliana

94. Tymieniecka, A-T. (ed.): *Phenomenology of Life - From the Animal Soul to the Human Mind. Book Two: The Human Soul in the Creative Transformation of the Mind.* 2007.	ISBN 978-1-4020-5181-6
95. Tymieniecka, A-T. (ed.): *Education in Human Creative Existential Planning.* 2008	ISBN 978-1-4020-6301-5
96. Tymieniecka, A-T. (ed.): *Virtues and Passions in Literature:* Excellence, Courage, Engagements, Wisdom, Fulfilment. 2008	ISBN 978-1-4020-6421-0

springer.com